YOTSUBA&!

9

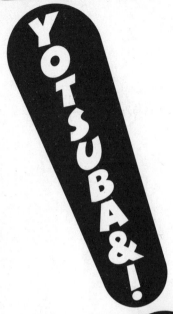

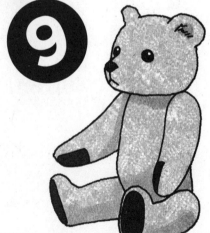

KIYOHIKO AZUMA

CONTENTS

YOTSUBA&!
KIYOHIKO AZUMA

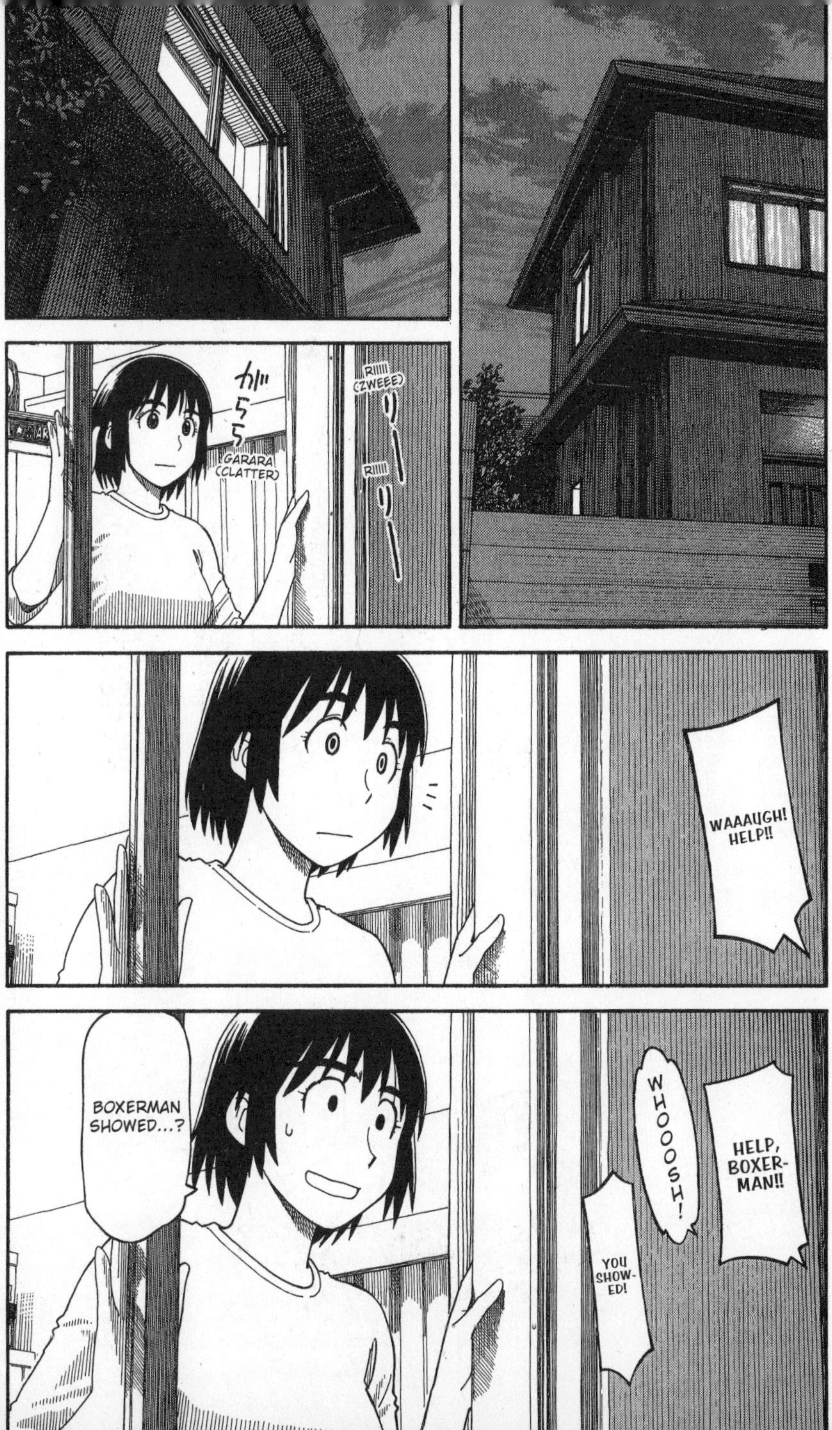
RIIIII (ZWEEE)
リー
RIIIII
リー
がらら
GARARA (CLATTER)
WAAAUGH! HELP!!
HELP, BOXER-MAN!!
WHOOOSH!
YOU SHOW-ED!
BOXERMAN SHOWED...?

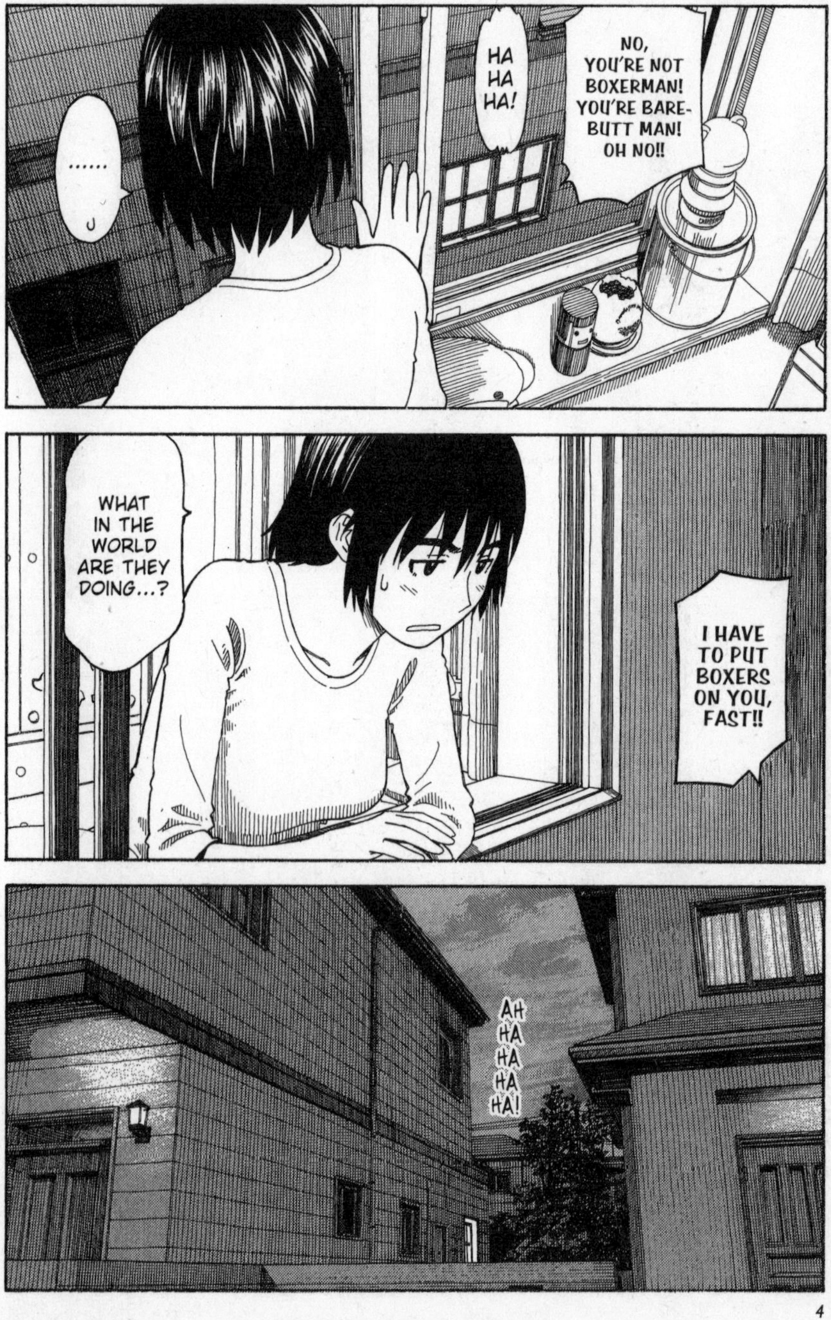
NO, YOU'RE NOT BOXERMAN! YOU'RE BARE-BUTT MAN! OH NO!!
HA HA HA!
......
I HAVE TO PUT BOXERS ON YOU, FAST!!
WHAT IN THE WORLD ARE THEY DOING...?
AH HA HA HA HA!

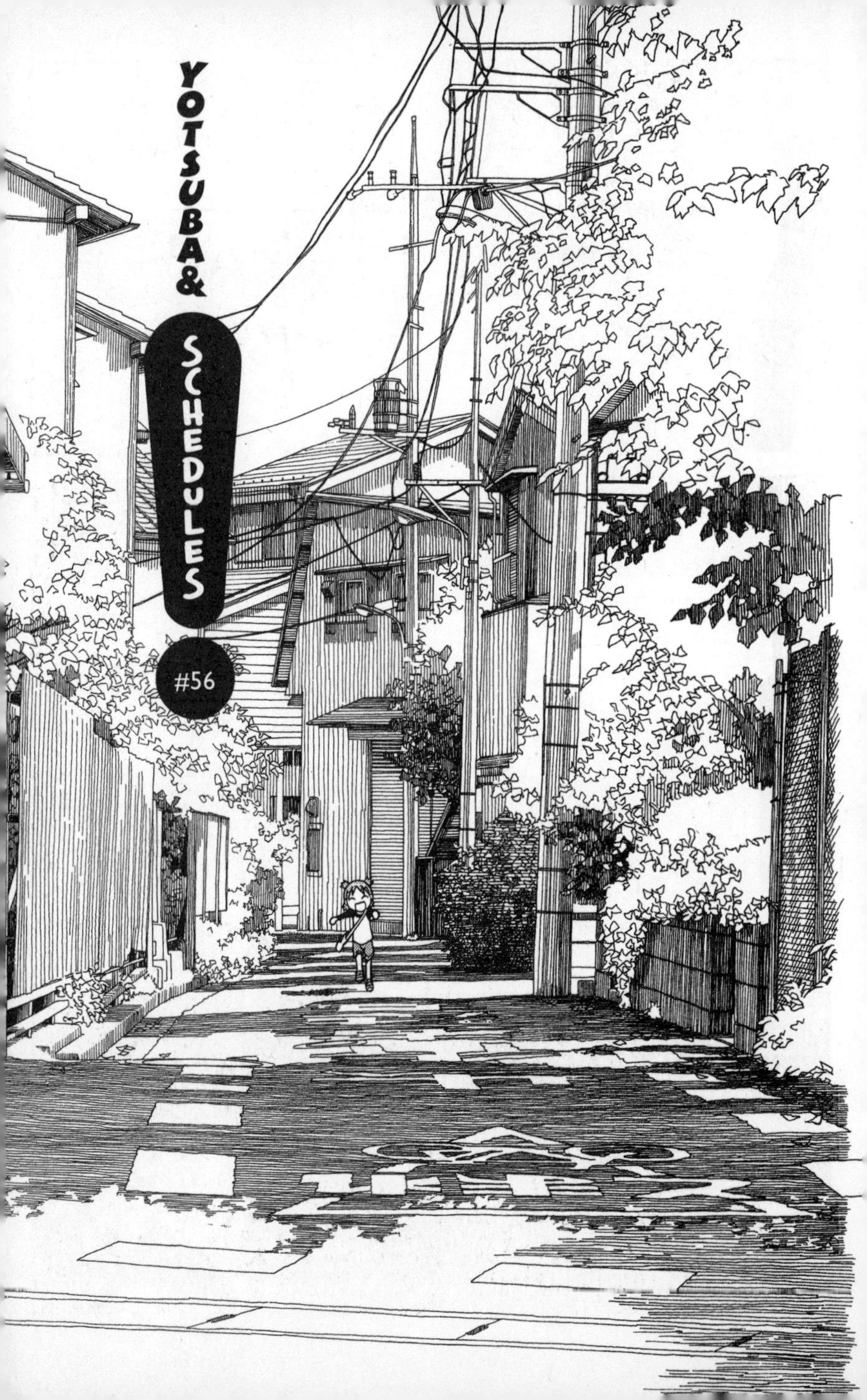
YOTSUBA&
SCHEDULES
#56

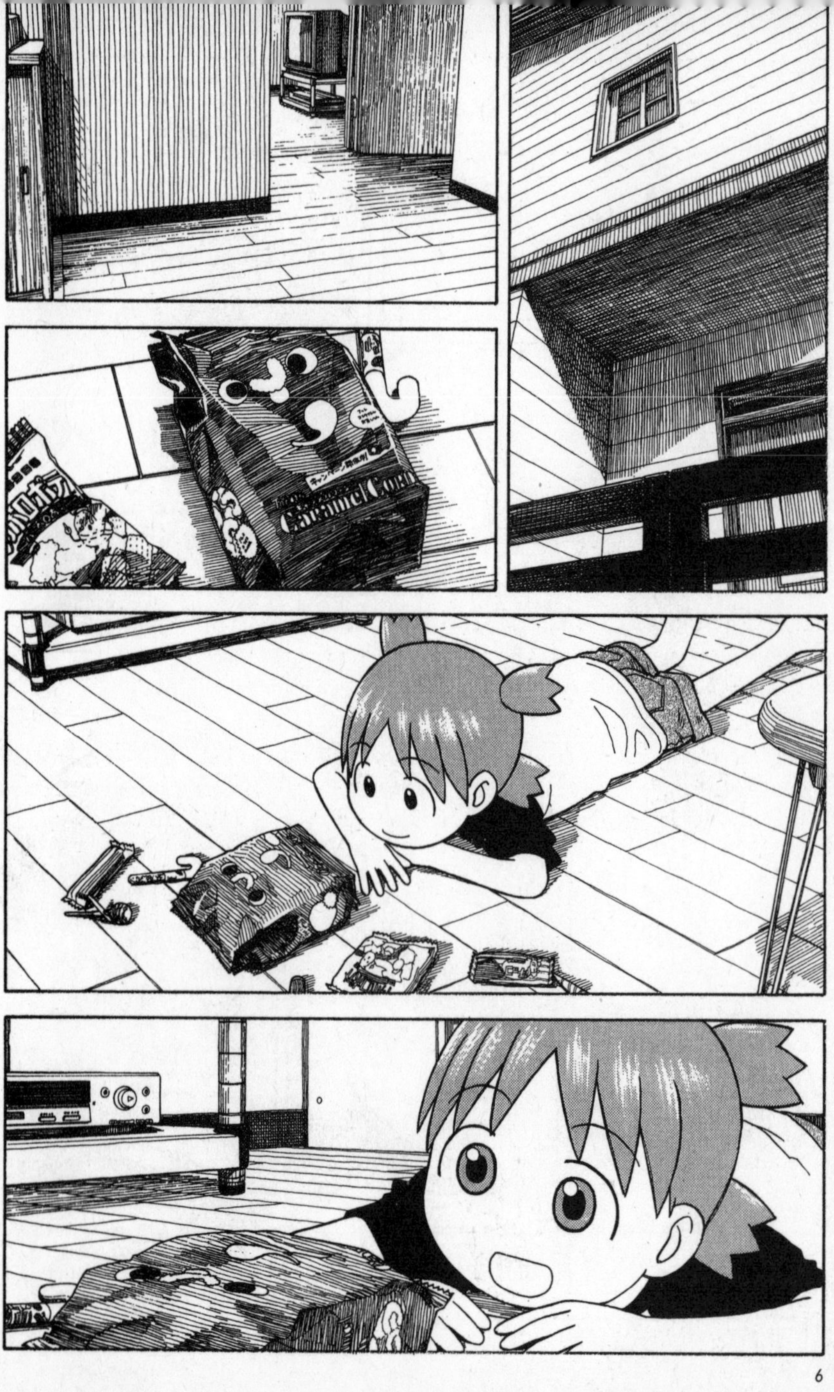
CaramelCorn

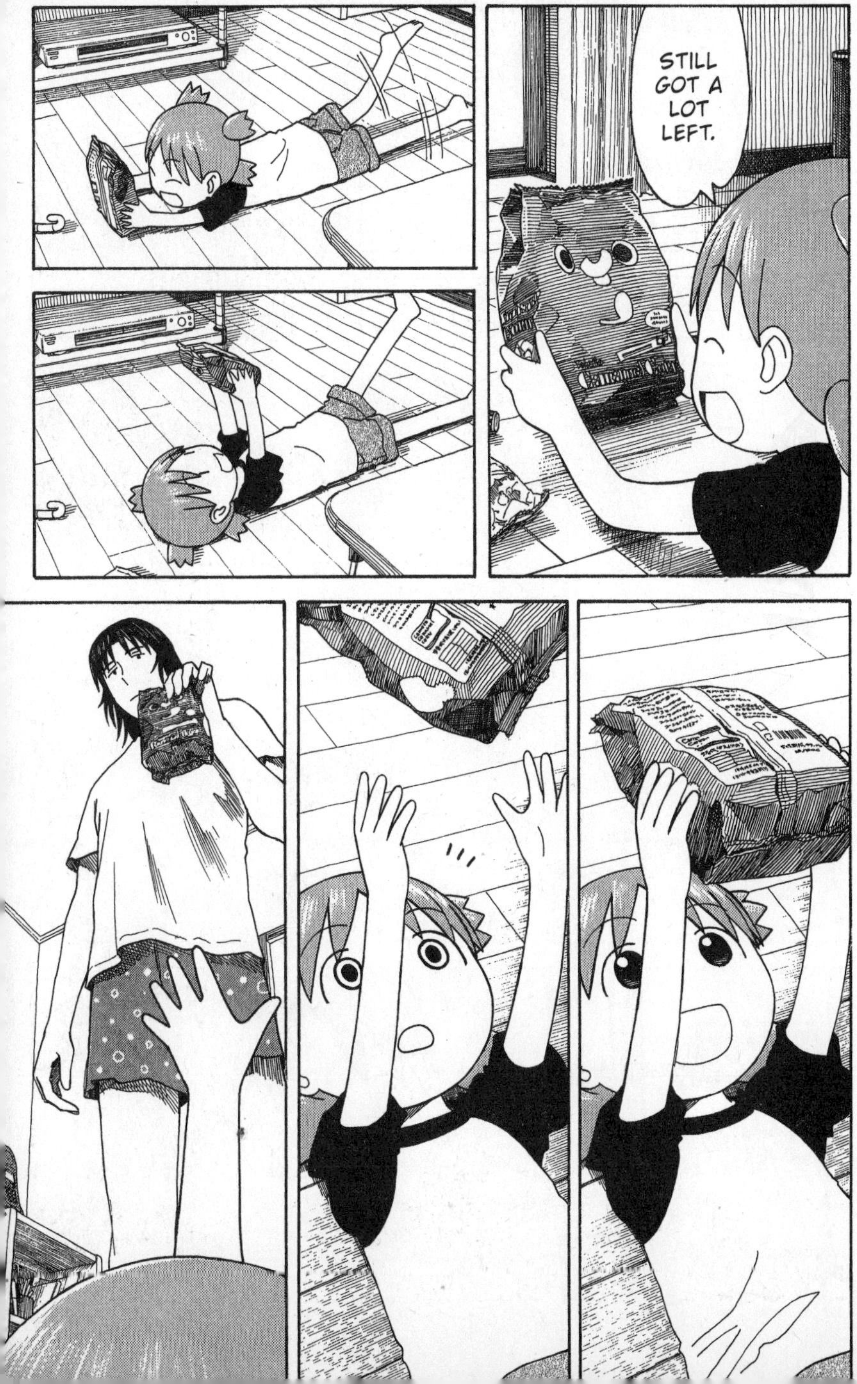
STILL GOT A LOT LEFT.

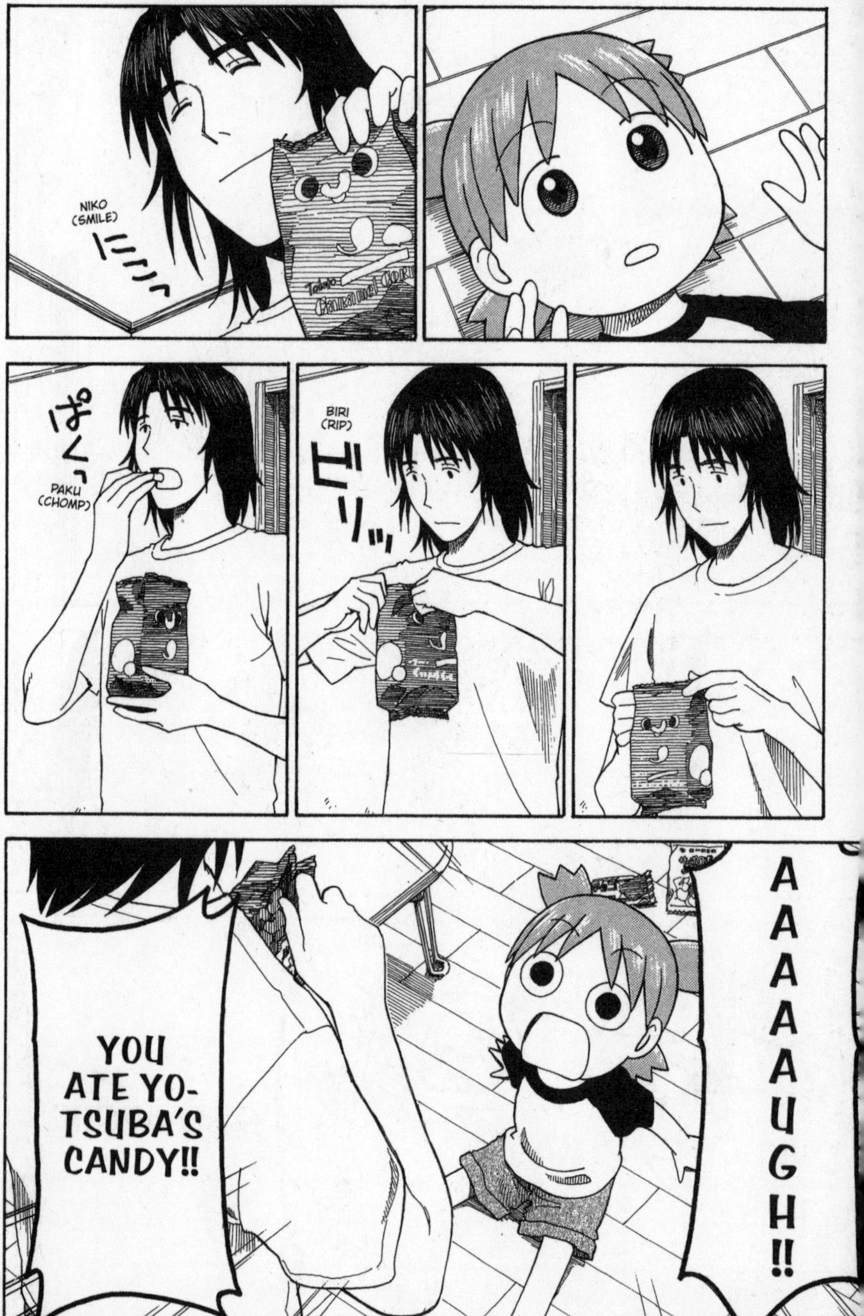
NIKO (SMILE)
にこっ
BIRI (RIP)
ビリッ
ぱくっ
PAKU (CHOMP)
AAAAAUGH!!
YOU ATE YO-TSUBA'S CANDY!!

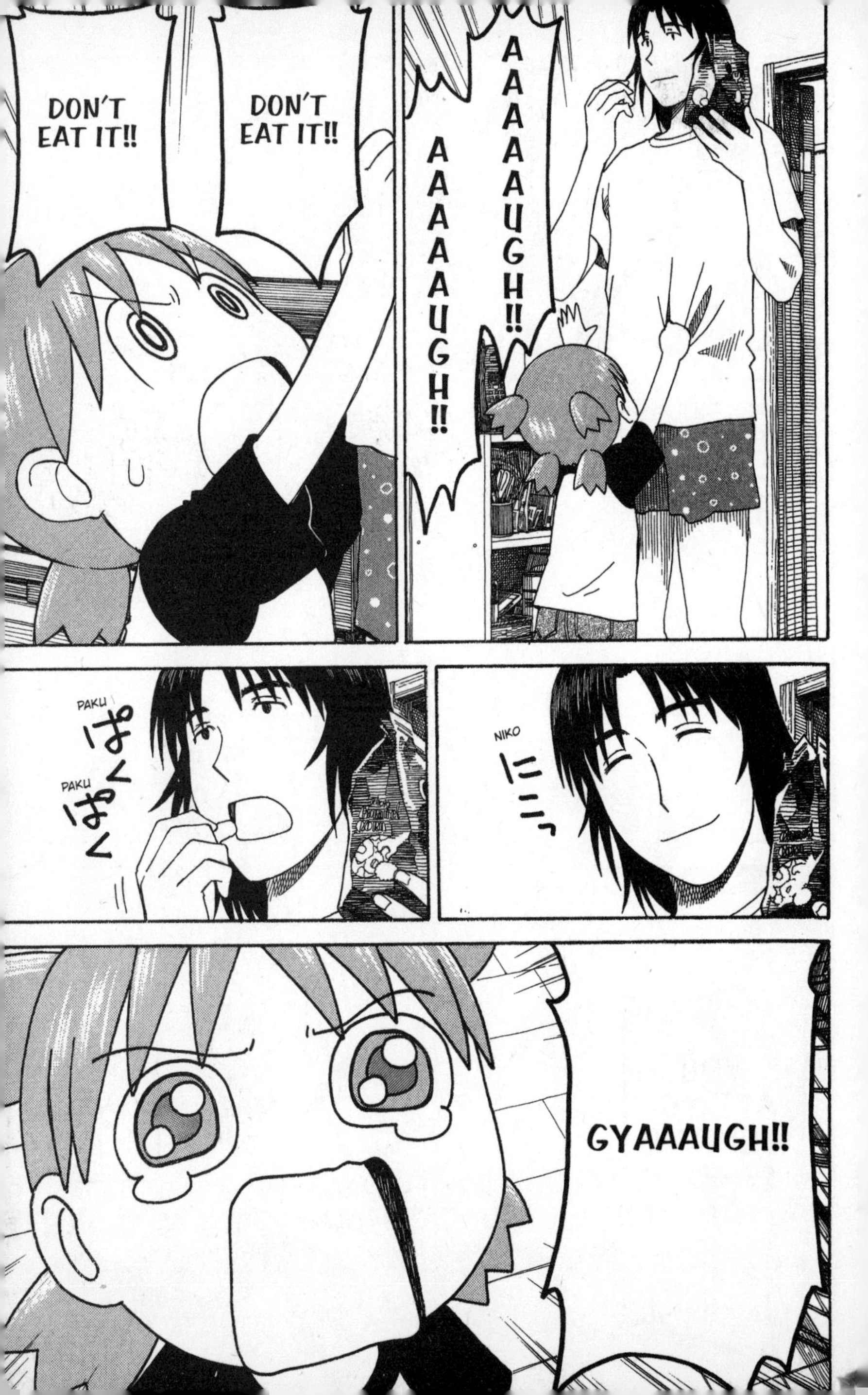
AAAAAUGH!!
AAAAAUGH!!
DON'T EAT IT!!
DON'T EAT IT!!
NIKO
にこっ
PAKU
ぱく
PAKU
ぱく
GYAAAUGH!!

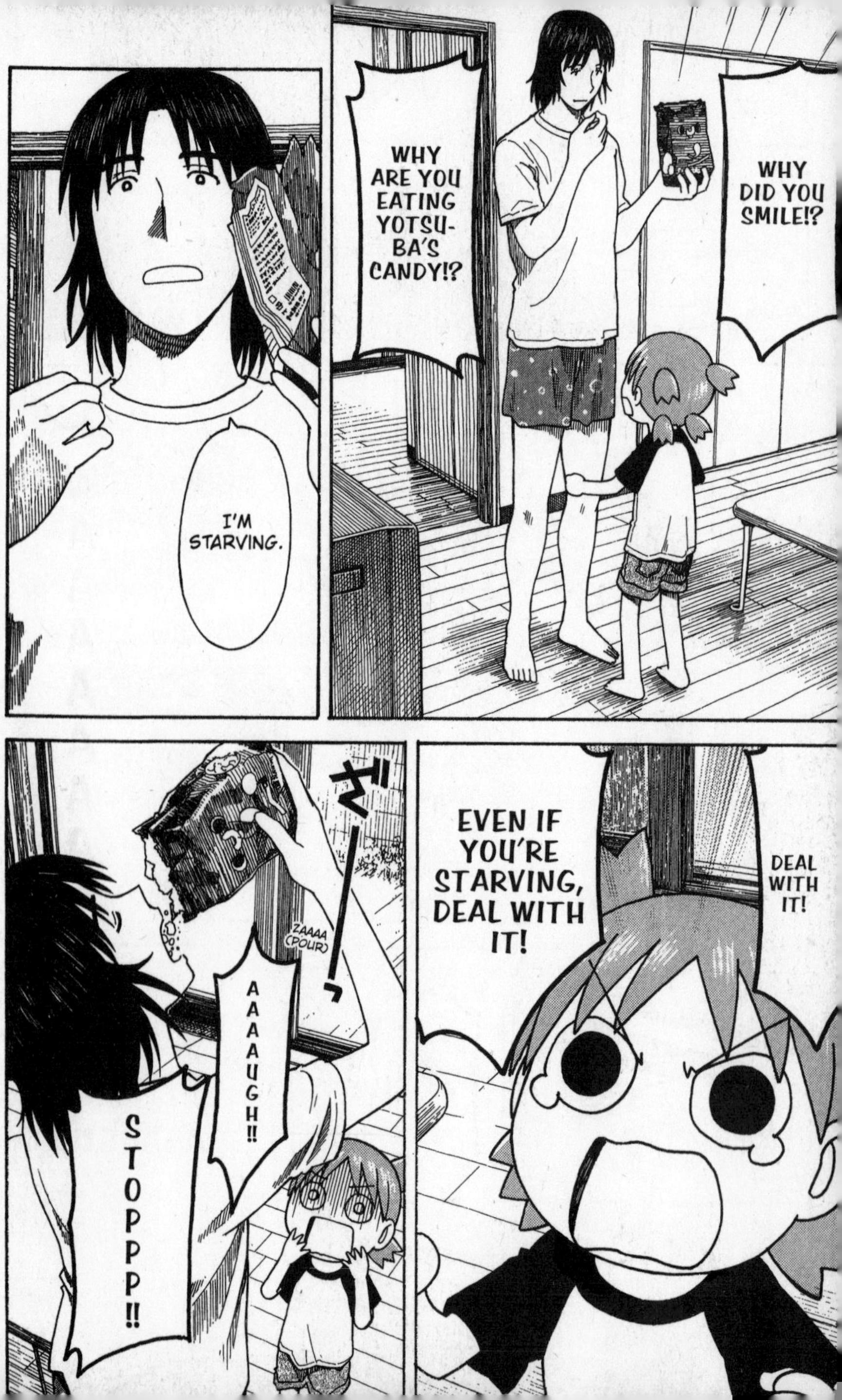
WHY DID YOU SMILE!?
WHY ARE YOU EATING YOTSUBA'S CANDY!?
I'M STARVING.
EVEN IF YOU'RE STARVING, DEAL WITH IT!
DEAL WITH IT!
ZAAAA (POUR)
AAAAAUGH!!
STOPPPP!!

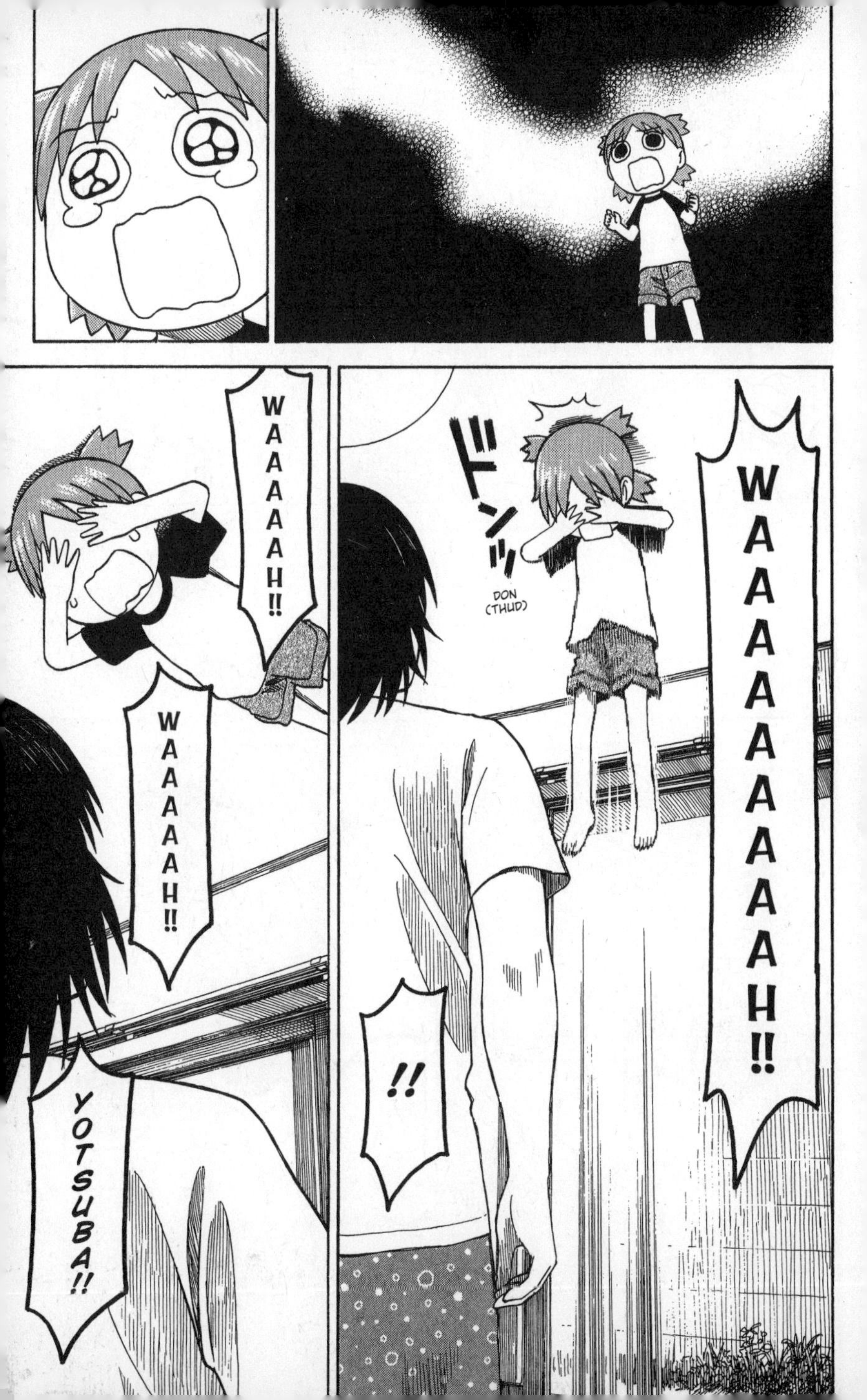
WAAAAAAAAAAAH!!
ドンッ
DON (THUD)
!!
WAAAAAAH!!
WAAAAAAH!!
YOTSUBA!!

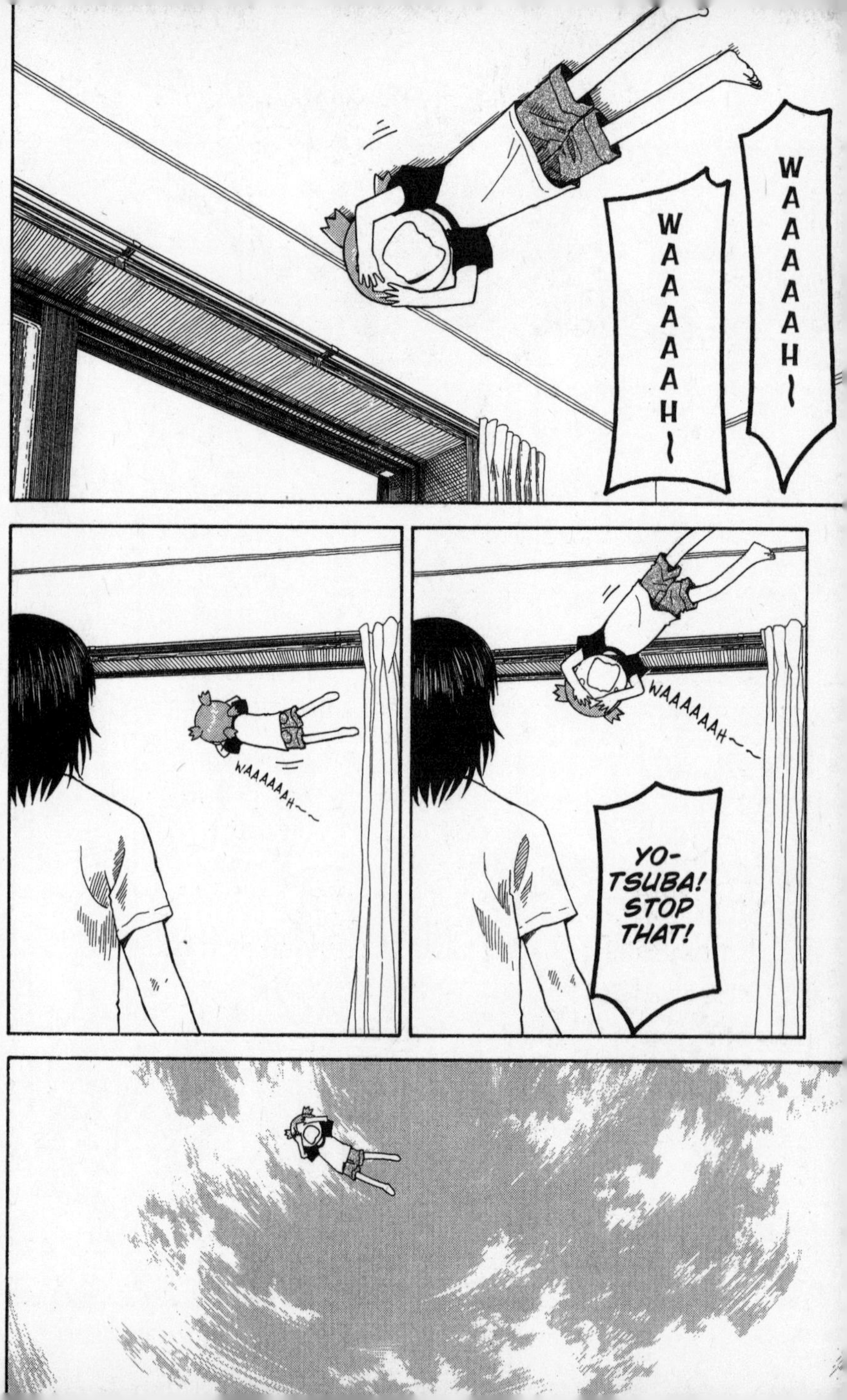
WAAAAAAH~
WAAAAAAH~
WAAAAAAH~~
YO-TSUBA! STOP THAT!
WAAAAAAH~~

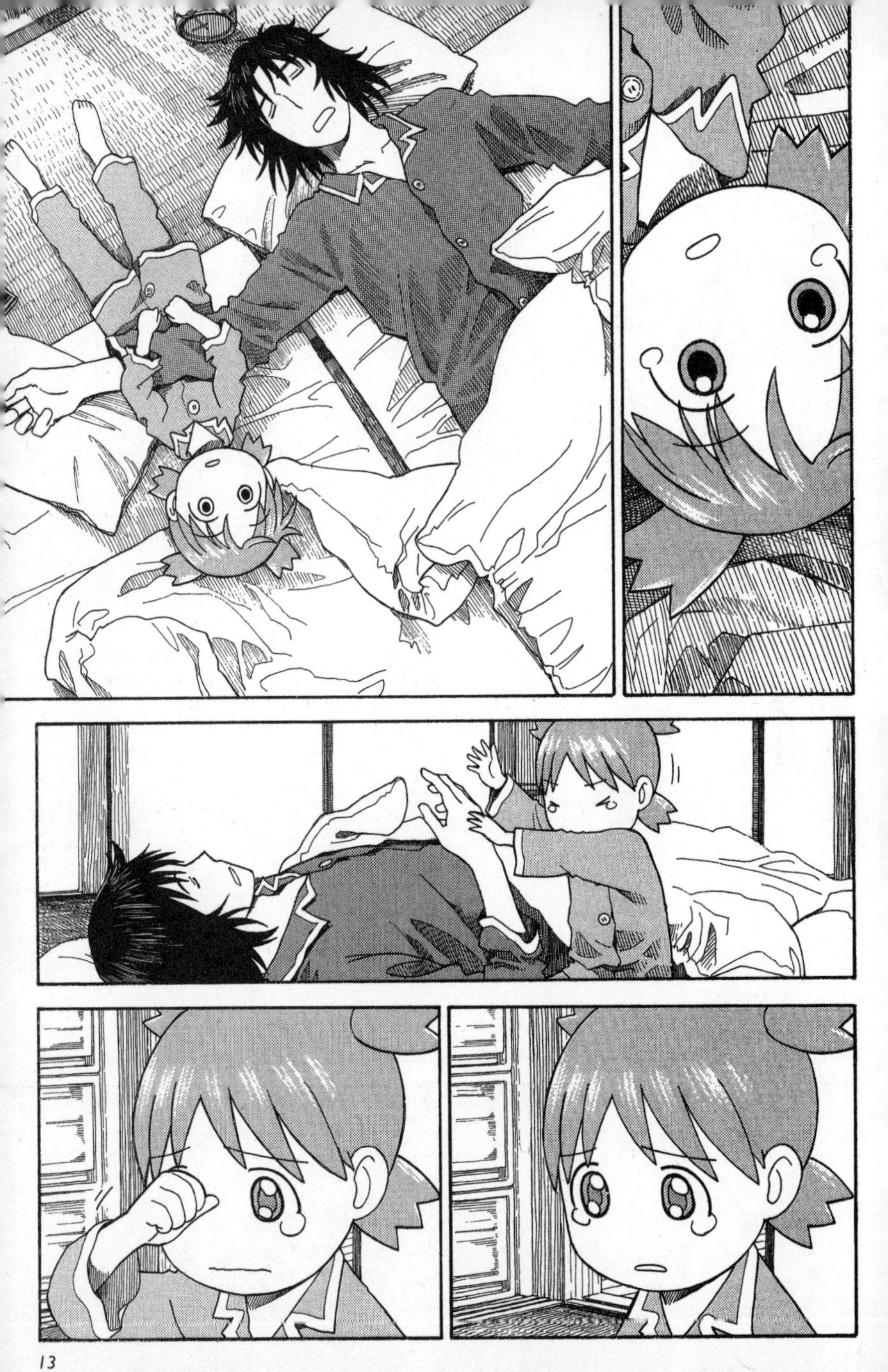

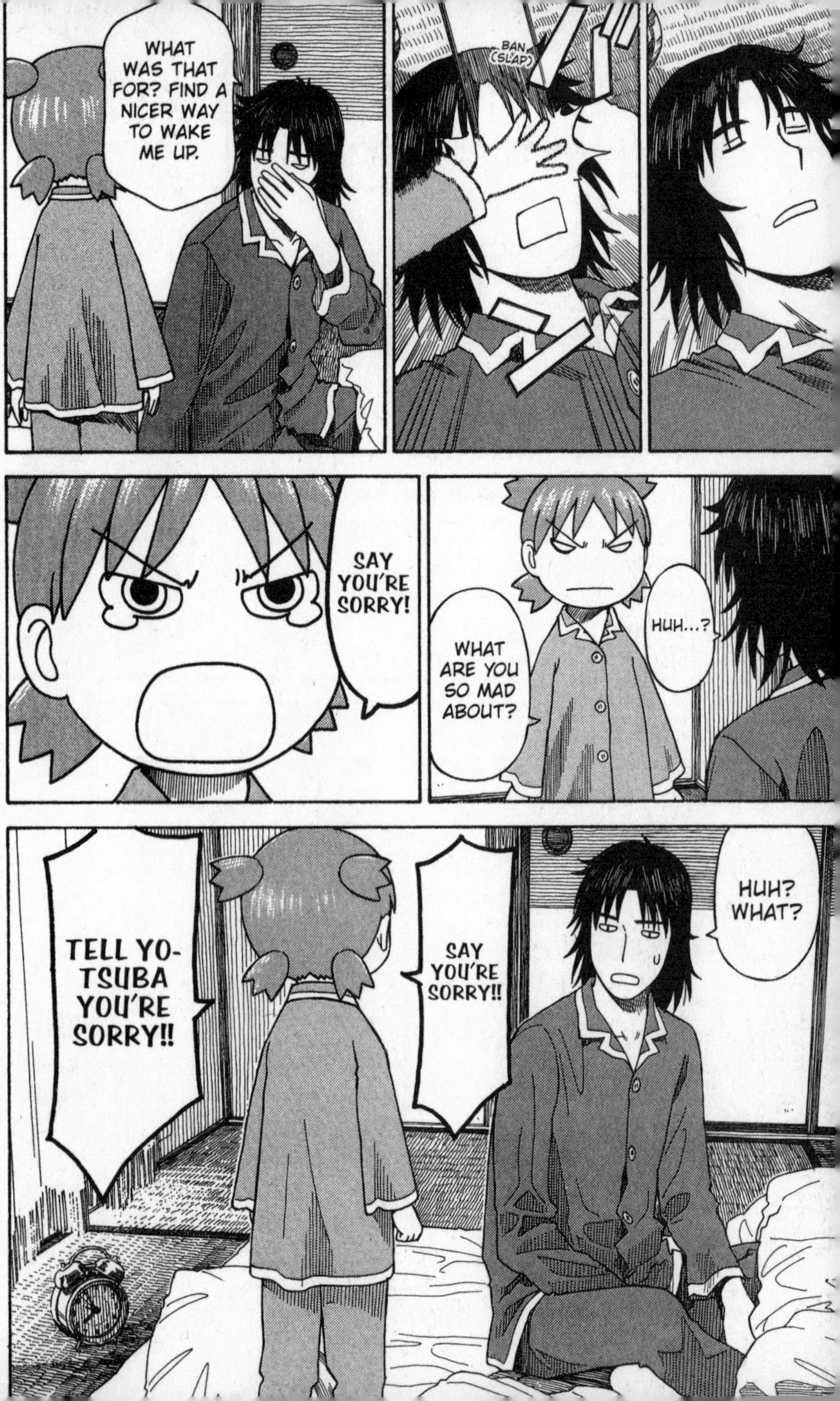
BAN (SLAP)
WHAT WAS THAT FOR? FIND A NICER WAY TO WAKE ME UP.
HUH...?
WHAT ARE YOU SO MAD ABOUT?
SAY YOU'RE SORRY!
HUH? WHAT?
SAY YOU'RE SORRY!!
TELL YO-TSUBA YOU'RE SORRY!!

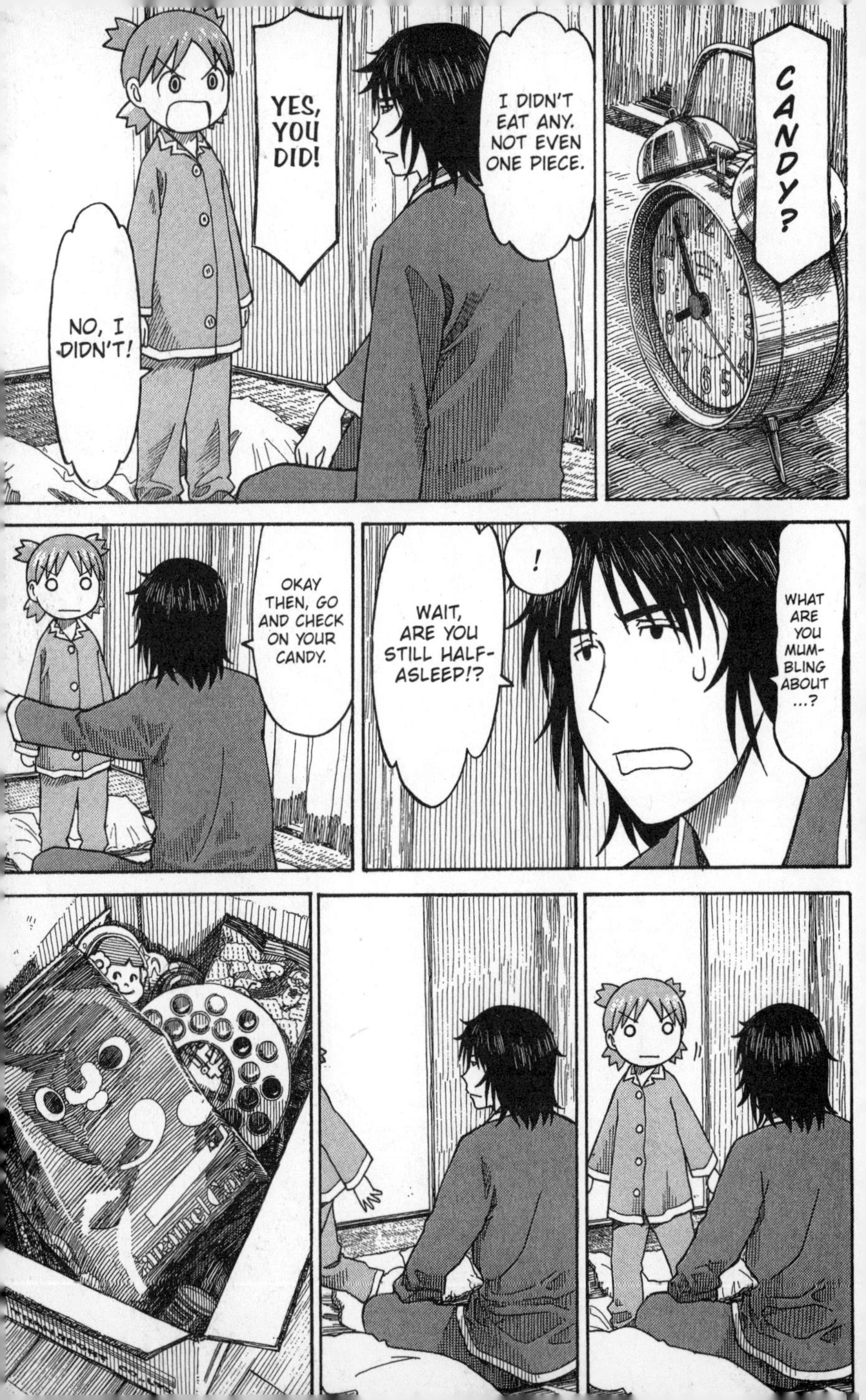
CANDY?
I DIDN'T EAT ANY. NOT EVEN ONE PIECE.
YES, YOU DID!
NO, I DIDN'T!
WHAT ARE YOU MUM-BLING ABOUT ...?
!
WAIT, ARE YOU STILL HALF-ASLEEP!?
OKAY THEN, GO AND CHECK ON YOUR CANDY.

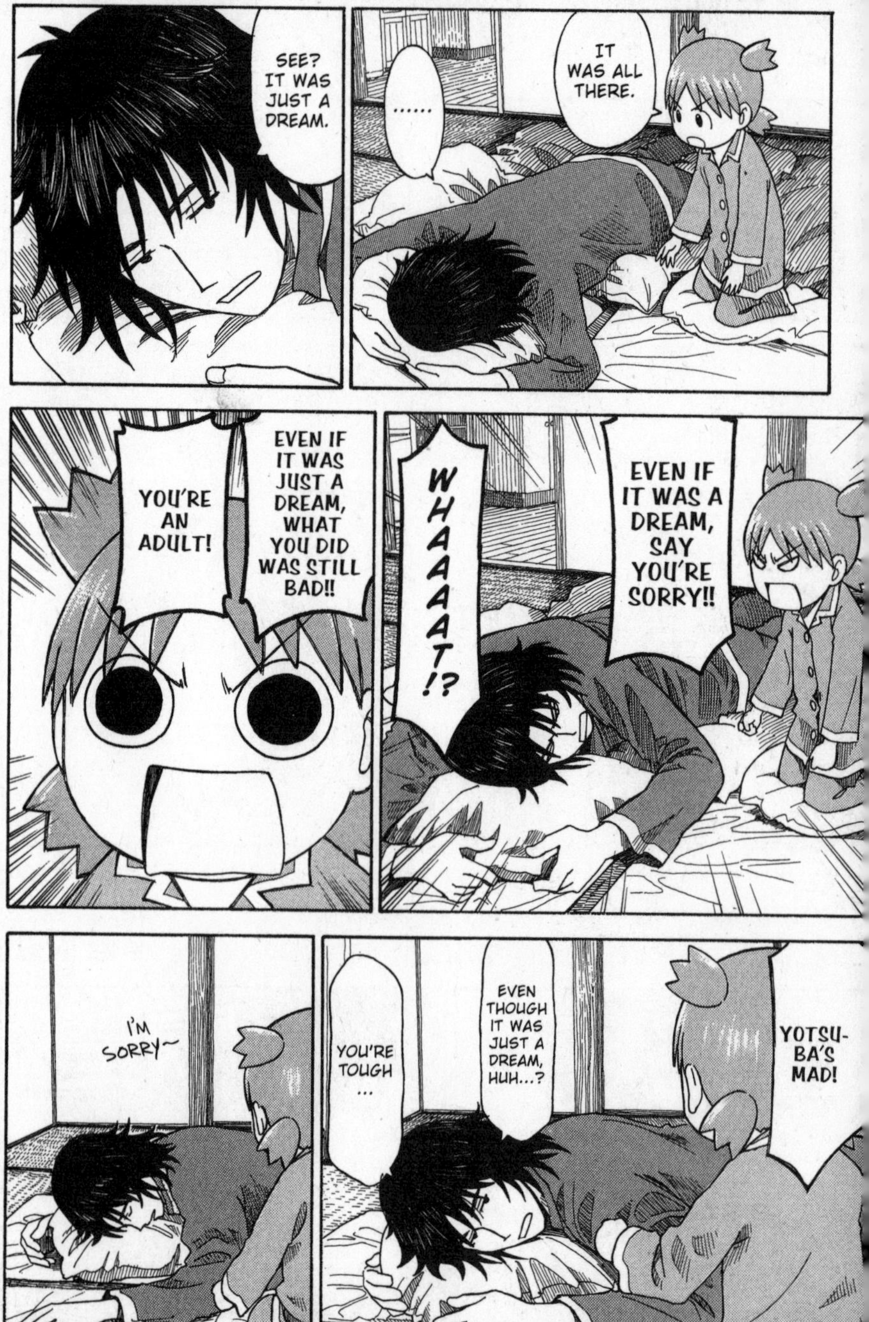
IT WAS ALL THERE.
......
SEE? IT WAS JUST A DREAM.
EVEN IF IT WAS A DREAM, SAY YOU'RE SORRY!!
WHAAAAAT!?
EVEN IF IT WAS JUST A DREAM, WHAT YOU DID WAS STILL BAD!!
YOU'RE AN ADULT!
YOTSU-BA'S MAD!
EVEN THOUGH IT WAS JUST A DREAM, HUH...?
YOU'RE TOUGH...
I'M SORRY~

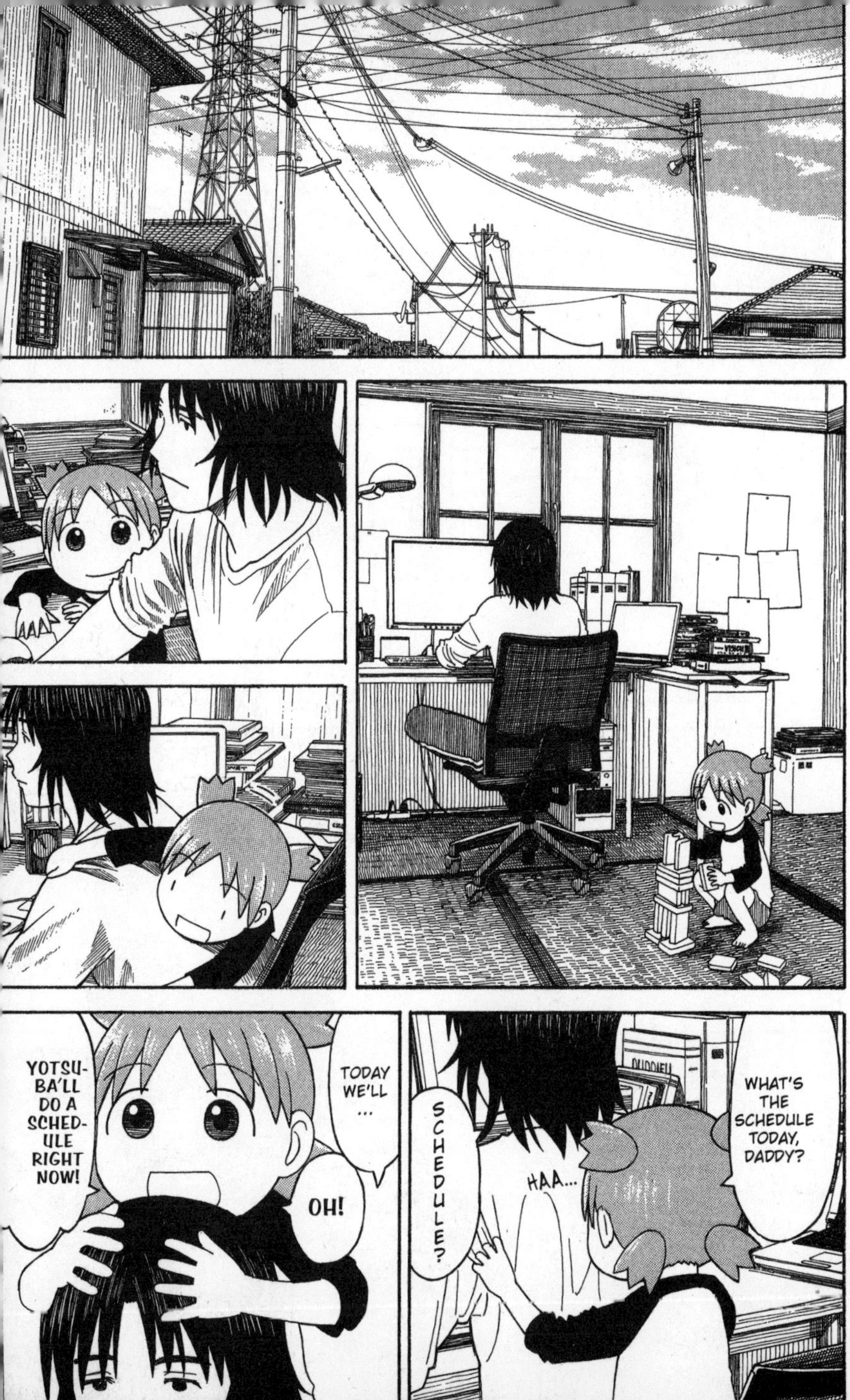
WHAT'S THE SCHEDULE TODAY, DADDY?
SCHEDULE?
HAA...
TODAY WE'LL ...
OH!
YOTSUBA'LL DO A SCHEDULE RIGHT NOW!

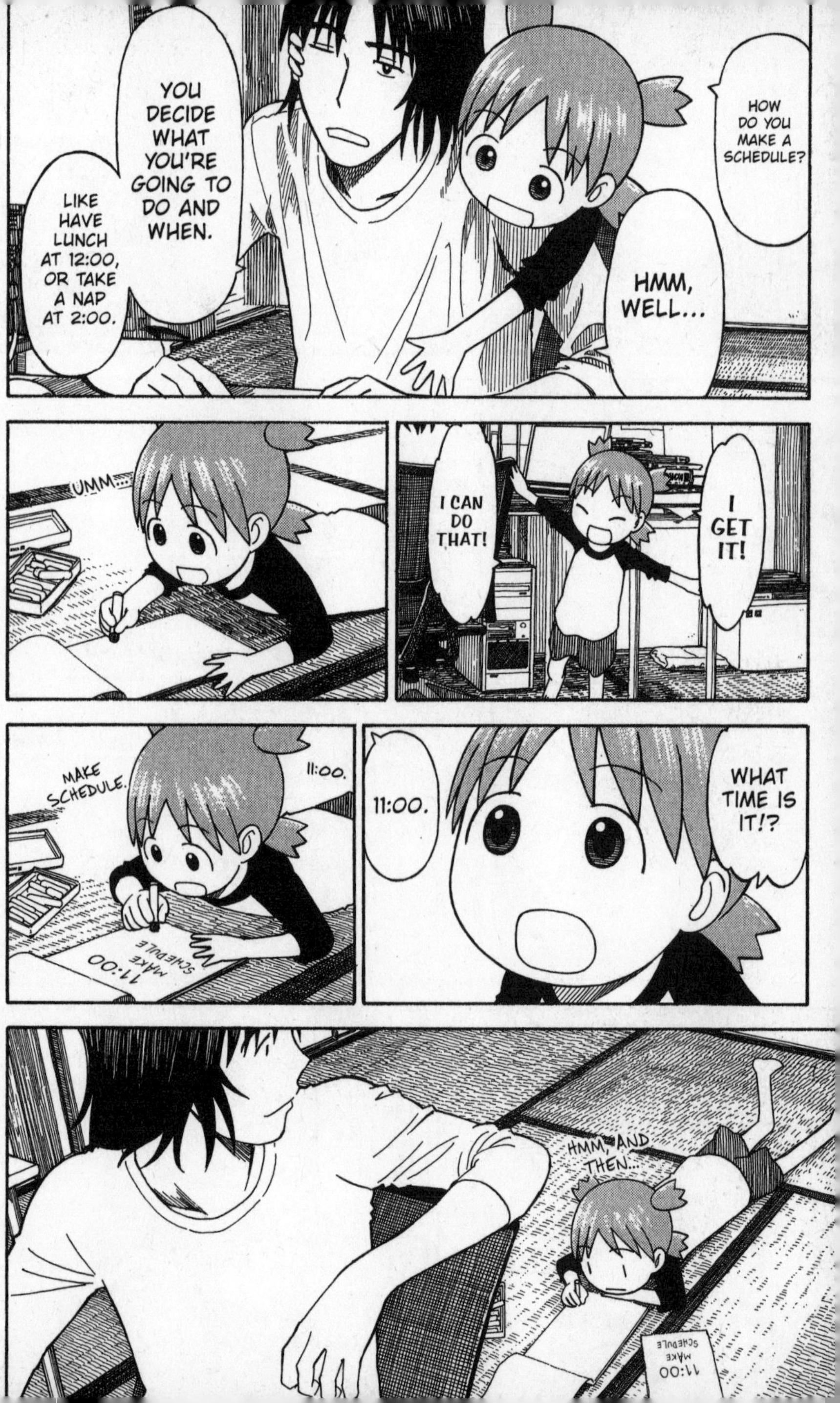
HOW DO YOU MAKE A SCHEDULE?
HMM, WELL...
YOU DECIDE WHAT YOU'RE GOING TO DO AND WHEN.
LIKE HAVE LUNCH AT 12:00, OR TAKE A NAP AT 2:00.
I GET IT!
I CAN DO THAT!
UMM...
WHAT TIME IS IT!?
11:00.
11:00.
MAKE SCHEDULE.
11:00 MAKE SCHEDULE
HMM, AND THEN...
11:00 MAKE SCHEDULE

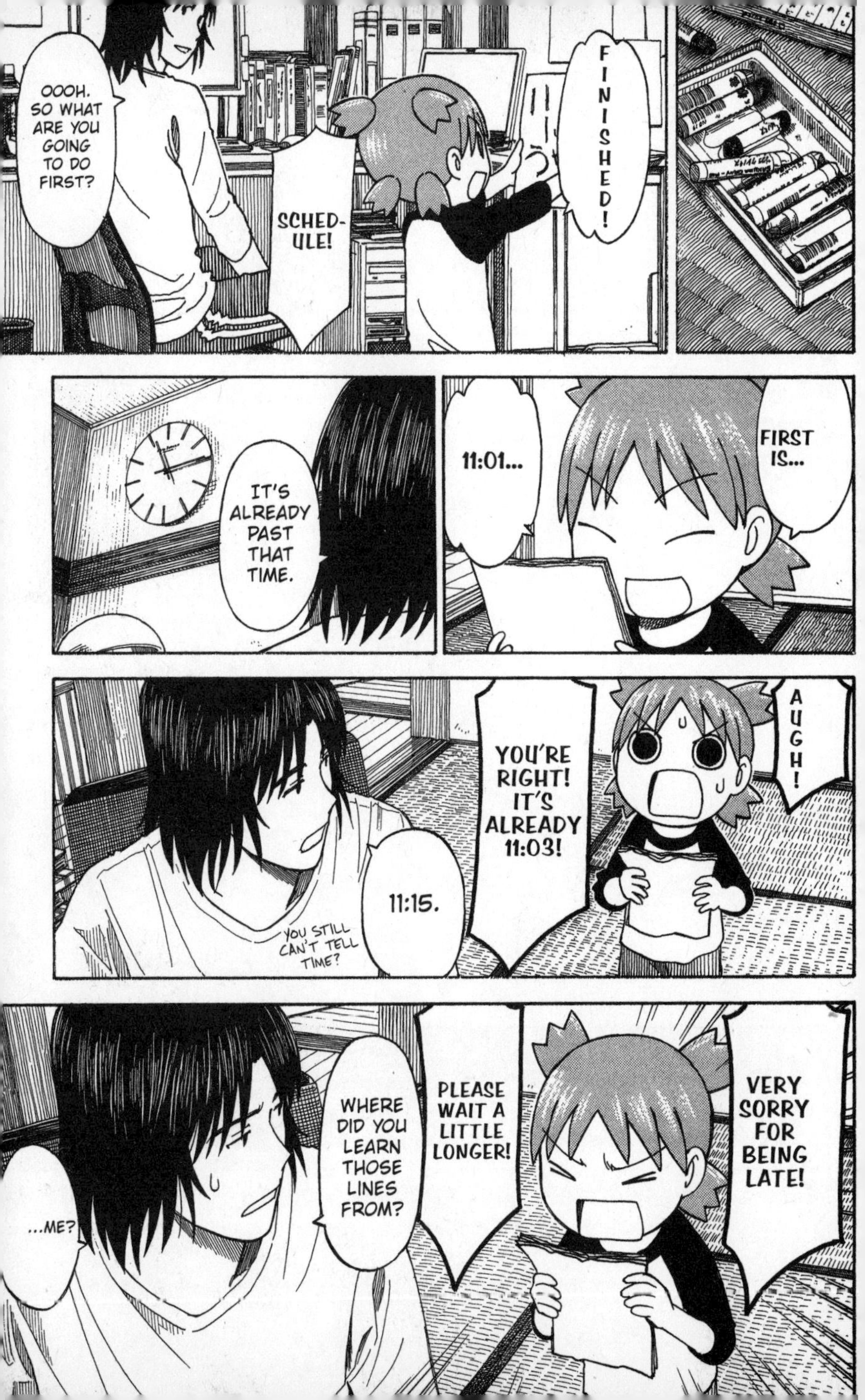
FINISHED!
SCHED-ULE!
OOOH. SO WHAT ARE YOU GOING TO DO FIRST?
FIRST IS...
11:01...
IT'S ALREADY PAST THAT TIME.
AUGH!
YOU'RE RIGHT! IT'S ALREADY 11:03!
11:15.
YOU STILL CAN'T TELL TIME?
VERY SORRY FOR BEING LATE!
PLEASE WAIT A LITTLE LONGER!
WHERE DID YOU LEARN THOSE LINES FROM?
...ME?

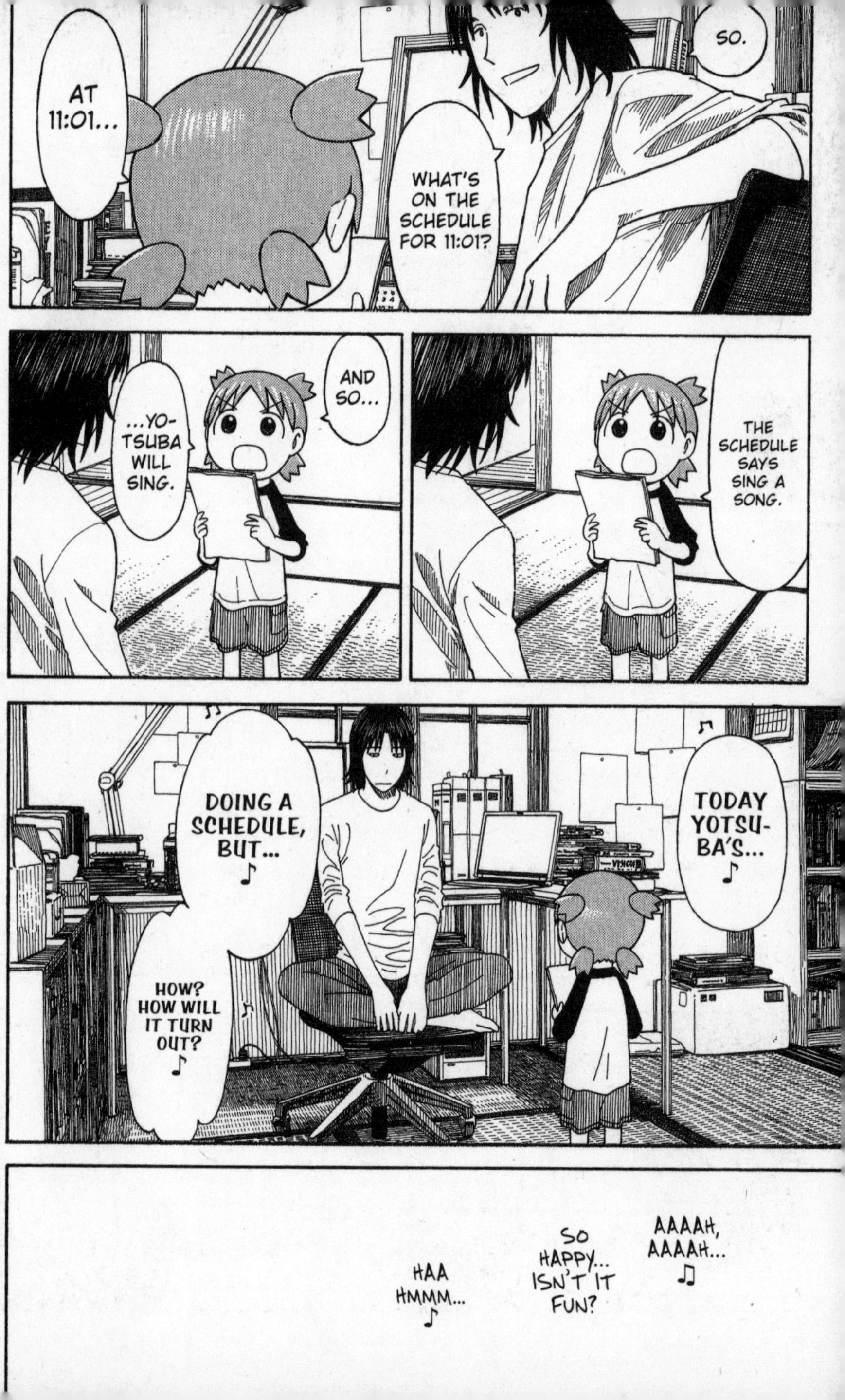
SO.
WHAT'S ON THE SCHEDULE FOR 11:01?
AT 11:01...
THE SCHEDULE SAYS SING A SONG.
AND SO...
...YO-TSUBA WILL SING.
TODAY YOTSU-BA'S... ♪
DOING A SCHEDULE, BUT... ♪
HOW? HOW WILL IT TURN OUT? ♪
AAAAH, AAAAH... ♫
SO HAPPY... ISN'T IT FUN?
HAA HMMM... ♪

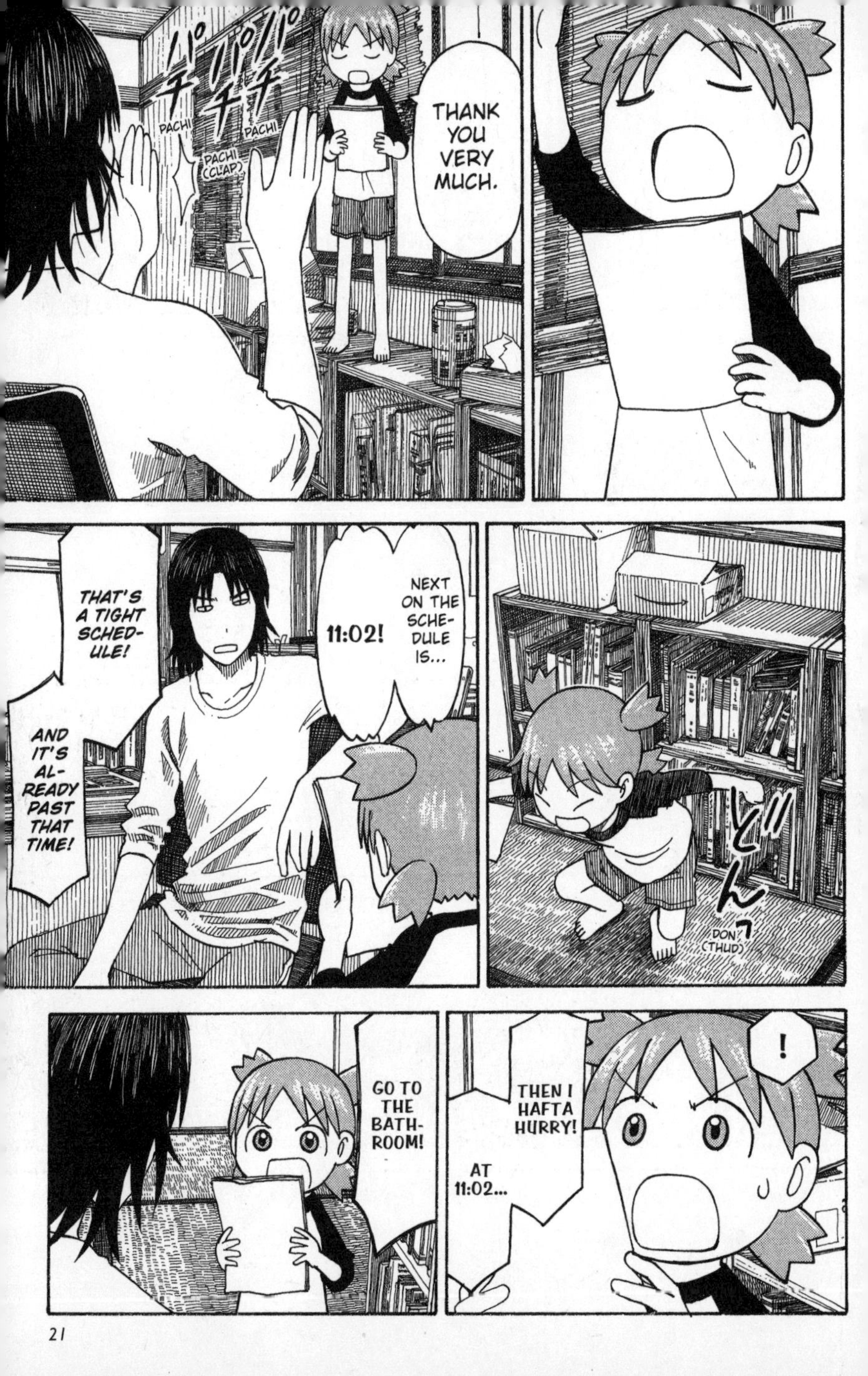
THANK YOU VERY MUCH.
パチパチパチ
PACHI PACHI PACHI (CLAP)
どん
DON (THUD)
NEXT ON THE SCHEDULE IS...
11:02!
THAT'S A TIGHT SCHEDULE!
AND IT'S ALREADY PAST THAT TIME!
!
THEN I HAFTA HURRY!
AT 11:02...
GO TO THE BATHROOM!

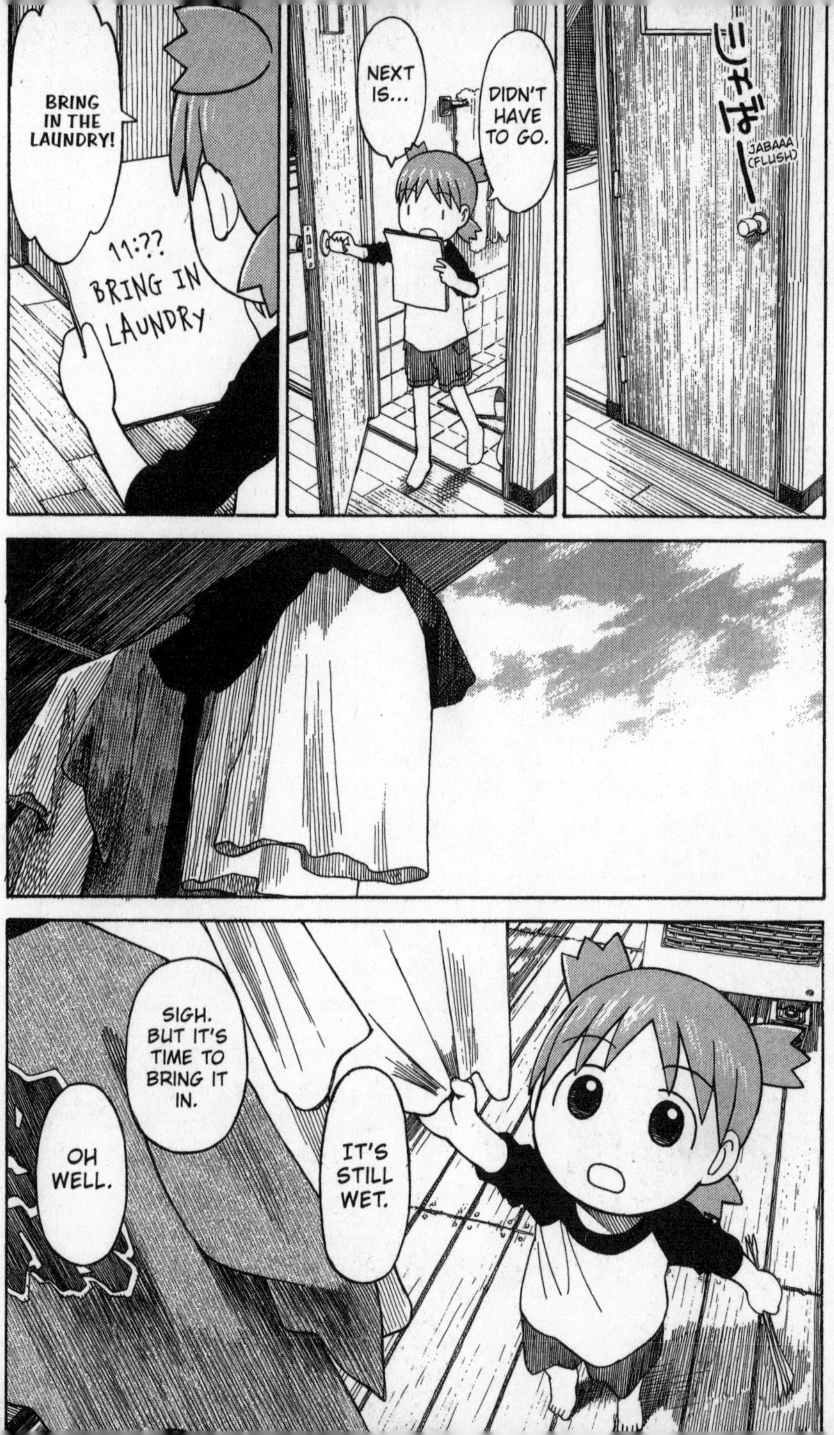
じゃばー
JABAAA (FLUSH)
DIDN'T HAVE TO GO.
NEXT IS...
BRING IN THE LAUNDRY!
11:?? BRING IN LAUNDRY
IT'S STILL WET.
SIGH. BUT IT'S TIME TO BRING IT IN.
OH WELL.

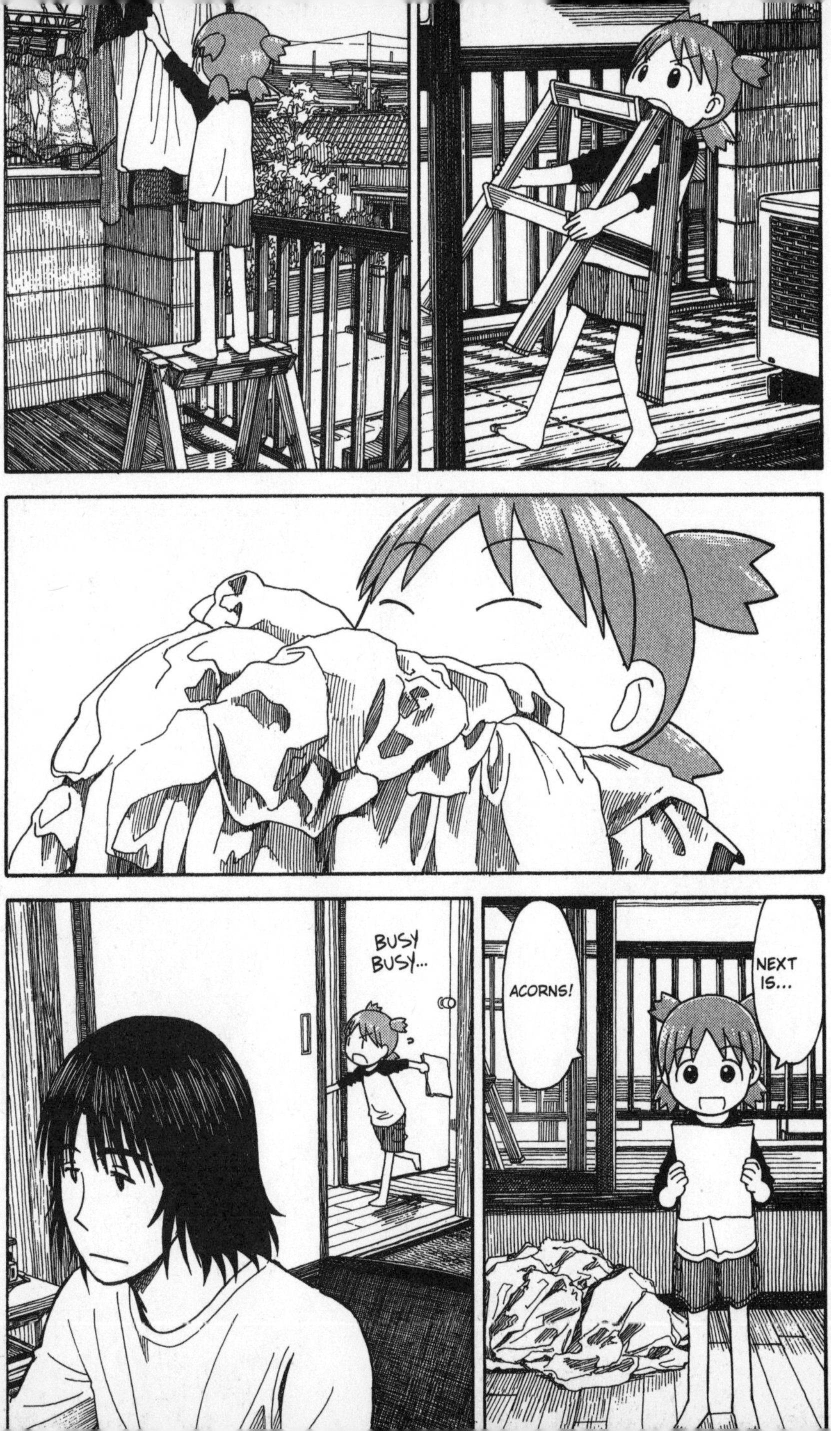
NEXT IS...
ACORNS!
BUSY BUSY...

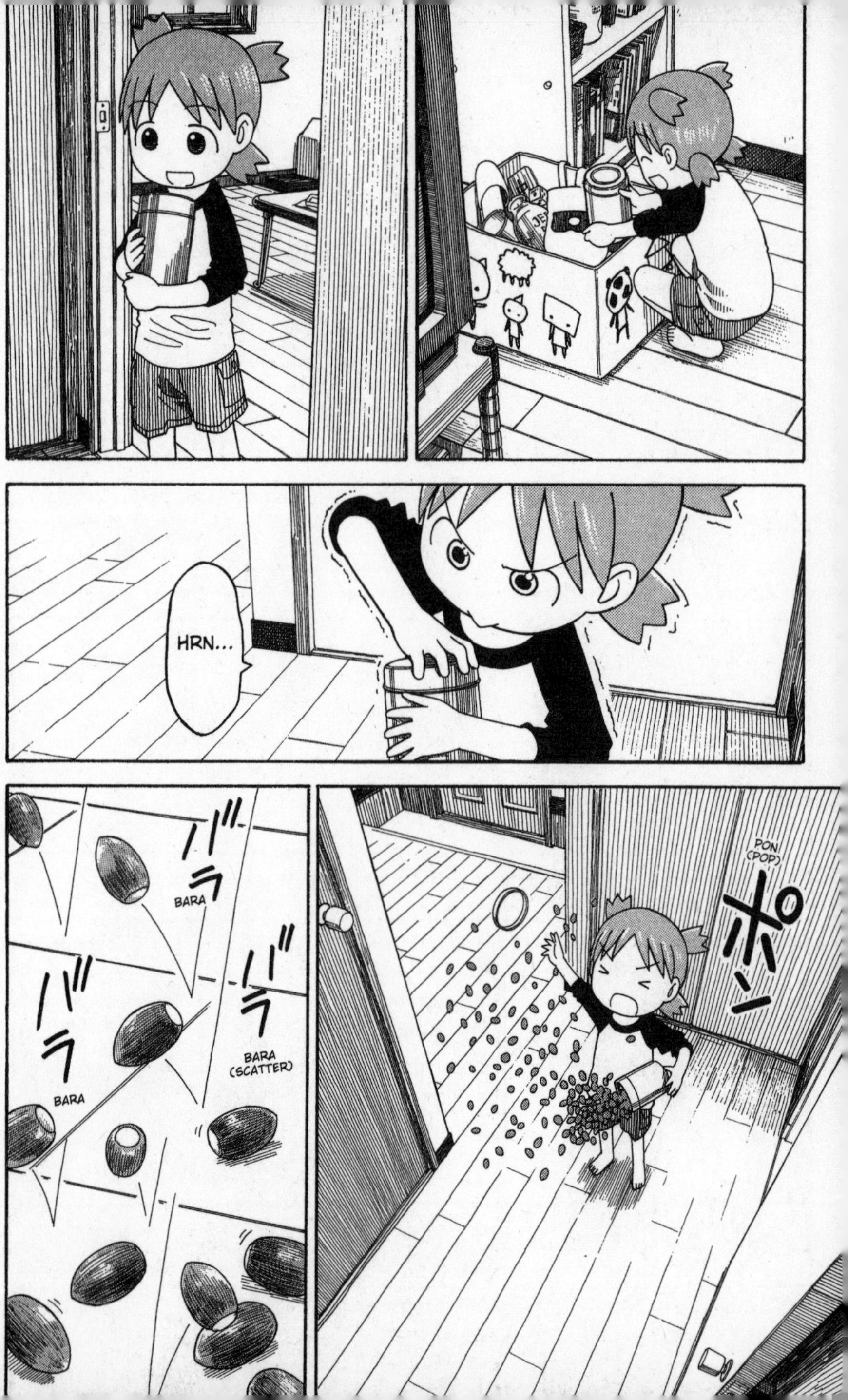
HRN...
ポン
PON (POP)
バラ
BARA
バラ
BARA (SCATTER)
バラ
BARA

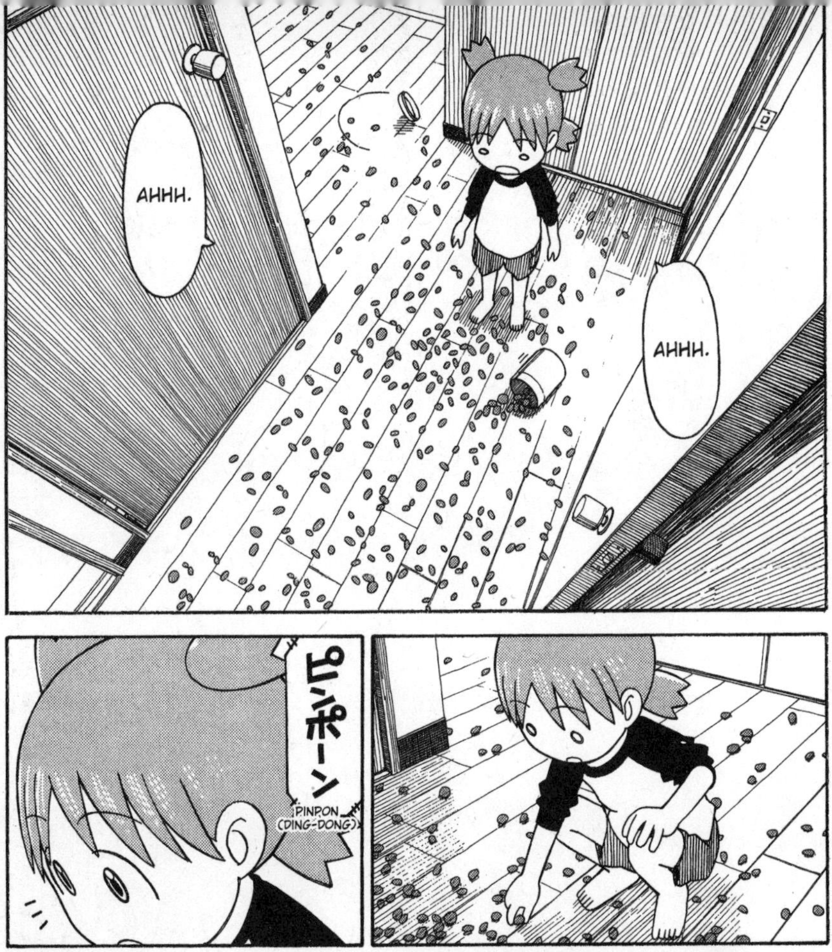
AHHH.
AHHH.
ピンポーン
PINPON (DING-DONG)

*THE STAMP YOTSUBA IS REFERRING TO IS A HANKO, A STAMP/SEAL THAT IS USED IN LIEU OF A SIGNATURE IN JAPAN.

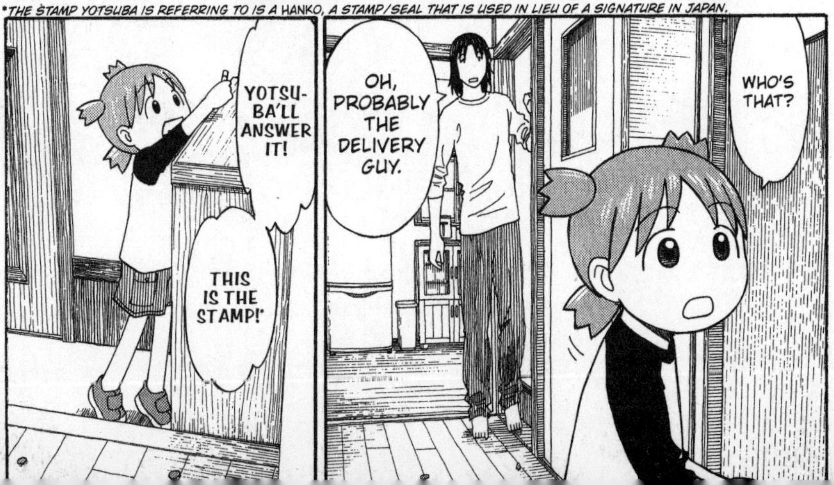
WHO'S THAT?
OH, PROBABLY THE DELIVERY GUY.
YOTSU-BA'LL ANSWER IT!
THIS IS THE STAMP!*

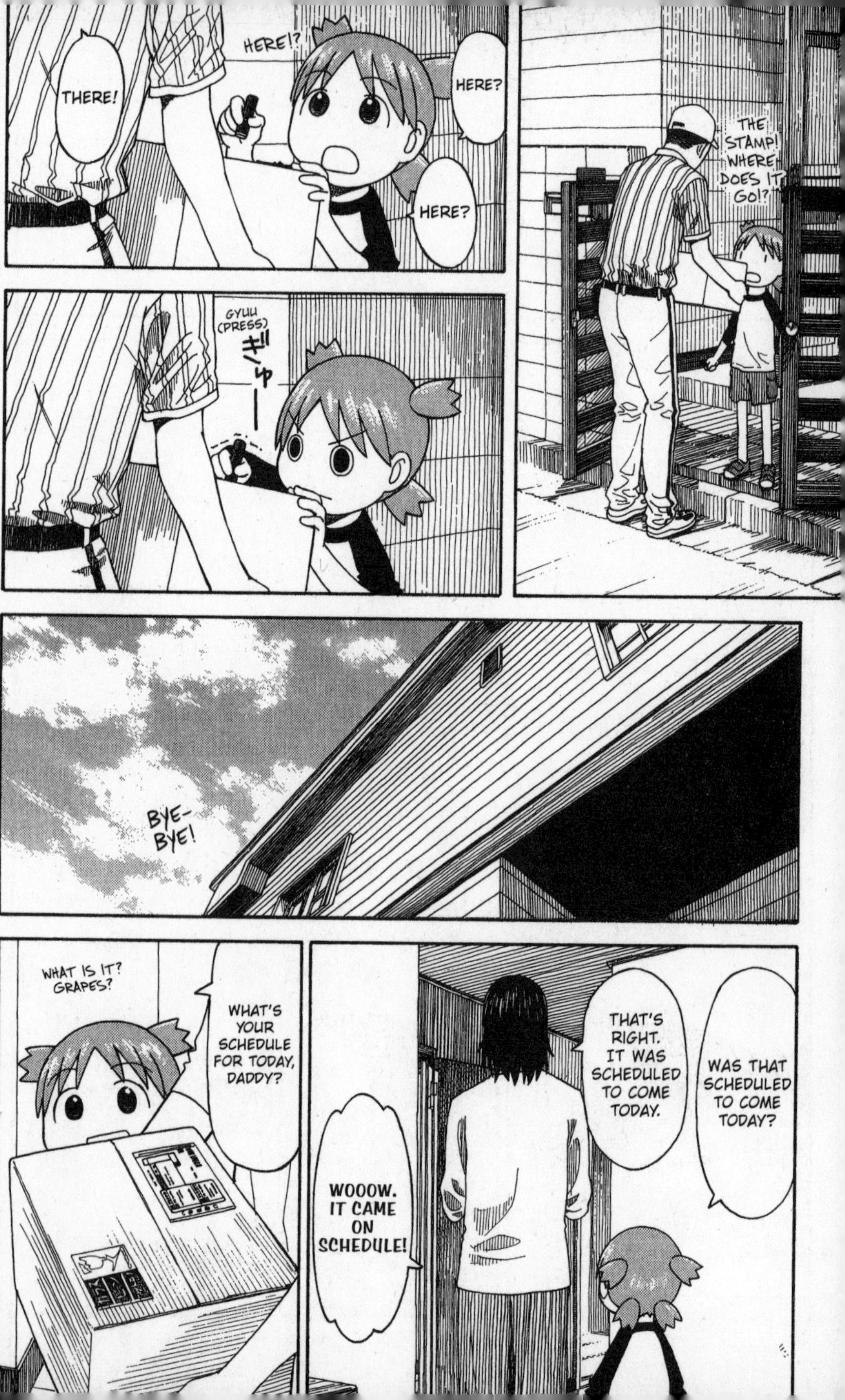
THE STAMP! WHERE DOES IT GO!?
HERE?
HERE?
THERE!
HERE!?
GYUU (PRESS)
ぎゅー
BYE-BYE!
WAS THAT SCHEDULED TO COME TODAY?
THAT'S RIGHT. IT WAS SCHEDULED TO COME TODAY.
WOOOW. IT CAME ON SCHEDULE!
WHAT'S YOUR SCHEDULE FOR TODAY, DADDY?
WHAT IS IT? GRAPES?

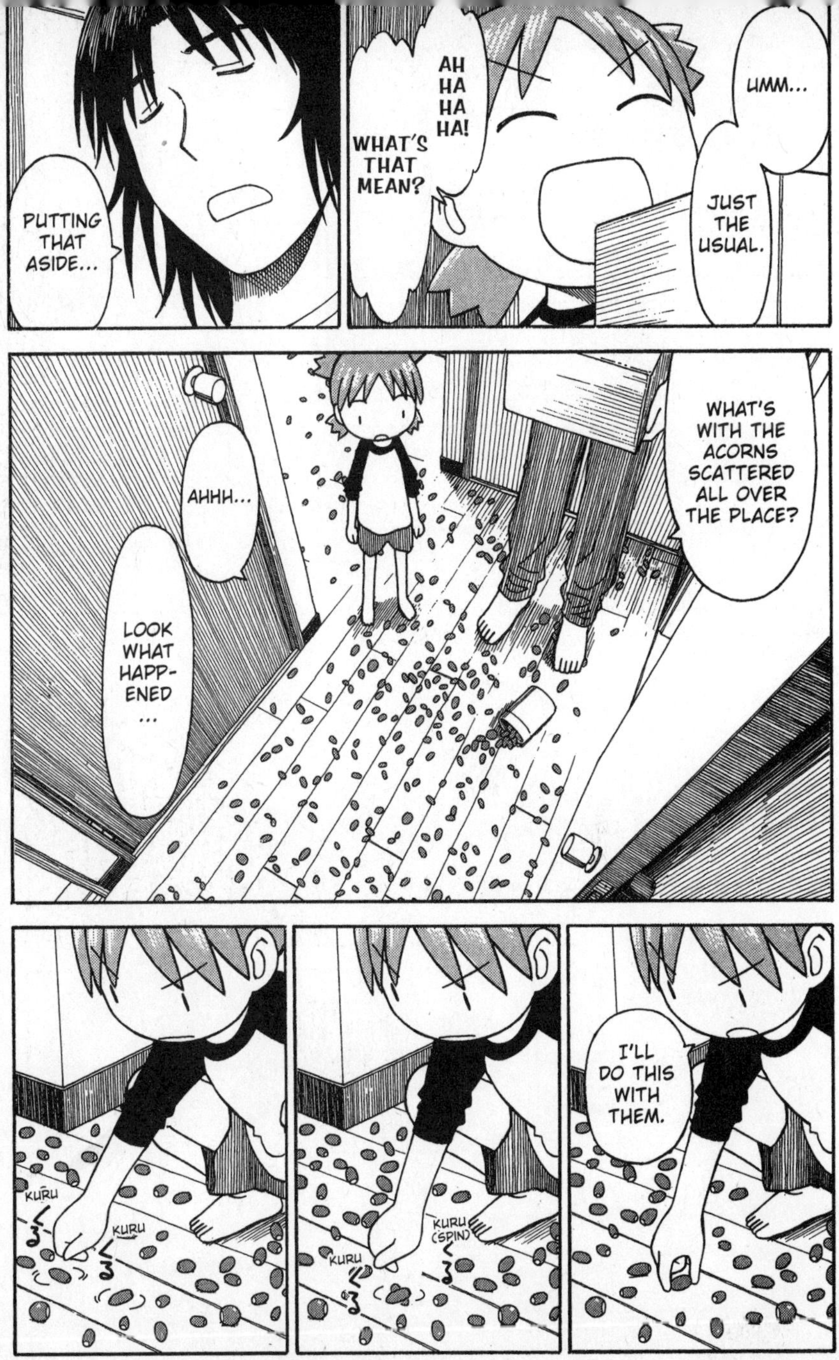
UMM...
JUST THE USUAL.
AH HA HA HA!
WHAT'S THAT MEAN?
PUTTING THAT ASIDE...
WHAT'S WITH THE ACORNS SCATTERED ALL OVER THE PLACE?
AHHH...
LOOK WHAT HAPPENED...
I'LL DO THIS WITH THEM.
KURU (SPIN)
KURU
KURU
KURU

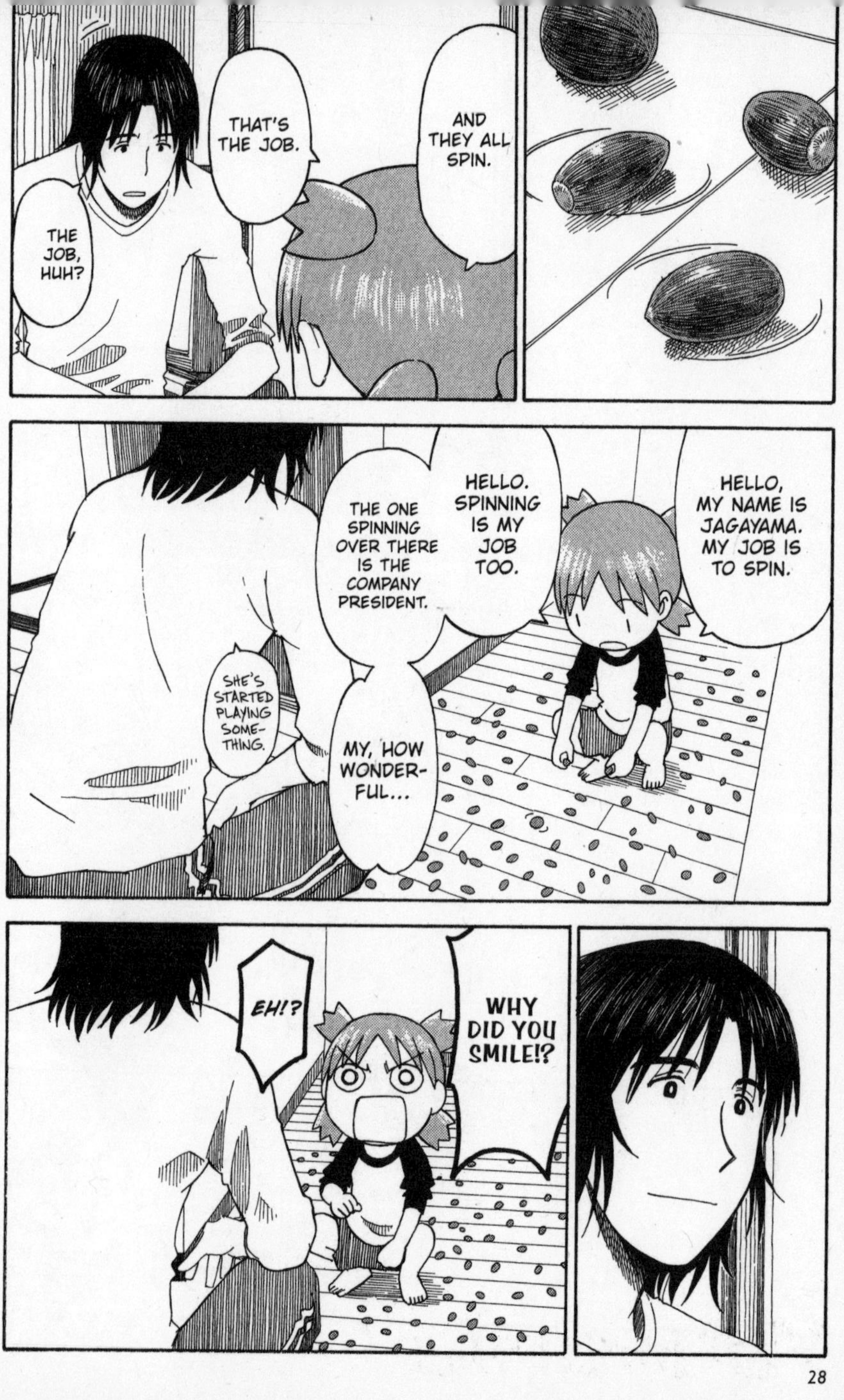
AND THEY ALL SPIN.
THAT'S THE JOB.
THE JOB, HUH?
HELLO, MY NAME IS JAGAYAMA. MY JOB IS TO SPIN.
HELLO. SPINNING IS MY JOB TOO.
THE ONE SPINNING OVER THERE IS THE COMPANY PRESIDENT.
MY, HOW WONDERFUL...
SHE'S STARTED PLAYING SOME-THING.
WHY DID YOU SMILE!?
EH!?

YOTSUBA&!

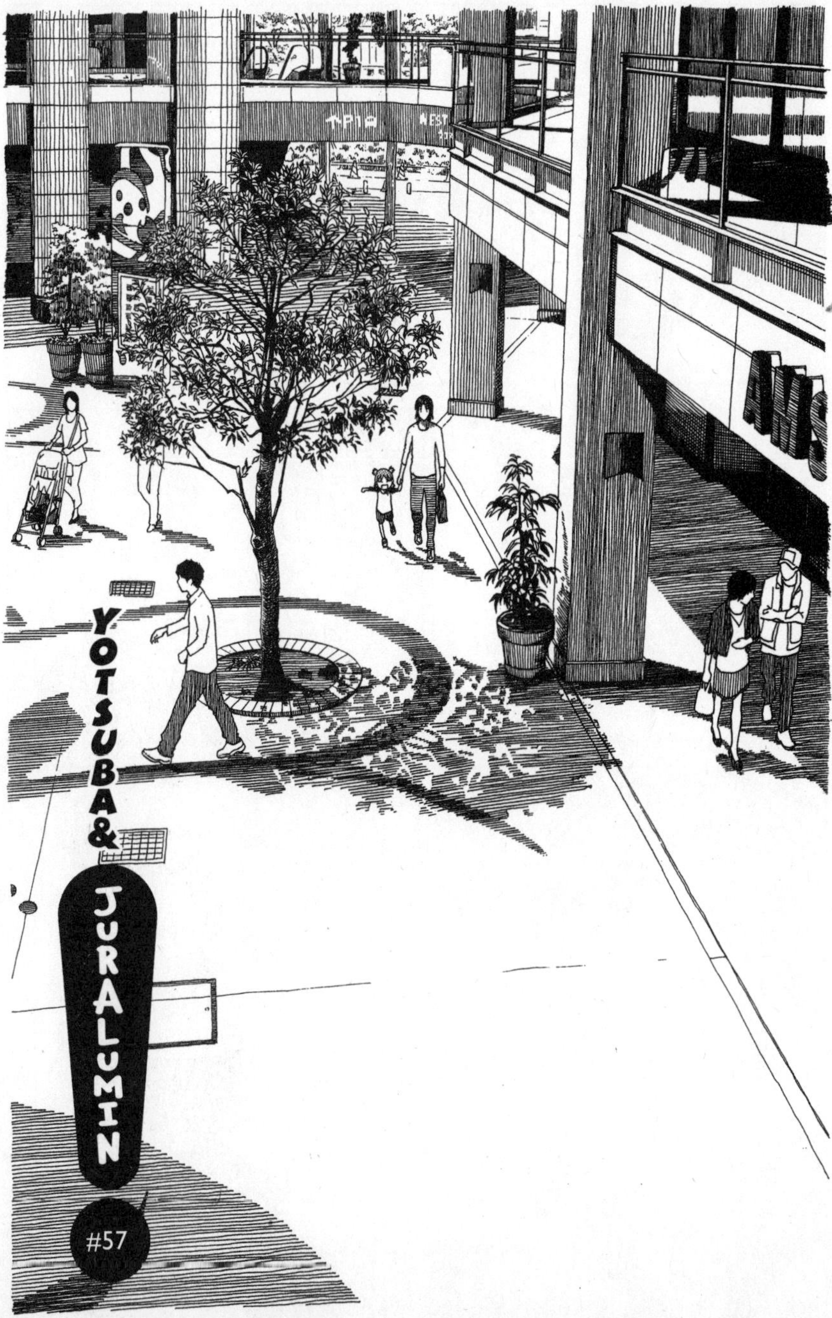
YOTSUBA&
JURALUMIN!
#57

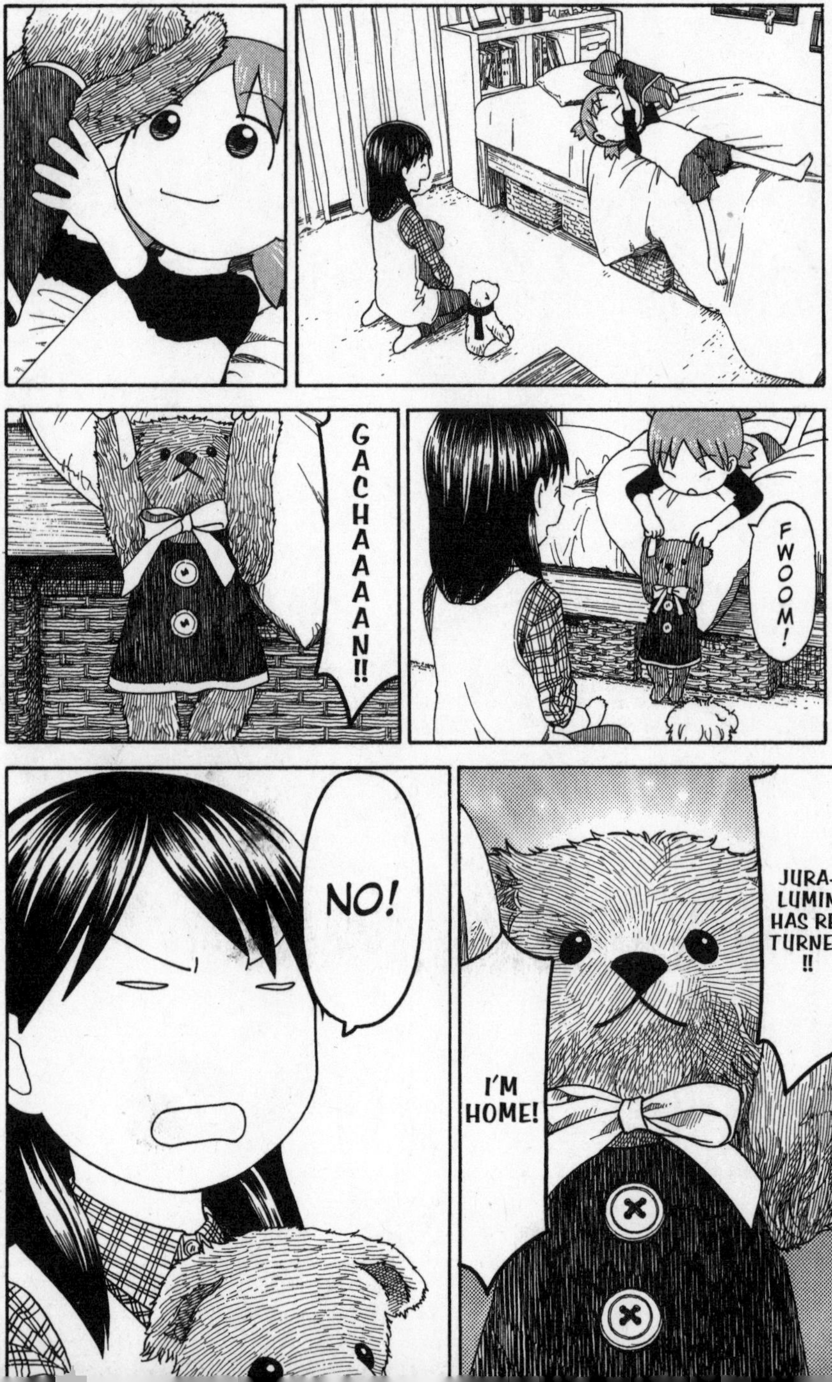
FWOOM!
GACHAAAAAN!!
JURA-LUMIN HAS RE-TURNED!!
I'M HOME!
NO!

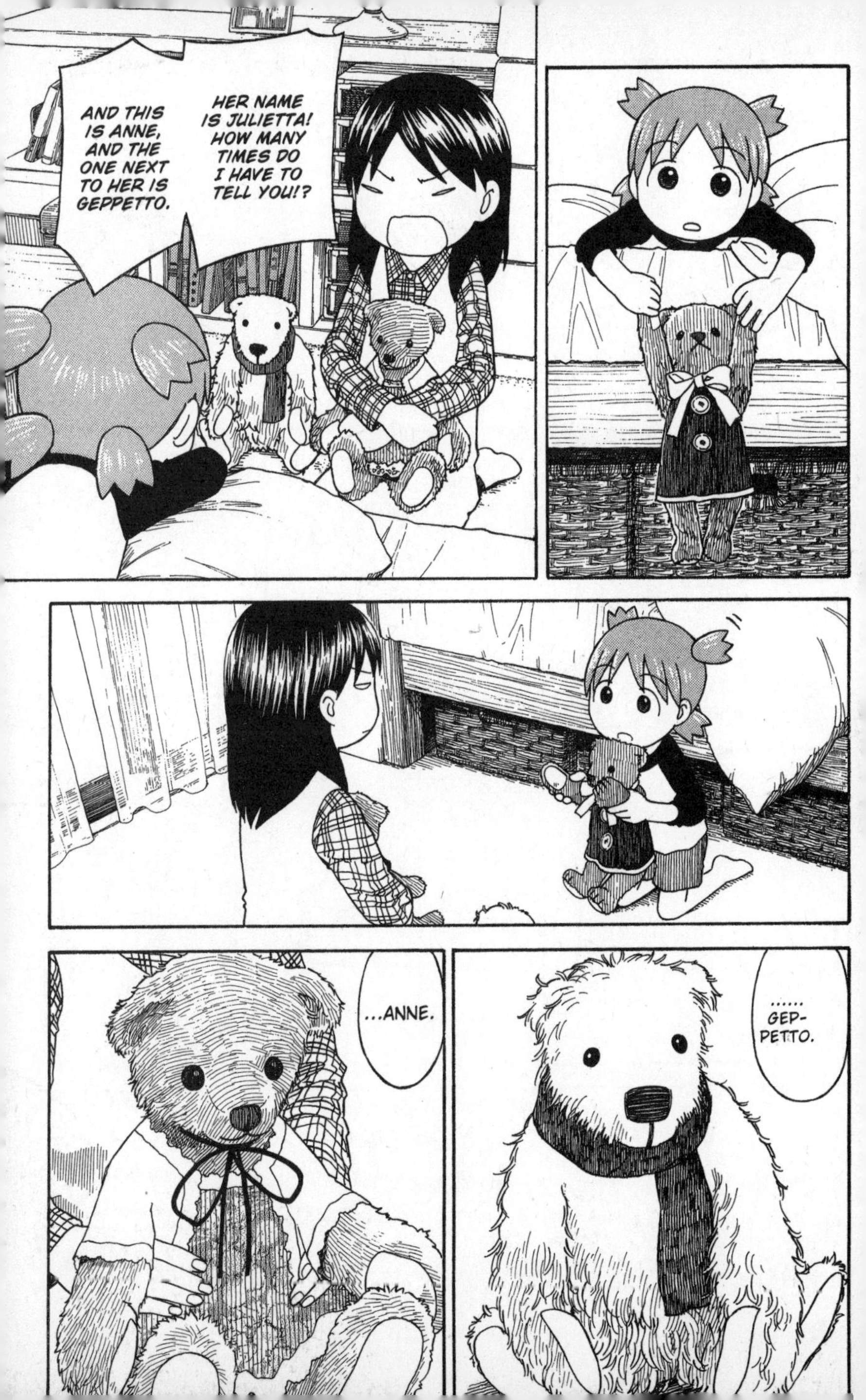
AND THIS IS ANNE, AND THE ONE NEXT TO HER IS GEPPETTO.
HER NAME IS JULIETTA! HOW MANY TIMES DO I HAVE TO TELL YOU!?
...... GEP-PETTO.
...ANNE.

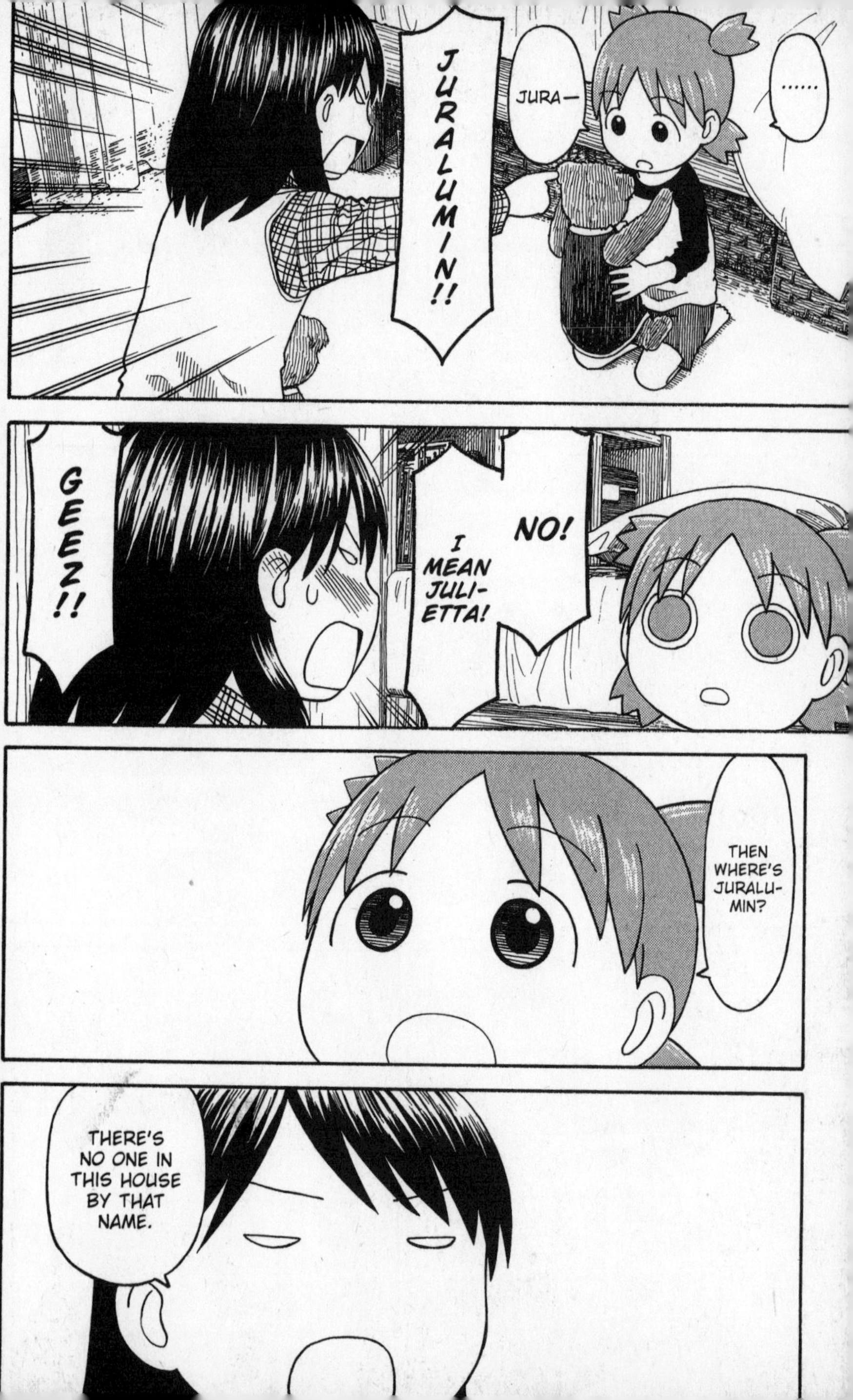
......
JURA—
JURALUMIN!!
NO! I MEAN JULI-ETTA!
GEEZ!!
THEN WHERE'S JURALU-MIN?
THERE'S NO ONE IN THIS HOUSE BY THAT NAME.

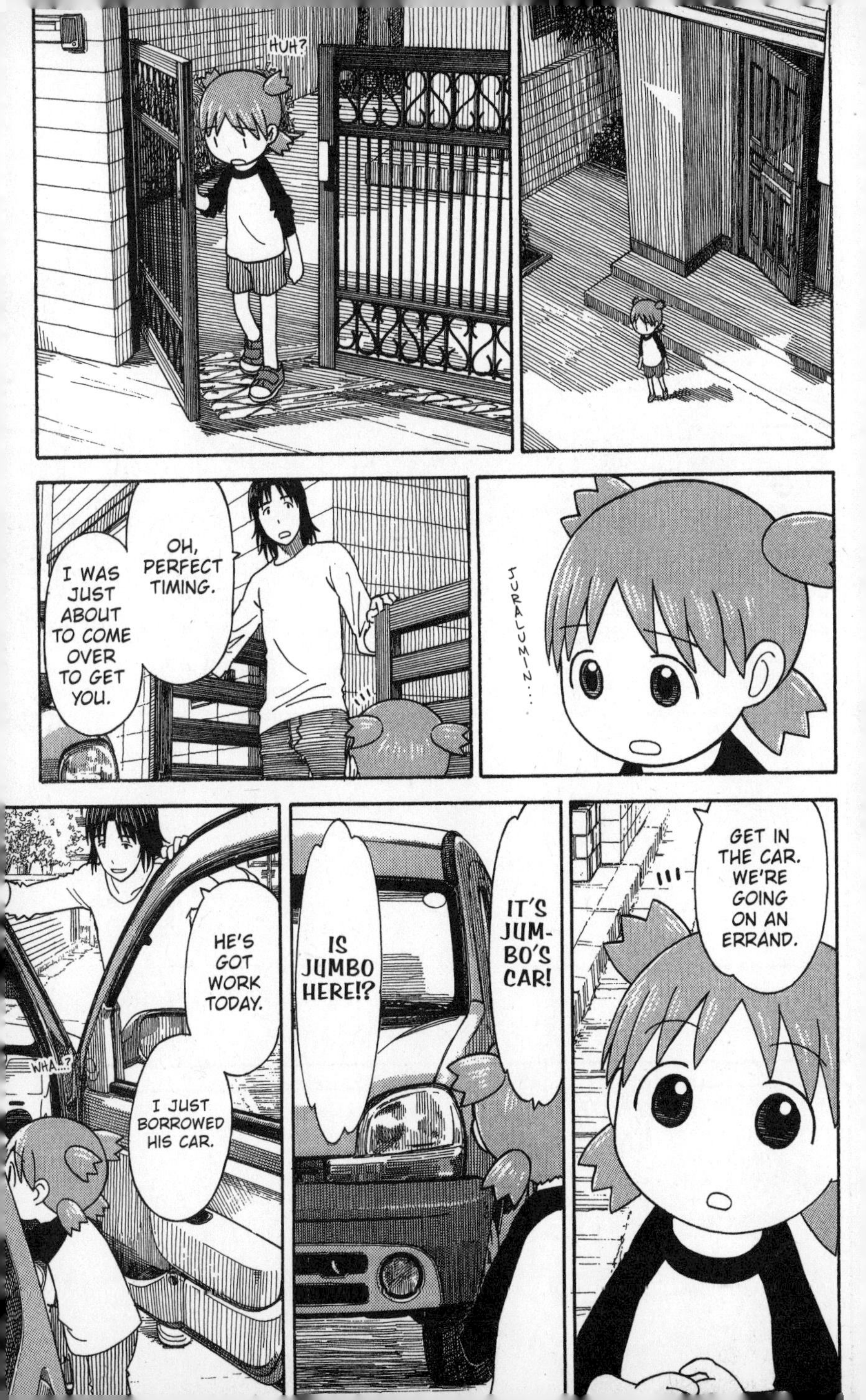

HUH?
JURALUMIN...
OH, PERFECT TIMING.
I WAS JUST ABOUT TO COME OVER TO GET YOU.
GET IN THE CAR. WE'RE GOING ON AN ERRAND.
!!!
IT'S JUMBO'S CAR!
IS JUMBO HERE!?
HE'S GOT WORK TODAY.
I JUST BORROWED HIS CAR.
WHA...?

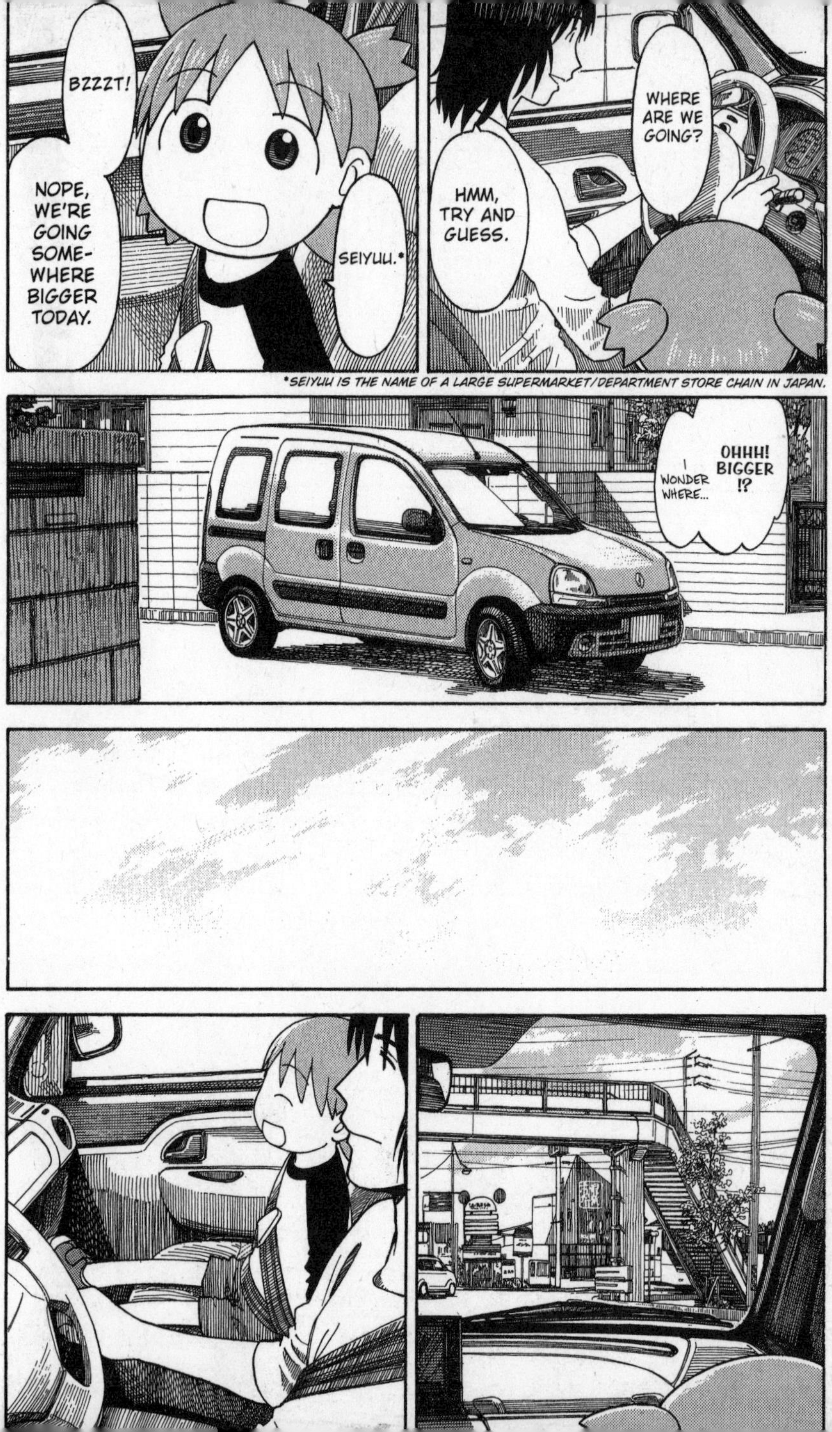
WHERE ARE WE GOING?
HMM, TRY AND GUESS.
SEIYUU.*
BZZZT!
NOPE, WE'RE GOING SOME-WHERE BIGGER TODAY.
OHHH! BIGGER!?
I WONDER WHERE...

*SEIYUU IS THE NAME OF A LARGE SUPERMARKET/DEPARTMENT STORE CHAIN IN JAPAN.

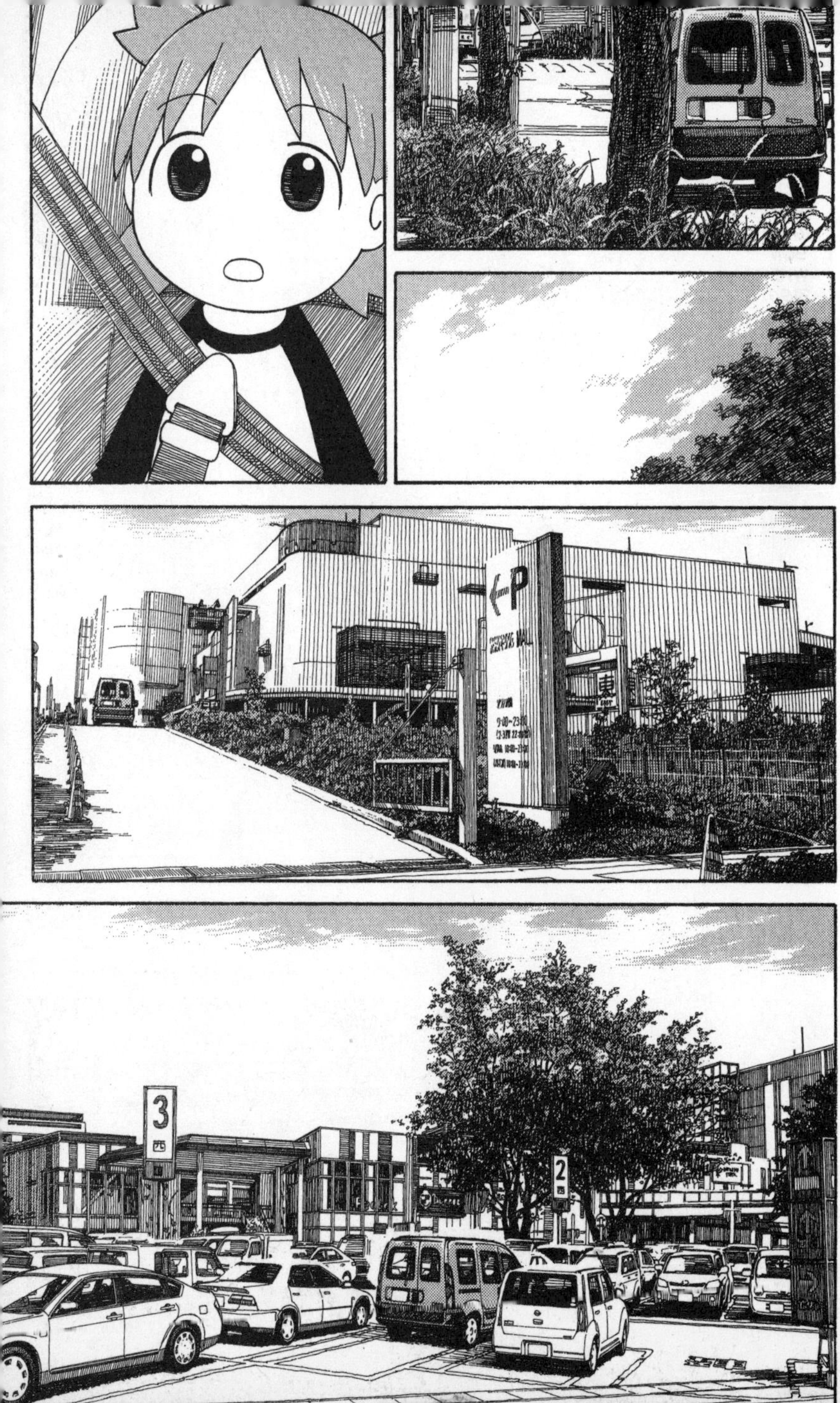
P
東
2
3

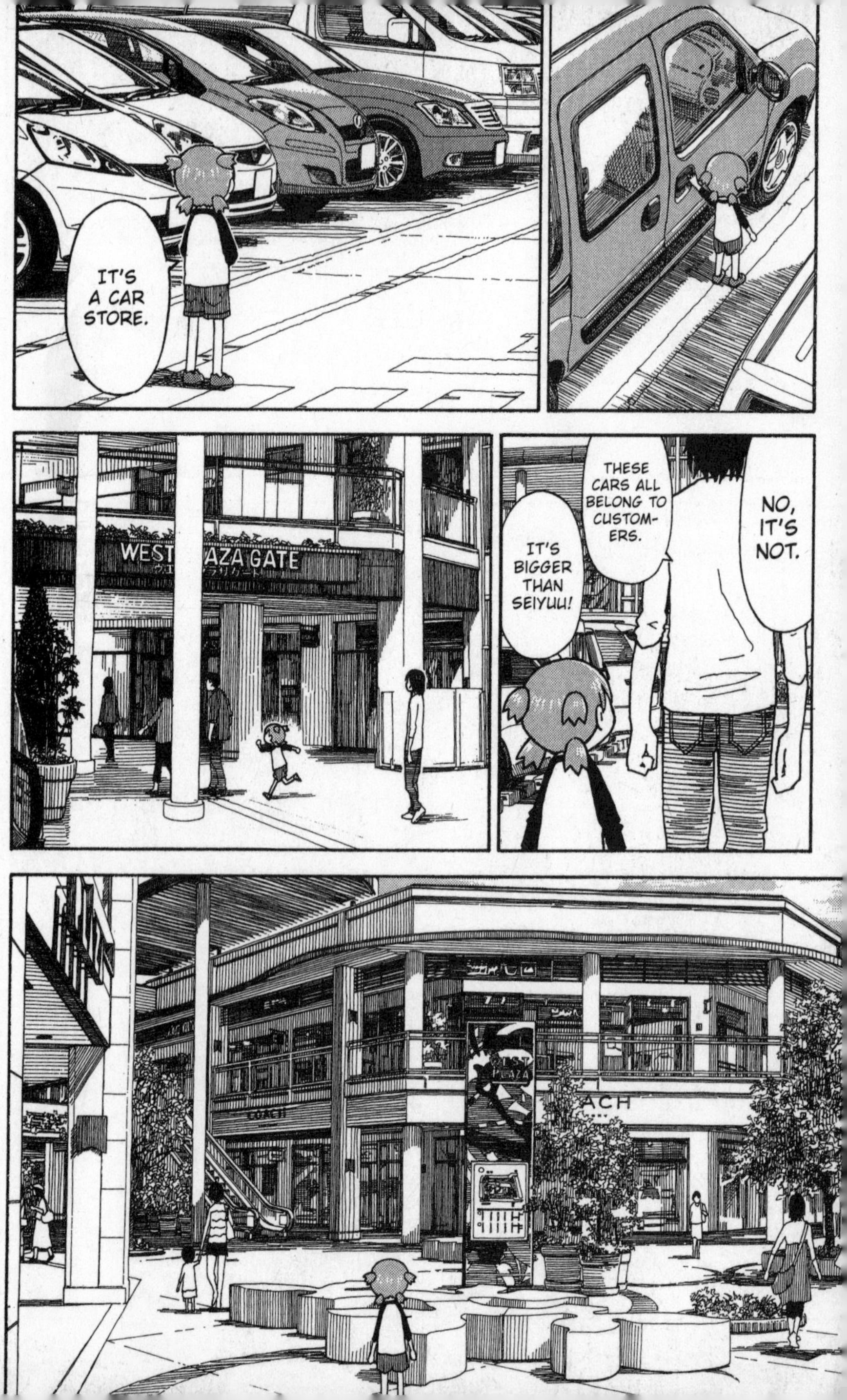
IT'S A CAR STORE.
NO, IT'S NOT.
THESE CARS ALL BELONG TO CUSTOM-ERS.
IT'S BIGGER THAN SEIYUU!
WEST
AZA GATE
COACH
ACH

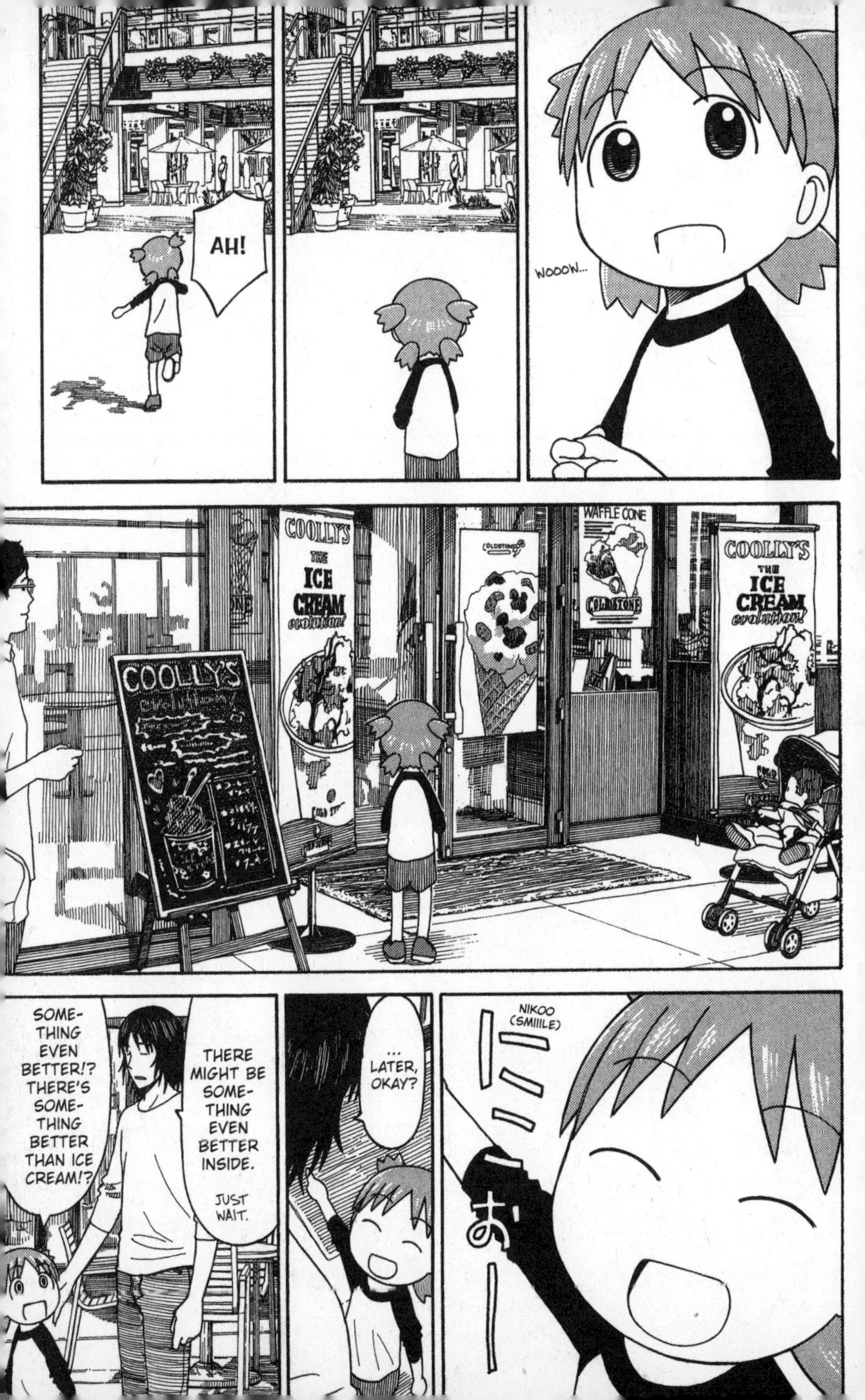
WOOOW...
AH!
COOLLY'S THE ICE CREAM evolution!
WAFFLE CONE
COLDSTONE
COOLLY'S THE ICE CREAM evolution!
COOLLY'S
NIKOO (SMIIILE)
おー
... LATER, OKAY?
THERE MIGHT BE SOME-THING EVEN BETTER INSIDE.
JUST WAIT.
SOME-THING EVEN BETTER!? THERE'S SOME-THING BETTER THAN ICE CREAM!?

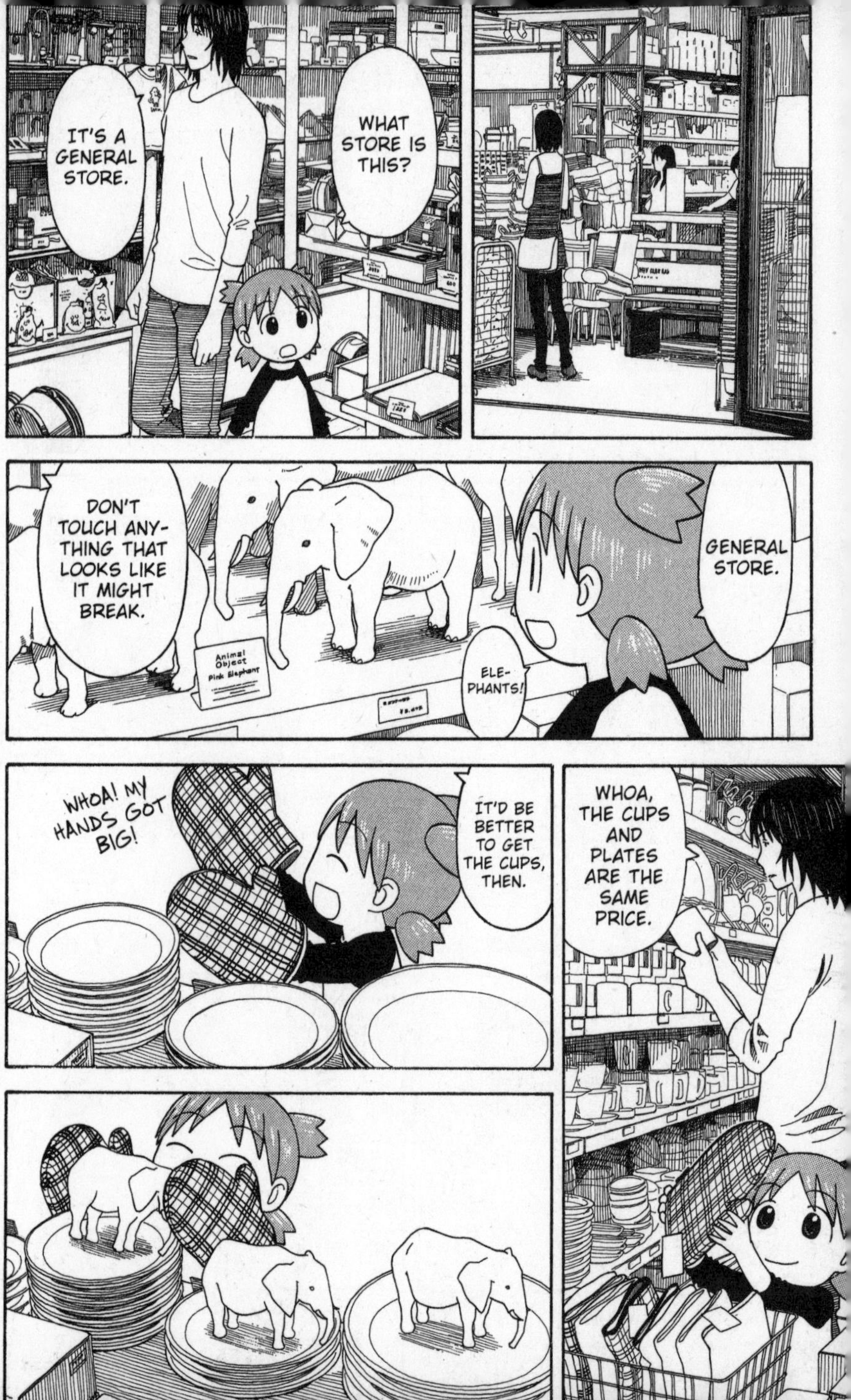
WHAT STORE IS THIS?
IT'S A GENERAL STORE.
GENERAL STORE.
ELE-PHANTS!
Animal Object
Pink Elephant
DON'T TOUCH ANY-THING THAT LOOKS LIKE IT MIGHT BREAK.
WHOA, THE CUPS AND PLATES ARE THE SAME PRICE.
IT'D BE BETTER TO GET THE CUPS, THEN.
WHOA! MY HANDS GOT BIG!

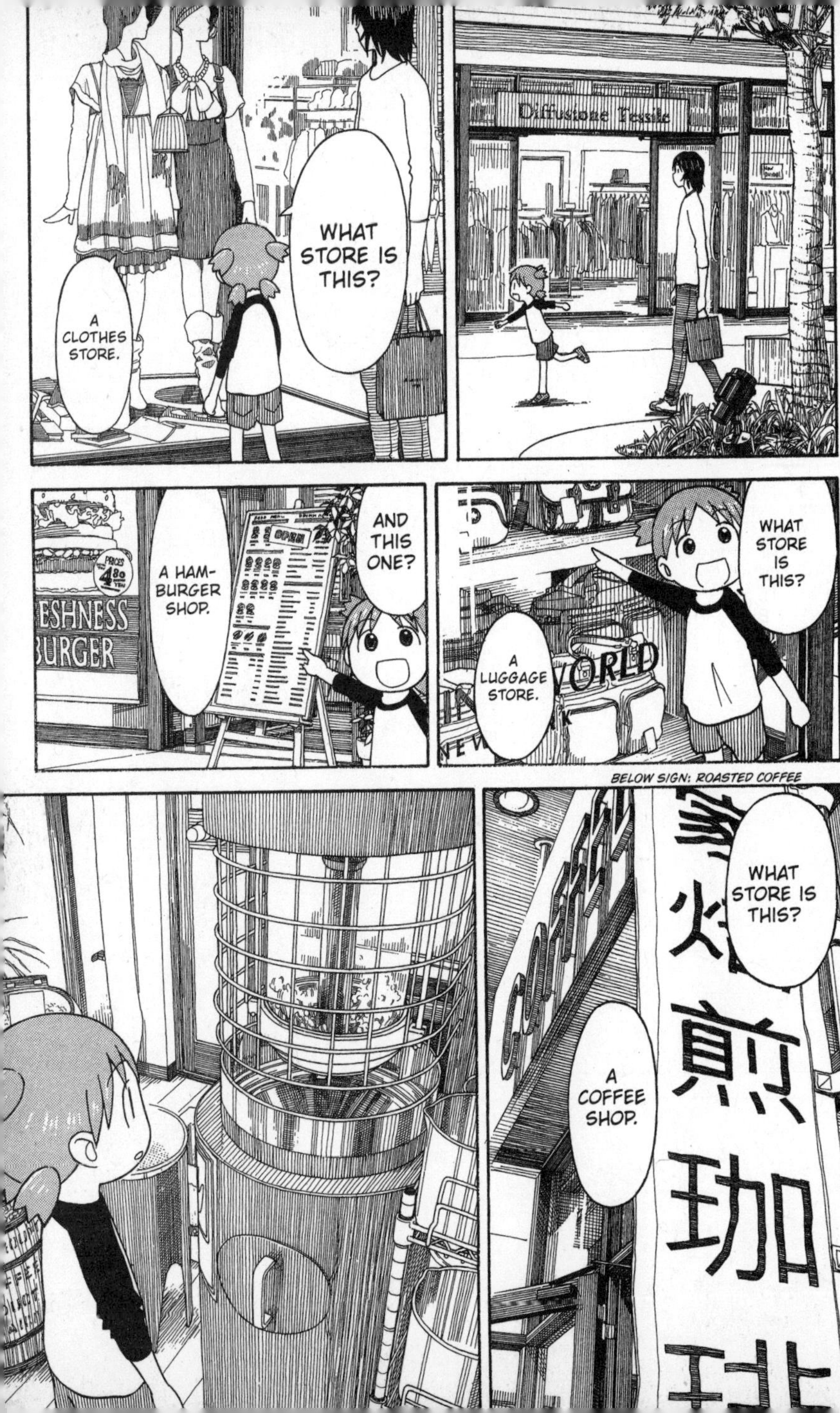
Diffusione Tessile
WHAT STORE IS THIS?
A CLOTHES STORE.
WHAT STORE IS THIS?
WORLD
A LUGGAGE STORE.
AND THIS ONE?
ESHNESS BURGER
A HAM-BURGER SHOP.
BELOW SIGN: ROASTED COFFEE
WHAT STORE IS THIS?
A COFFEE SHOP.

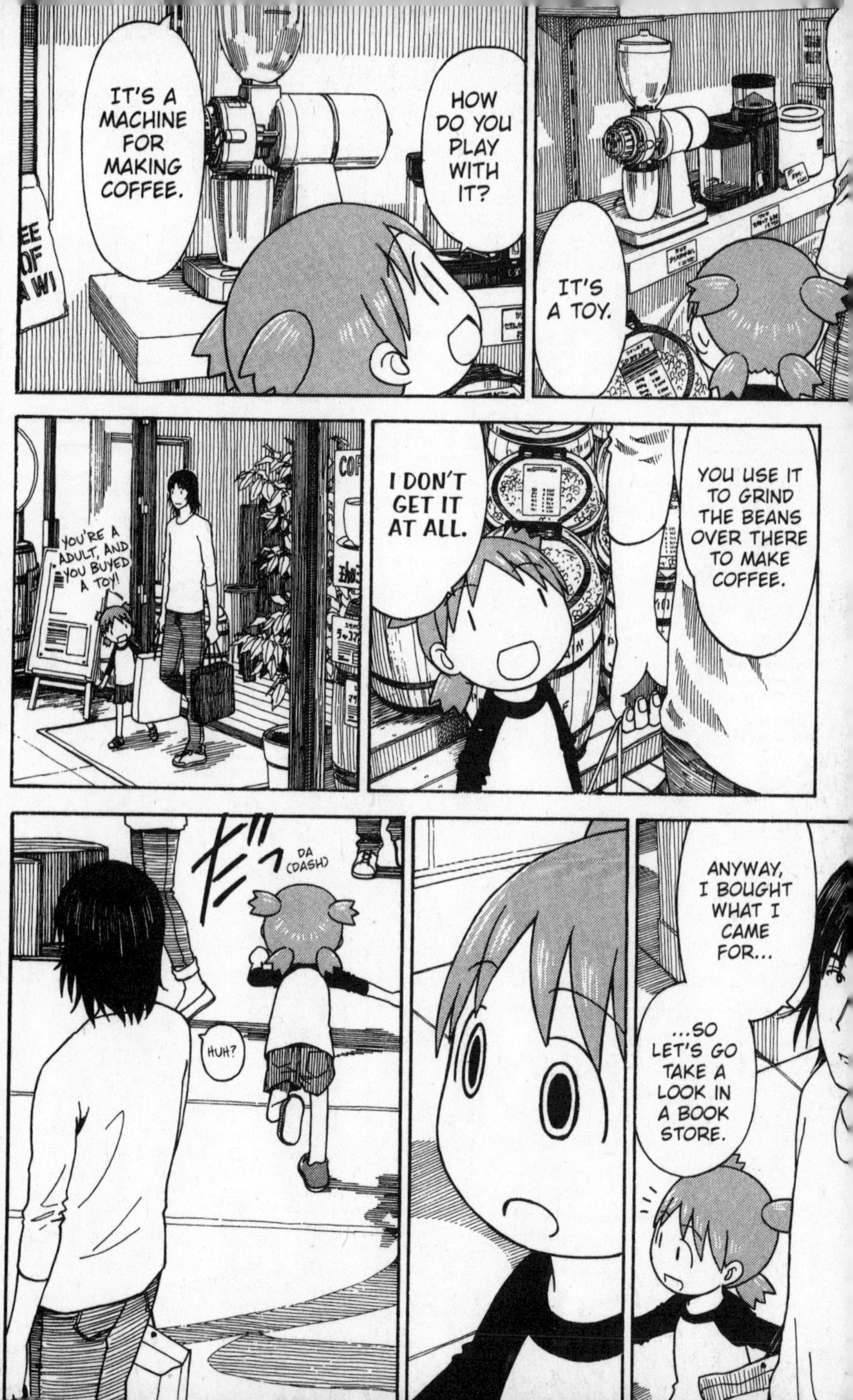
IT'S A TOY.
HOW DO YOU PLAY WITH IT?
IT'S A MACHINE FOR MAKING COFFEE.
YOU USE IT TO GRIND THE BEANS OVER THERE TO MAKE COFFEE.
I DON'T GET IT AT ALL.
YOU'RE A ADULT, AND YOU BUYED A TOY!
ANYWAY, I BOUGHT WHAT I CAME FOR...
...SO LET'S GO TAKE A LOOK IN A BOOK STORE.
DA (DASH)
HUH?

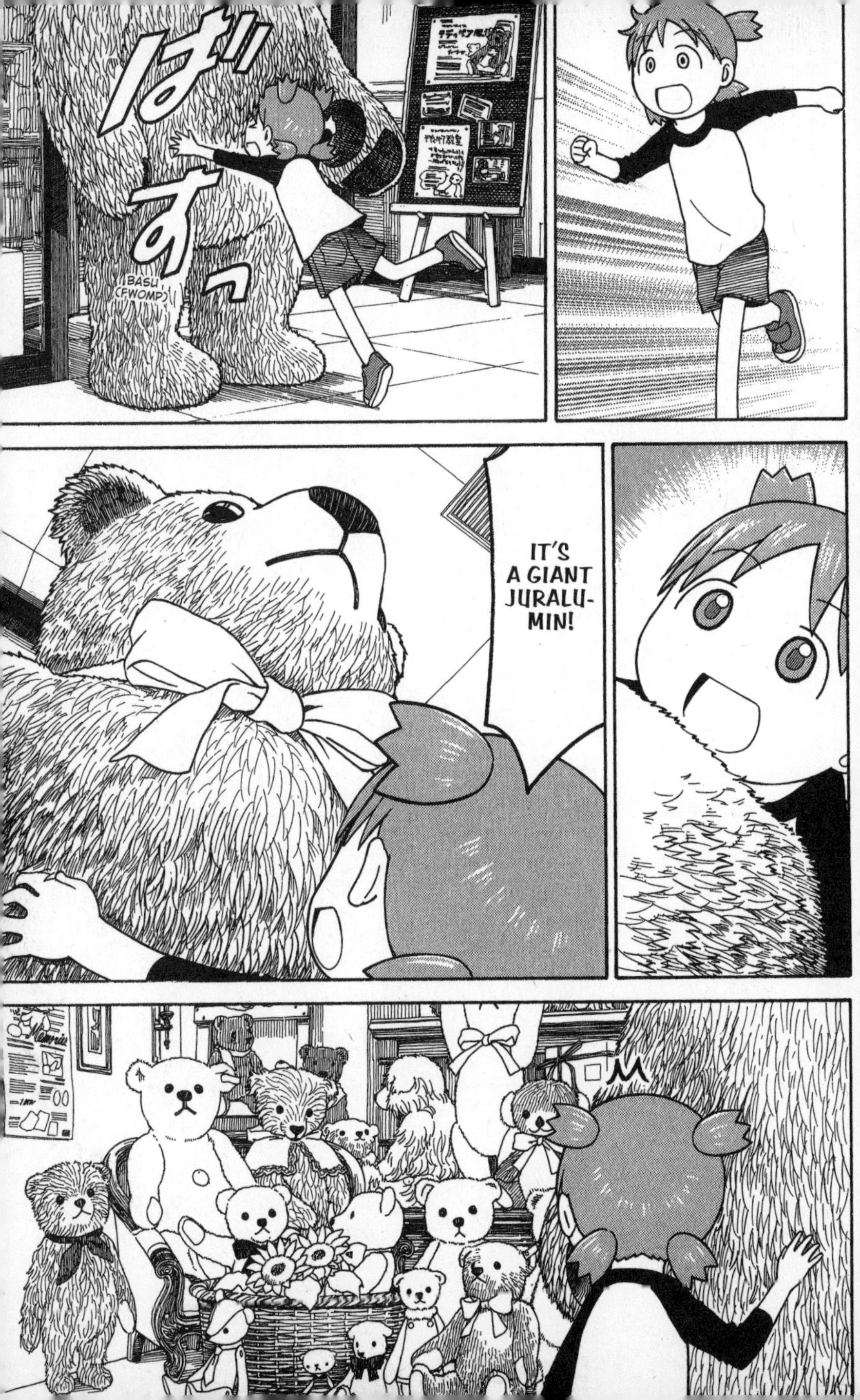
ばすっ
BASU (FWOMP)
IT'S A GIANT JURALU-MIN!

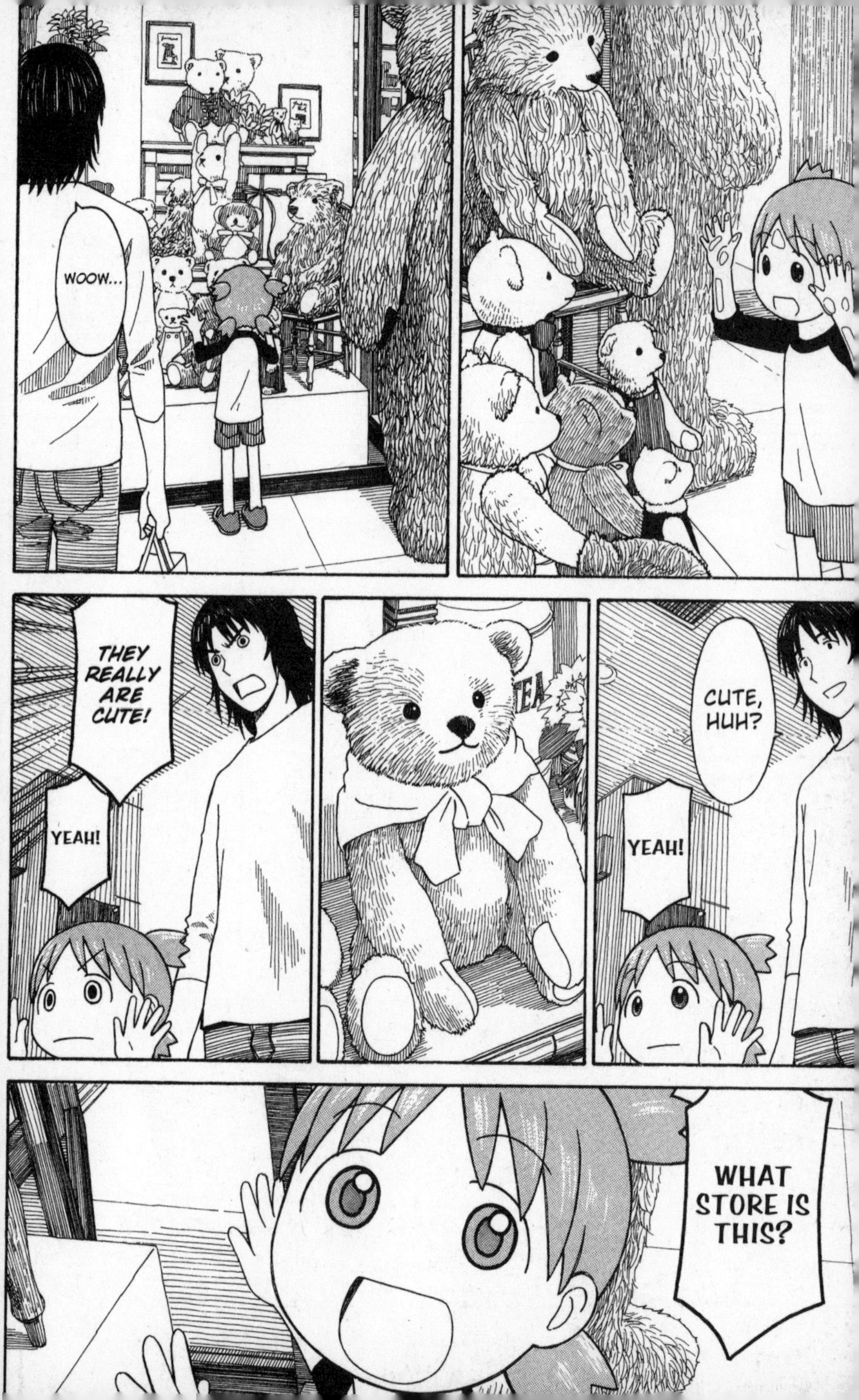
WOOW...
CUTE, HUH?
YEAH!
TEA
THEY REALLY ARE CUTE!
YEAH!
WHAT STORE IS THIS?

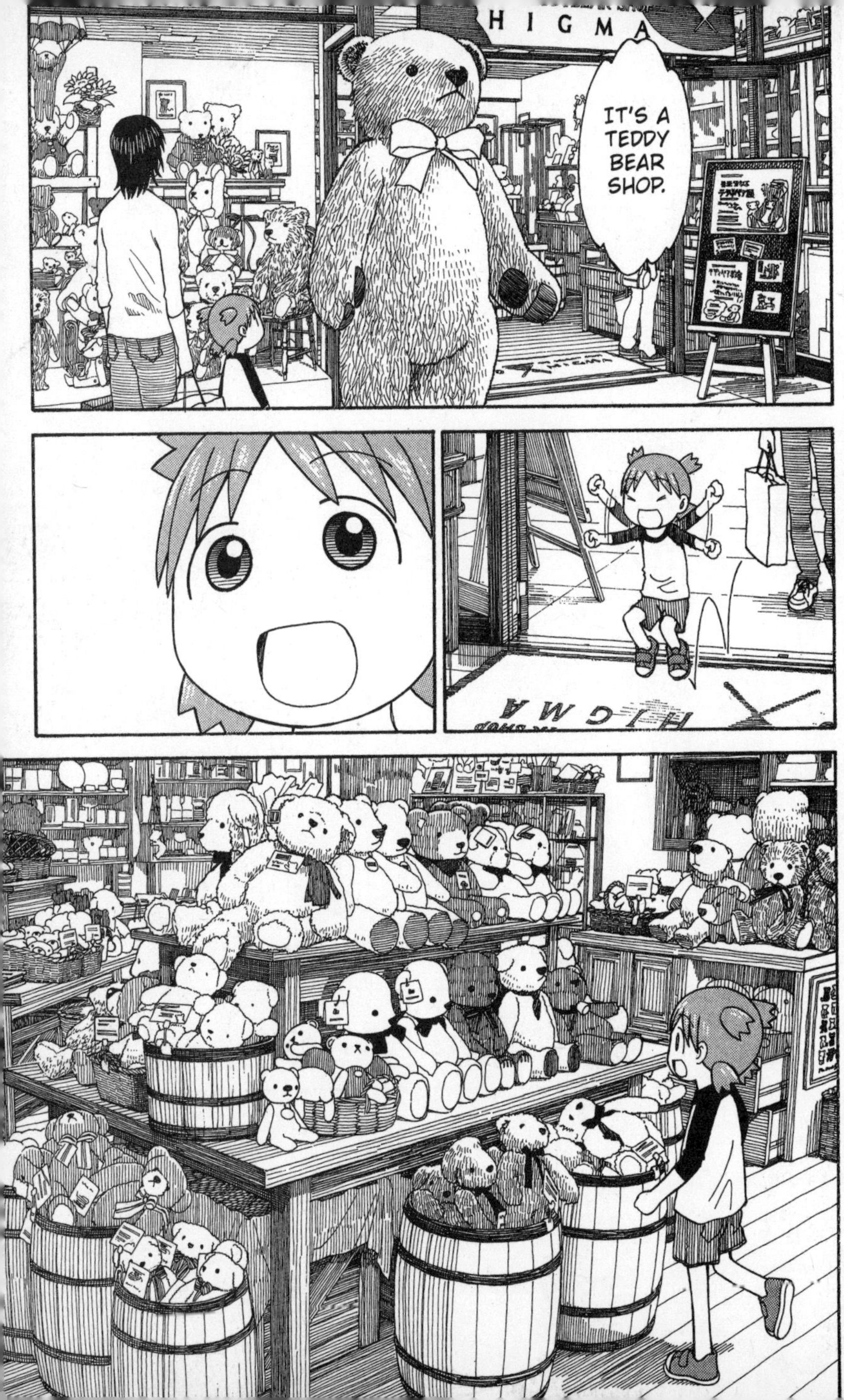
HIGMA
IT'S A TEDDY BEAR SHOP.
HIGMA

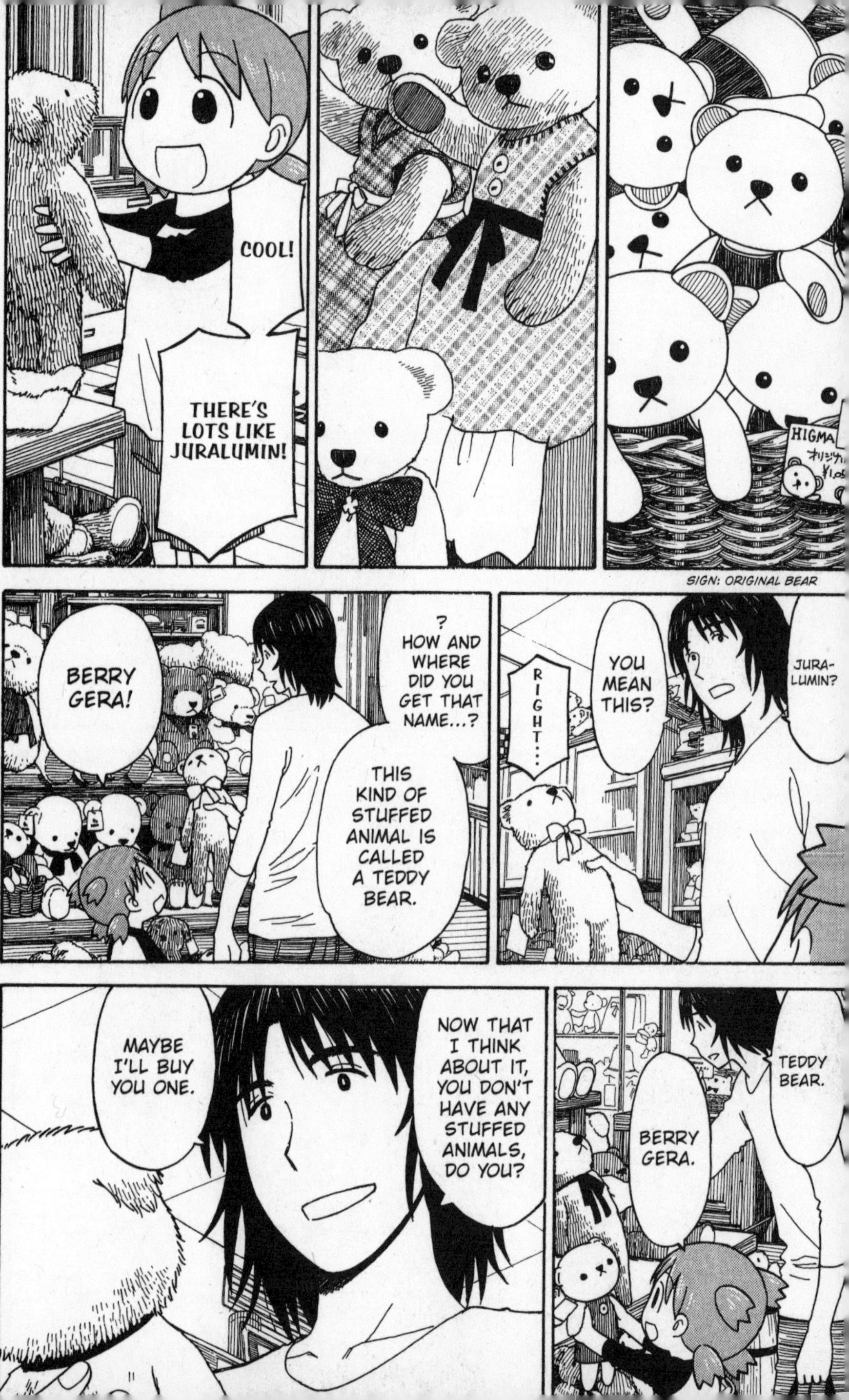
HIGMA
SIGN: ORIGINAL BEAR
COOL!
THERE'S LOTS LIKE JURALUMIN!
JURA-LUMIN?
YOU MEAN THIS?
RIGHT...
? HOW AND WHERE DID YOU GET THAT NAME...?
THIS KIND OF STUFFED ANIMAL IS CALLED A TEDDY BEAR.
BERRY GERA!
TEDDY BEAR.
BERRY GERA.
NOW THAT I THINK ABOUT IT, YOU DON'T HAVE ANY STUFFED ANIMALS, DO YOU?
MAYBE I'LL BUY YOU ONE.

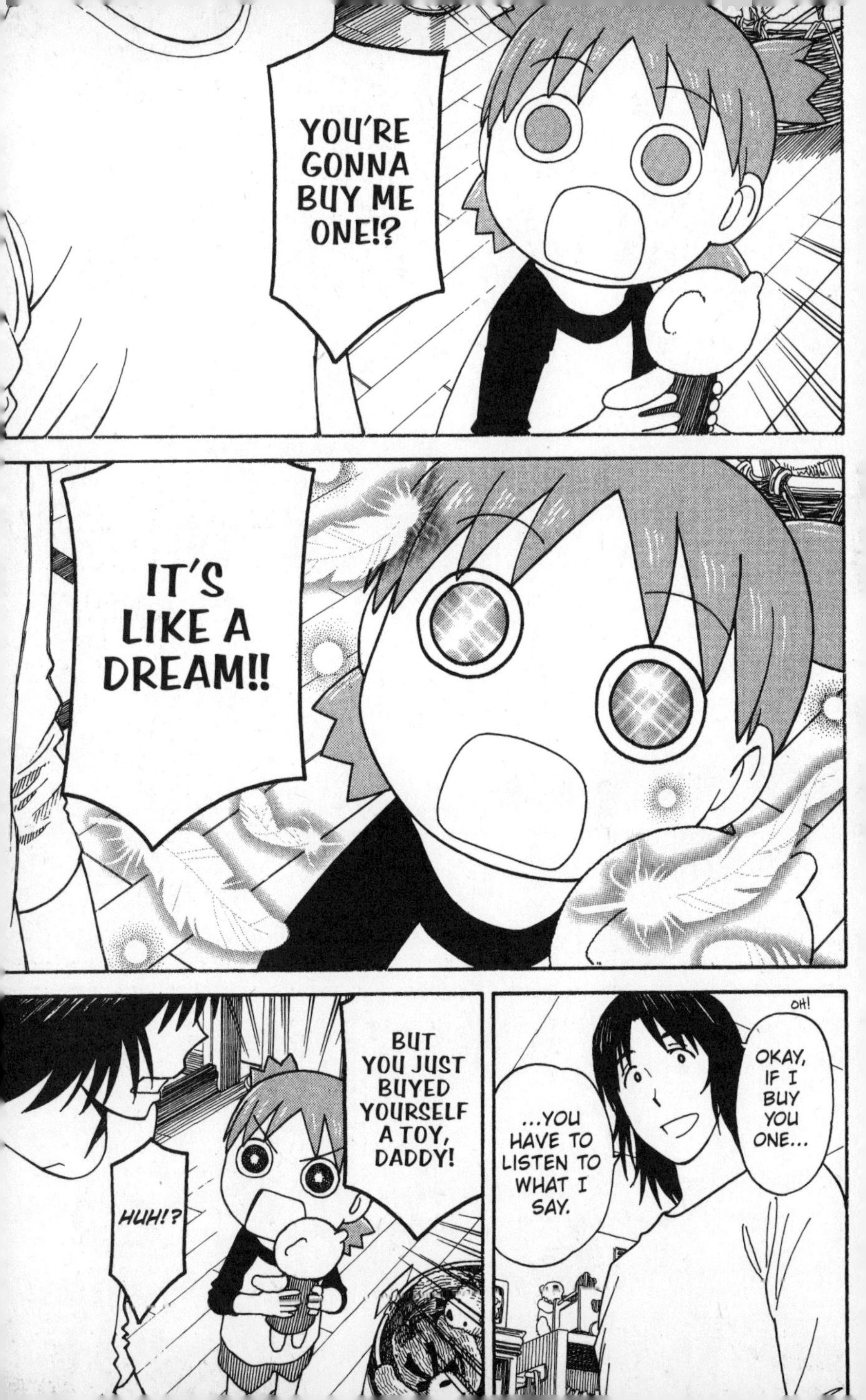
YOU'RE GONNA BUY ME ONE!?
IT'S LIKE A DREAM!!
OH!
OKAY, IF I BUY YOU ONE...
...YOU HAVE TO LISTEN TO WHAT I SAY.
BUT YOU JUST BUYED YOURSELF A TOY, DADDY!
HUH!?

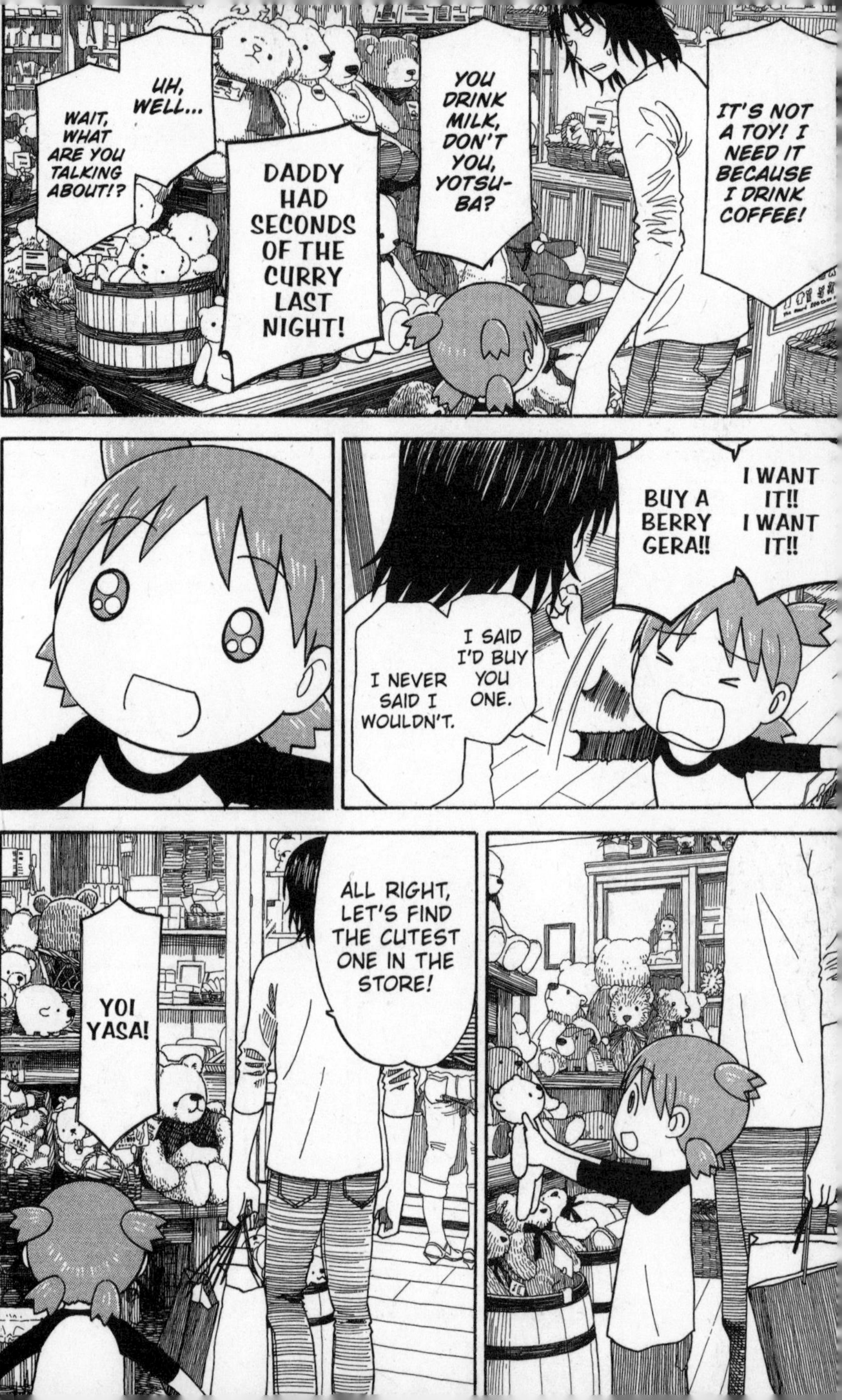
IT'S NOT A TOY! I NEED IT BECAUSE I DRINK COFFEE!
YOU DRINK MILK, DON'T YOU, YOTSUBA?
DADDY HAD SECONDS OF THE CURRY LAST NIGHT!
UH, WELL...
WAIT, WHAT ARE YOU TALKING ABOUT!?
I WANT IT!! I WANT IT!!
BUY A BERRY GERA!!
I SAID I'D BUY YOU ONE.
I NEVER SAID I WOULDN'T.
ALL RIGHT, LET'S FIND THE CUTEST ONE IN THE STORE!
YOI YASA!

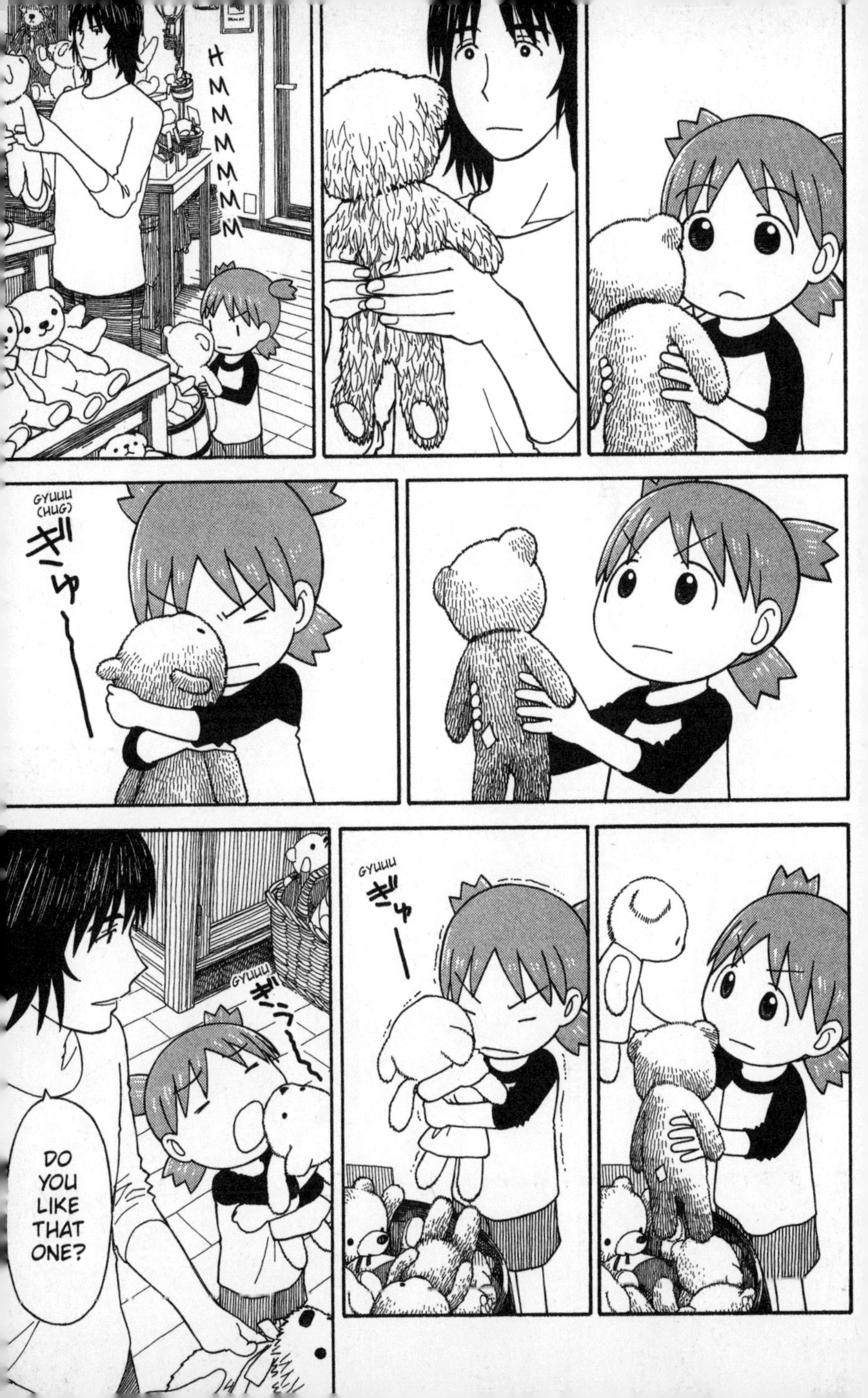

HMMMMMMM
GYUUU (HUG)
ぎゅ〜
GYUUU
ぎゅー
GYUUU
ぎゅ〜〜
DO YOU LIKE THAT ONE?

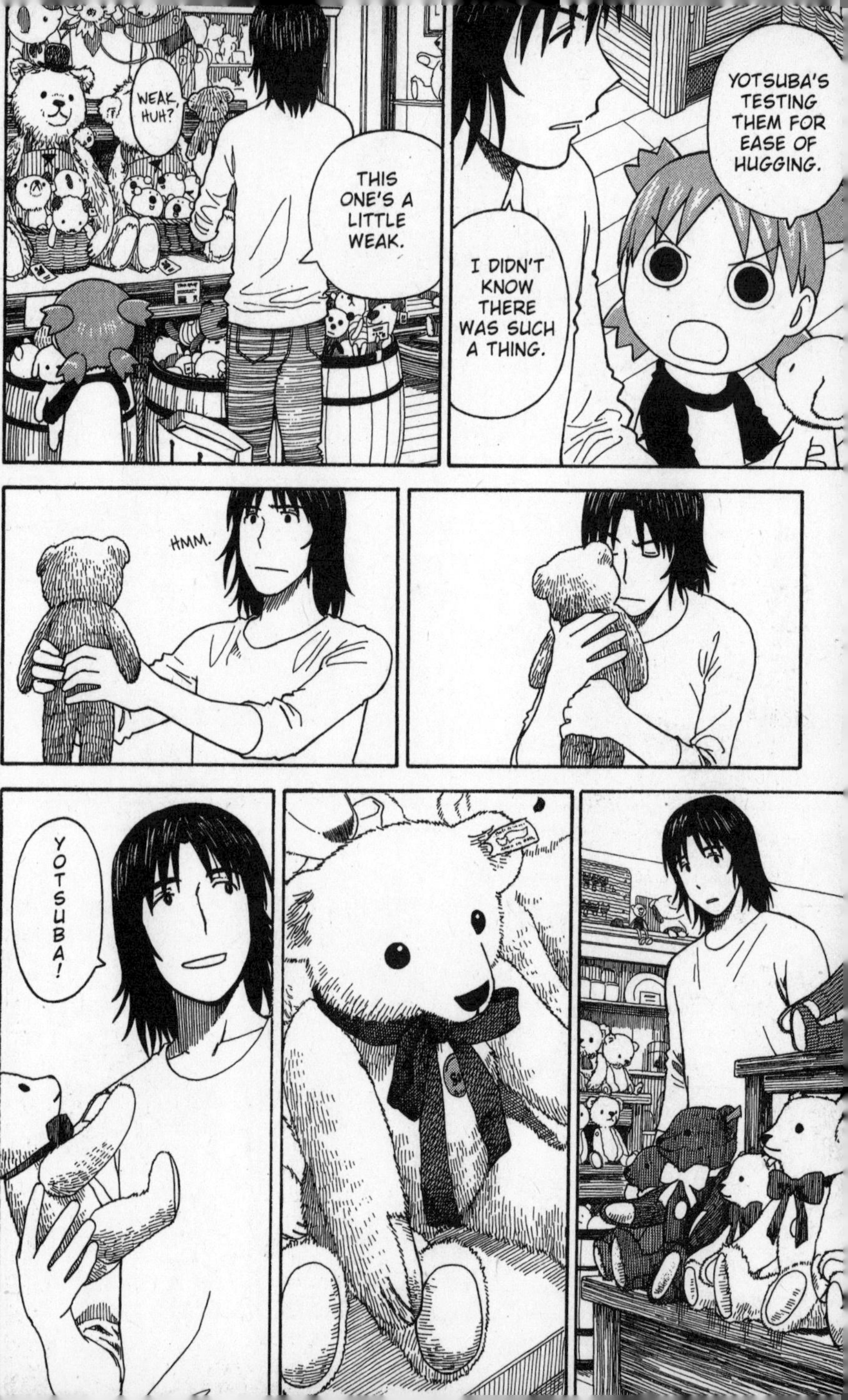
YOTSUBA'S TESTING THEM FOR EASE OF HUGGING.
I DIDN'T KNOW THERE WAS SUCH A THING.
THIS ONE'S A LITTLE WEAK.
WEAK, HUH?
HMM.
YOTSUBA!

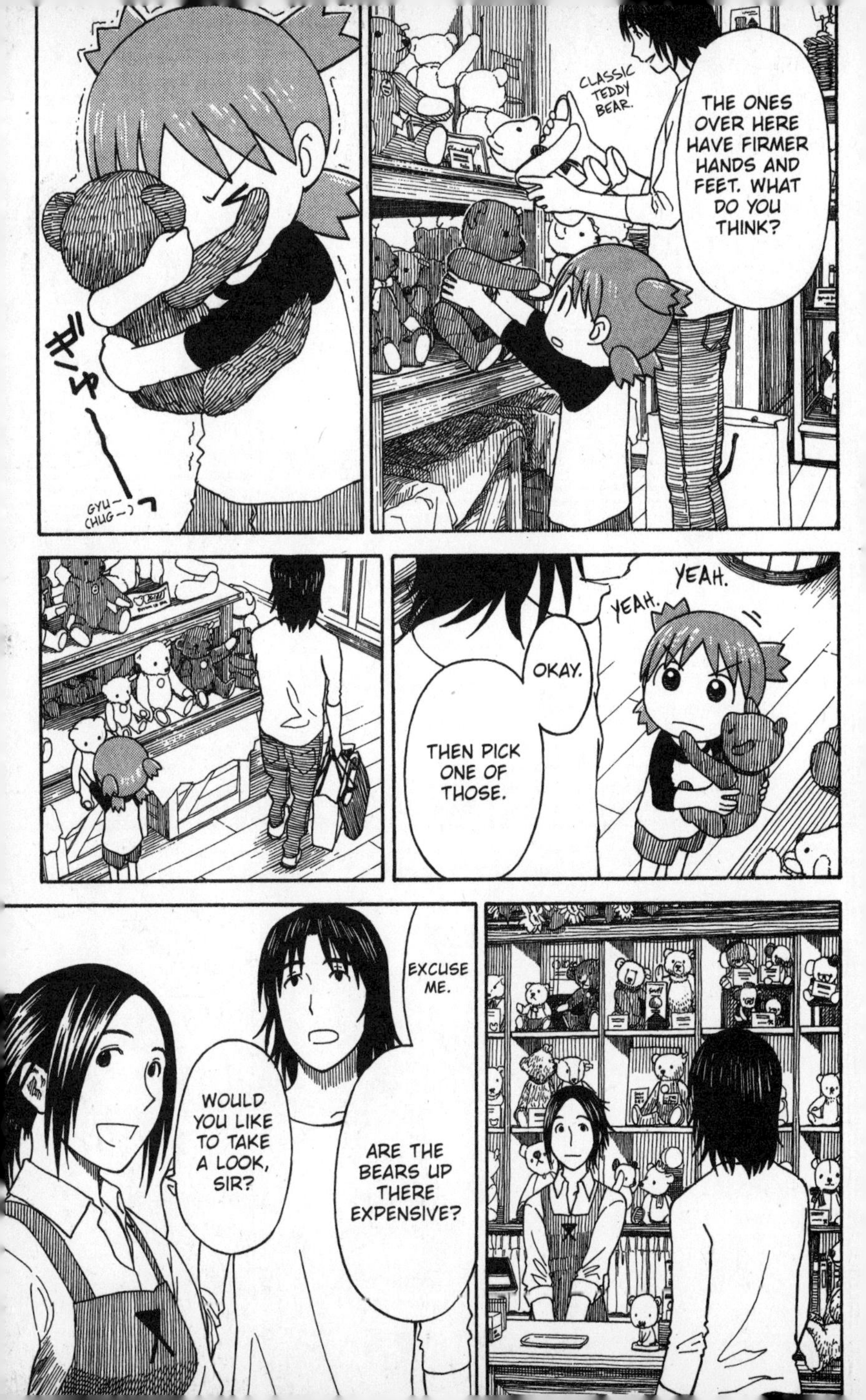
CLASSIC TEDDY BEAR.
THE ONES OVER HERE HAVE FIRMER HANDS AND FEET. WHAT DO YOU THINK?
GYU— CHUG—
YEAH.
YEAH.
OKAY.
THEN PICK ONE OF THOSE.
EXCUSE ME.
ARE THE BEARS UP THERE EXPENSIVE?
WOULD YOU LIKE TO TAKE A LOOK, SIR?

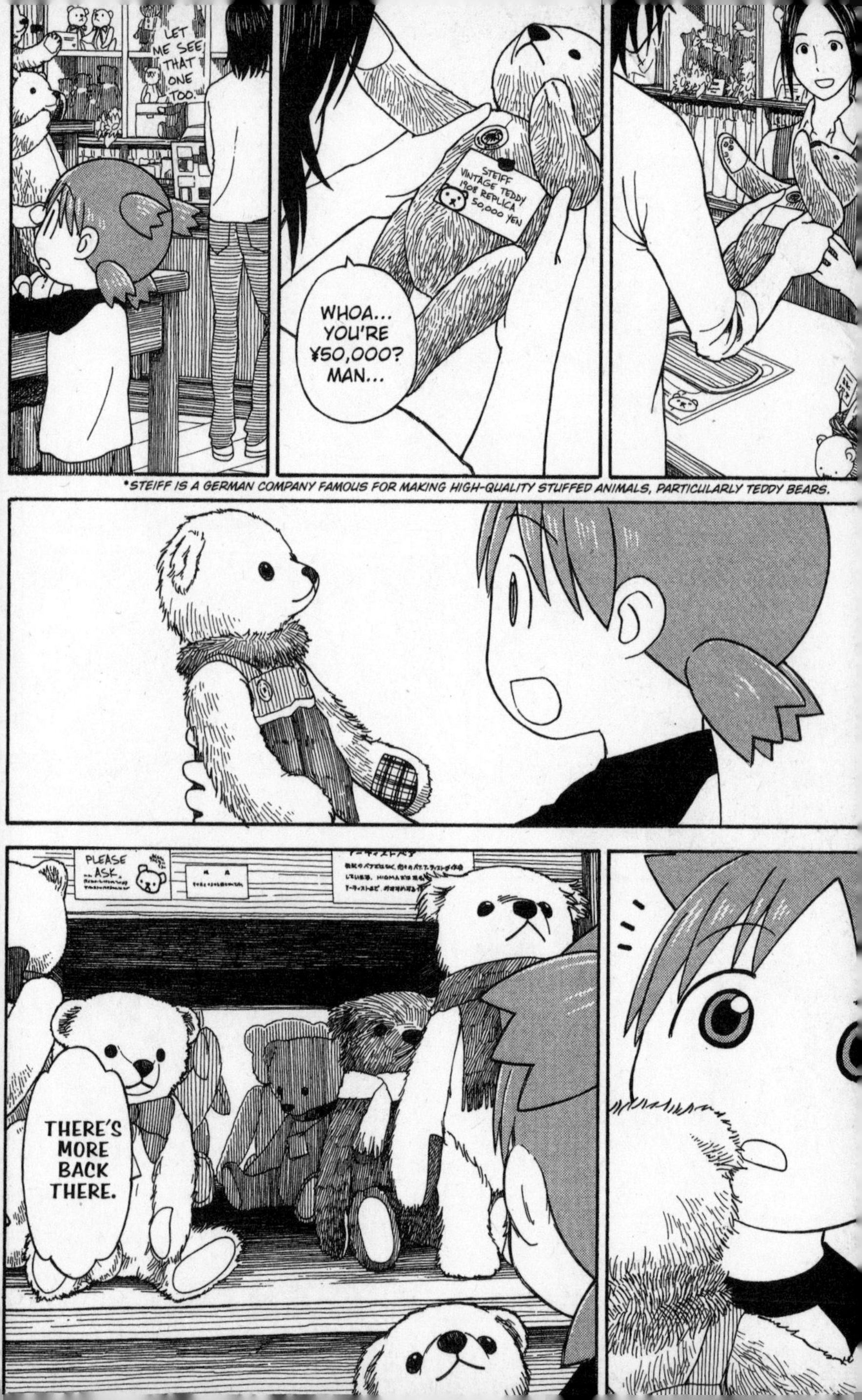
STEIFF VINTAGE TEDDY 1908 REPLICA 50,000 YEN
WHOA... YOU'RE ¥50,000? MAN...
LET ME SEE THAT ONE TOO.
PLEASE ASK.
THERE'S MORE BACK THERE.
*STEIFF IS A GERMAN COMPANY FAMOUS FOR MAKING HIGH-QUALITY STUFFED ANIMALS, PARTICULARLY TEDDY BEARS.

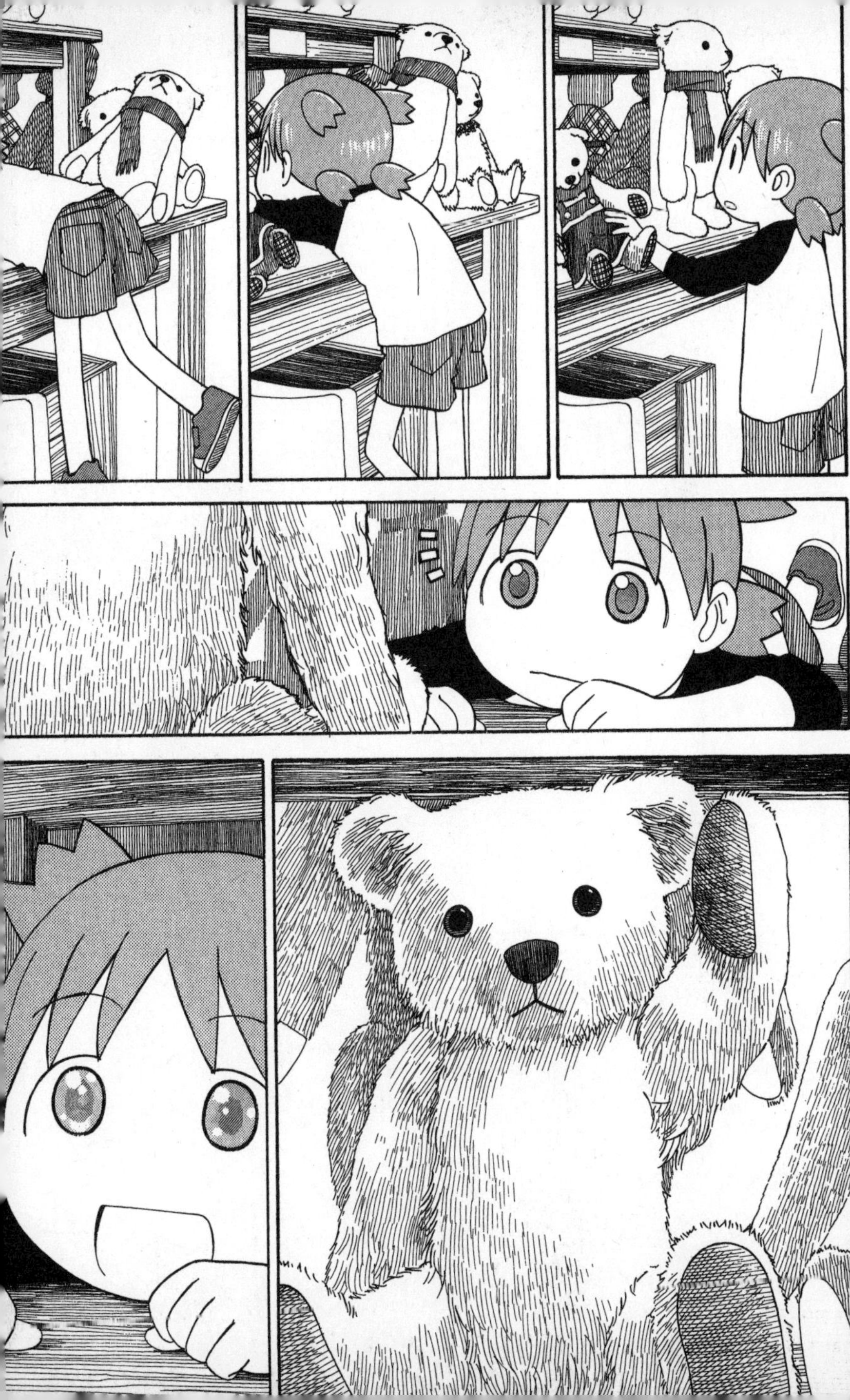

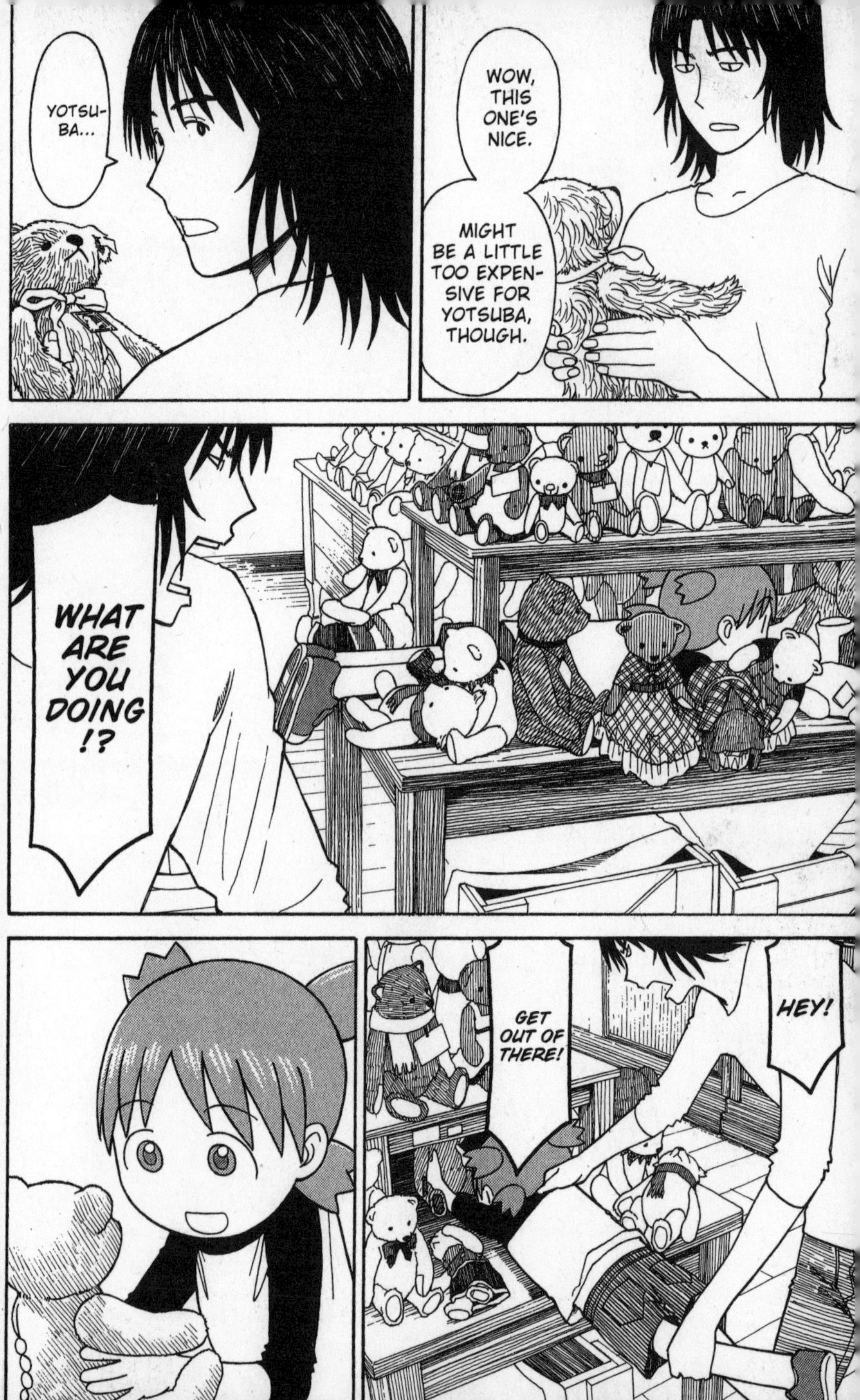
WOW, THIS ONE'S NICE.
MIGHT BE A LITTLE TOO EXPENSIVE FOR YOTSUBA, THOUGH.
YOTSUBA...
WHAT ARE YOU DOING!?
HEY!
GET OUT OF THERE!

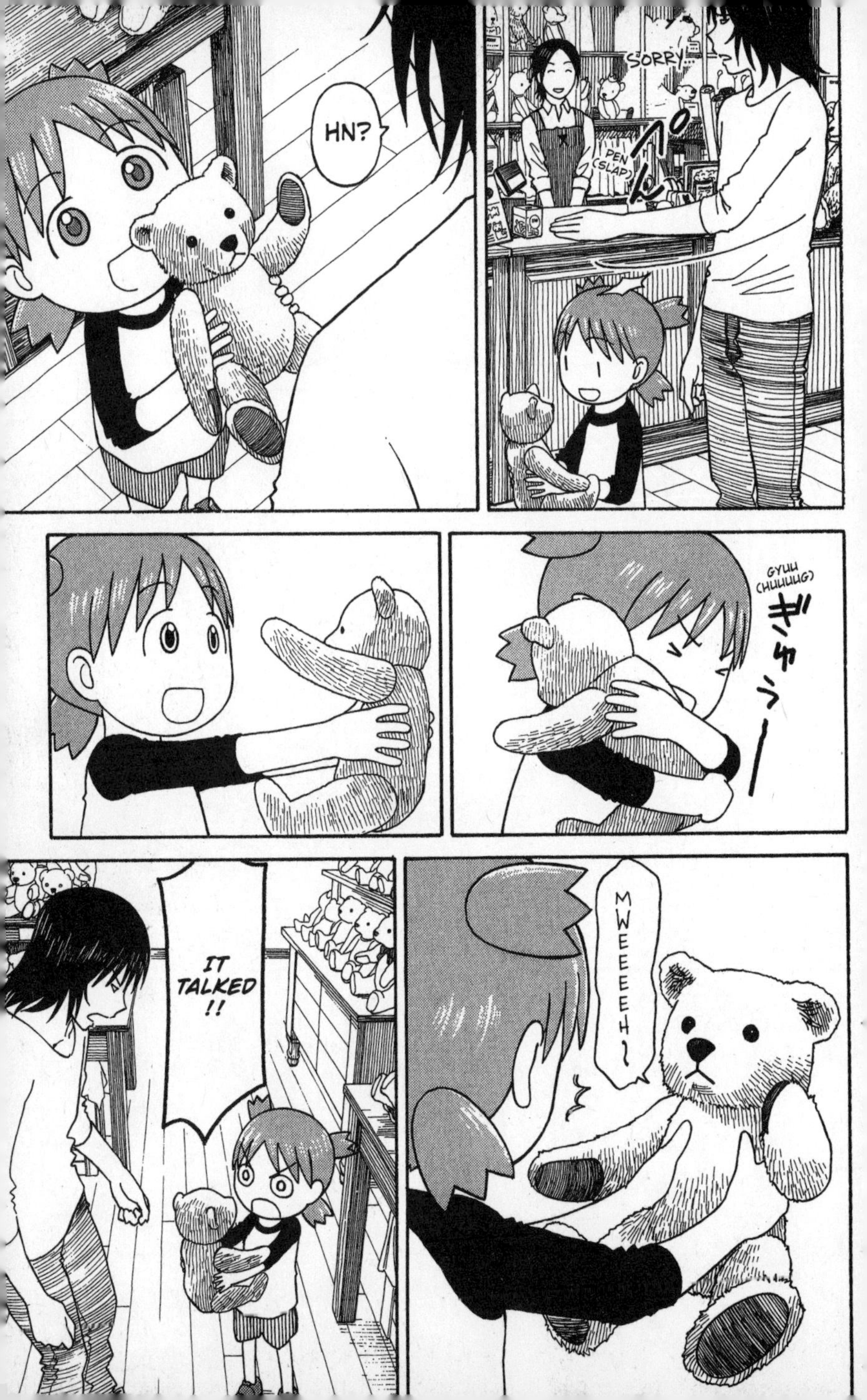
SORRY...
?
PEN (SLAP)
ぺん
HN?
GYUU (HUUUUG)
ぎゅうー
MWEEEEH~
IT TALKED !!

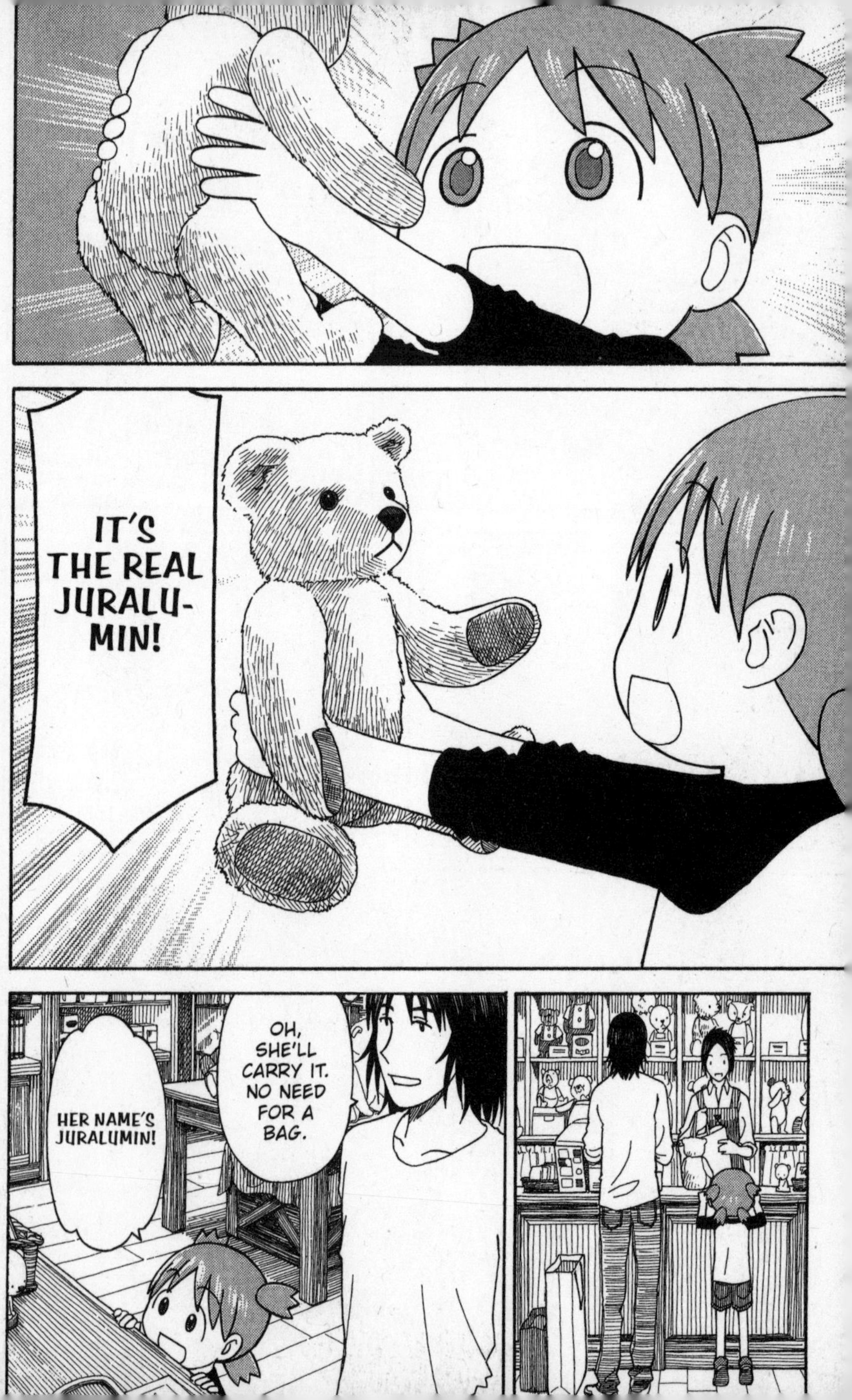
IT'S THE REAL JURALU-MIN!
OH, SHE'LL CARRY IT. NO NEED FOR A BAG.
HER NAME'S JURALUMIN!

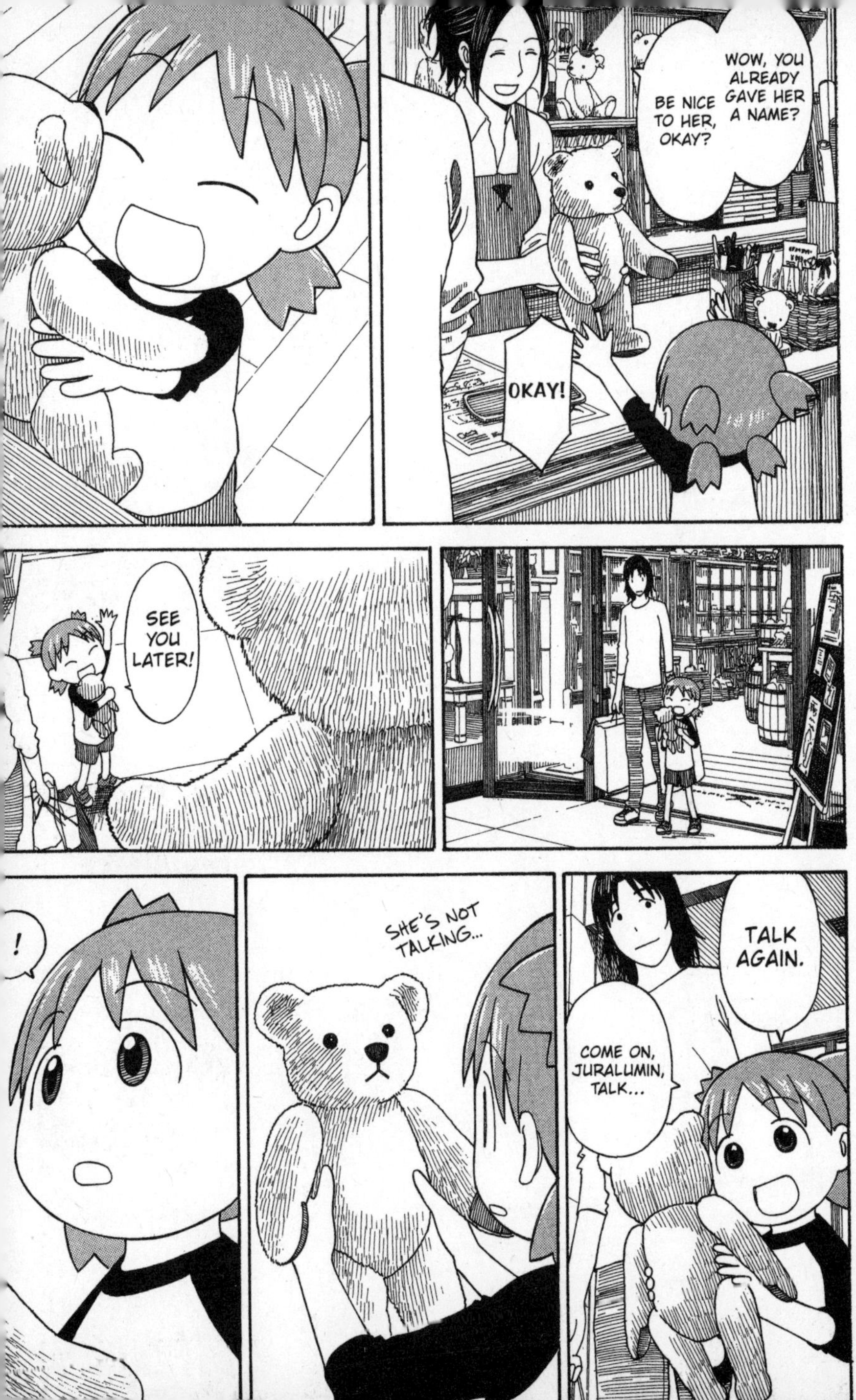
WOW, YOU ALREADY GAVE HER A NAME?
BE NICE TO HER, OKAY?
OKAY!
SEE YOU LATER!
TALK AGAIN.
COME ON, JURALUMIN, TALK...
SHE'S NOT TALKING...
!

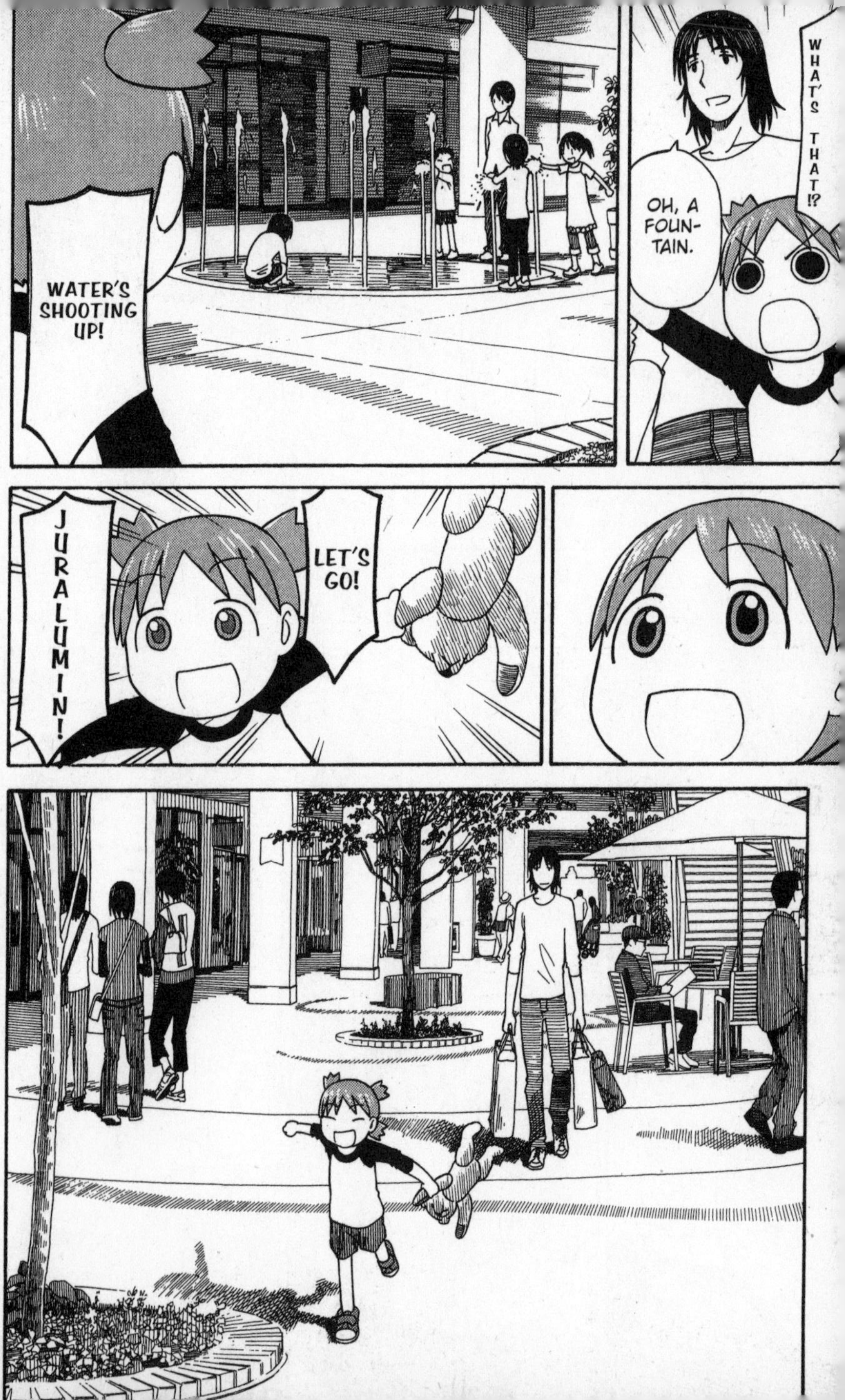
WHAT'S THAT!?
OH, A FOUN-TAIN.
WATER'S SHOOTING UP!
LET'S GO!
JURALUMIN!

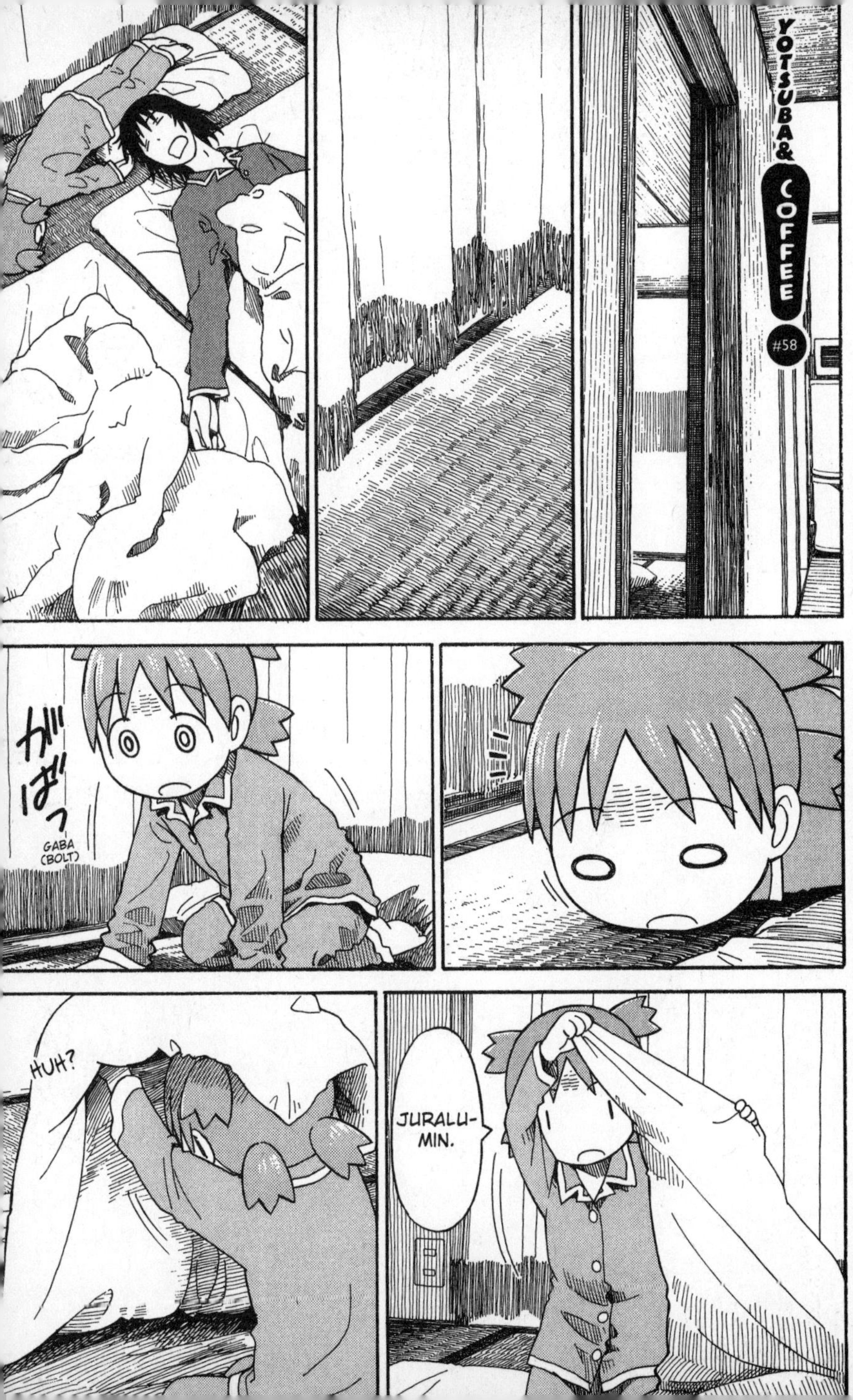
YOTSUBA&
COFFEE
#58
がばっ
GABA (BOLT)
JURALUMIN.
HUH?

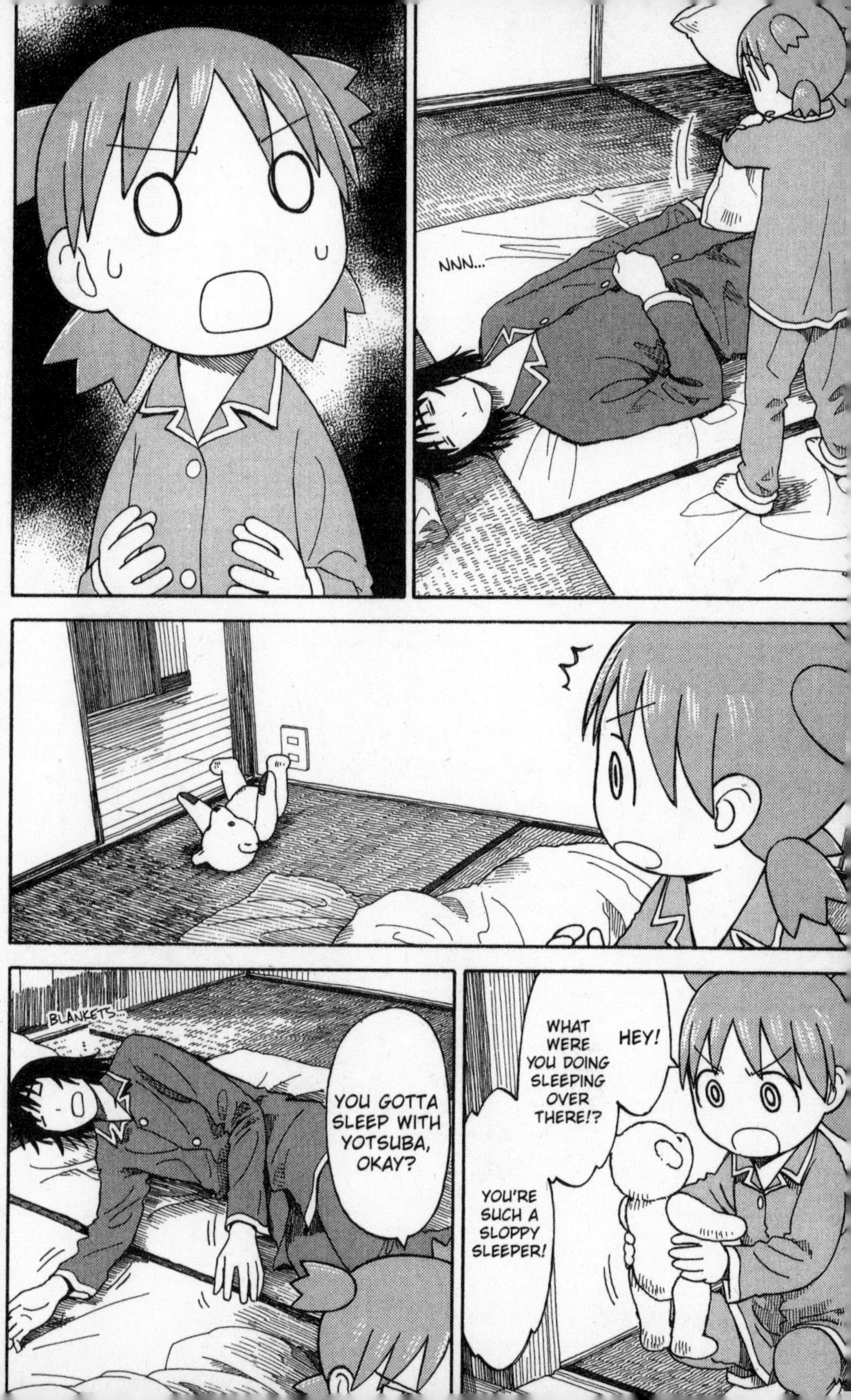
NNN...
HEY!
WHAT WERE YOU DOING SLEEPING OVER THERE!?
YOU'RE SUCH A SLOPPY SLEEPER!
YOU GOTTA SLEEP WITH YOTSUBA, OKAY?
BLANKETS...

YOTSUBA&!

COFFEE

#58

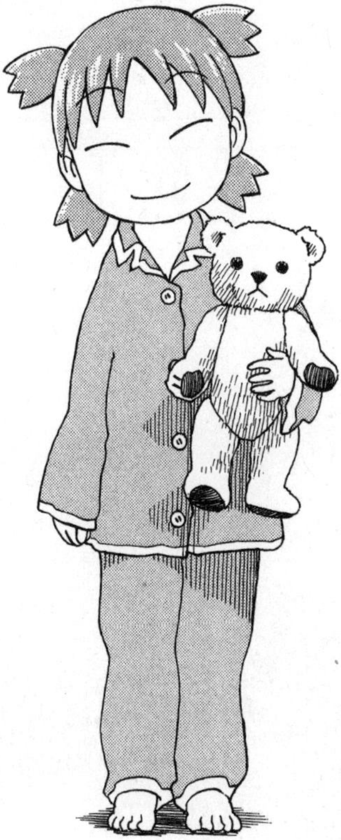

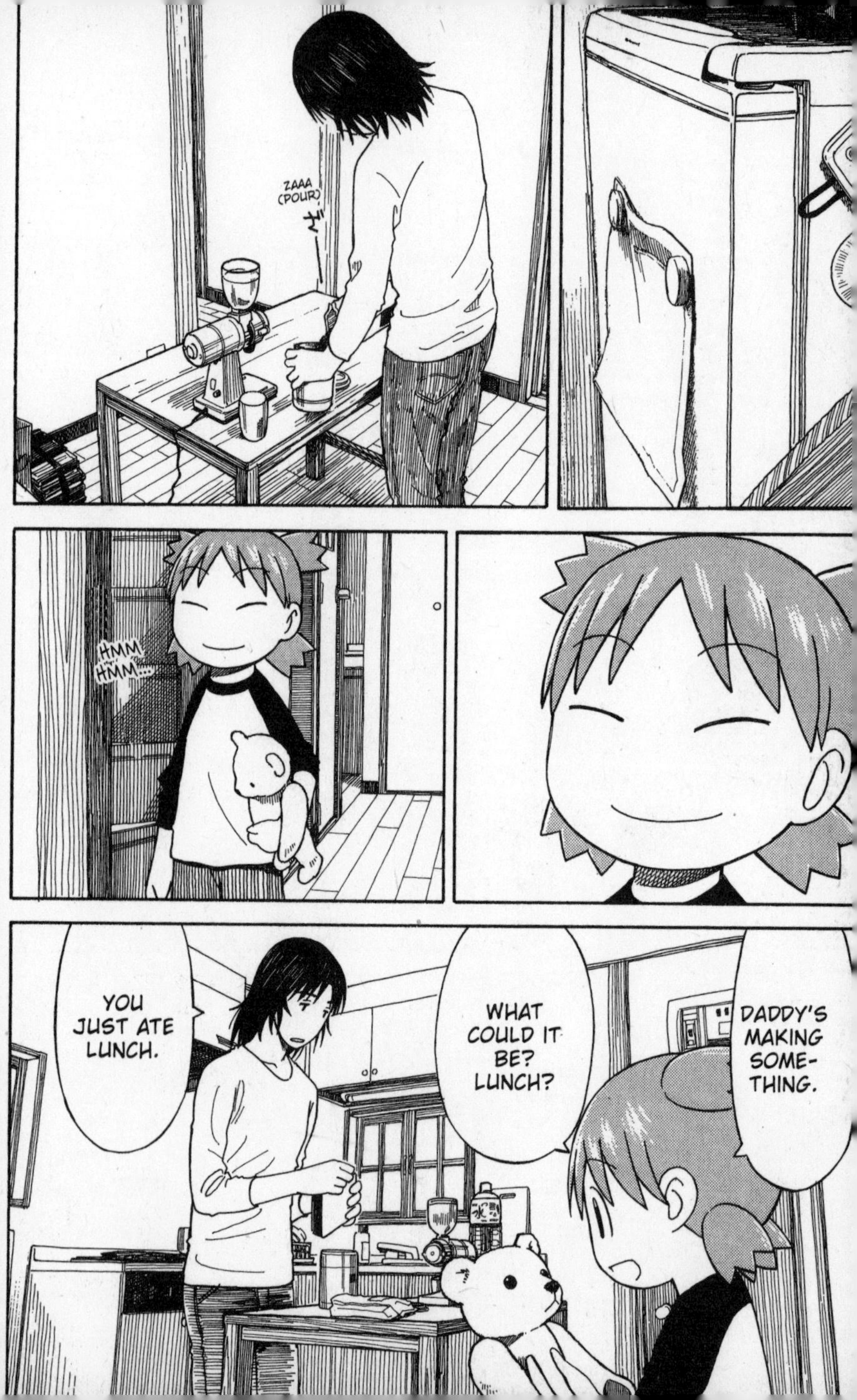
ZAAA (POUR)
HMM HMM...
DADDY'S MAKING SOME-THING.
WHAT COULD IT BE? LUNCH?
YOU JUST ATE LUNCH.

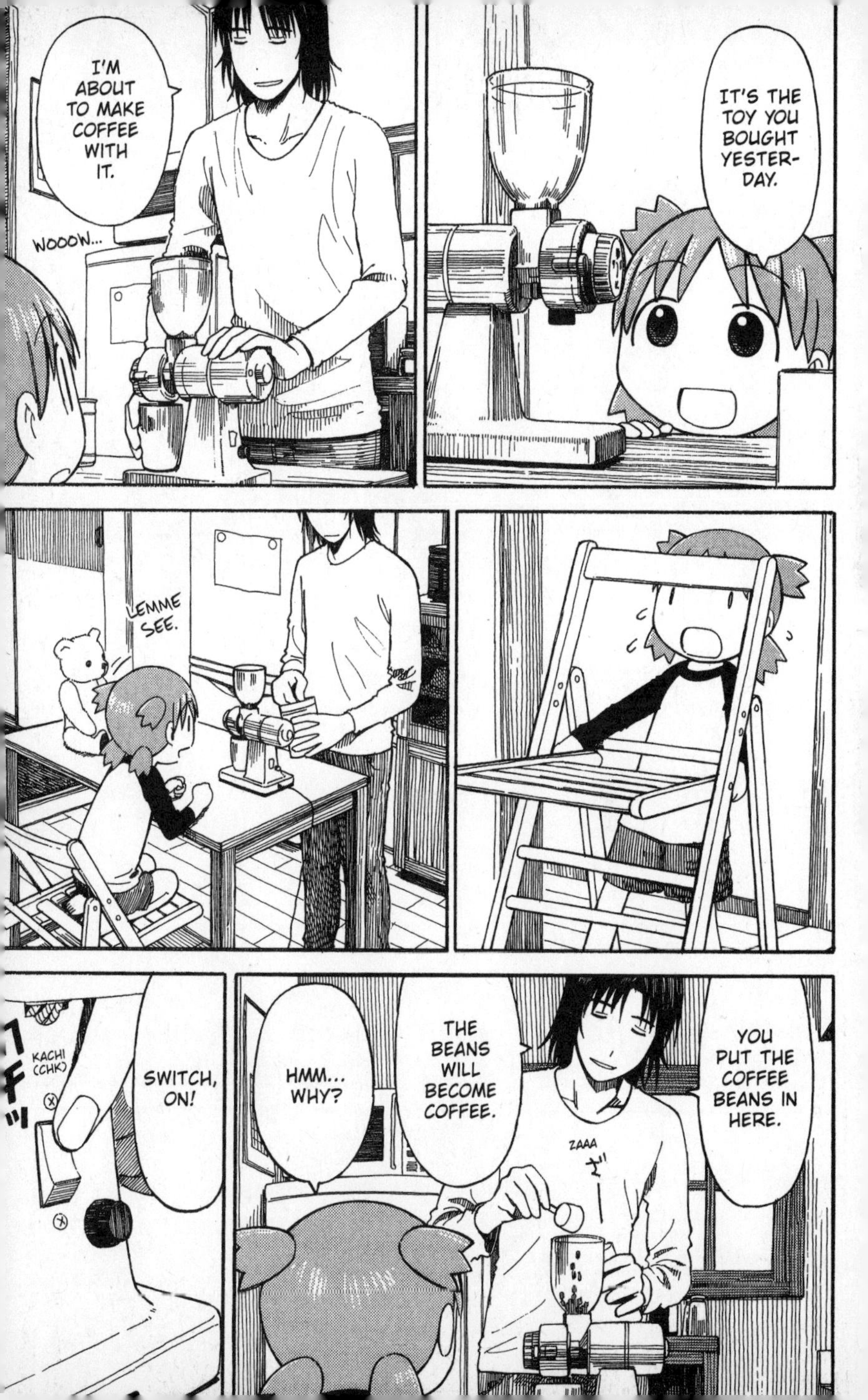
IT'S THE TOY YOU BOUGHT YESTER-DAY.
I'M ABOUT TO MAKE COFFEE WITH IT.
WOOOW...
LEMME SEE.
YOU PUT THE COFFEE BEANS IN HERE.
ZAAA
THE BEANS WILL BECOME COFFEE.
HMM... WHY?
SWITCH, ON!
KACHI (CHK)

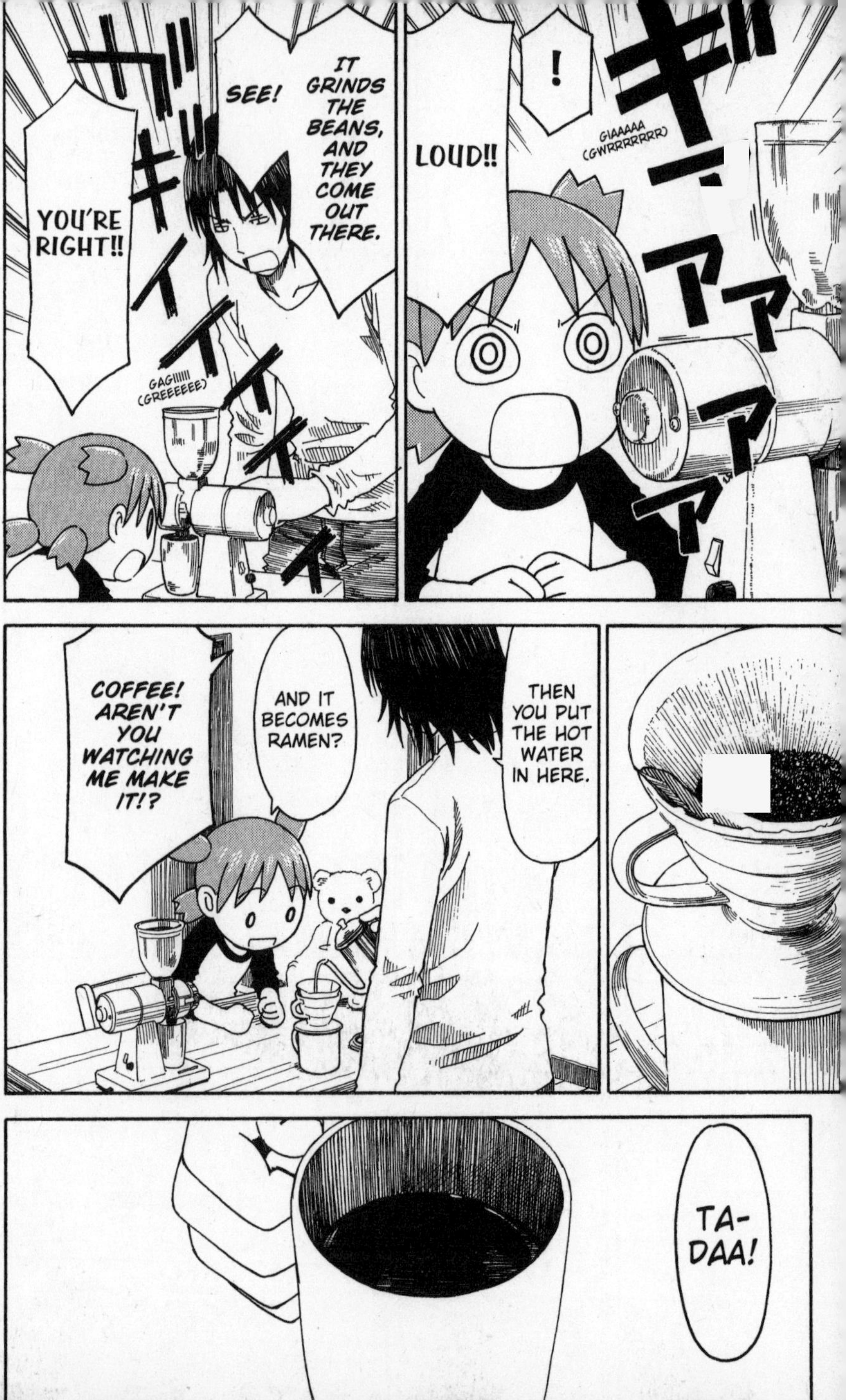
!
GIAAAAA (GWRRRRRRR)
LOUD!!
IT GRINDS THE BEANS, AND THEY COME OUT THERE.
SEE!
YOU'RE RIGHT!!
GAGIIIIII (GREEEEEE)
THEN YOU PUT THE HOT WATER IN HERE.
AND IT BECOMES RAMEN?
COFFEE! AREN'T YOU WATCHING ME MAKE IT!?
TA-DAA!

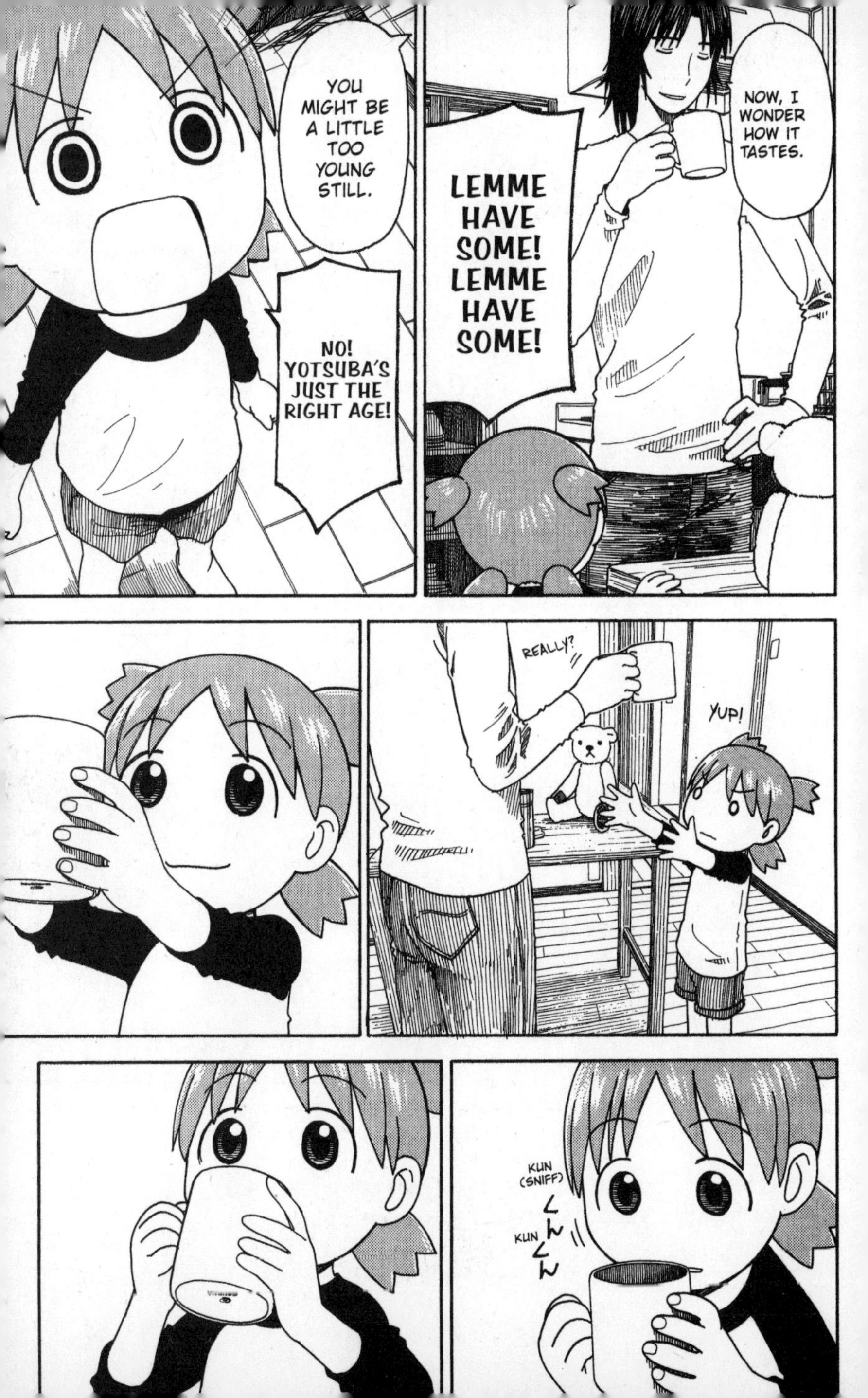

NOW, I WONDER HOW IT TASTES.
LEMME HAVE SOME! LEMME HAVE SOME!
YOU MIGHT BE A LITTLE TOO YOUNG STILL.
NO! YOTSUBA'S JUST THE RIGHT AGE!
REALLY?
YUP!
くん
KUN (SNIFF)
くん
KUN

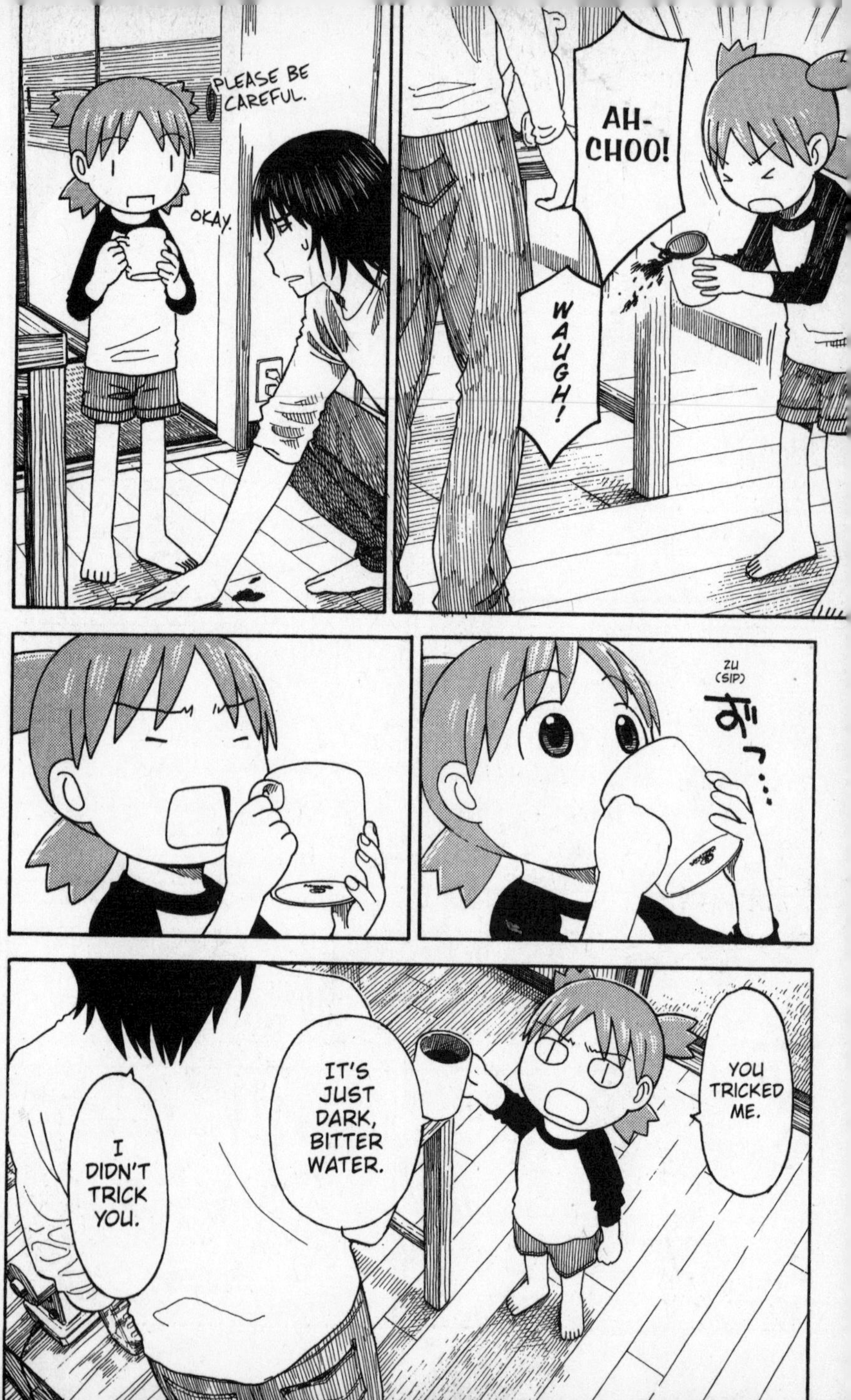
AH-CHOO!
WAUGH!
PLEASE BE CAREFUL.
OKAY.
ZU (SIP)
ずっ…
YOU TRICKED ME.
IT'S JUST DARK, BITTER WATER.
I DIDN'T TRICK YOU.

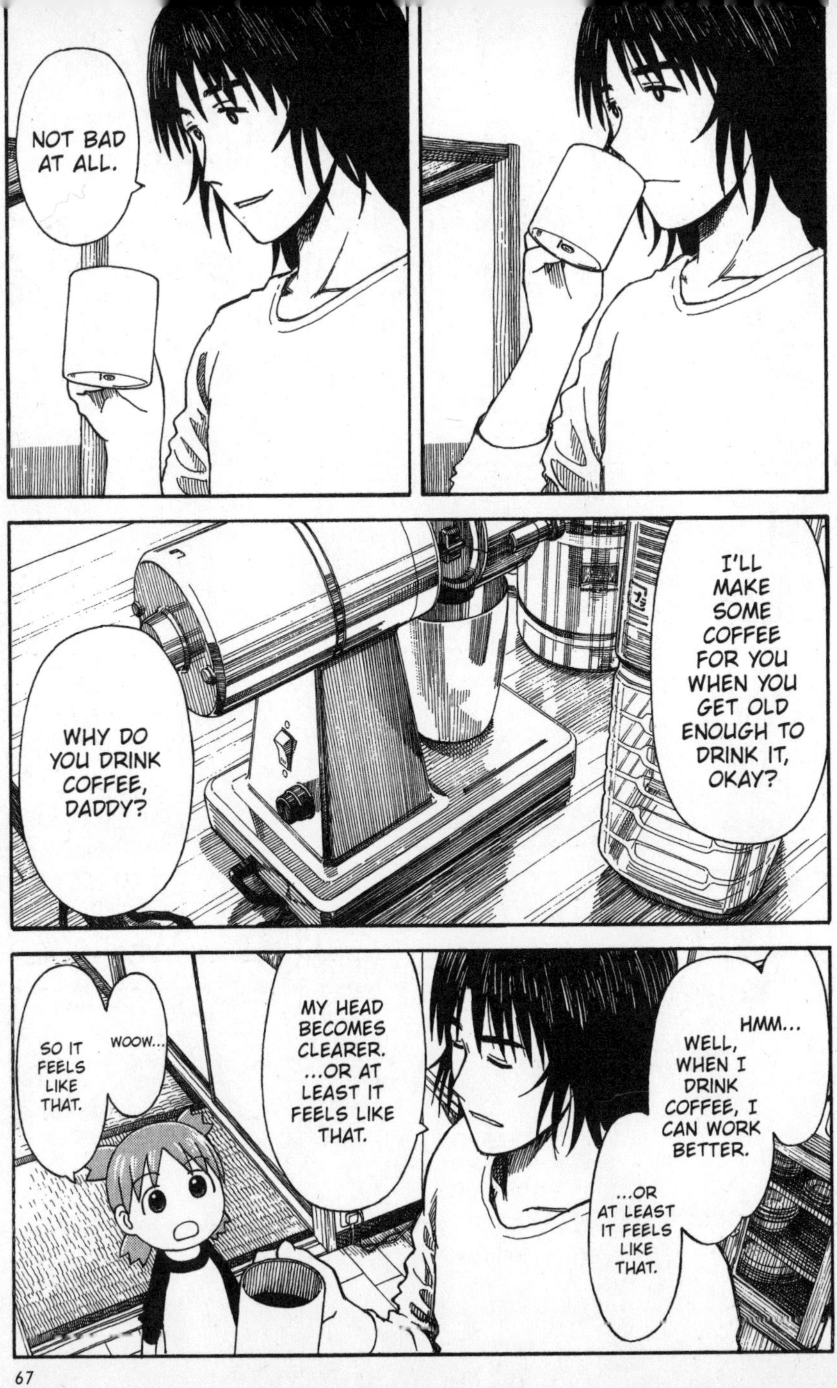
NOT BAD AT ALL.
I'LL MAKE SOME COFFEE FOR YOU WHEN YOU GET OLD ENOUGH TO DRINK IT, OKAY?
WHY DO YOU DRINK COFFEE, DADDY?
HMM... WELL, WHEN I DRINK COFFEE, I CAN WORK BETTER.
...OR AT LEAST IT FEELS LIKE THAT.
MY HEAD BECOMES CLEARER. ...OR AT LEAST IT FEELS LIKE THAT.
WOOW...
SO IT FEELS LIKE THAT.

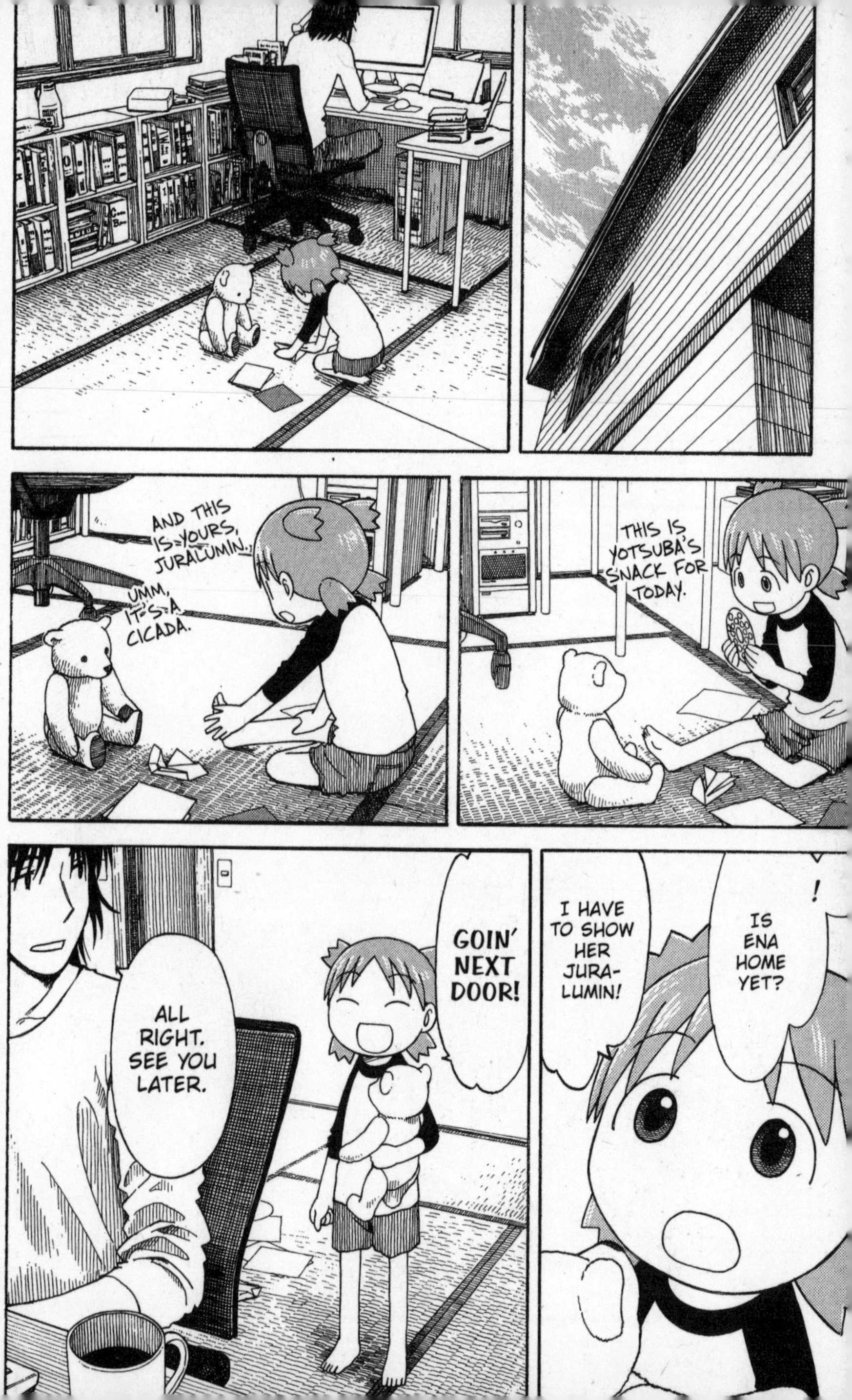
THIS IS YOTSUBA'S SNACK FOR TODAY.
AND THIS IS YOURS, JURALUMIN.
UMM, IT'S A CICADA.
!
IS ENA HOME YET?
I HAVE TO SHOW HER JURA-LUMIN!
GOIN' NEXT DOOR!
ALL RIGHT. SEE YOU LATER.

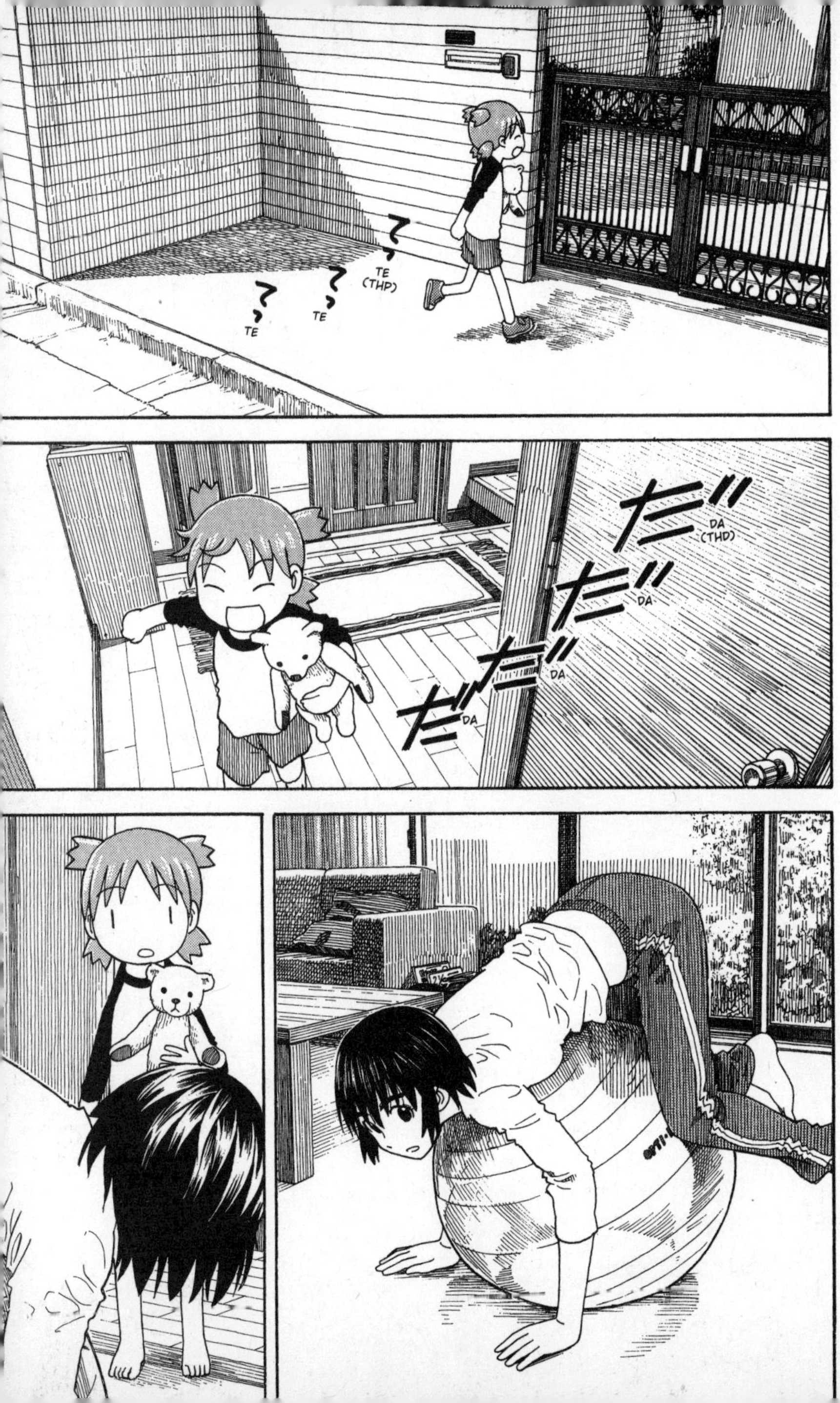
TE
(THP)
TE
TE
DA
(THD)
DA
DA
DA

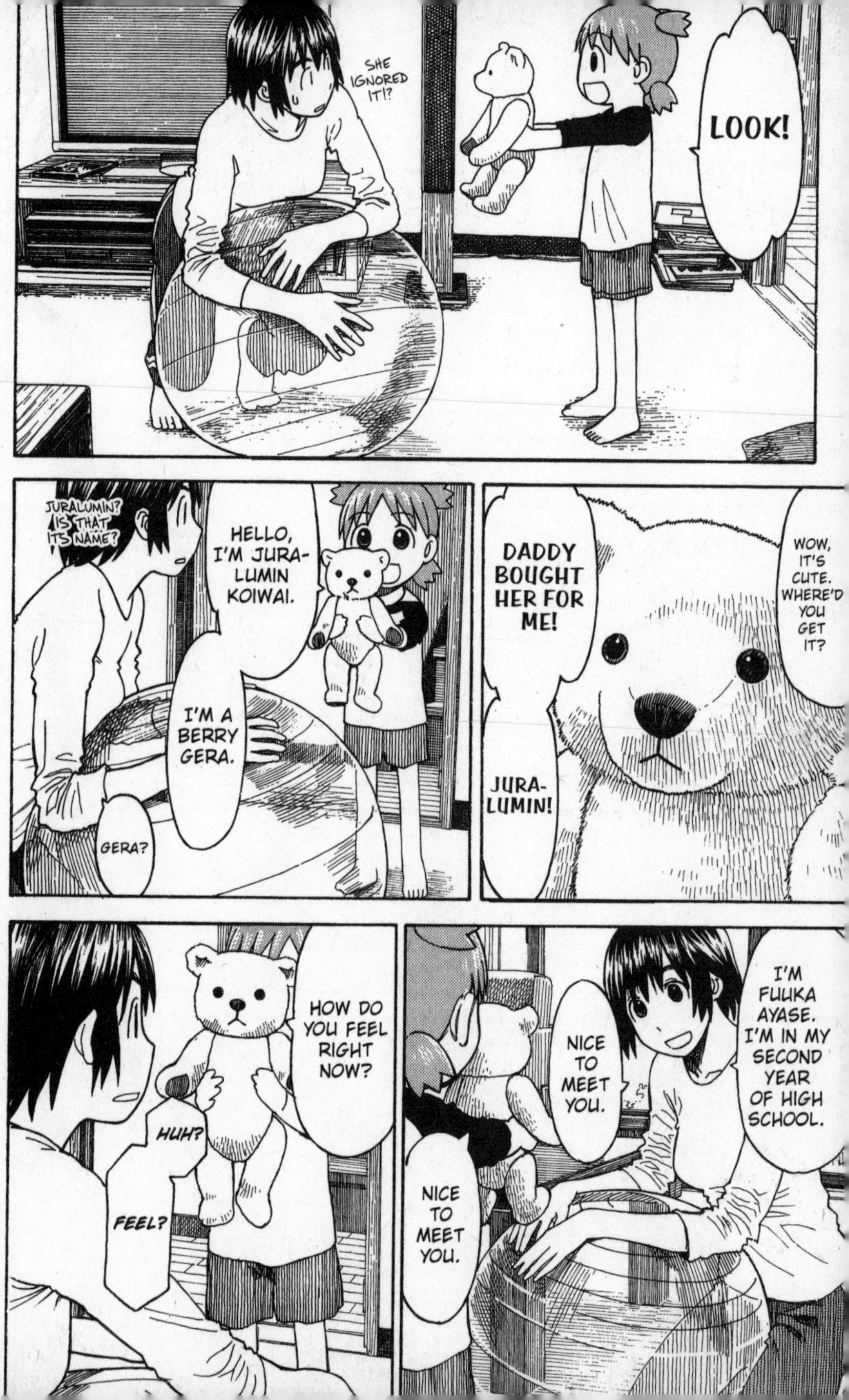
LOOK!
SHE IGNORED IT!?
WOW, IT'S CUTE. WHERE'D YOU GET IT?
DADDY BOUGHT HER FOR ME!
JURA-LUMIN!
HELLO, I'M JURA-LUMIN KOIWAI.
JURALUMIN? IS THAT ITS NAME?
I'M A BERRY GERA.
GERA?
I'M FUUKA AYASE. I'M IN MY SECOND YEAR OF HIGH SCHOOL.
NICE TO MEET YOU.
NICE TO MEET YOU.
HOW DO YOU FEEL RIGHT NOW?
HUH?
FEEL?

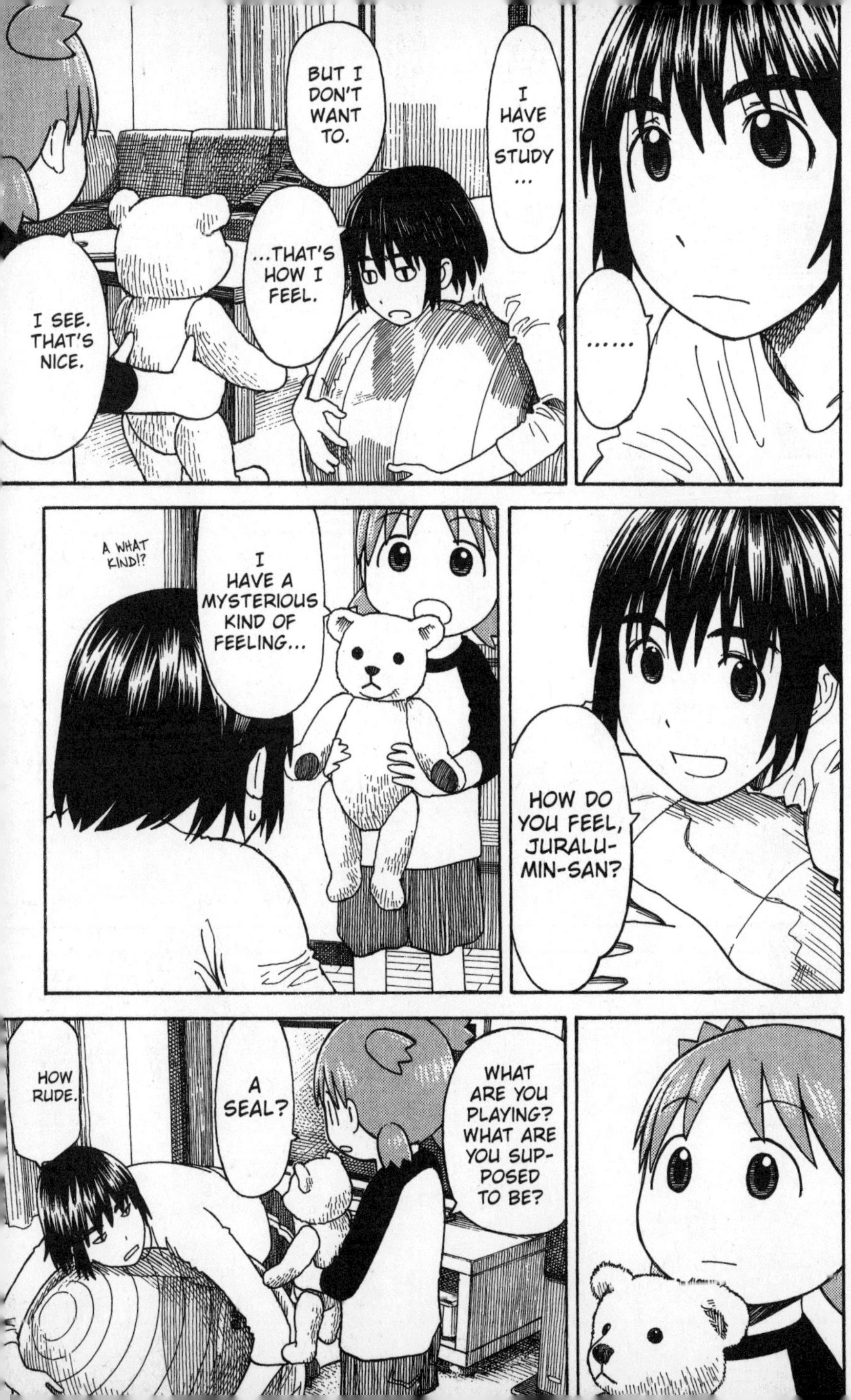
......
I HAVE TO STUDY ...
BUT I DON'T WANT TO.
...THAT'S HOW I FEEL.
I SEE. THAT'S NICE.
HOW DO YOU FEEL, JURALU-MIN-SAN?
I HAVE A MYSTERIOUS KIND OF FEELING...
A WHAT KIND!?
WHAT ARE YOU PLAYING? WHAT ARE YOU SUP-POSED TO BE?
A SEAL?
HOW RUDE.

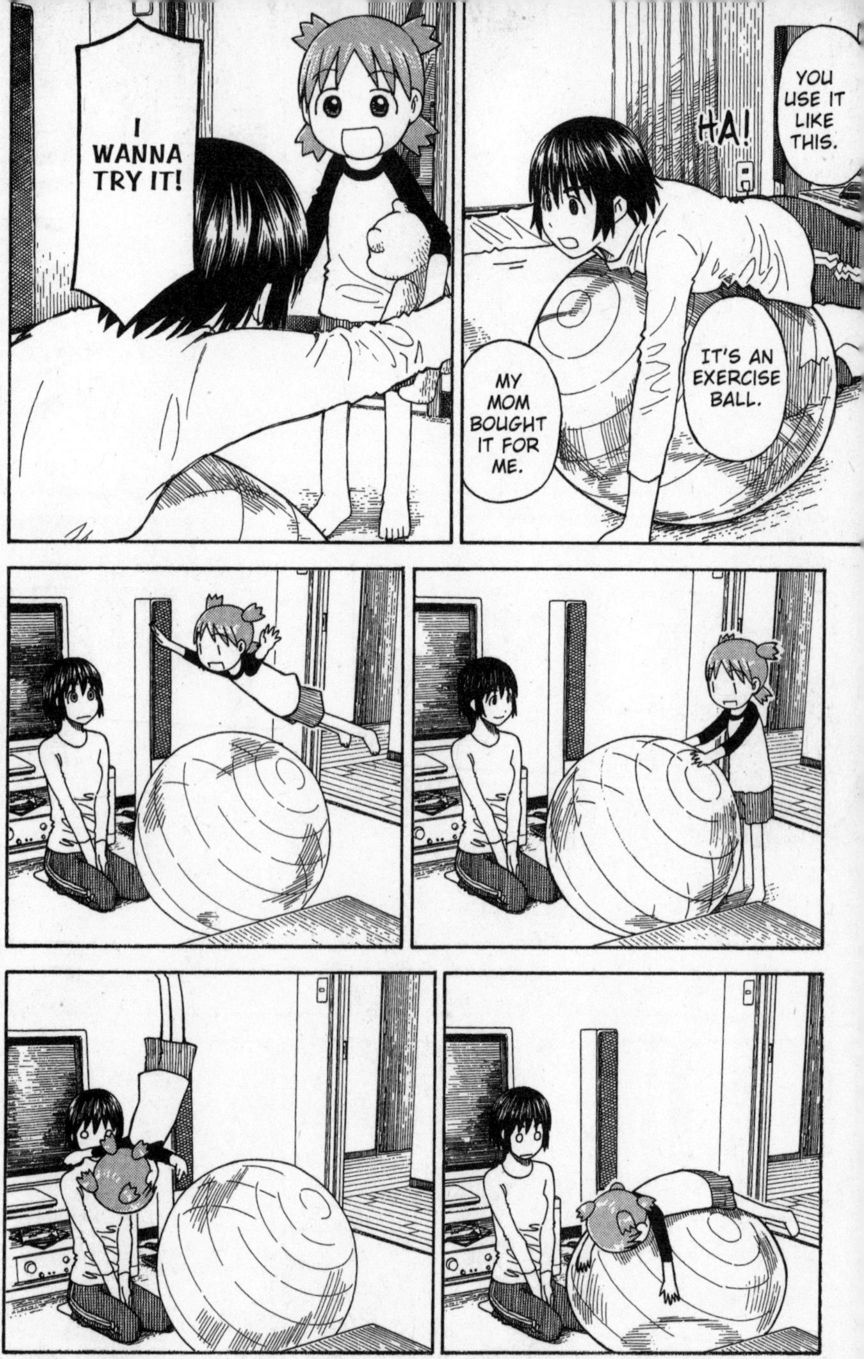
YOU USE IT LIKE THIS.
HA!
IT'S AN EXERCISE BALL.
MY MOM BOUGHT IT FOR ME.
I WANNA TRY IT!

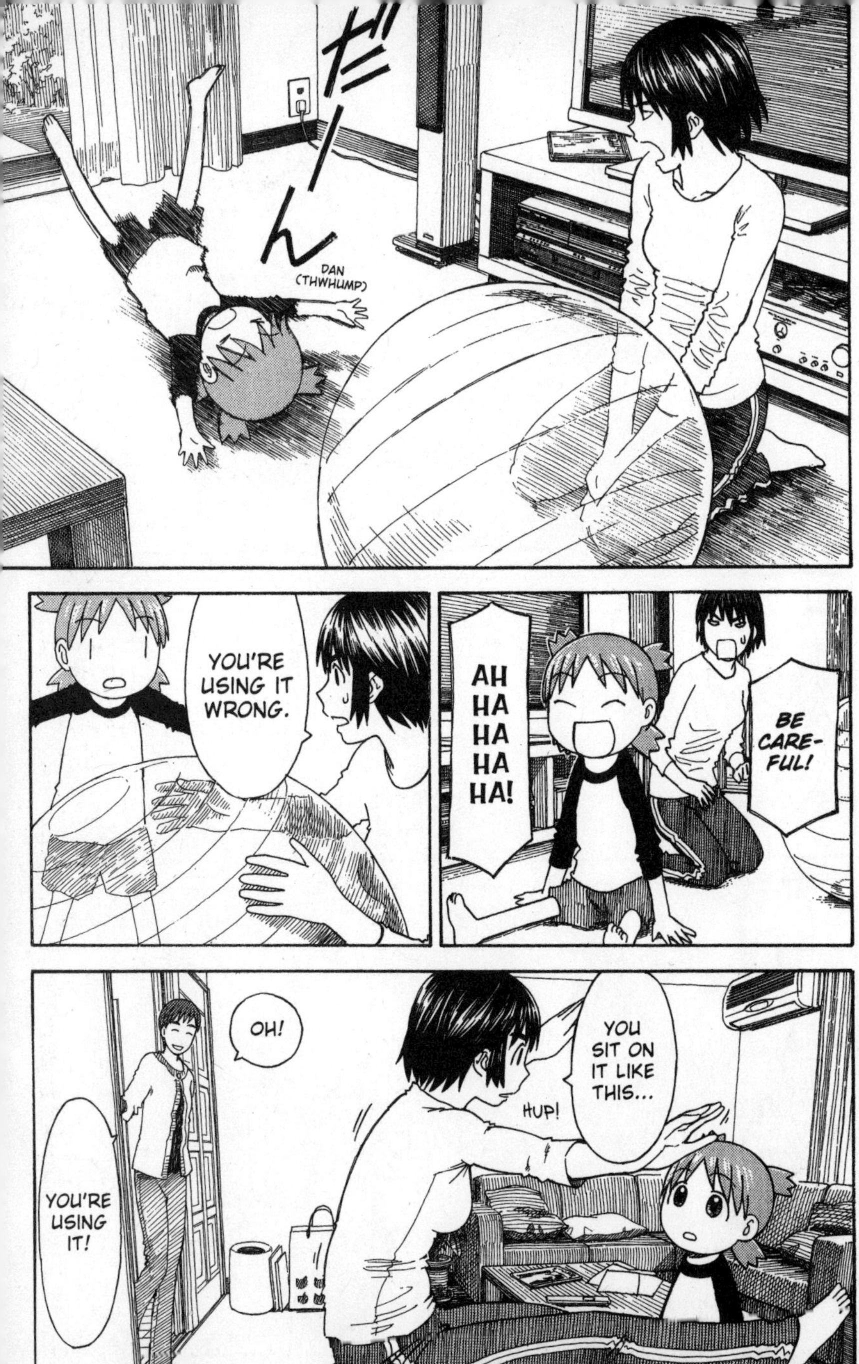
だーん
DAN (THWHUMP)
BE CARE-FUL!
AH HA HA HA HA!
YOU'RE USING IT WRONG.
YOU SIT ON IT LIKE THIS...
HUP!
OH!
YOU'RE USING IT!

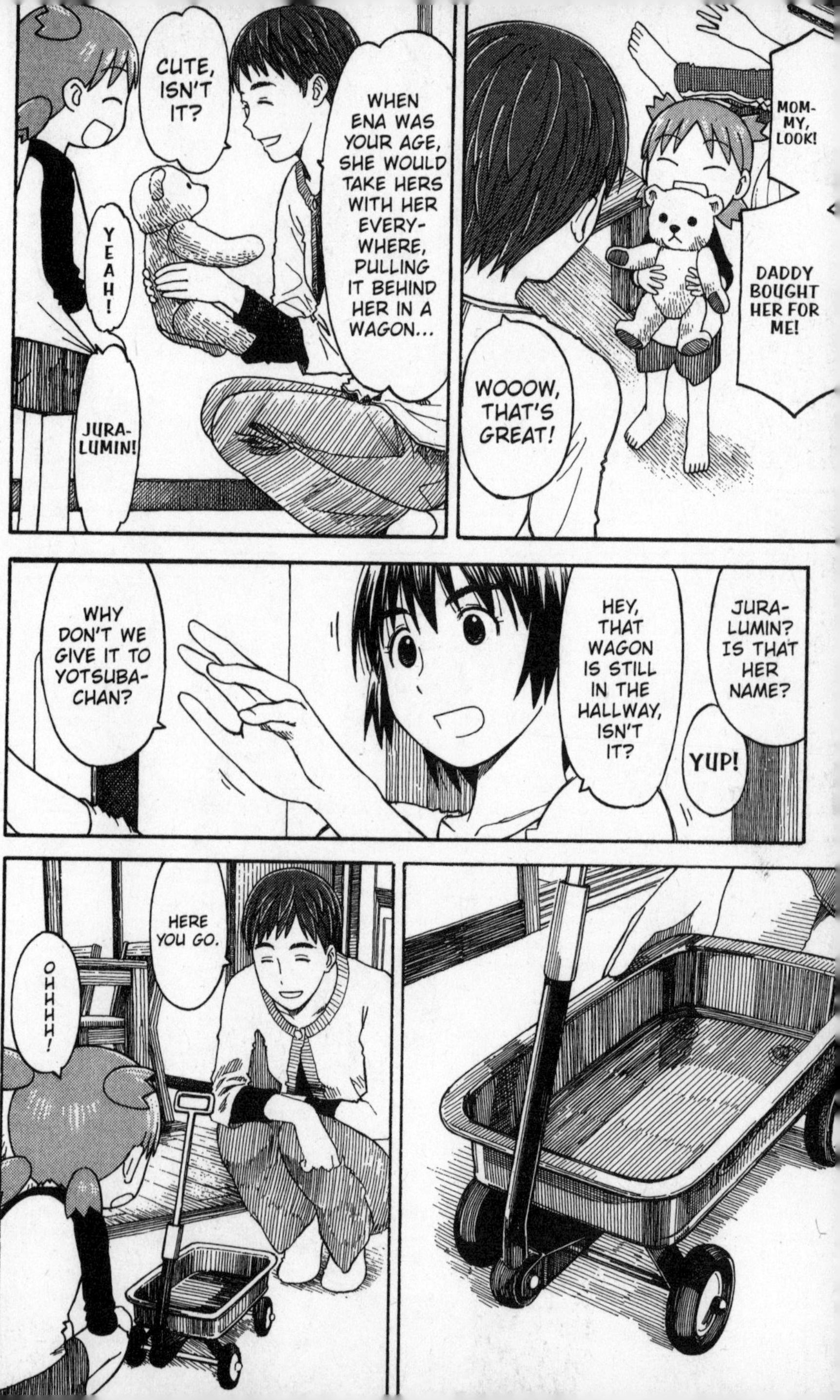
MOM-
MY, LOOK!
DADDY BOUGHT HER FOR ME!
WOOOW, THAT'S GREAT!
WHEN ENA WAS YOUR AGE, SHE WOULD TAKE HERS WITH HER EVERY-WHERE, PULLING IT BEHIND HER IN A WAGON...
CUTE, ISN'T IT?
YEAH!
JURA-LUMIN!
JURA-LUMIN? IS THAT HER NAME?
YUP!
HEY, THAT WAGON IS STILL IN THE HALLWAY, ISN'T IT?
WHY DON'T WE GIVE IT TO YOTSUBA-CHAN?
HERE YOU GO.
OHHHH!

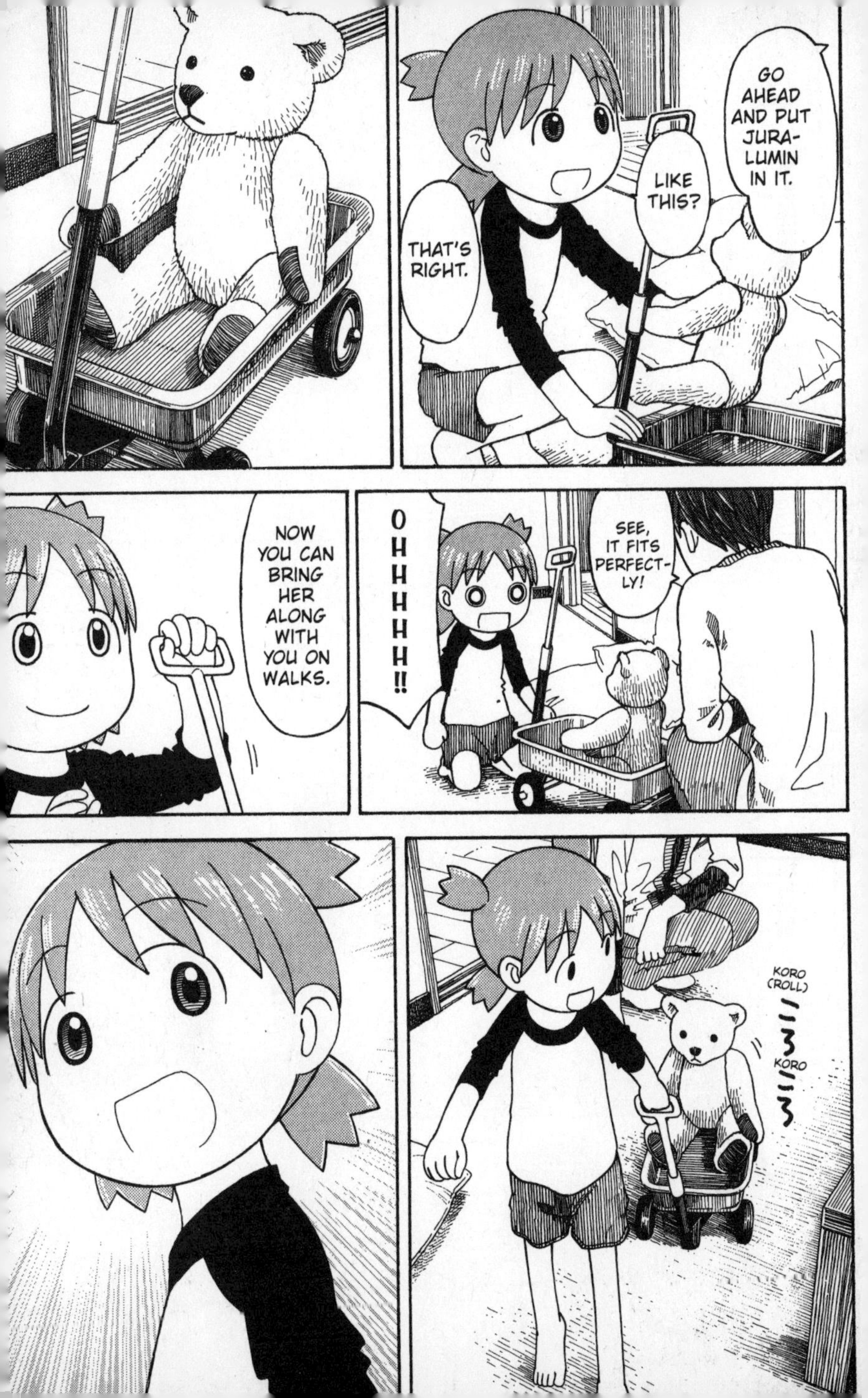
GO AHEAD AND PUT JURA-LUMIN IN IT.
LIKE THIS?
THAT'S RIGHT.
SEE, IT FITS PERFECT-LY!
OHHHHHH!!
NOW YOU CAN BRING HER ALONG WITH YOU ON WALKS.
KORO (ROLL)
KORO

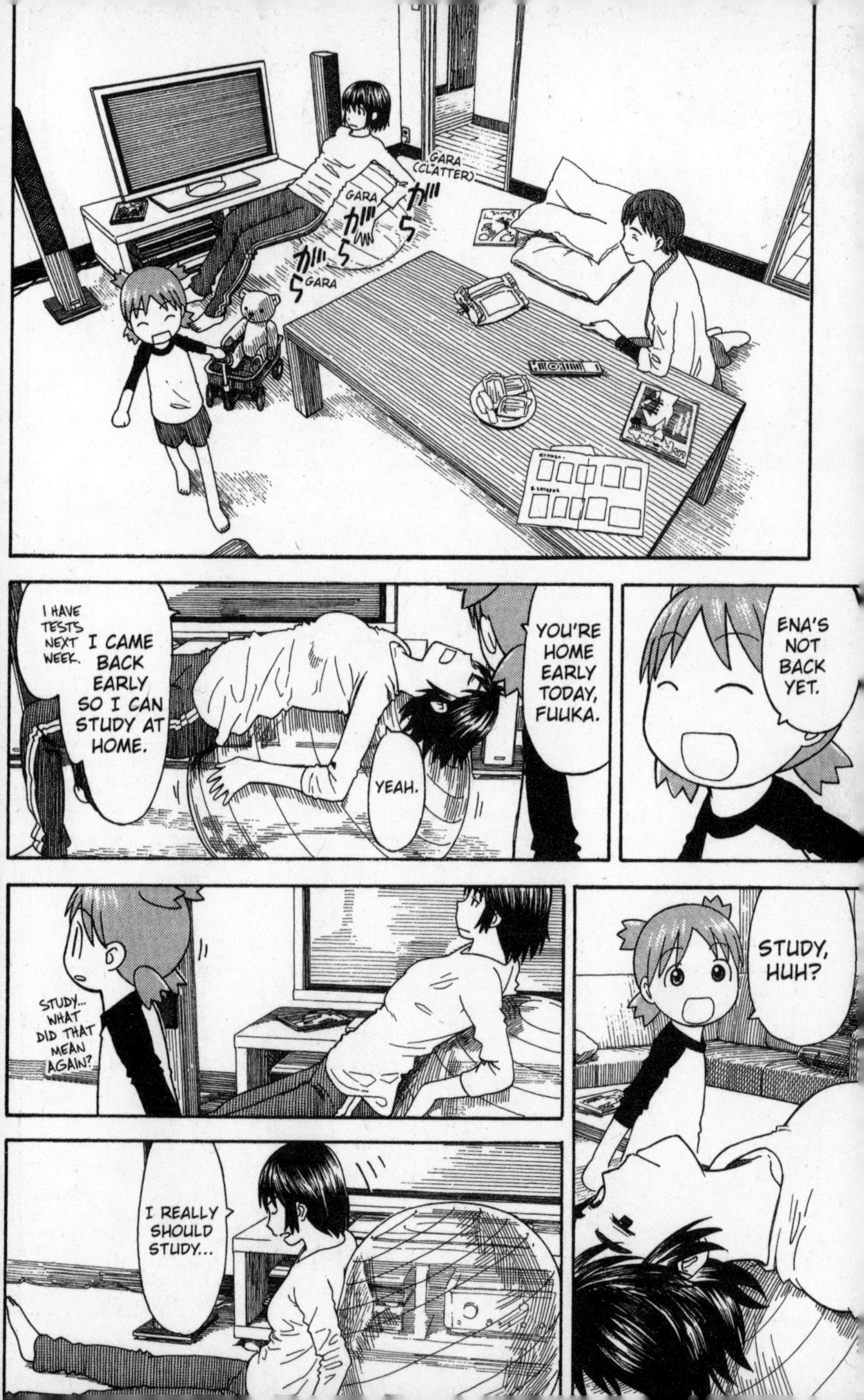
GARA (CLATTER)
がら
GARA
がら
がら
GARA
ENA'S NOT BACK YET.
YOU'RE HOME EARLY TODAY, FUUKA.
YEAH.
I CAME BACK EARLY SO I CAN STUDY AT HOME.
I HAVE TESTS NEXT WEEK.
STUDY, HUH?
STUDY... WHAT DID THAT MEAN AGAIN?
I REALLY SHOULD STUDY...

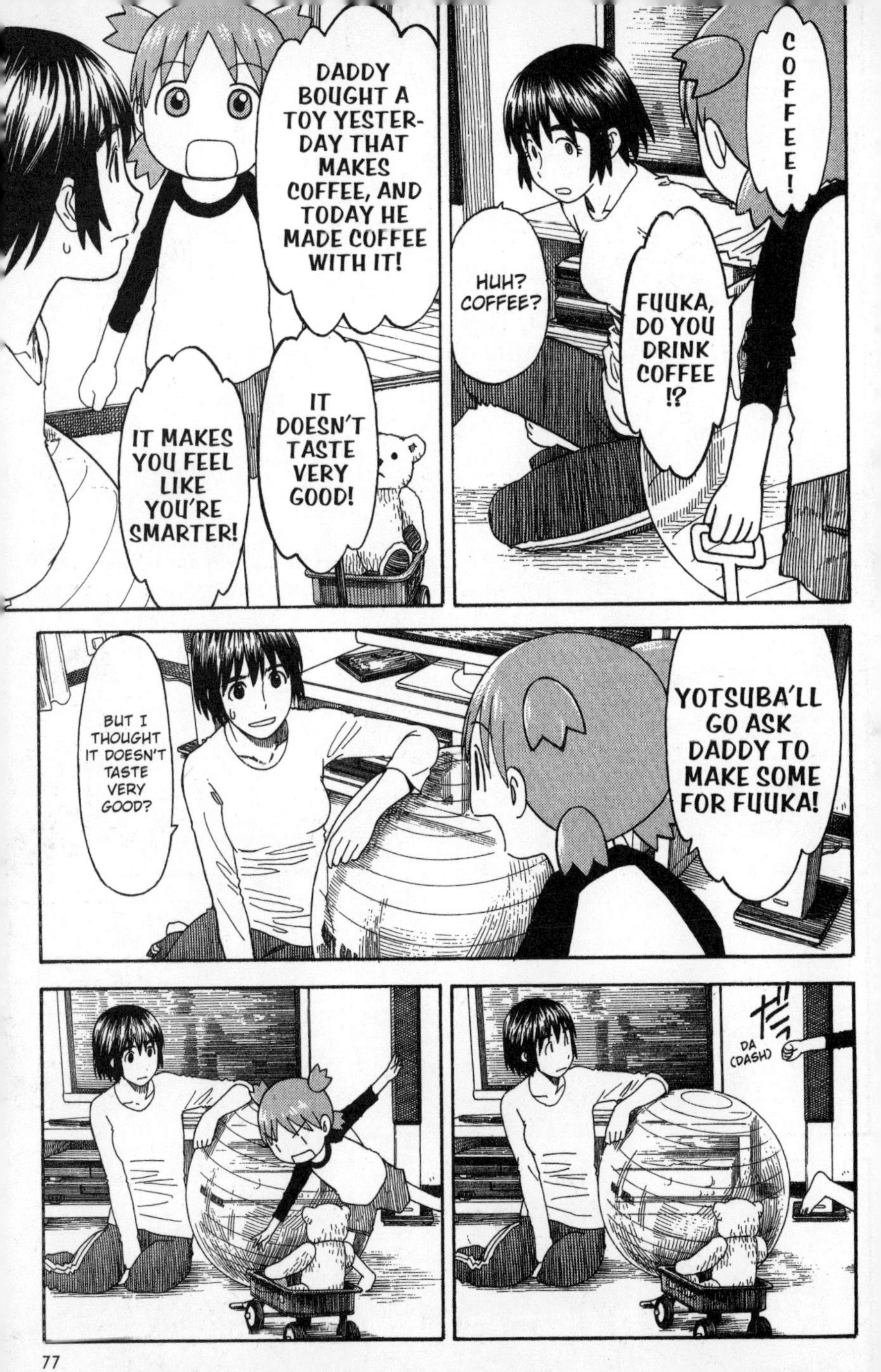
COFFEE!
FUUKA, DO YOU DRINK COFFEE !?
HUH? COFFEE?
DADDY BOUGHT A TOY YESTER-DAY THAT MAKES COFFEE, AND TODAY HE MADE COFFEE WITH IT!
IT DOESN'T TASTE VERY GOOD!
IT MAKES YOU FEEL LIKE YOU'RE SMARTER!
YOTSUBA'LL GO ASK DADDY TO MAKE SOME FOR FUUKA!
BUT I THOUGHT IT DOESN'T TASTE VERY GOOD?
DA (DASH)

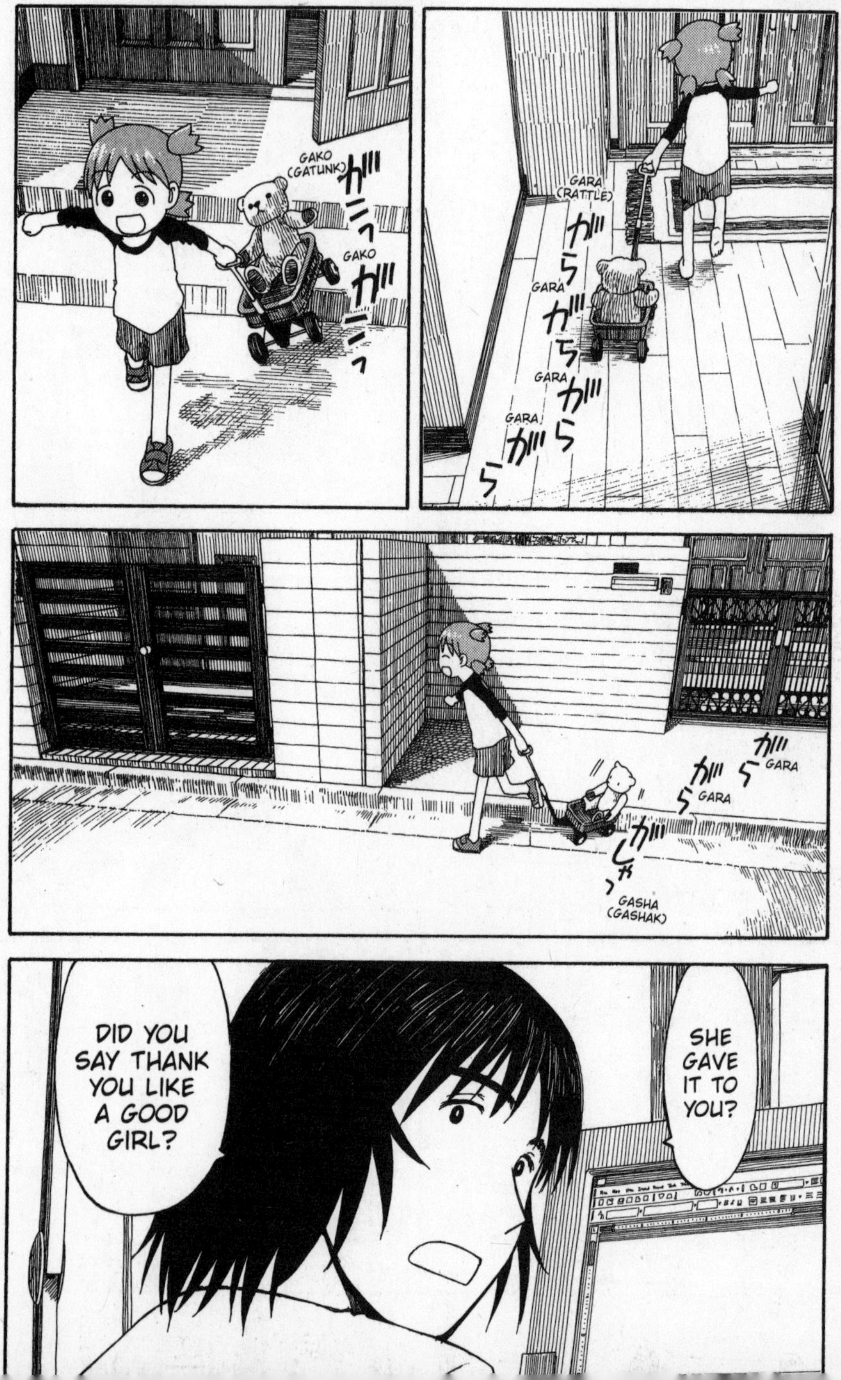
GARA (RATTLE)
がら
GARA
がら
GARA
がら
GARA
がら
GAKO (GATUNK)
ガコッ
GAKO
ガコッ
GARA
がら
GARA
がら
GASHA (GASHAK)
がしゃっ
SHE GAVE IT TO YOU?
DID YOU SAY THANK YOU LIKE A GOOD GIRL?

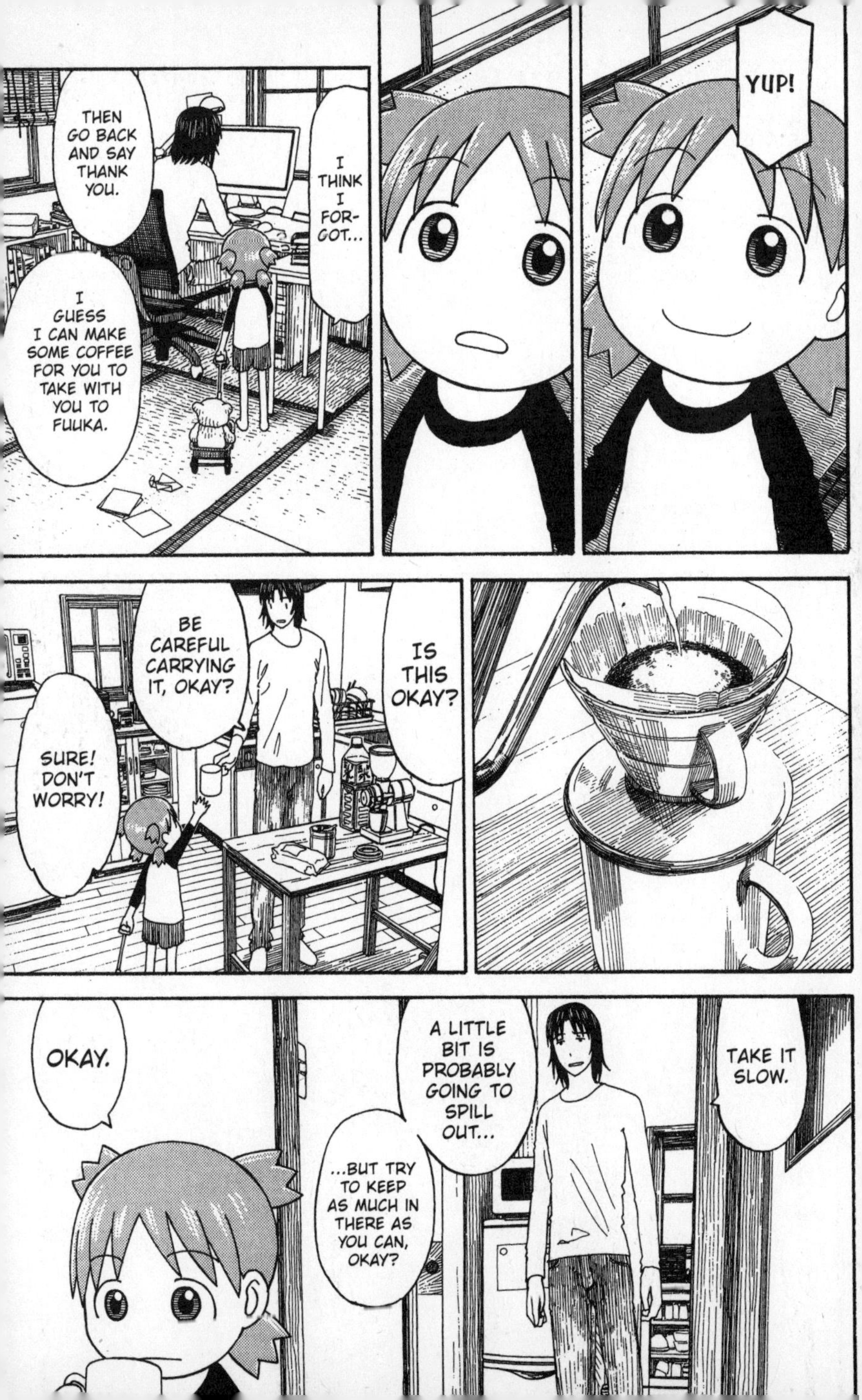
YUP!
I THINK I FORGOT...
THEN GO BACK AND SAY THANK YOU.
I GUESS I CAN MAKE SOME COFFEE FOR YOU TO TAKE WITH YOU TO FUUKA.
IS THIS OKAY?
BE CAREFUL CARRYING IT, OKAY?
SURE! DON'T WORRY!
TAKE IT SLOW.
A LITTLE BIT IS PROBABLY GOING TO SPILL OUT...
...BUT TRY TO KEEP AS MUCH IN THERE AS YOU CAN, OKAY?
OKAY.

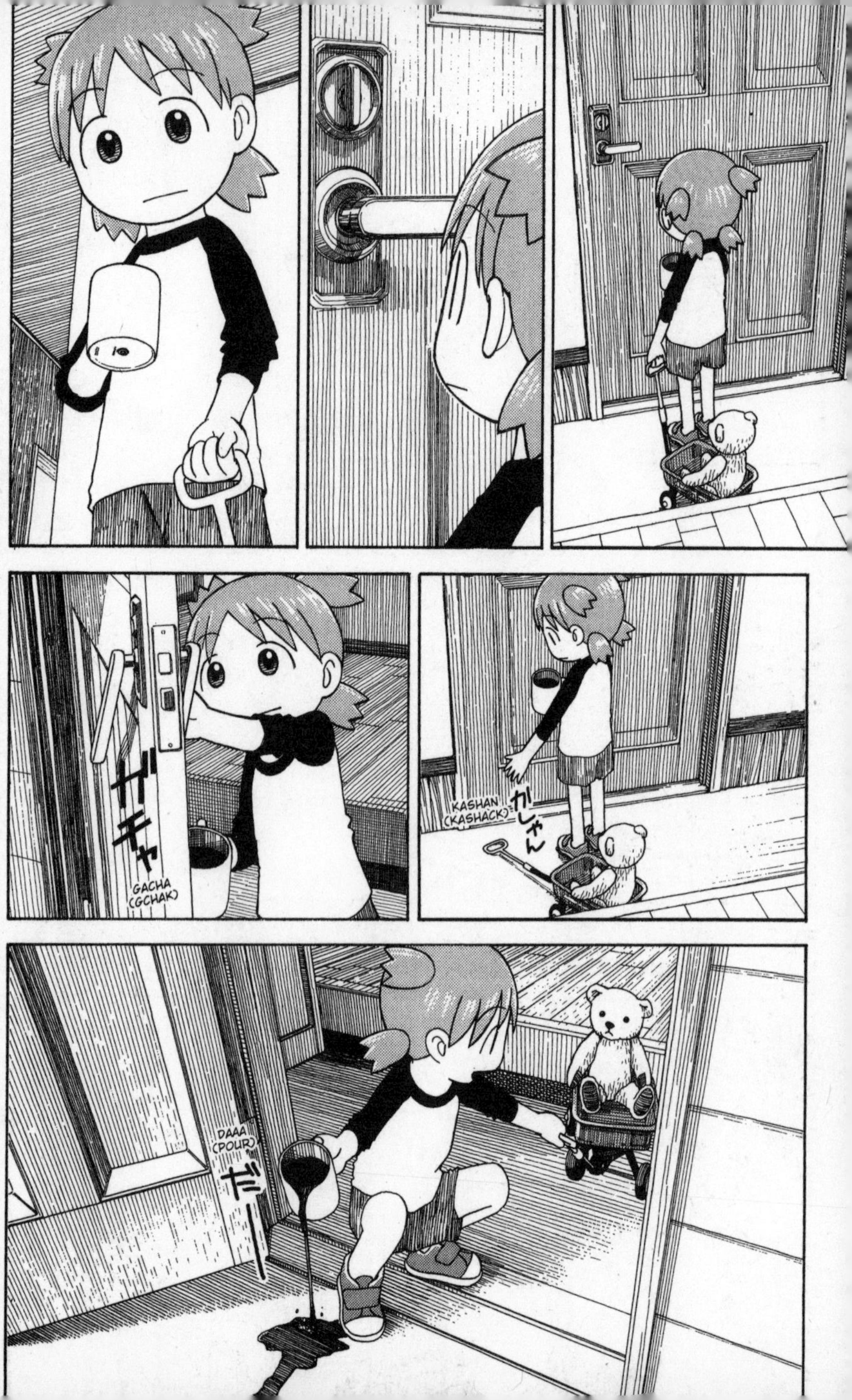
KASHAN (KASHACK)
かしゃん
GACHA (GCHAK)
ガチャ
DAAA (POUR)
だー

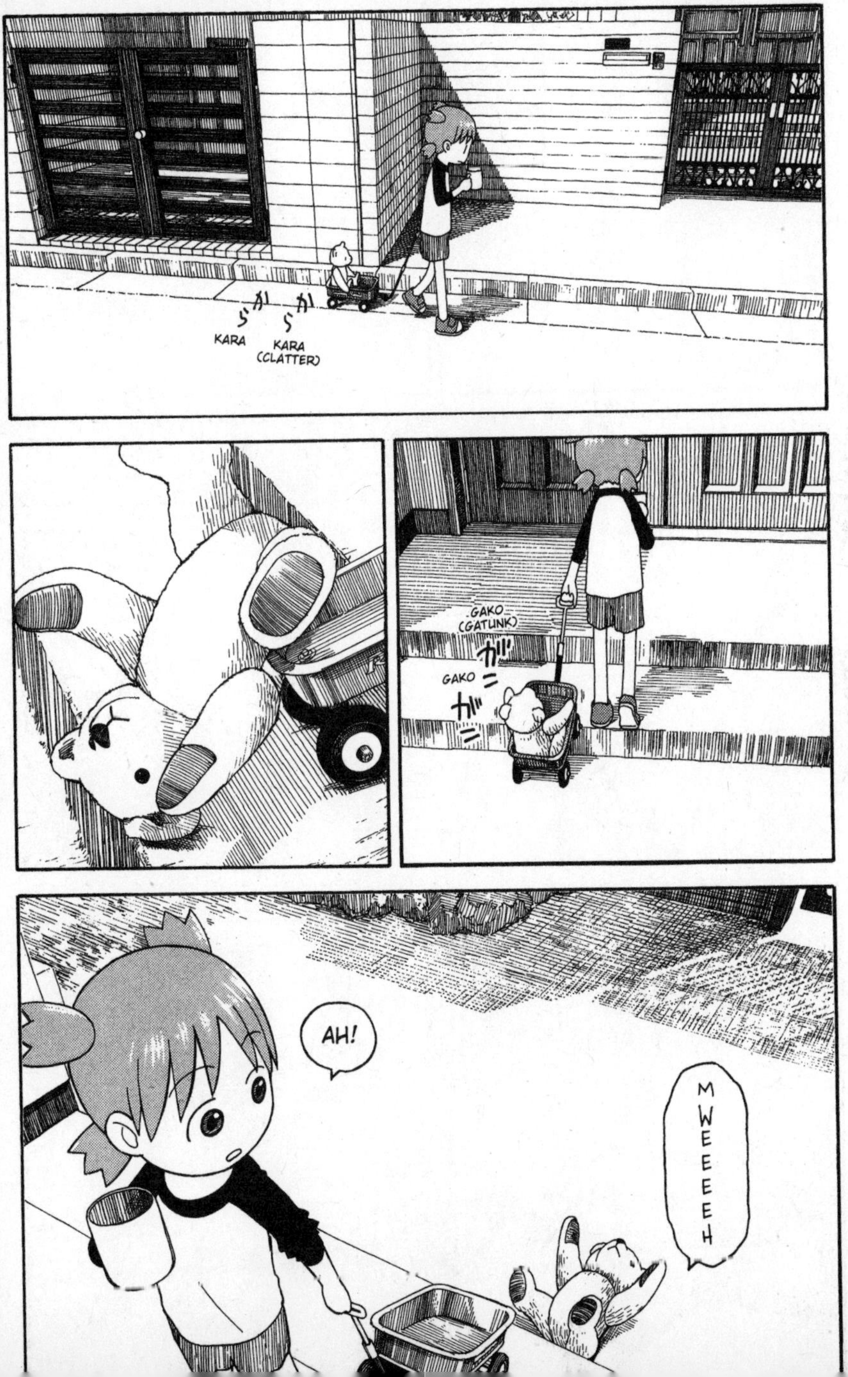

から
から
KARA
KARA (CLATTER)
GAKO (GATUNK)
GAKO
MWEEEEH
AH!

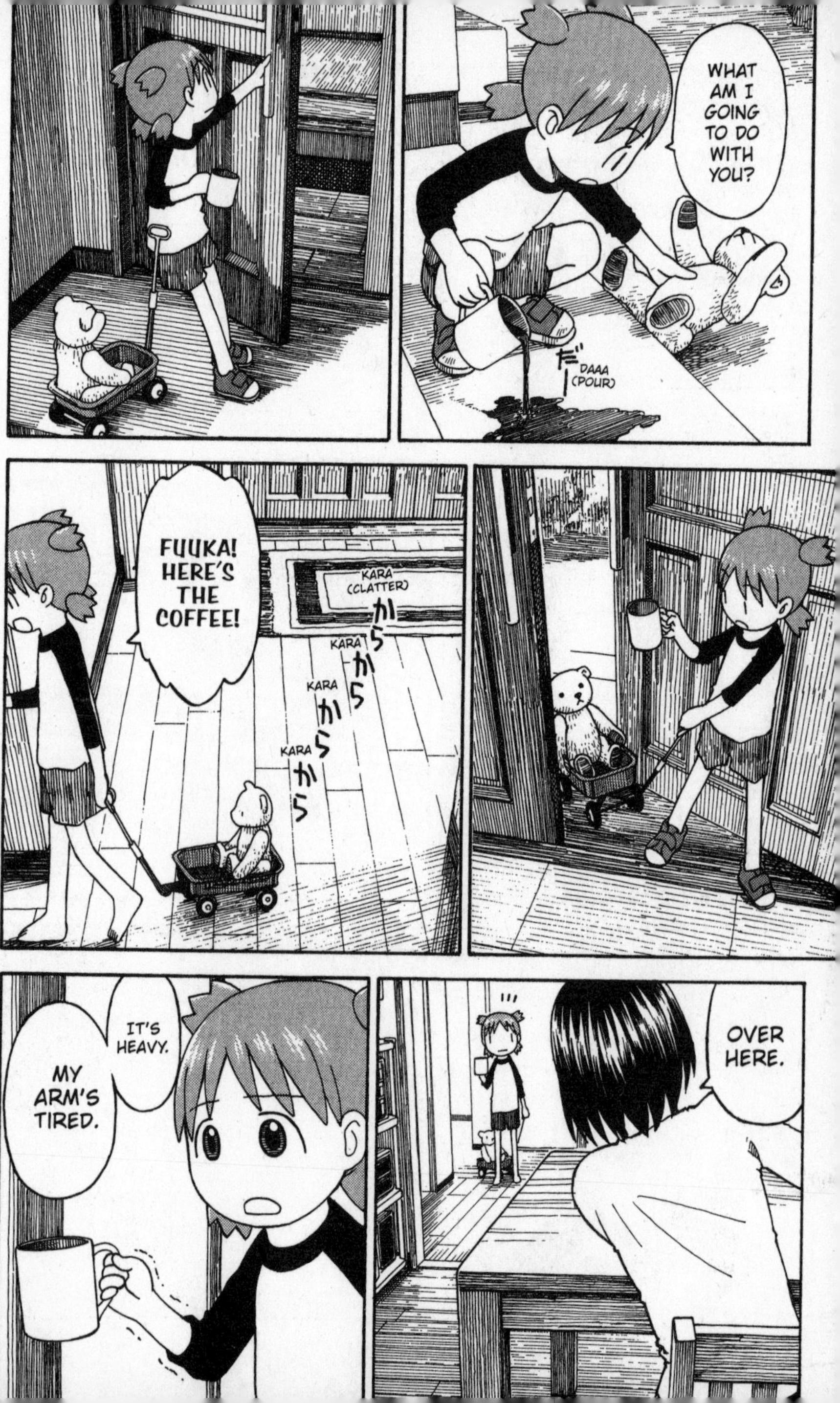
WHAT AM I GOING TO DO WITH YOU?
だー
DAAA (POUR)
FUUKA! HERE'S THE COFFEE!
KARA (CLATTER)
から
KARA
から
KARA
から
KARA
から
OVER HERE.
IT'S HEAVY.
MY ARM'S TIRED.

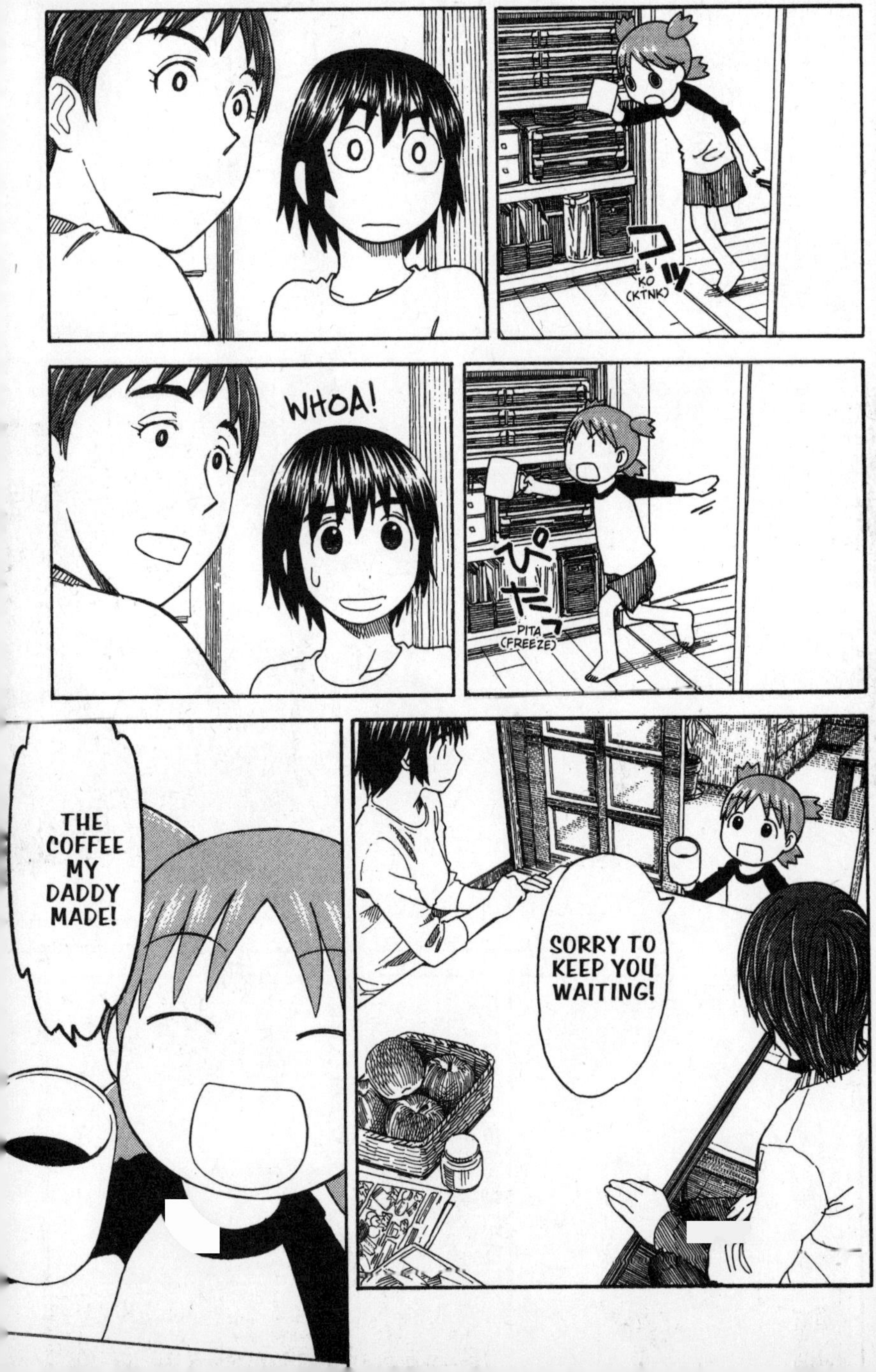
コッ
KO (KTNK)
ぴたっ
PITA (FREEZE)
WHOA!
SORRY TO KEEP YOU WAITING!
THE COFFEE MY DADDY MADE!

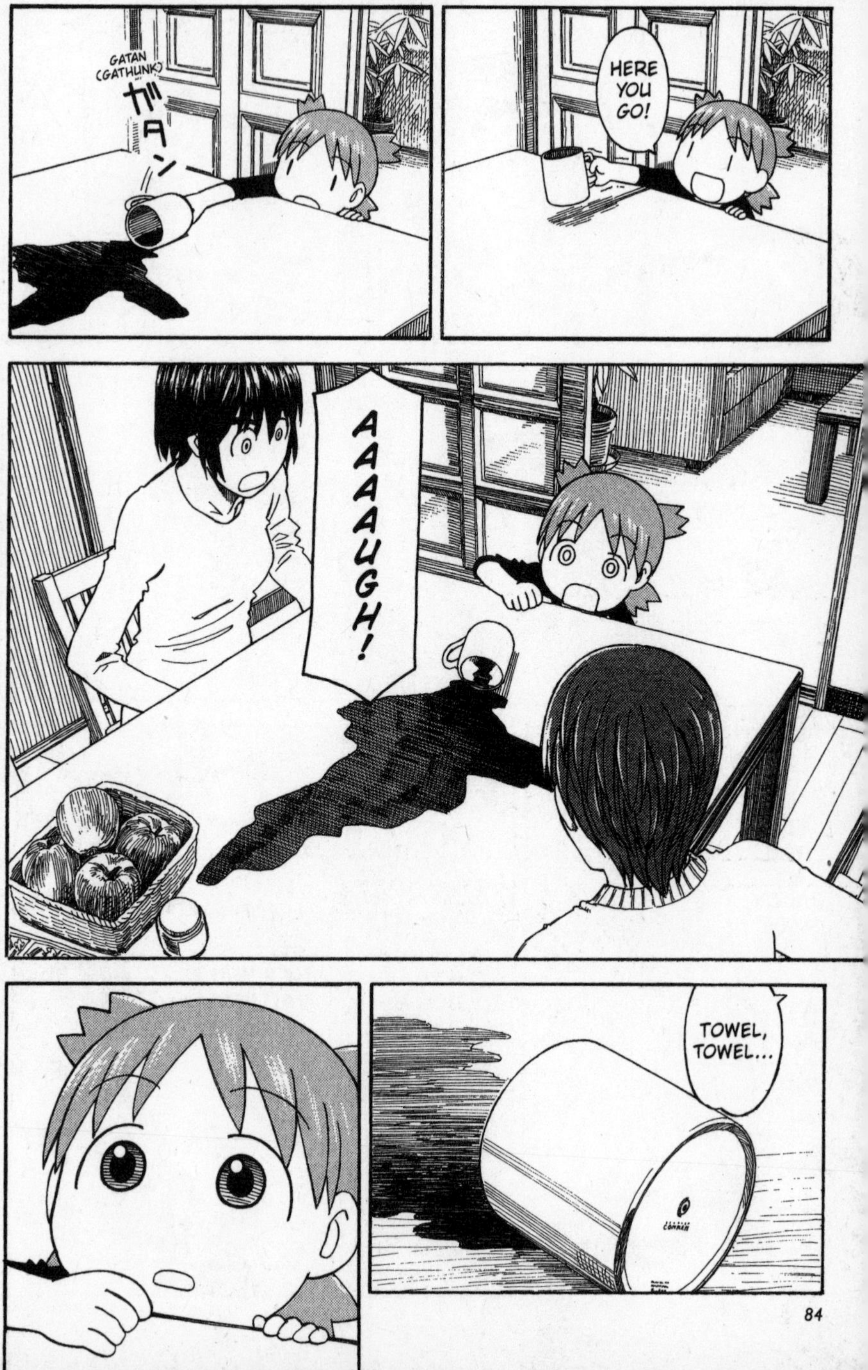
HERE YOU GO!
GATAN (GATHUNK)
ガタン
AAAAAUGH!
TOWEL, TOWEL...

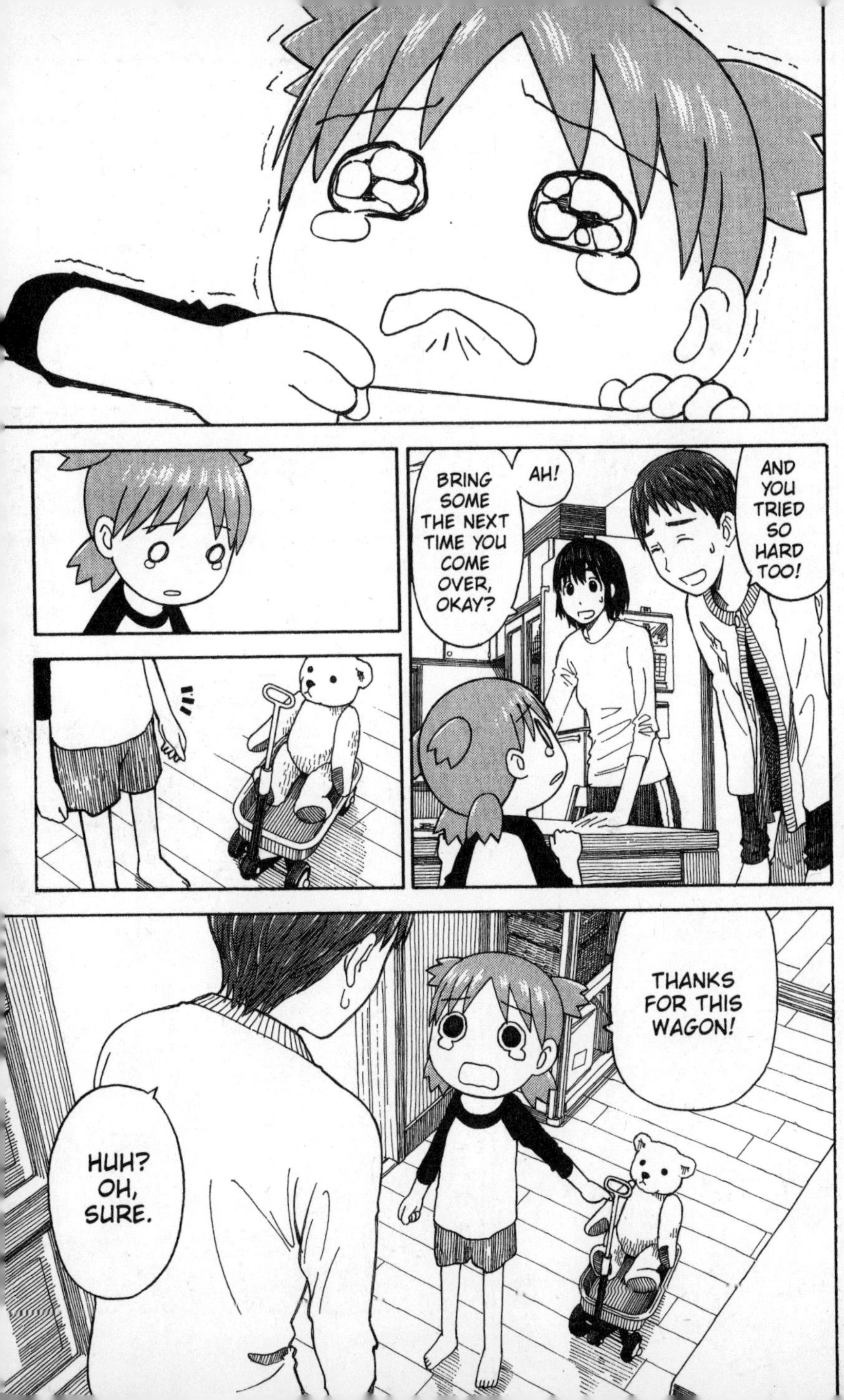
AND YOU TRIED SO HARD TOO!
AH!
BRING SOME THE NEXT TIME YOU COME OVER, OKAY?
THANKS FOR THIS WAGON!
HUH? OH, SURE.

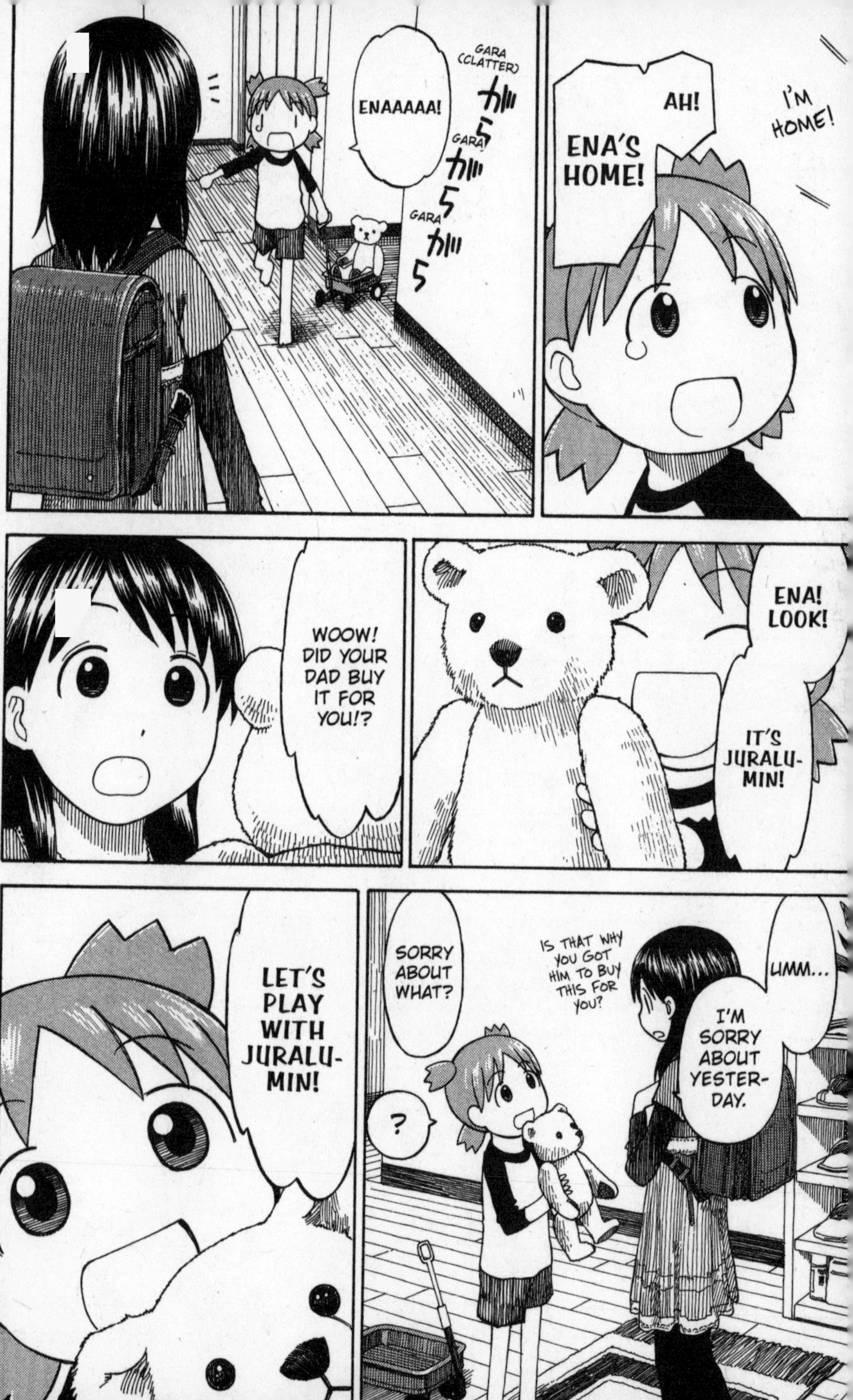
I'M HOME!
AH!
ENA'S HOME!
GARA (CLATTER)
がら
GARA
がら
GARA
がら
ENAAAAA!
ENA! LOOK!
IT'S JURALU-MIN!
WOOW! DID YOUR DAD BUY IT FOR YOU!?
UMM...
I'M SORRY ABOUT YESTER-DAY.
IS THAT WHY YOU GOT HIM TO BUY THIS FOR YOU?
SORRY ABOUT WHAT?
?
LET'S PLAY WITH JURALU-MIN!

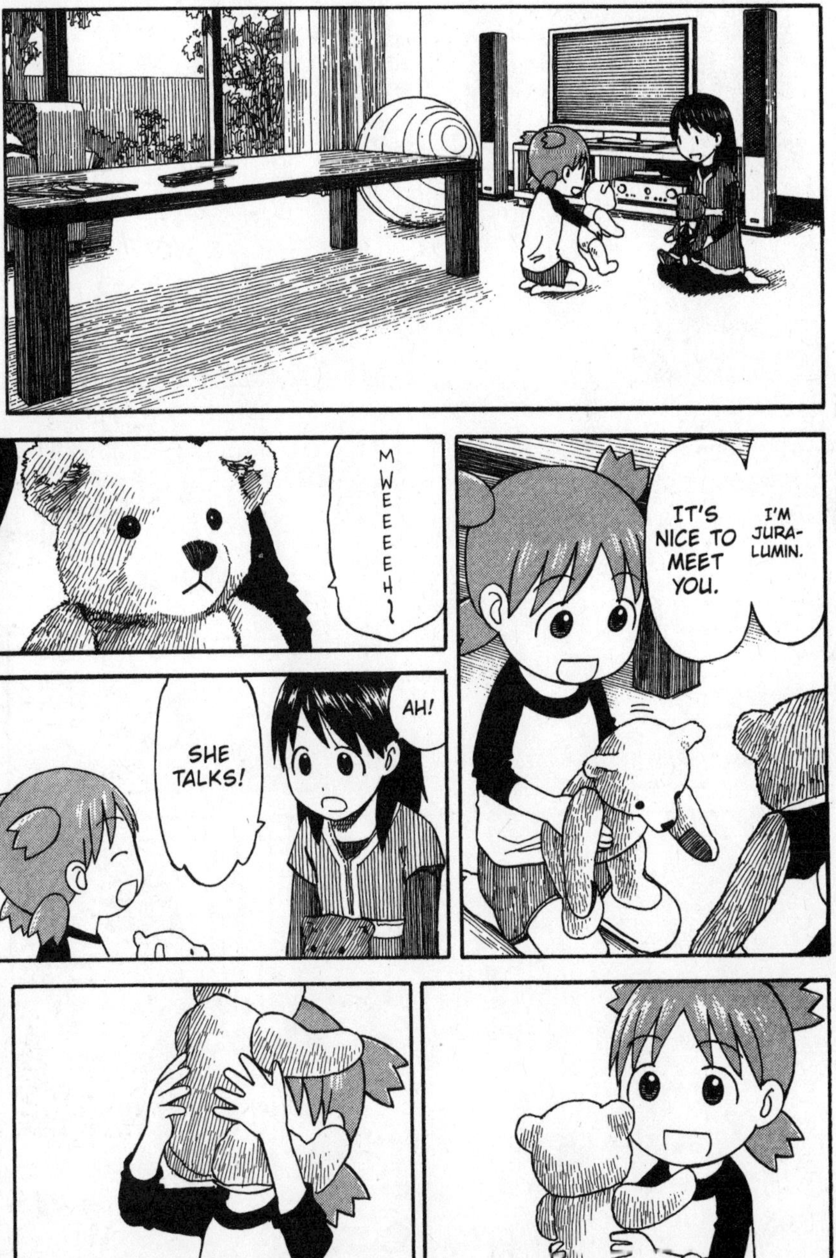
I'M JURALUMIN.
IT'S NICE TO MEET YOU.
MWEEEEEH~
AH!
SHE TALKS!

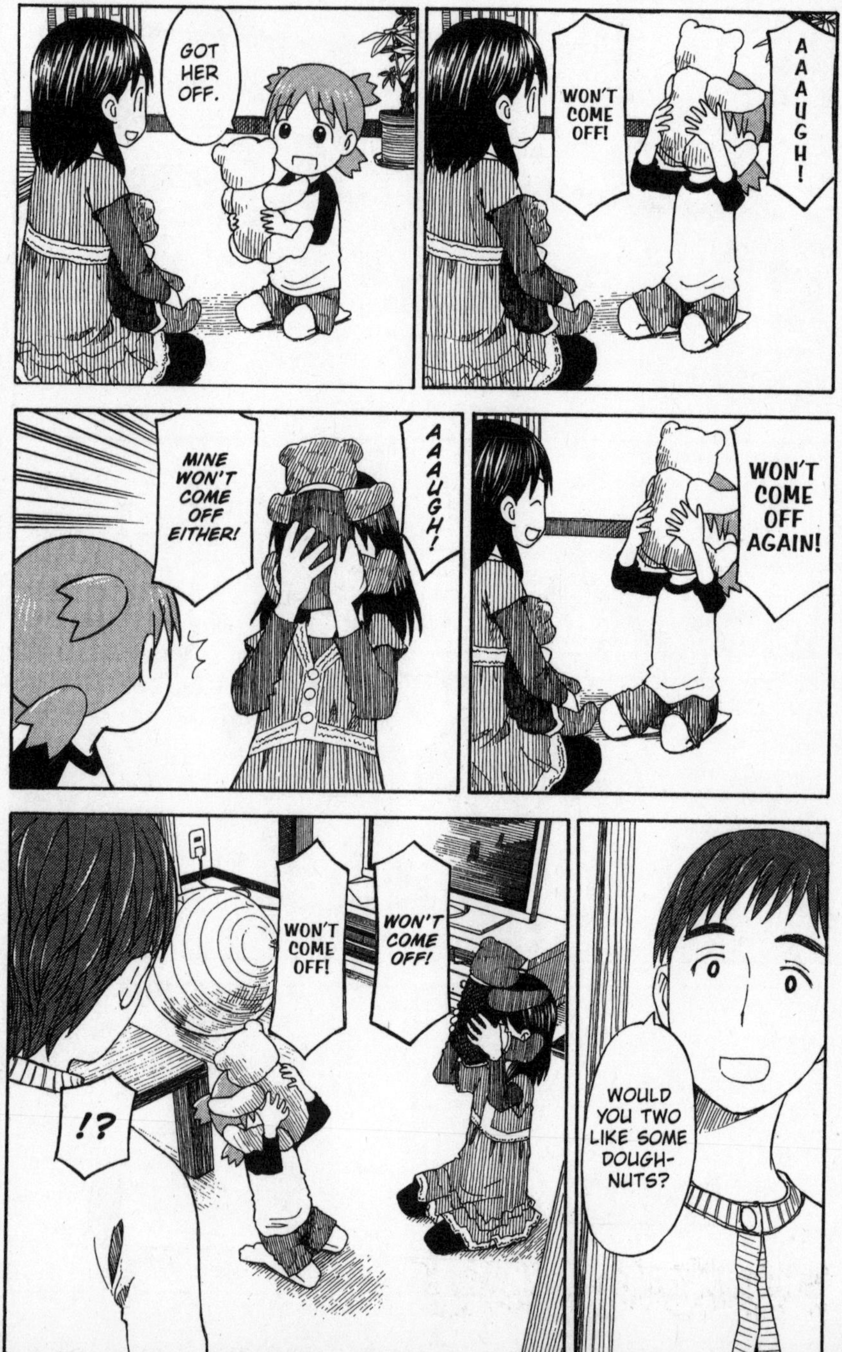
AAAAUGH!
WON'T COME OFF!
GOT HER OFF.
WON'T COME OFF AGAIN!
AAAUGH!
MINE WON'T COME OFF EITHER!
WOULD YOU TWO LIKE SOME DOUGH-NUTS?
WON'T COME OFF!
WON'T COME OFF!
!?

YOTSUBA&!

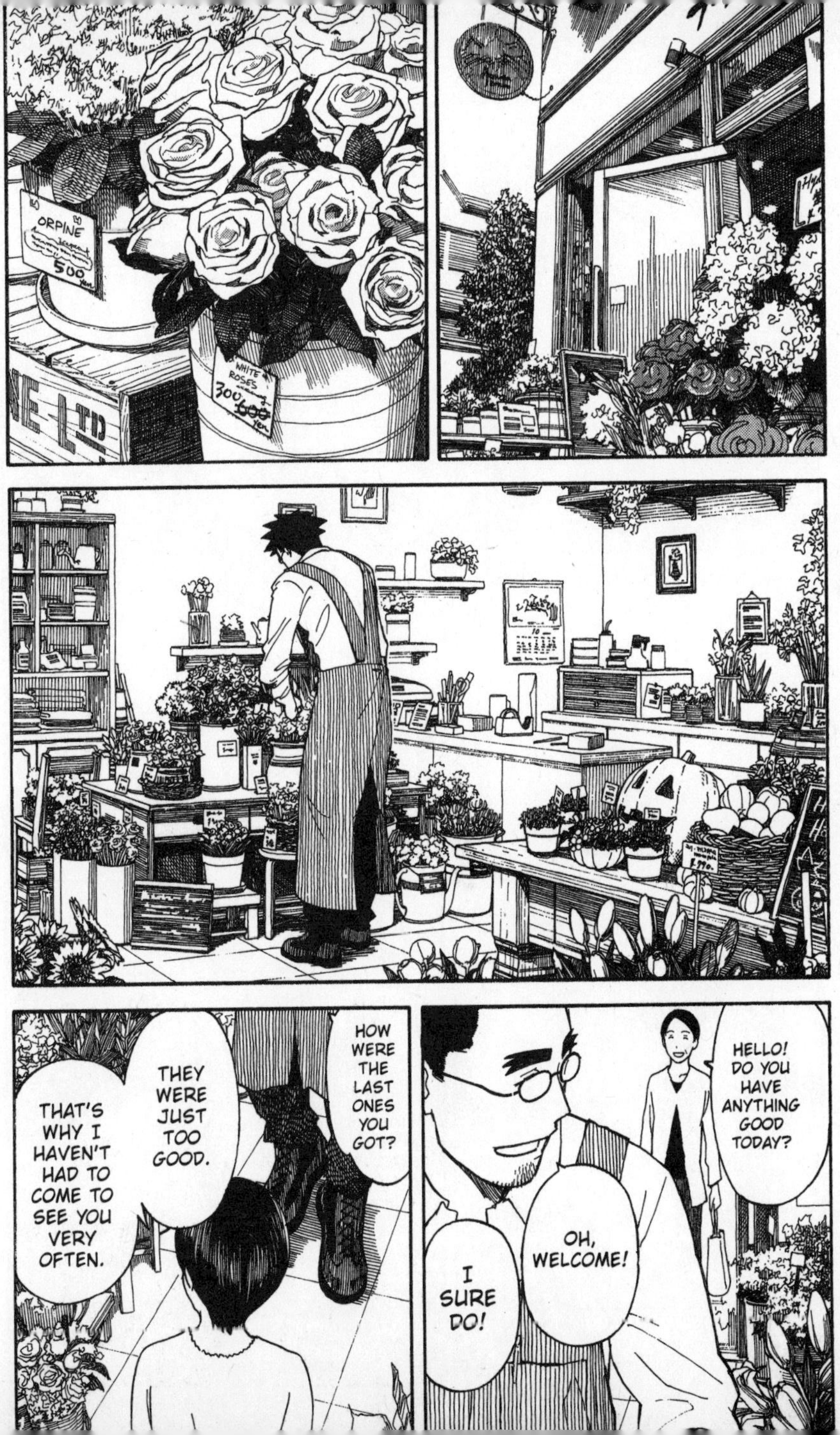
ORPINE
500 yen
WHITE ROSES
300 600 yen
HELLO! DO YOU HAVE ANYTHING GOOD TODAY?
OH, WELCOME!
I SURE DO!
HOW WERE THE LAST ONES YOU GOT?
THEY WERE JUST TOO GOOD.
THAT'S WHY I HAVEN'T HAD TO COME TO SEE YOU VERY OFTEN.

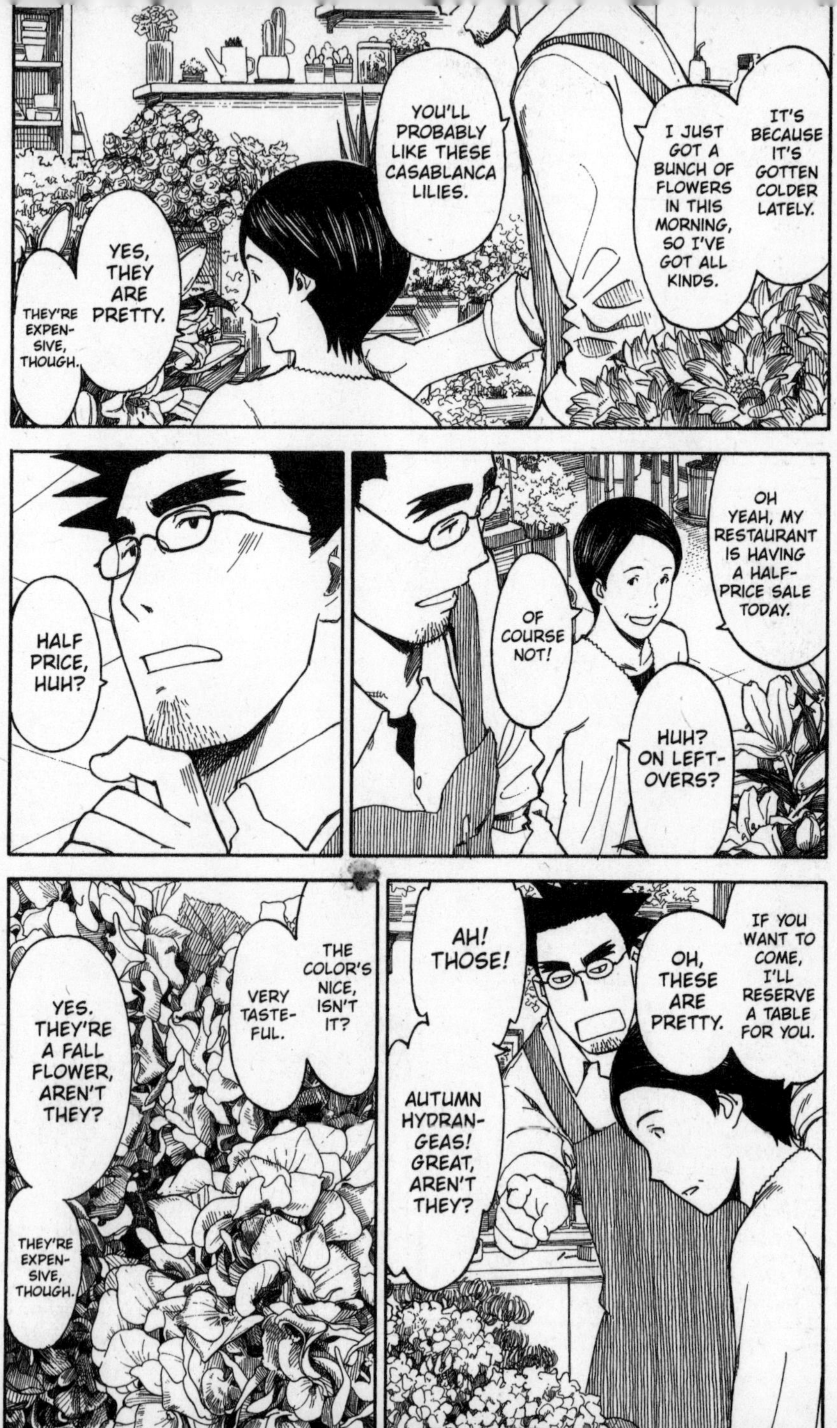
IT'S BECAUSE IT'S GOTTEN COLDER LATELY.
I JUST GOT A BUNCH OF FLOWERS IN THIS MORNING, SO I'VE GOT ALL KINDS.
YOU'LL PROBABLY LIKE THESE CASABLANCA LILIES.
YES, THEY ARE PRETTY.
THEY'RE EXPENSIVE, THOUGH.
OH YEAH, MY RESTAURANT IS HAVING A HALF-PRICE SALE TODAY.
HUH? ON LEFTOVERS?
OF COURSE NOT!
HALF PRICE, HUH?
IF YOU WANT TO COME, I'LL RESERVE A TABLE FOR YOU.
OH, THESE ARE PRETTY.
AH! THOSE!
AUTUMN HYDRANGEAS! GREAT, AREN'T THEY?
THE COLOR'S NICE, ISN'T IT?
VERY TASTEFUL.
YES. THEY'RE A FALL FLOWER, AREN'T THEY?
THEY'RE EXPENSIVE, THOUGH.

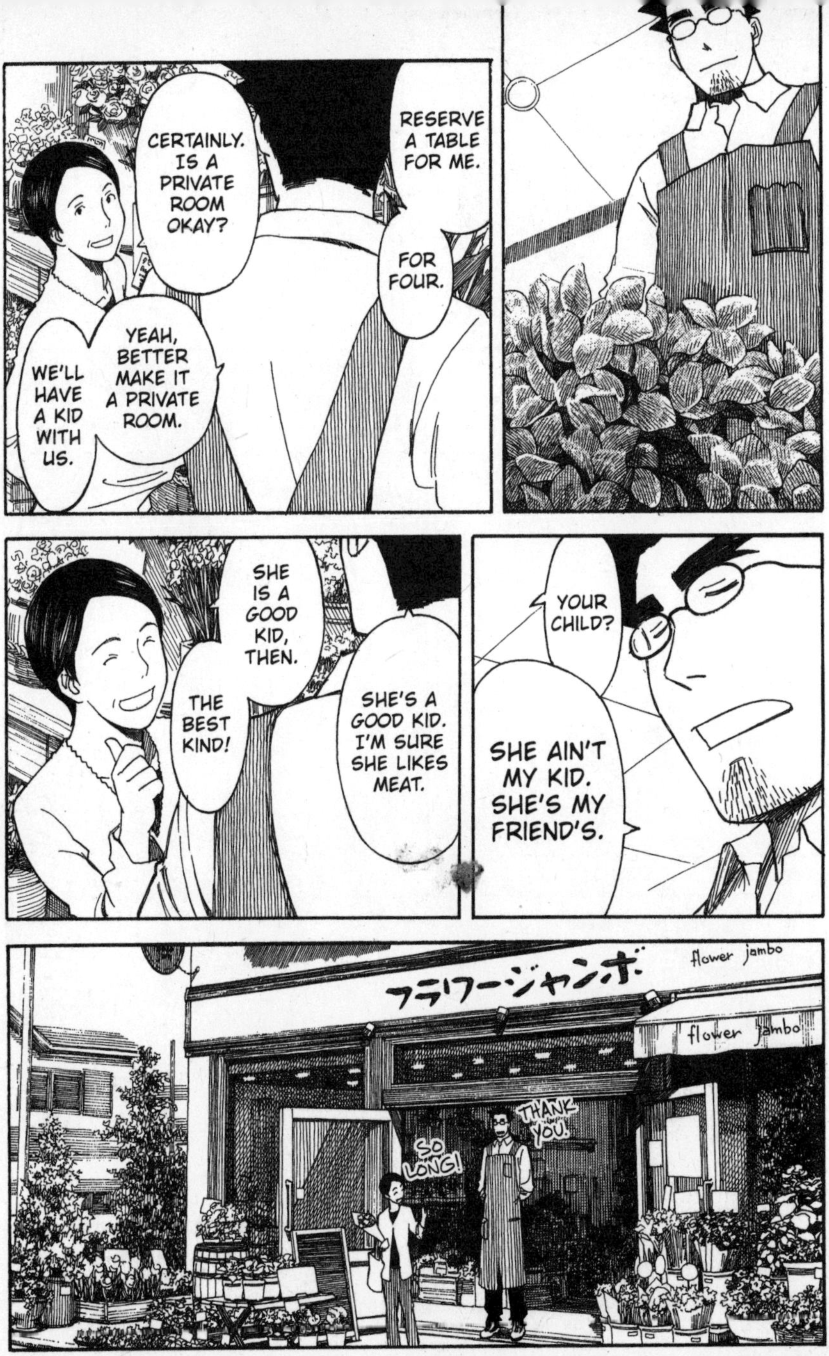
RESERVE A TABLE FOR ME.
FOR FOUR.
CERTAINLY. IS A PRIVATE ROOM OKAY?
YEAH, BETTER MAKE IT A PRIVATE ROOM.
WE'LL HAVE A KID WITH US.
YOUR CHILD?
SHE AIN'T MY KID. SHE'S MY FRIEND'S.
SHE'S A GOOD KID. I'M SURE SHE LIKES MEAT.
SHE IS A GOOD KID, THEN.
THE BEST KIND!
flower jambo
フラワージャンボ
flower jambo
THANK YOU!
SO LONG!

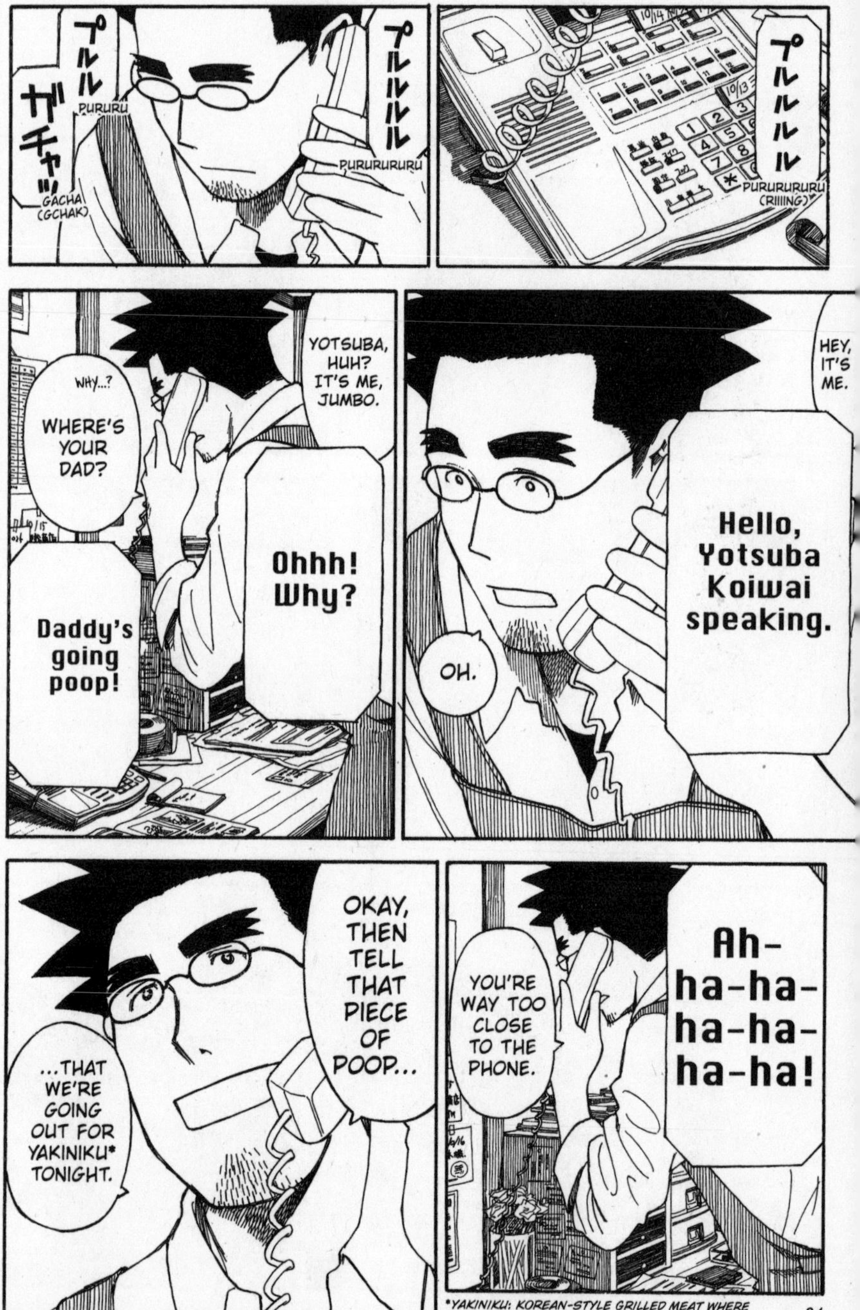
プルルルル
PURURURURU (RIIIING)
プルルルル
PURURURURU
プルル
PURURU
ガチャッ
GACHA (GCHAK)
HEY, IT'S ME.
Hello, Yotsuba Koiwai speaking.
OH.
YOTSUBA, HUH? IT'S ME, JUMBO.
Ohhh! Why?
WHY...?
WHERE'S YOUR DAD?
Daddy's going poop!
Ah-ha-ha-ha-ha-ha-ha!
YOU'RE WAY TOO CLOSE TO THE PHONE.
OKAY, THEN TELL THAT PIECE OF POOP...
...THAT WE'RE GOING OUT FOR YAKINIKU* TONIGHT.

*YAKINIKU: KOREAN-STYLE GRILLED MEAT WHERE CUSTOMERS COOK THE MEAT THEMSELVES AT A GRILL BUILD INTO THEIR TABLE.

YOTSUBA&

YAKINIKU!

#59

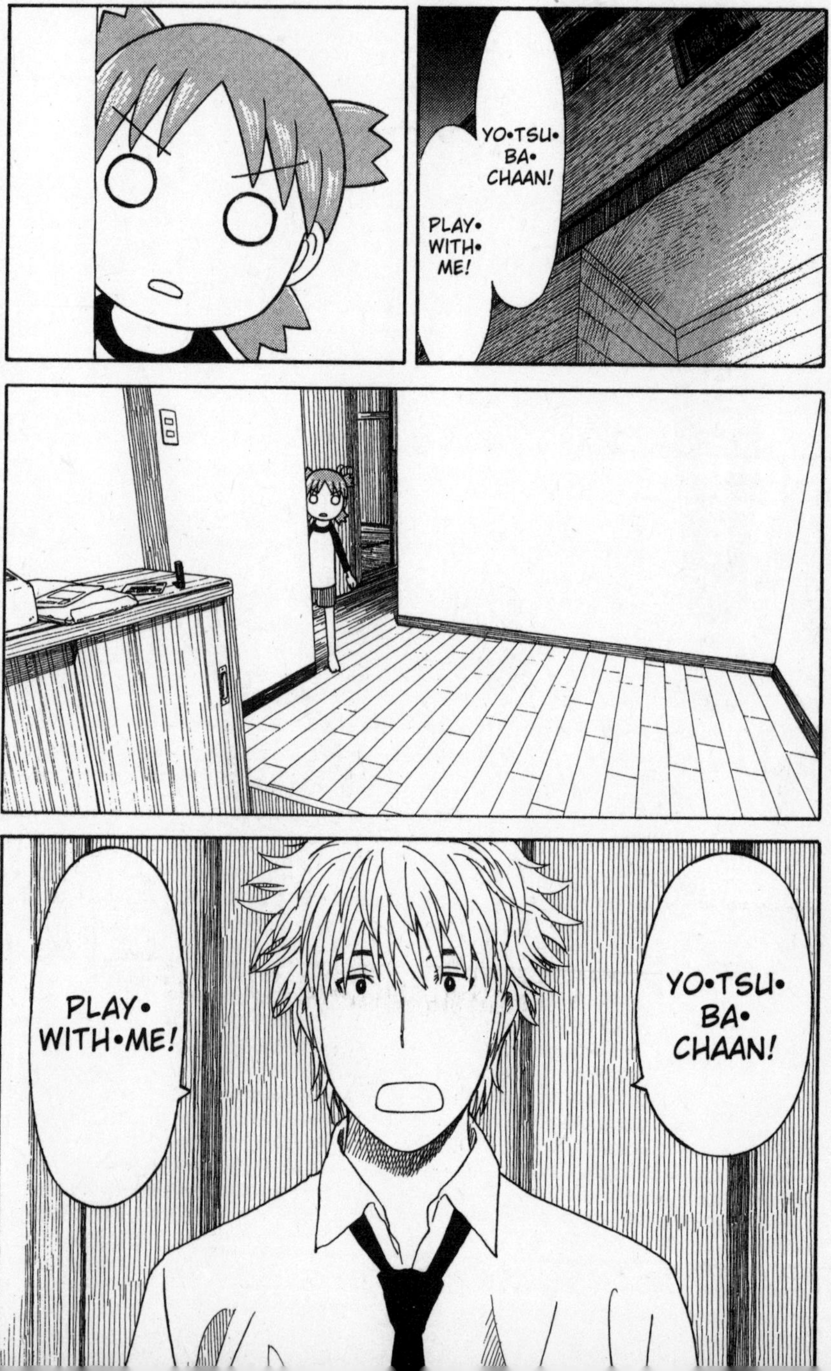
YO•TSU•BA•CHAAN!
PLAY•WITH•ME!
YO•TSU•BA•CHAAN!
PLAY•WITH•ME!

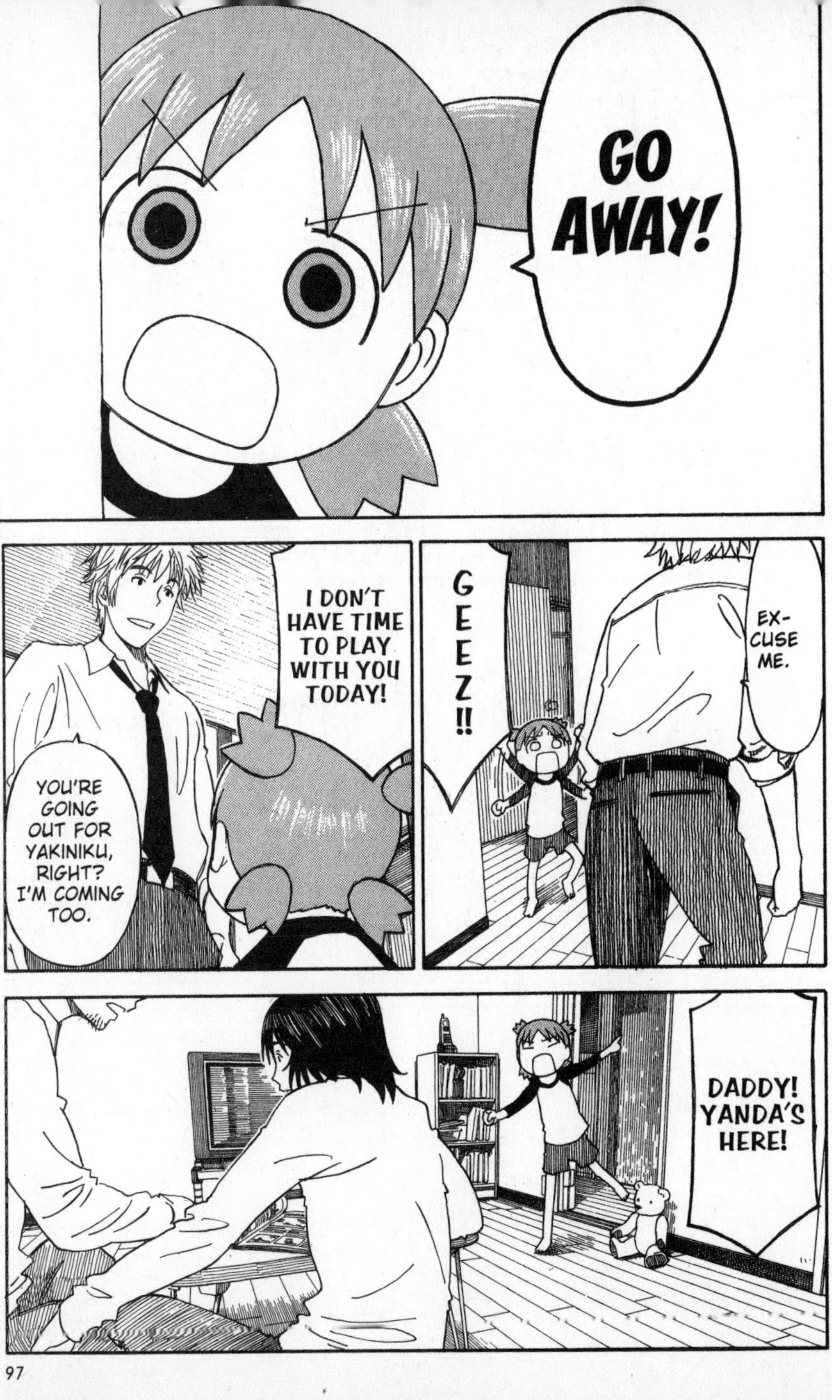
GO AWAY!
EX-CUSE ME.
GEEZ!!
I DON'T HAVE TIME TO PLAY WITH YOU TODAY!
YOU'RE GOING OUT FOR YAKINIKU, RIGHT? I'M COMING TOO.
DADDY! YANDA'S HERE!

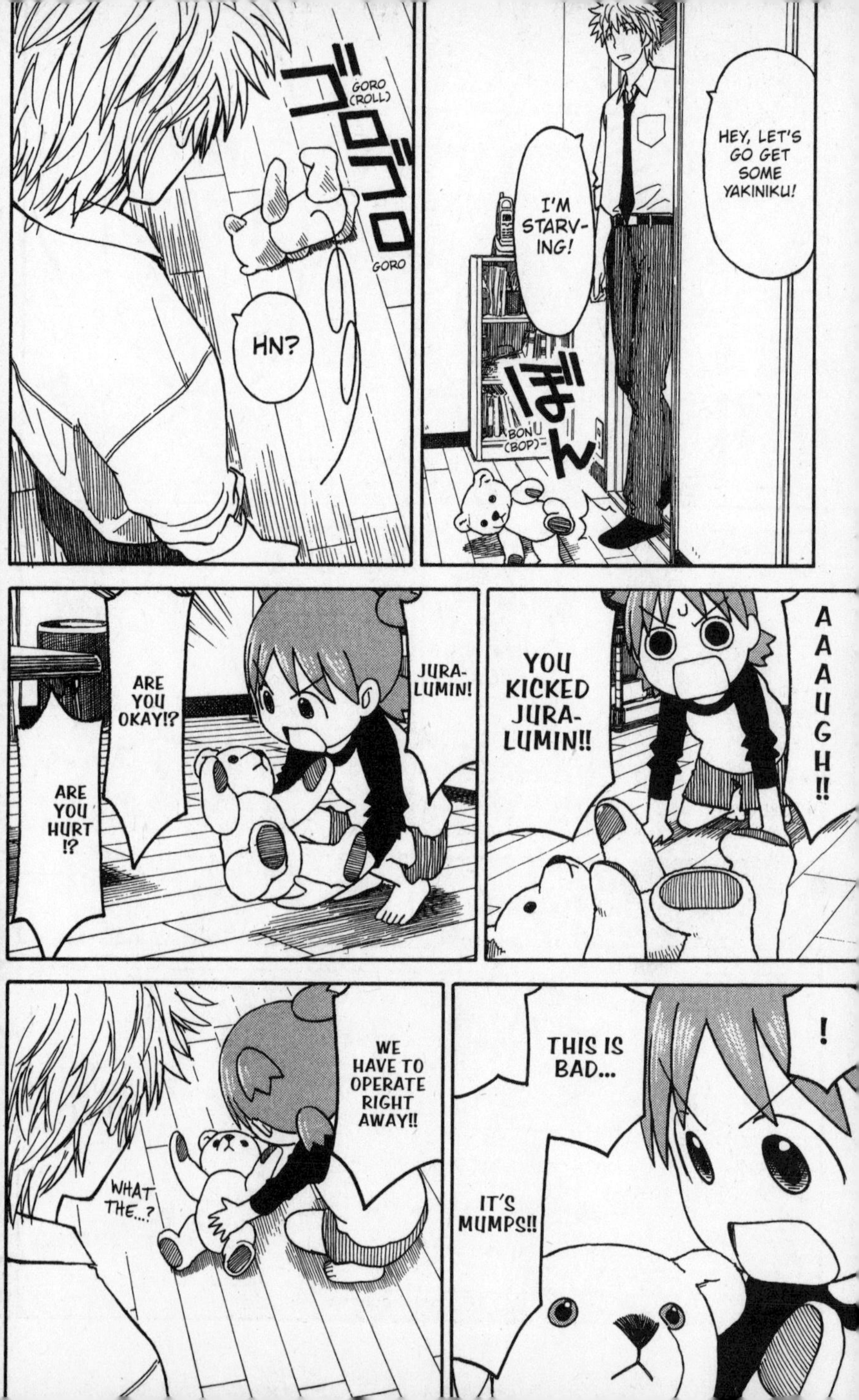
HEY, LET'S GO GET SOME YAKINIKU!
I'M STARV-ING!
BON (BOP)
GORO (ROLL)
GORO
HN?
AAAAUGH!!
YOU KICKED JURA-LUMIN!!
JURA-LUMIN!
ARE YOU OKAY!?
ARE YOU HURT!?
!
THIS IS BAD...
IT'S MUMPS!!
WE HAVE TO OPERATE RIGHT AWAY!!
WHAT THE...?

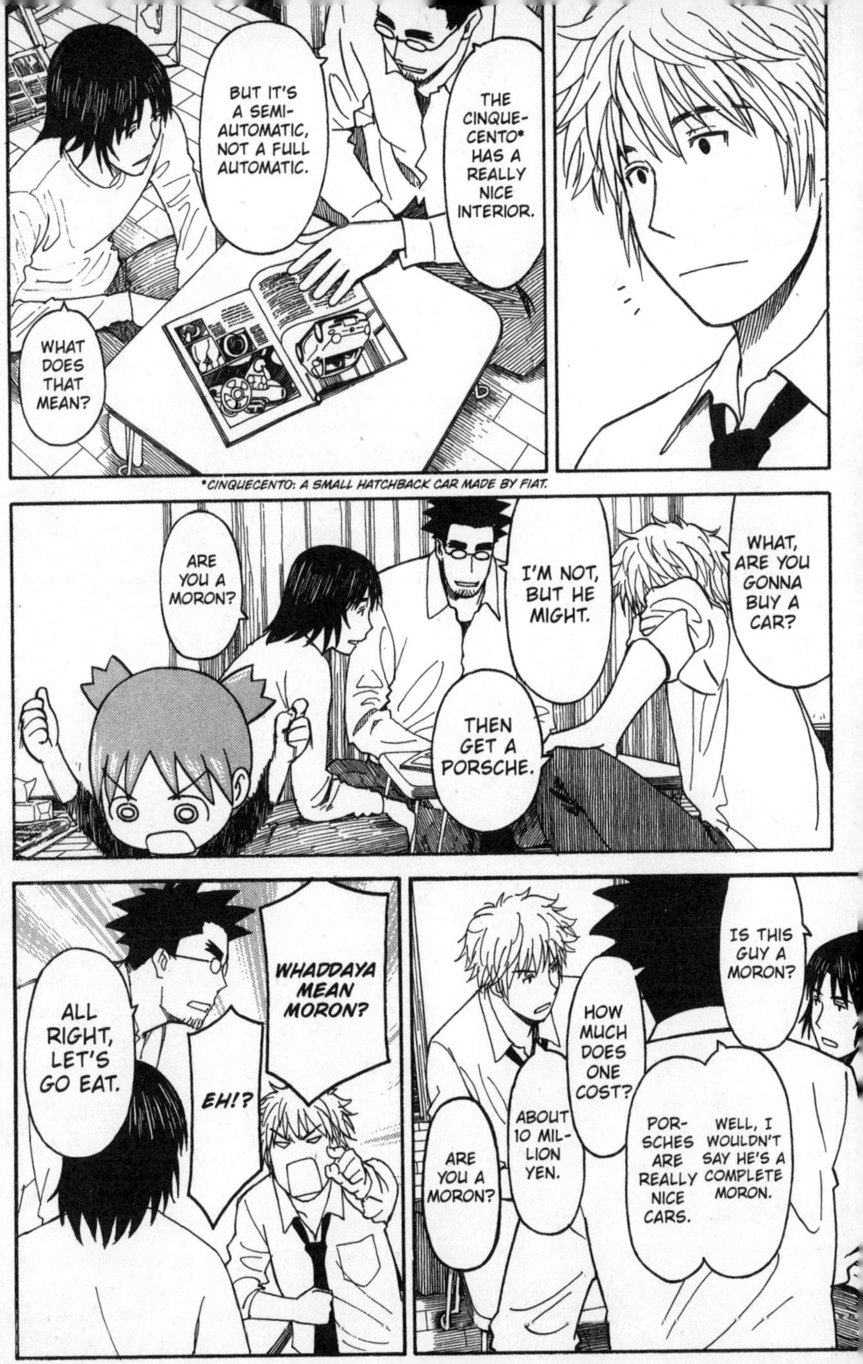
THE CINQUECENTO* HAS A REALLY NICE INTERIOR.
BUT IT'S A SEMI-AUTOMATIC, NOT A FULL AUTOMATIC.
WHAT DOES THAT MEAN?
WHAT, ARE YOU GONNA BUY A CAR?
I'M NOT, BUT HE MIGHT.
THEN GET A PORSCHE.
ARE YOU A MORON?
IS THIS GUY A MORON?
HOW MUCH DOES ONE COST?
WELL, I WOULDN'T SAY HE'S A COMPLETE MORON.
PORSCHES ARE REALLY NICE CARS.
ABOUT 10 MILLION YEN.
ARE YOU A MORON?
WHADDAYA MEAN MORON?
EH!?
ALL RIGHT, LET'S GO EAT.

*CINQUECENTO: A SMALL HATCHBACK CAR MADE BY FIAT.

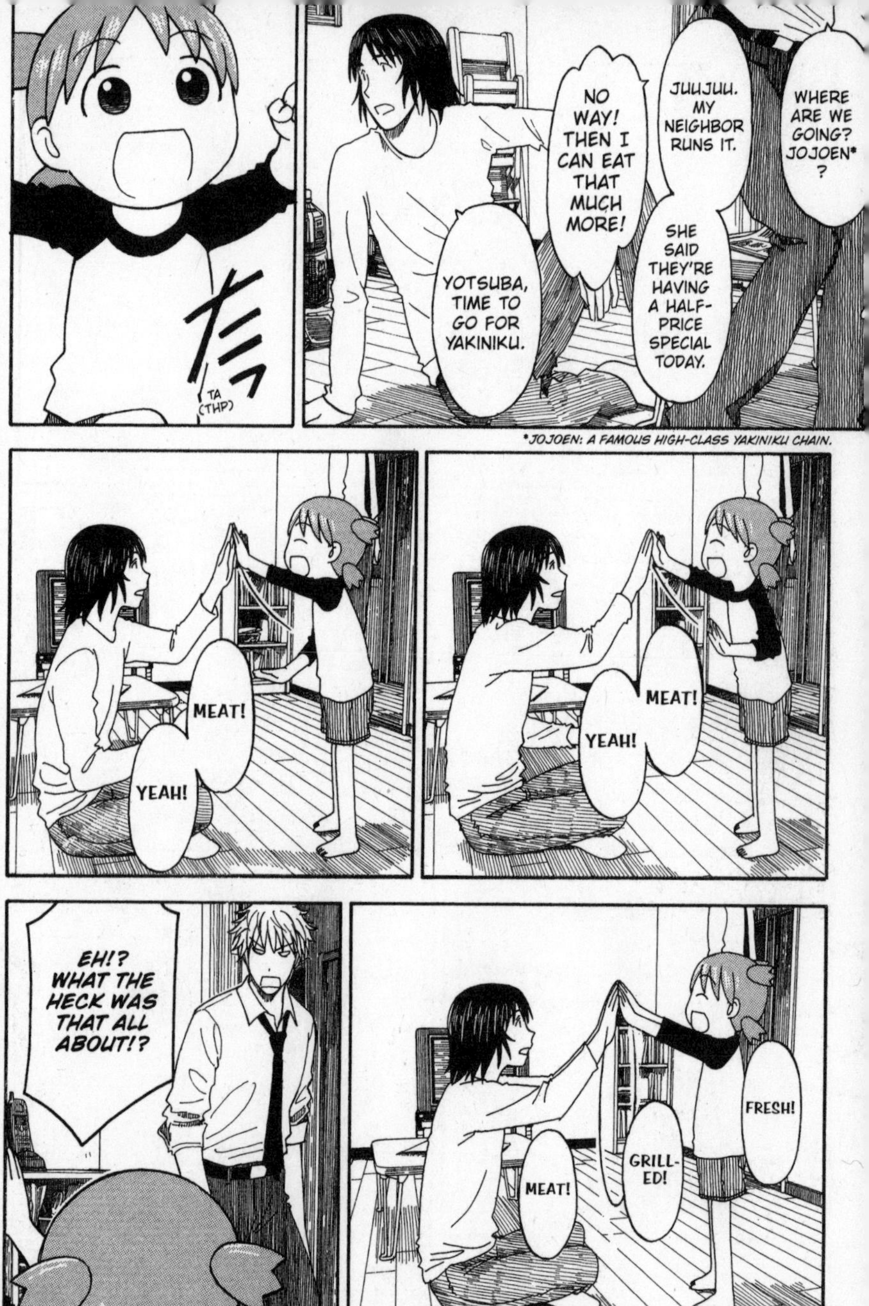
WHERE ARE WE GOING? JOJOEN*?
JUUJUU. MY NEIGHBOR RUNS IT.
SHE SAID THEY'RE HAVING A HALF-PRICE SPECIAL TODAY.
NO WAY! THEN I CAN EAT THAT MUCH MORE!
YOTSUBA, TIME TO GO FOR YAKINIKU.
TA (THP)
MEAT!
YEAH!
MEAT!
YEAH!
FRESH!
GRILL-ED!
MEAT!
EH!? WHAT THE HECK WAS THAT ALL ABOUT!?

*JOJOEN: A FAMOUS HIGH-CLASS YAKINIKU CHAIN.

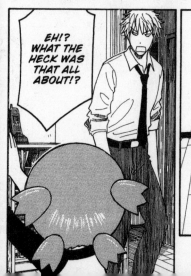

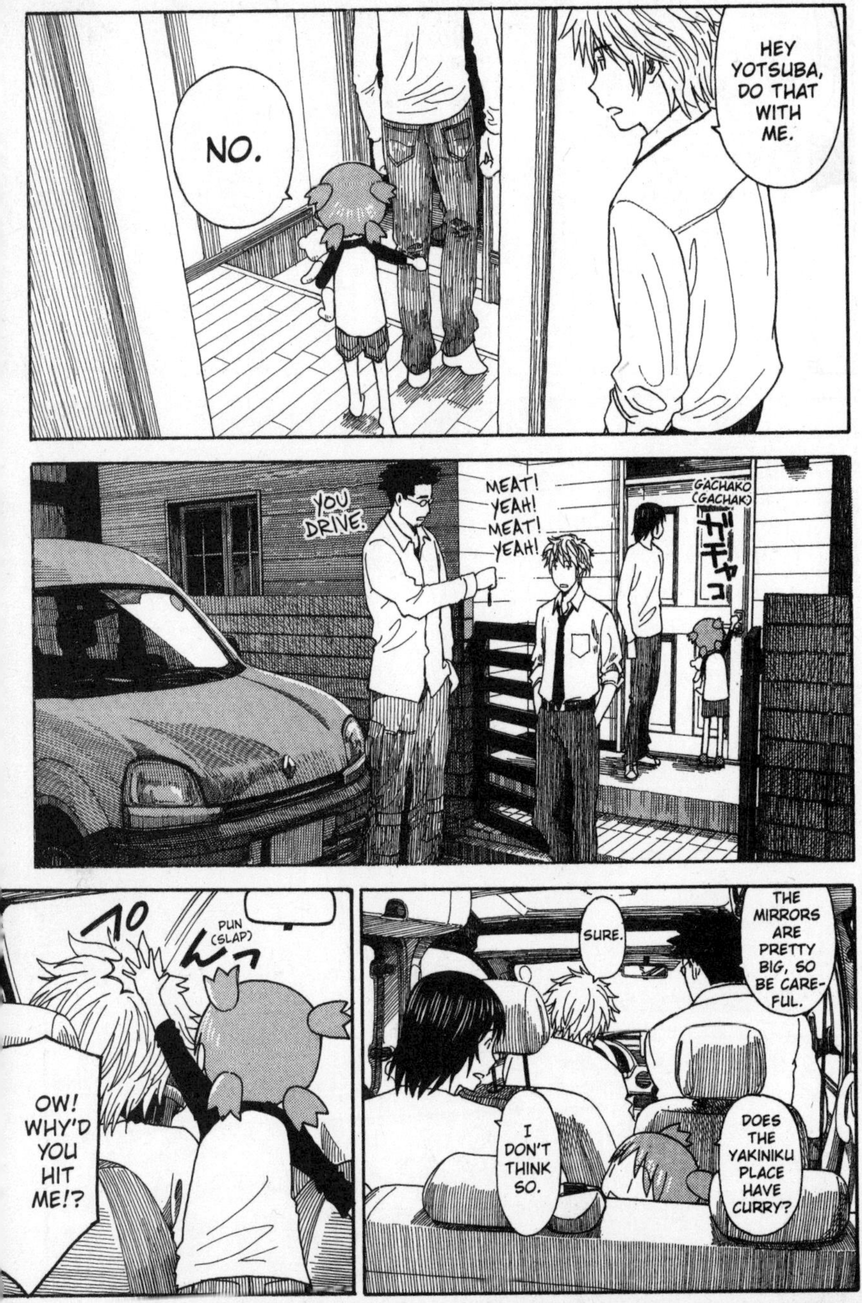

HEY YOTSUBA, DO THAT WITH ME.
NO.
GACHAKO (GACHAK)
ガチャコ
MEAT! YEAH! MEAT! YEAH!
YOU DRIVE.
THE MIRRORS ARE PRETTY BIG, SO BE CARE-FUL.
SURE.
DOES THE YAKINIKU PLACE HAVE CURRY?
I DON'T THINK SO.
PUN (SLAP)
OW! WHY'D YOU HIT ME!?

*THE NUMBER "10" IS "JUU" IN JAPANESE, SO OCTOBER 10TH WOULD BE "JUUJUU," WHICH IS THE NAME OF THE RESTAURANT.

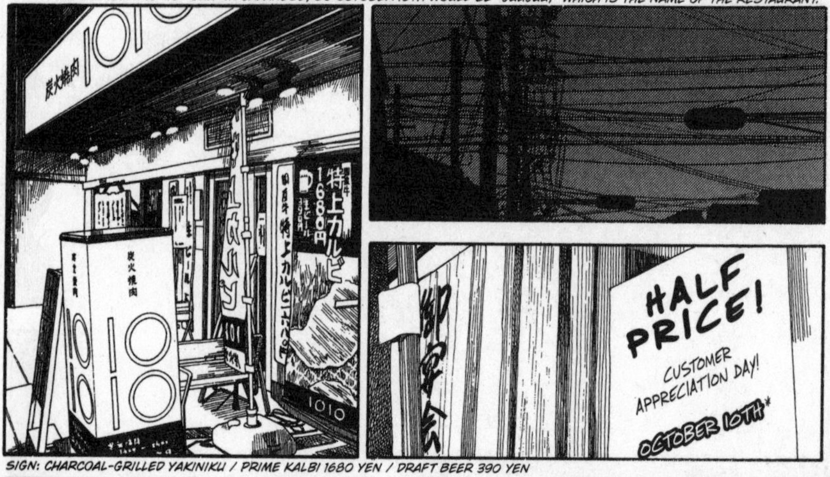
HALF PRICE!
CUSTOMER APPRECIATION DAY!
OCTOBER 10TH*
1010

SIGN: CHARCOAL-GRILLED YAKINIKU / PRIME KALBI 1680 YEN / DRAFT BEER 390 YEN

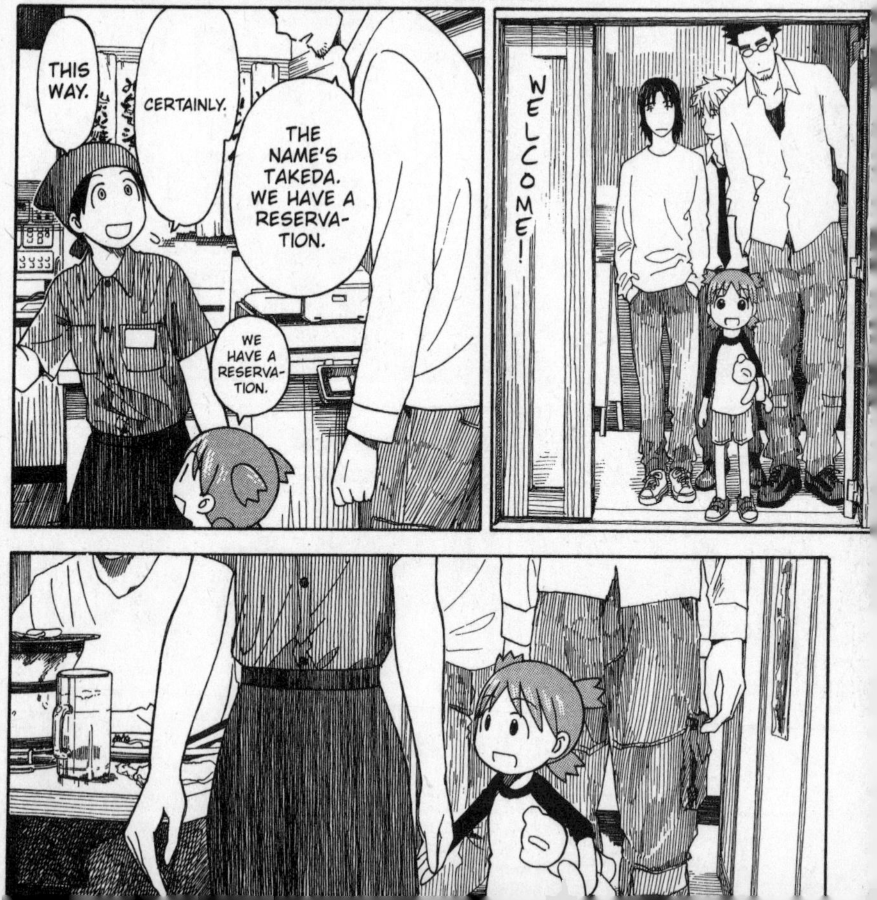
WELCOME!
THE NAME'S TAKEDA. WE HAVE A RESERVATION.
CERTAINLY.
THIS WAY.
WE HAVE A RESERVATION.

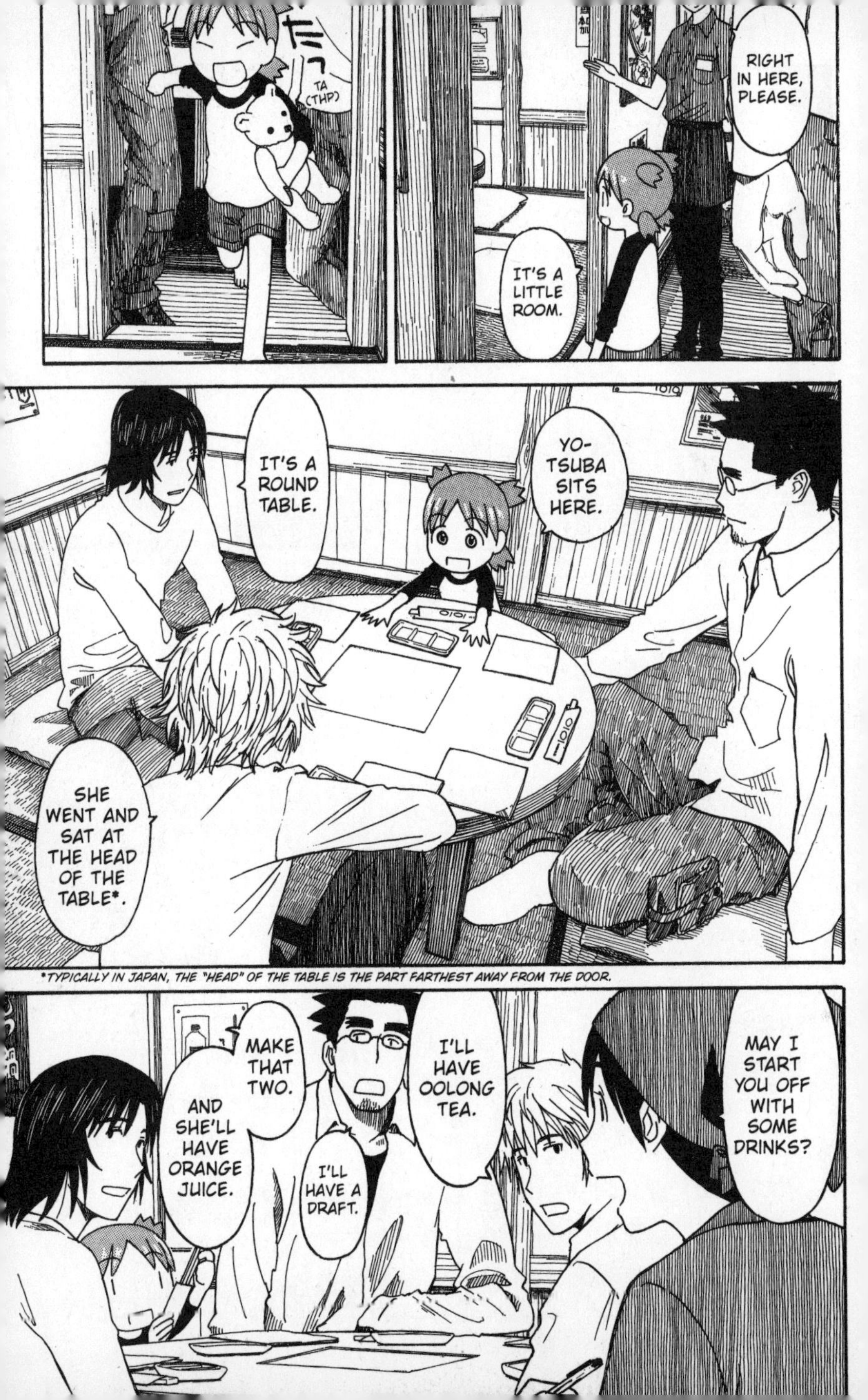
RIGHT IN HERE, PLEASE.
IT'S A LITTLE ROOM.
TA (THP)
YO-TSUBA SITS HERE.
IT'S A ROUND TABLE.
SHE WENT AND SAT AT THE HEAD OF THE TABLE*.
MAY I START YOU OFF WITH SOME DRINKS?
I'LL HAVE OOLONG TEA.
I'LL HAVE A DRAFT.
MAKE THAT TWO.
AND SHE'LL HAVE ORANGE JUICE.

*TYPICALLY IN JAPAN, THE "HEAD" OF THE TABLE IS THE PART FARTHEST AWAY FROM THE DOOR.

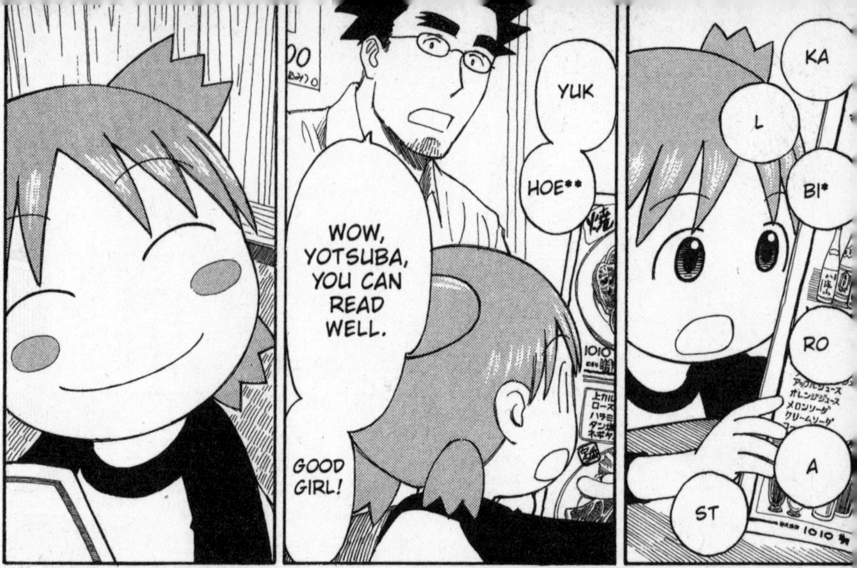
KA
L
BI*
RO
A
ST
YUK
HOE**
WOW, YOTSUBA, YOU CAN READ WELL.
GOOD GIRL!

**YUKHOE: A KOREAN DISH OF SEASONED RAW BEEF.

*KALBI: MARINATED SHORT RIBS IN A KOREAN SOY-BASED SAUCE.

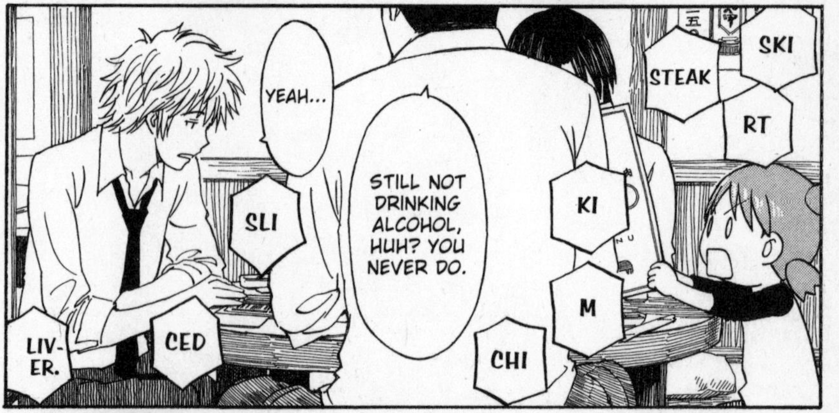
SKI
STEAK
RT
KI
M
CHI
YEAH...
STILL NOT DRINKING ALCOHOL, HUH? YOU NEVER DO.
SLI
CED
LIV-ER.

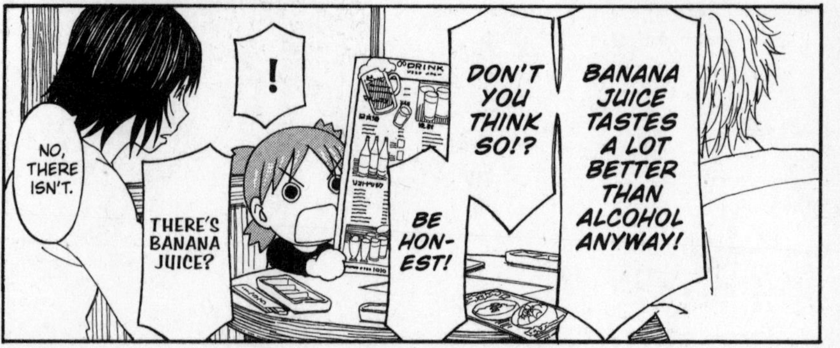
BANANA JUICE TASTES A LOT BETTER THAN ALCOHOL ANYWAY!
DON'T YOU THINK SO!?
BE HON-EST!
!
THERE'S BANANA JUICE?
NO, THERE ISN'T.

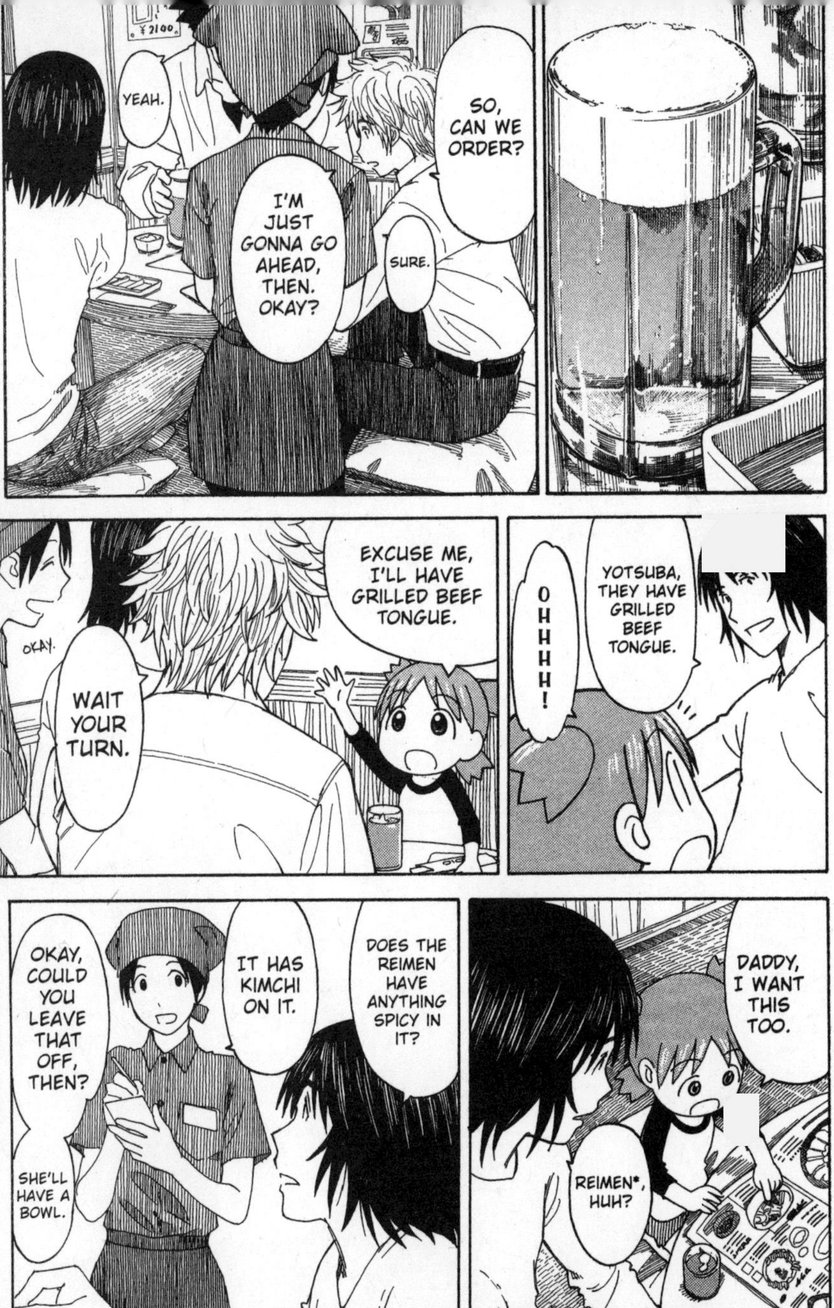

SO, CAN WE ORDER?
YEAH.
I'M JUST GONNA GO AHEAD, THEN. OKAY?
SURE.
YOTSUBA, THEY HAVE GRILLED BEEF TONGUE.
OHHHH!
EXCUSE ME, I'LL HAVE GRILLED BEEF TONGUE.
OKAY.
WAIT YOUR TURN.
DADDY, I WANT THIS TOO.
REIMEN*, HUH?
DOES THE REIMEN HAVE ANYTHING SPICY IN IT?
IT HAS KIMCHI ON IT.
OKAY, COULD YOU LEAVE THAT OFF, THEN?
SHE'LL HAVE A BOWL.

*REIMEN: KOREAN STYLE COLD NOODLES SERVED IN A COLD BROTH WITH TOPPINGS.

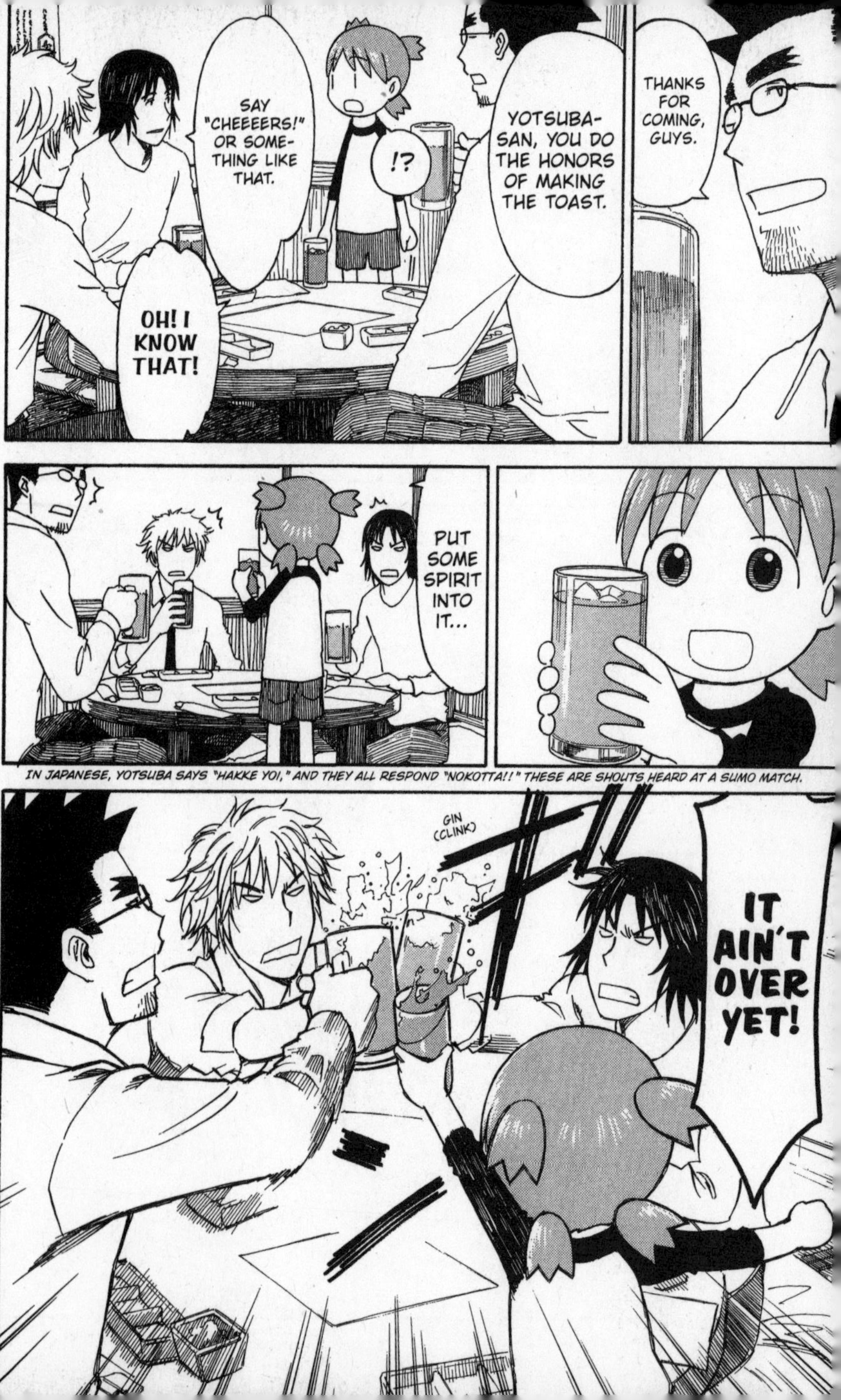
THANKS FOR COMING, GUYS.
YOTSUBA-SAN, YOU DO THE HONORS OF MAKING THE TOAST.
!?
SAY "CHEEEERS!" OR SOMETHING LIKE THAT.
OH! I KNOW THAT!
PUT SOME SPIRIT INTO IT...
IT AIN'T OVER YET!
GIN (CLINK)

IN JAPANESE, YOTSUBA SAYS "HAKKE YOI," AND THEY ALL RESPOND "NOKOTTA!!" THESE ARE SHOUTS HEARD AT A SUMO MATCH.

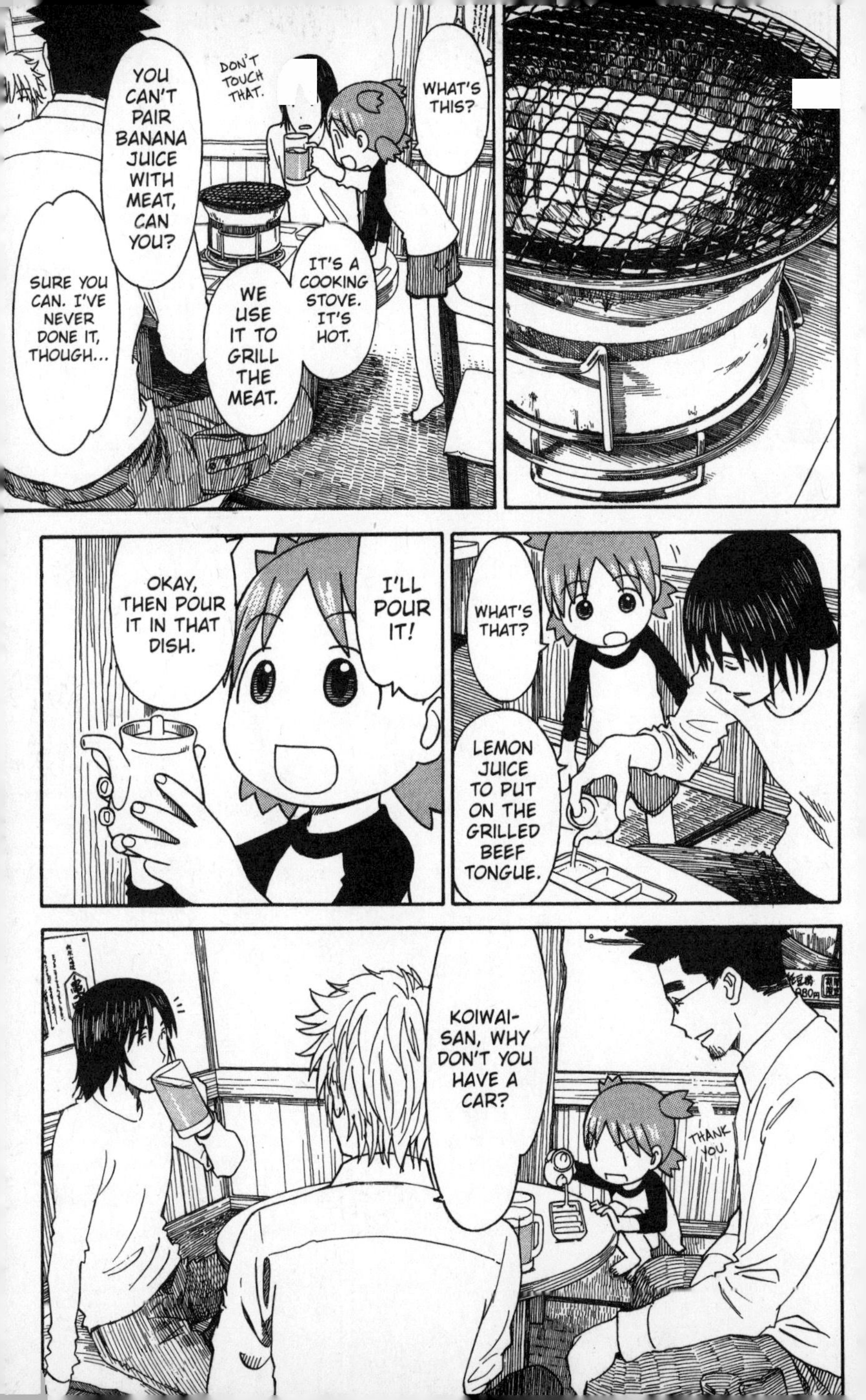
WHAT'S THIS?
DON'T TOUCH THAT.
YOU CAN'T PAIR BANANA JUICE WITH MEAT, CAN YOU?
IT'S A COOKING STOVE. IT'S HOT.
WE USE IT TO GRILL THE MEAT.
SURE YOU CAN. I'VE NEVER DONE IT, THOUGH...
WHAT'S THAT?
LEMON JUICE TO PUT ON THE GRILLED BEEF TONGUE.
I'LL POUR IT!
OKAY, THEN POUR IT IN THAT DISH.
THANK YOU.
KOIWAI-SAN, WHY DON'T YOU HAVE A CAR?

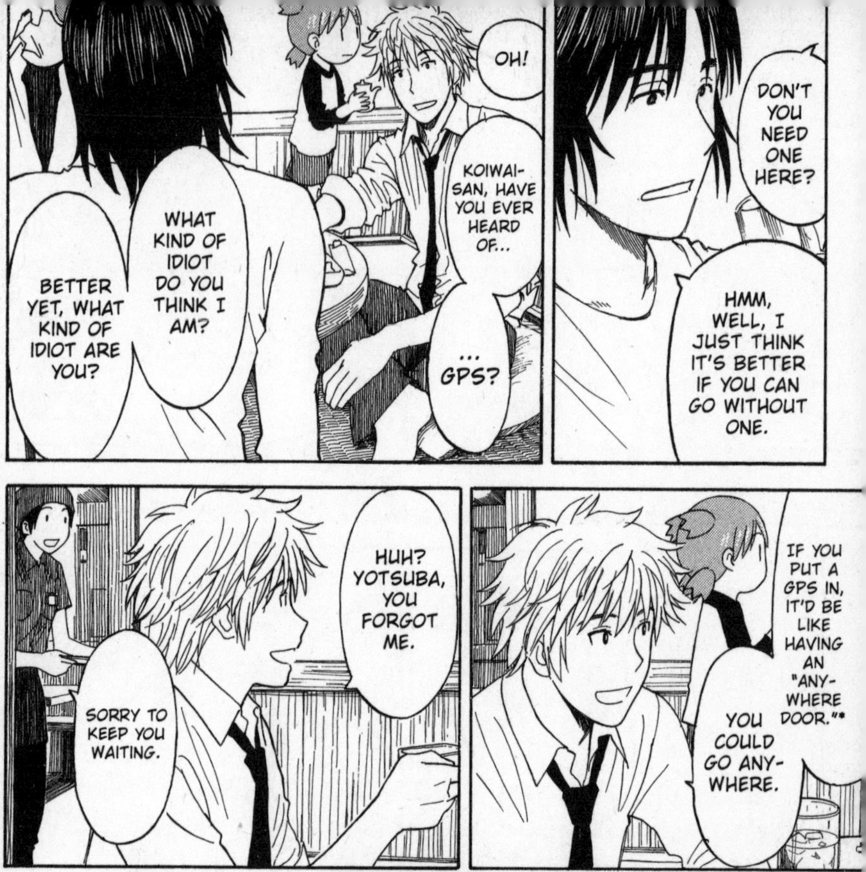
DON'T YOU NEED ONE HERE?
HMM, WELL, I JUST THINK IT'S BETTER IF YOU CAN GO WITHOUT ONE.
OH!
KOIWAI-SAN, HAVE YOU EVER HEARD OF...
... GPS?
WHAT KIND OF IDIOT DO YOU THINK I AM?
BETTER YET, WHAT KIND OF IDIOT ARE YOU?
IF YOU PUT A GPS IN, IT'D BE LIKE HAVING AN "ANY-WHERE DOOR."*
YOU COULD GO ANY-WHERE.
HUH? YOTSUBA, YOU FORGOT ME.
SORRY TO KEEP YOU WAITING.

*THE DOOR THAT ALLOWS THE CHARACTERS TO GO ANYWHERE IN THE KIDS MANGA AND ANIME SERIES DORAEMON.

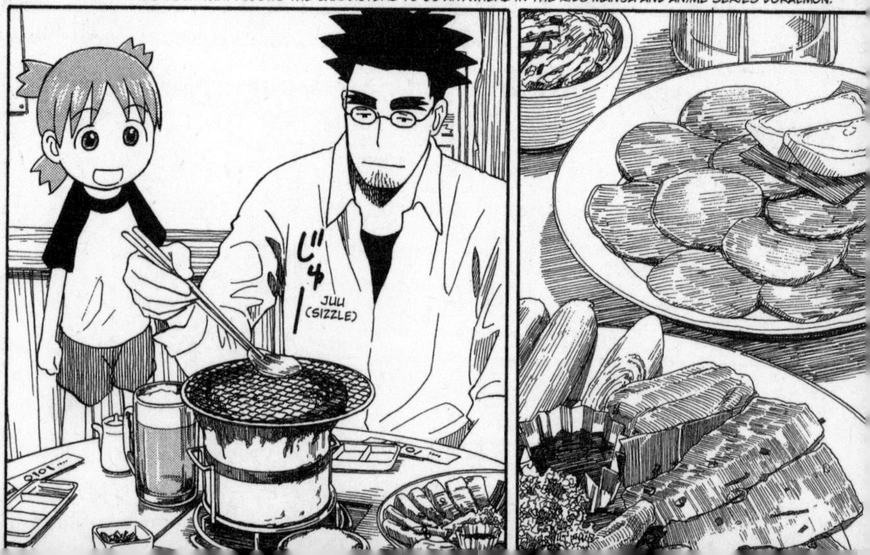
じゅ
JUU (SIZZLE)

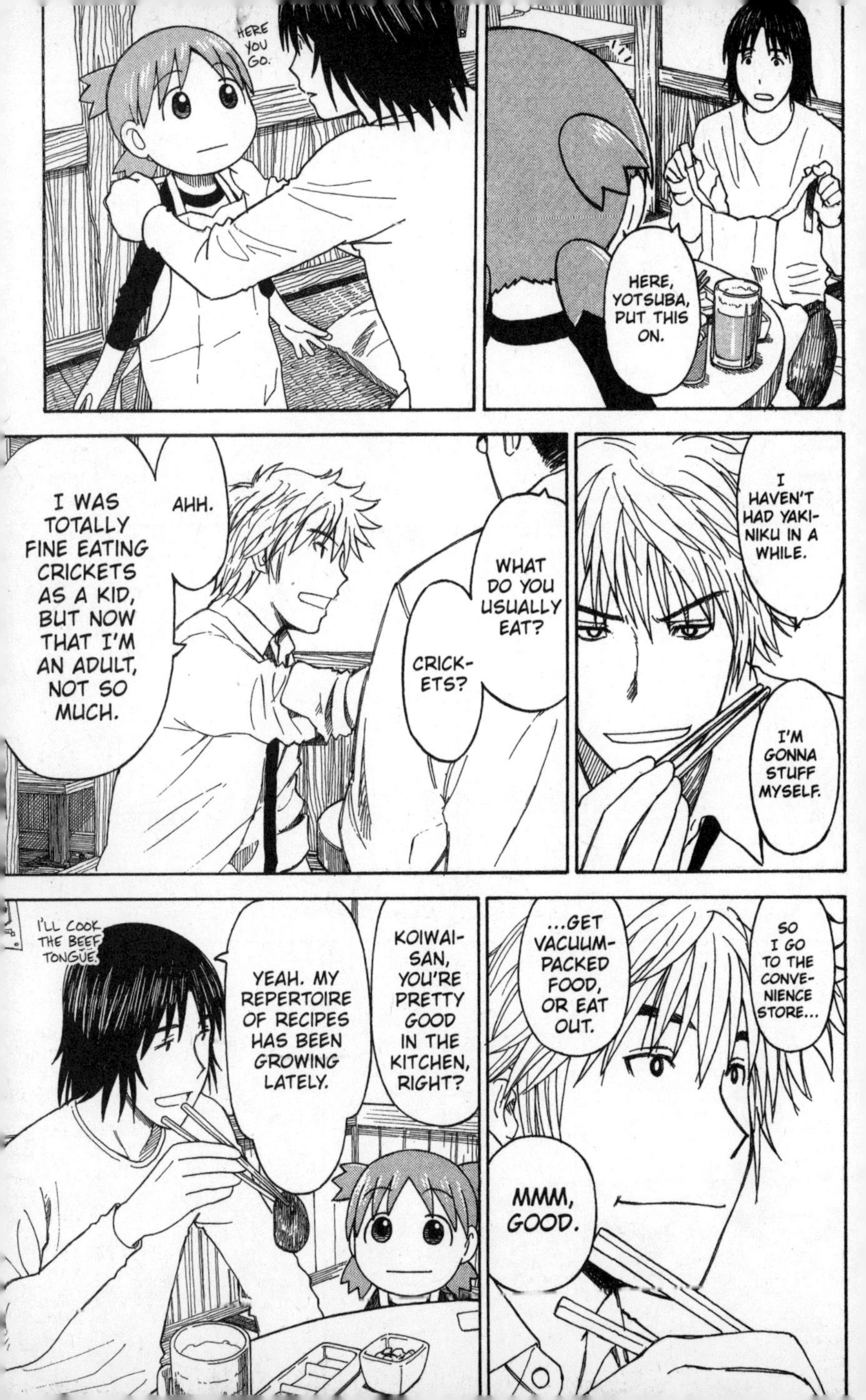
HERE, YOTSUBA, PUT THIS ON.
HERE YOU GO.
I HAVEN'T HAD YAKI-NIKU IN A WHILE.
I'M GONNA STUFF MYSELF.
WHAT DO YOU USUALLY EAT?
CRICK-ETS?
AHH.
I WAS TOTALLY FINE EATING CRICKETS AS A KID, BUT NOW THAT I'M AN ADULT, NOT SO MUCH.
SO I GO TO THE CONVE-NIENCE STORE...
...GET VACUUM-PACKED FOOD, OR EAT OUT.
MMM, GOOD.
KOIWAI-SAN, YOU'RE PRETTY GOOD IN THE KITCHEN, RIGHT?
YEAH. MY REPERTOIRE OF RECIPES HAS BEEN GROWING LATELY.
I'LL COOK THE BEEF TONGUE.

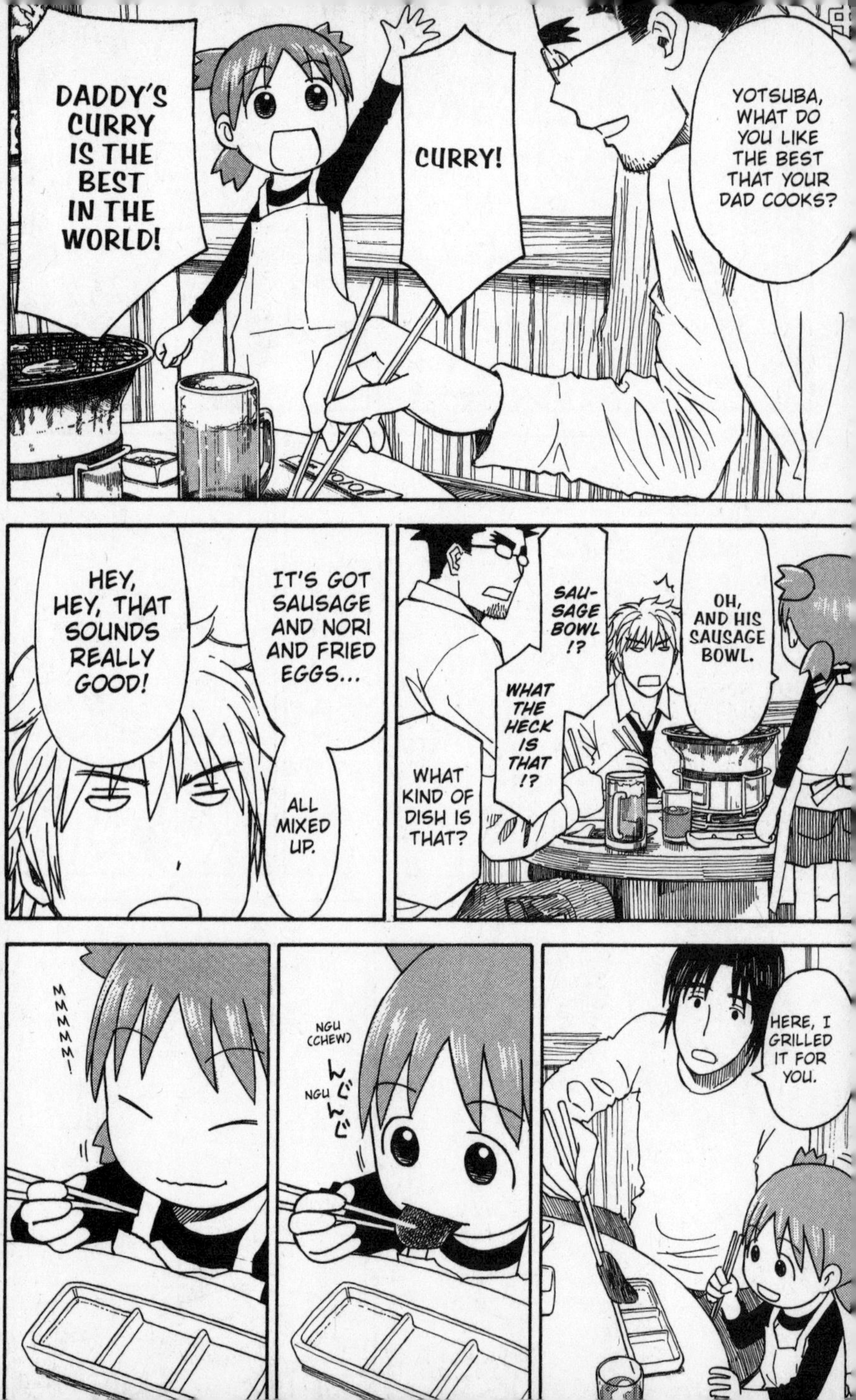
YOTSUBA, WHAT DO YOU LIKE THE BEST THAT YOUR DAD COOKS?
CURRY!
DADDY'S CURRY IS THE BEST IN THE WORLD!
OH, AND HIS SAUSAGE BOWL.
SAU-SAGE BOWL !?
WHAT THE HECK IS THAT !?
WHAT KIND OF DISH IS THAT?
IT'S GOT SAUSAGE AND NORI AND FRIED EGGS...
ALL MIXED UP.
HEY, HEY, THAT SOUNDS REALLY GOOD!
HERE, I GRILLED IT FOR YOU.
NGU (CHEW)
んぐんぐ
NGU
MMMMM!

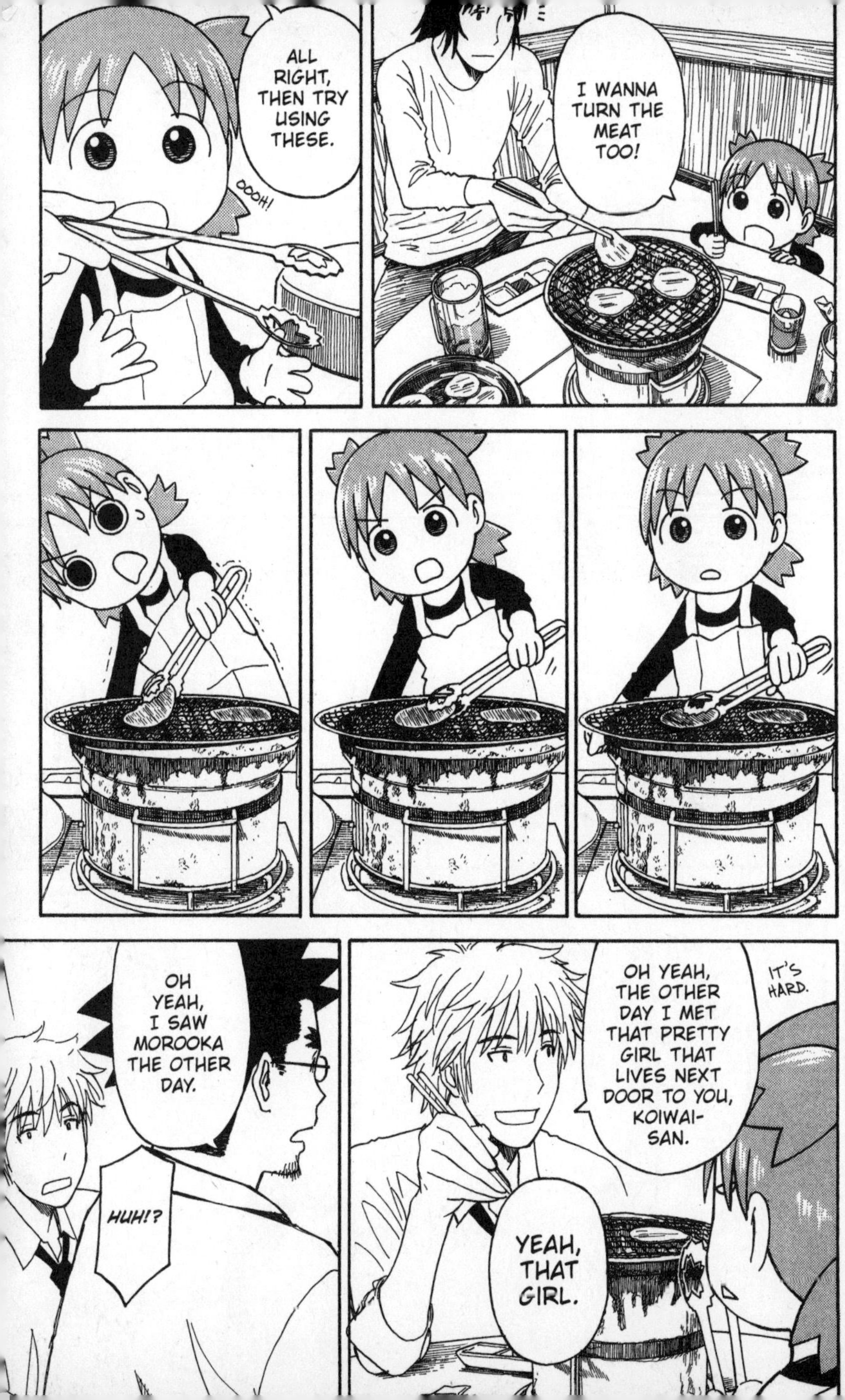
I WANNA TURN THE MEAT TOO!
ALL RIGHT, THEN TRY USING THESE.
OOOH!
IT'S HARD.
OH YEAH, THE OTHER DAY I MET THAT PRETTY GIRL THAT LIVES NEXT DOOR TO YOU, KOIWAI-SAN.
YEAH, THAT GIRL.
OH YEAH, I SAW MOROOKA THE OTHER DAY.
HUH!?

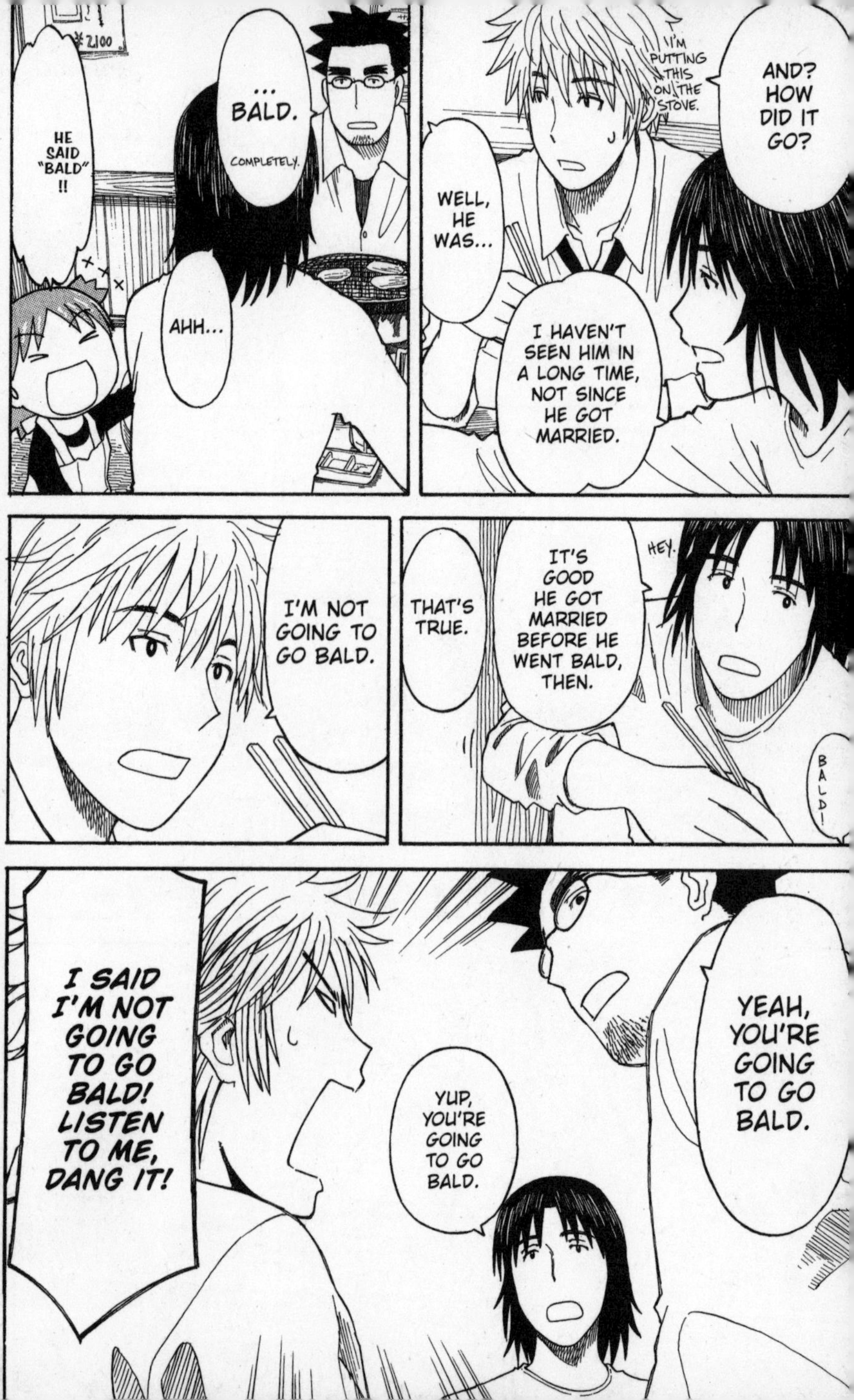
AND? HOW DID IT GO?
I'M PUTTING THIS ON THE STOVE.
WELL, HE WAS...
I HAVEN'T SEEN HIM IN A LONG TIME, NOT SINCE HE GOT MARRIED.
¥2100
... BALD.
COMPLETELY.
HE SAID "BALD" !!
AHH...
HEY.
IT'S GOOD HE GOT MARRIED BEFORE HE WENT BALD, THEN.
BALD!
THAT'S TRUE.
I'M NOT GOING TO GO BALD.
YEAH, YOU'RE GOING TO GO BALD.
YUP, YOU'RE GOING TO GO BALD.
I SAID I'M NOT GOING TO GO BALD! LISTEN TO ME, DANG IT!

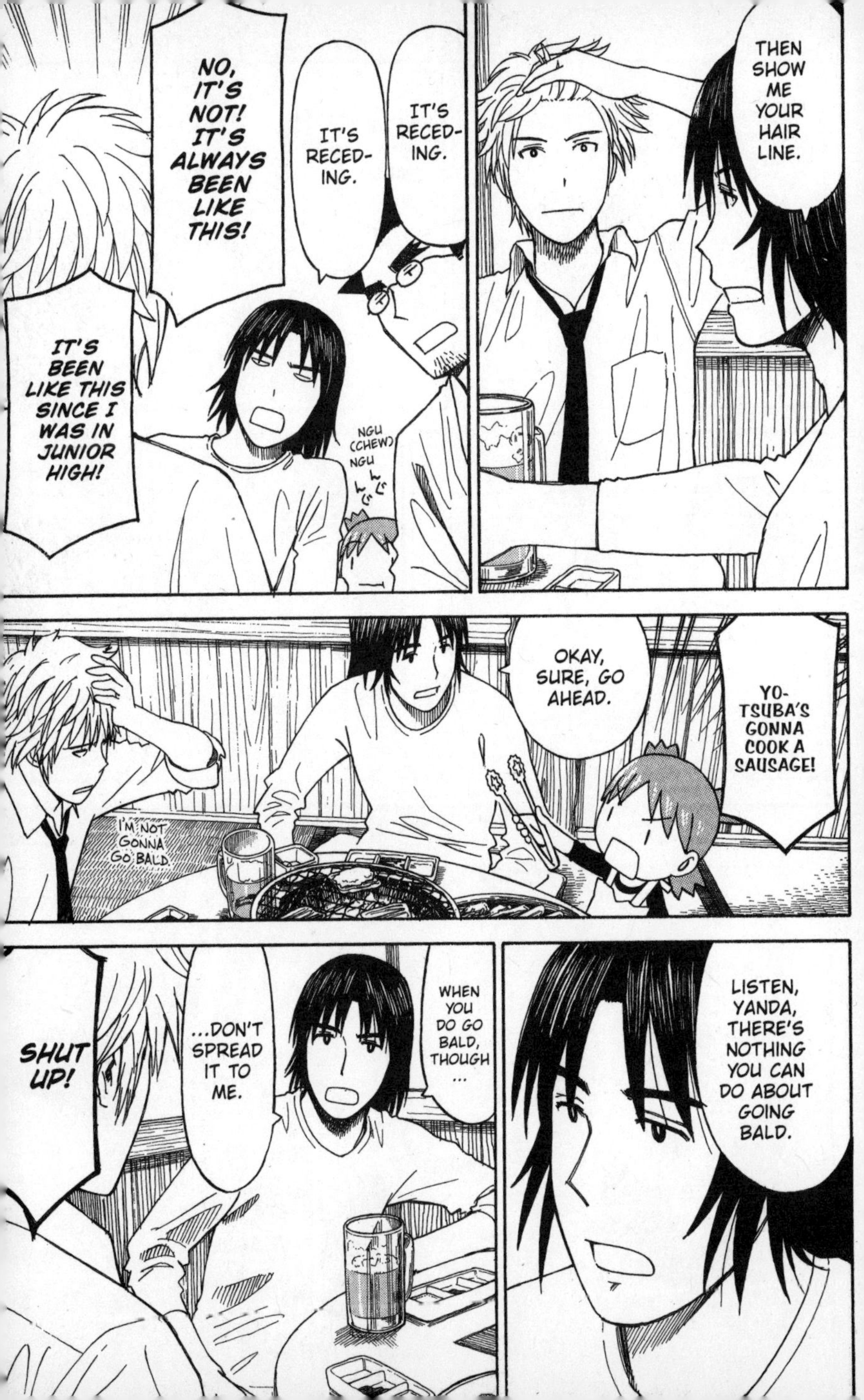
THEN SHOW ME YOUR HAIR LINE.
IT'S RECED-ING.
IT'S RECED-ING.
NO, IT'S NOT! IT'S ALWAYS BEEN LIKE THIS!
NGU (CHEW) NGU
IT'S BEEN LIKE THIS SINCE I WAS IN JUNIOR HIGH!
YO-TSUBA'S GONNA COOK A SAUSAGE!
OKAY, SURE, GO AHEAD.
I'M NOT GONNA GO BALD.
LISTEN, YANDA, THERE'S NOTHING YOU CAN DO ABOUT GOING BALD.
WHEN YOU DO GO BALD, THOUGH ...
...DON'T SPREAD IT TO ME.
SHUT UP!

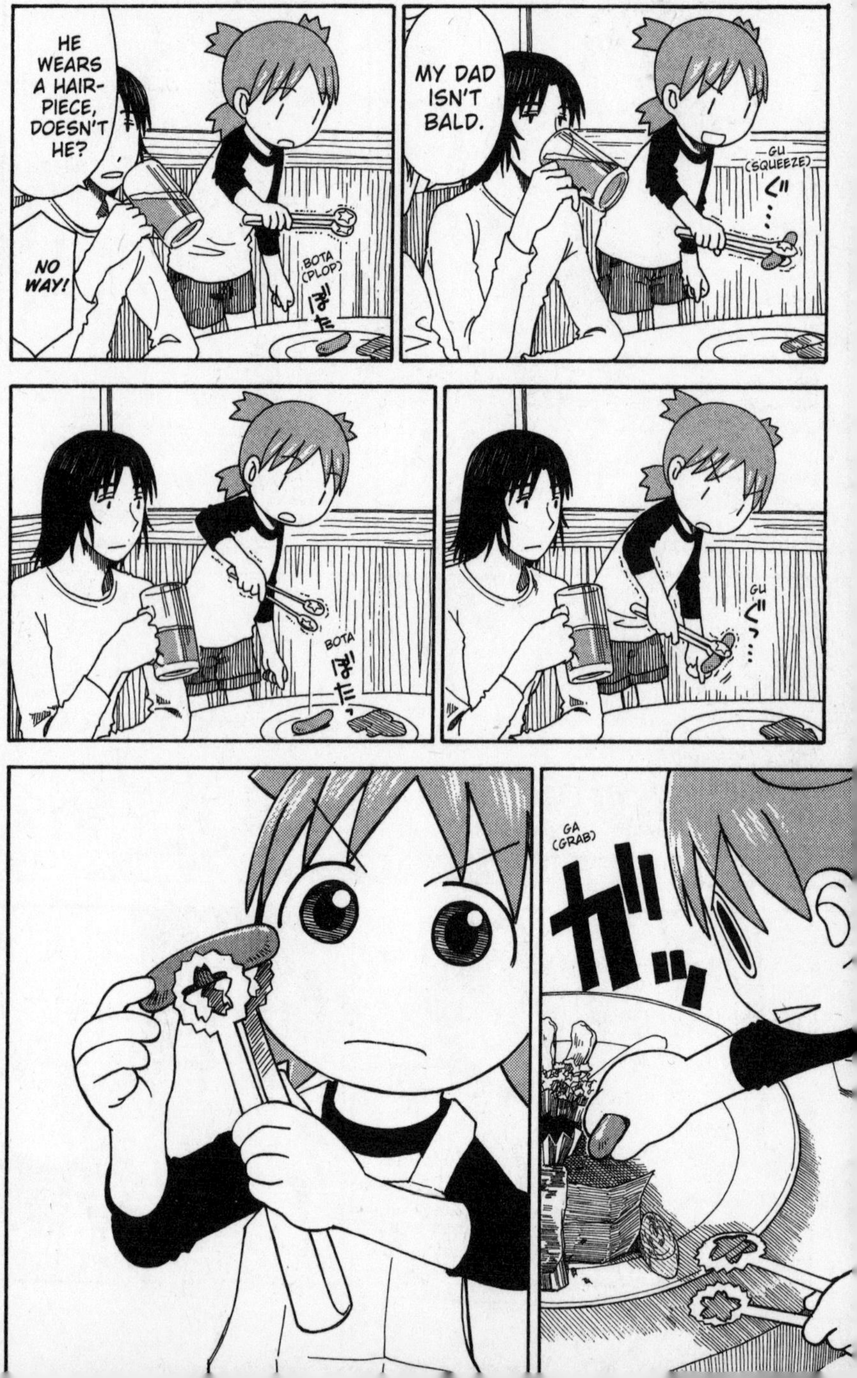
MY DAD ISN'T BALD.
GU (SQUEEZE)
ぐ…
HE WEARS A HAIR-PIECE, DOESN'T HE?
NO WAY!
BOTA (PLOP)
ぼた
GU
ぐっ…
BOTA
ぼた
GA (GRAB)
ガッ

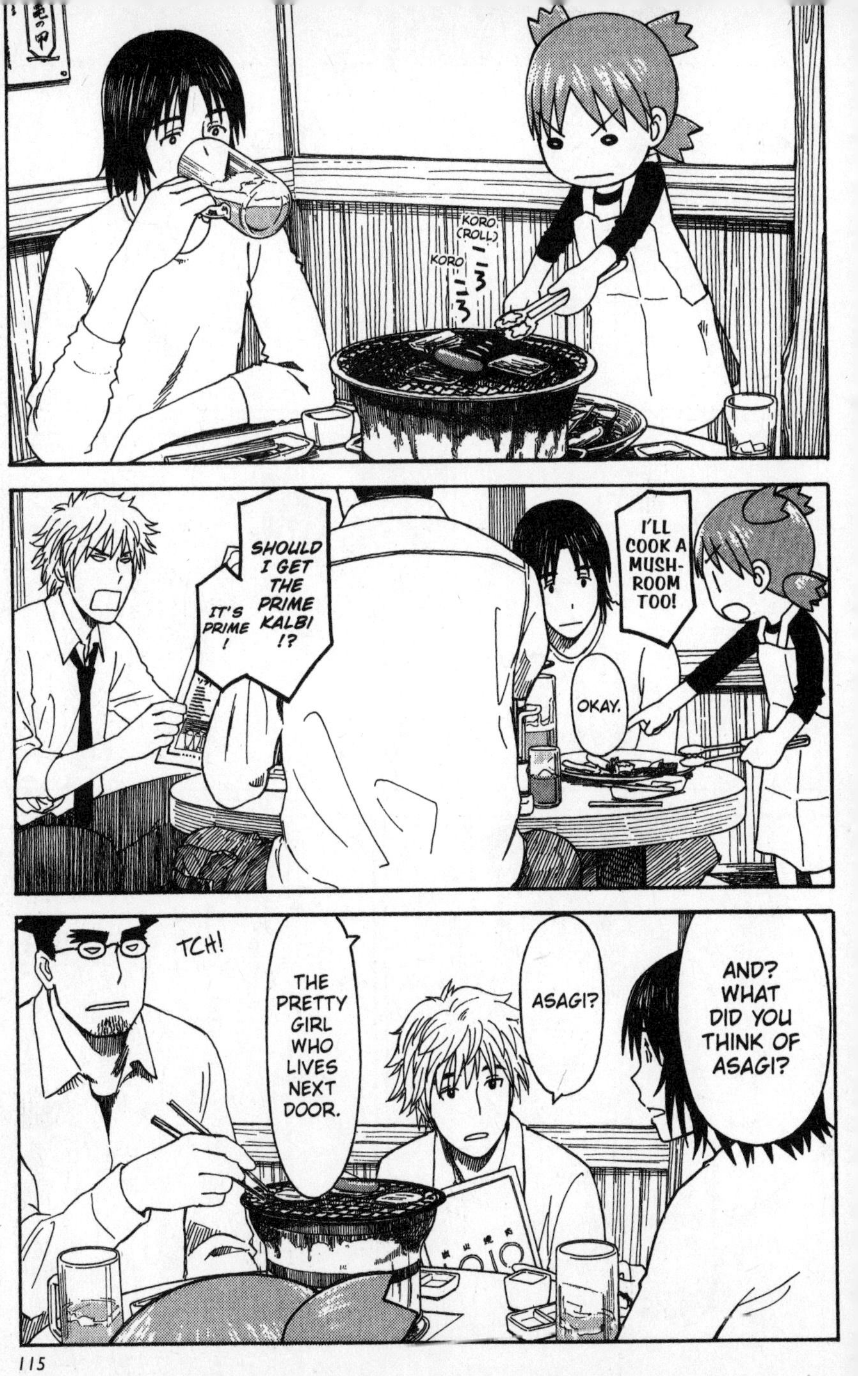
KORO (ROLL)
KORO
I'LL COOK A MUSHROOM TOO!
OKAY.
SHOULD I GET THE PRIME KALBI!?
IT'S PRIME!
AND? WHAT DID YOU THINK OF ASAGI?
ASAGI?
THE PRETTY GIRL WHO LIVES NEXT DOOR.
TCH!

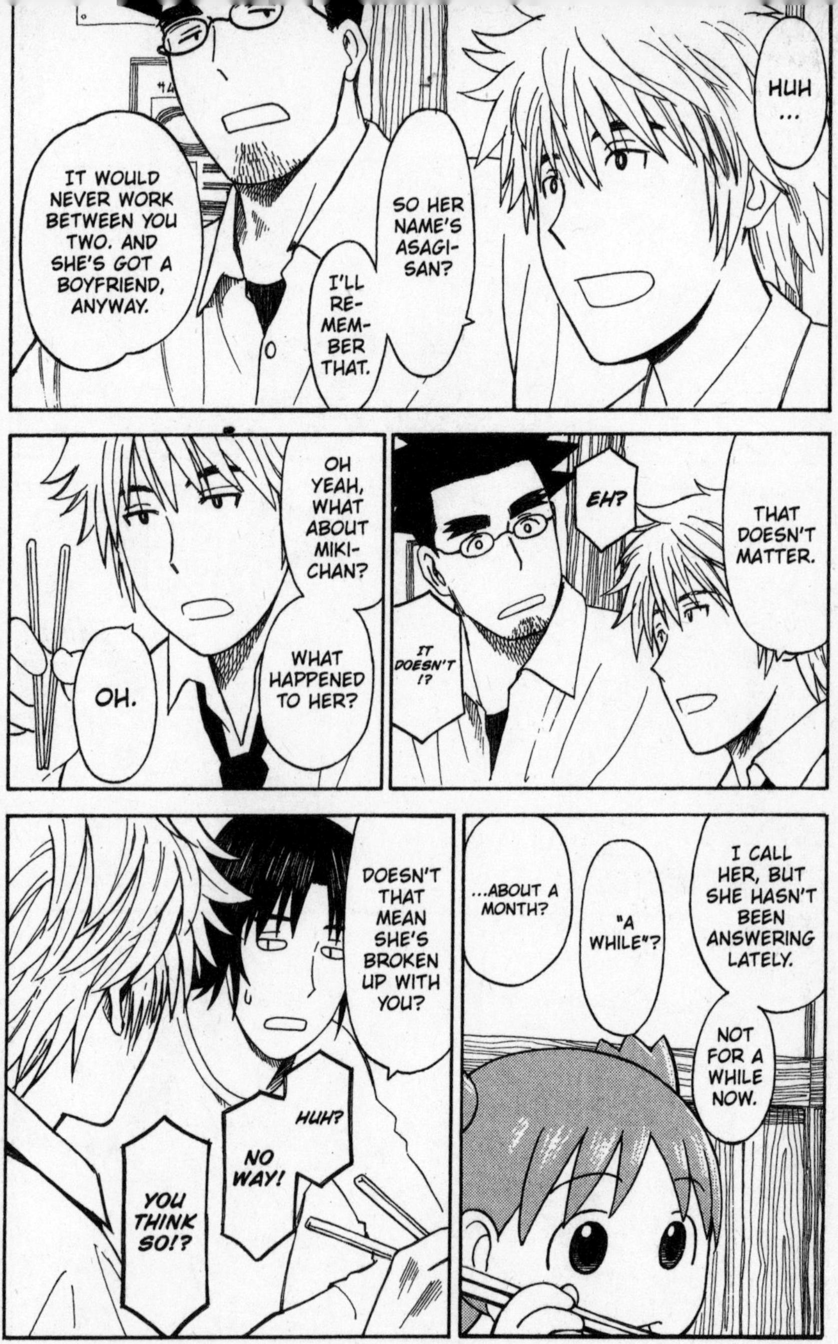
HUH ...
SO HER NAME'S ASAGI-SAN?
I'LL RE-MEMBER THAT.
IT WOULD NEVER WORK BETWEEN YOU TWO. AND SHE'S GOT A BOYFRIEND, ANYWAY.
THAT DOESN'T MATTER.
EH?
IT DOESN'T !?
OH YEAH, WHAT ABOUT MIKI-CHAN?
WHAT HAPPENED TO HER?
OH.
I CALL HER, BUT SHE HASN'T BEEN ANSWERING LATELY.
NOT FOR A WHILE NOW.
"A WHILE"?
...ABOUT A MONTH?
DOESN'T THAT MEAN SHE'S BROKEN UP WITH YOU?
HUH? NO WAY!
YOU THINK SO!?

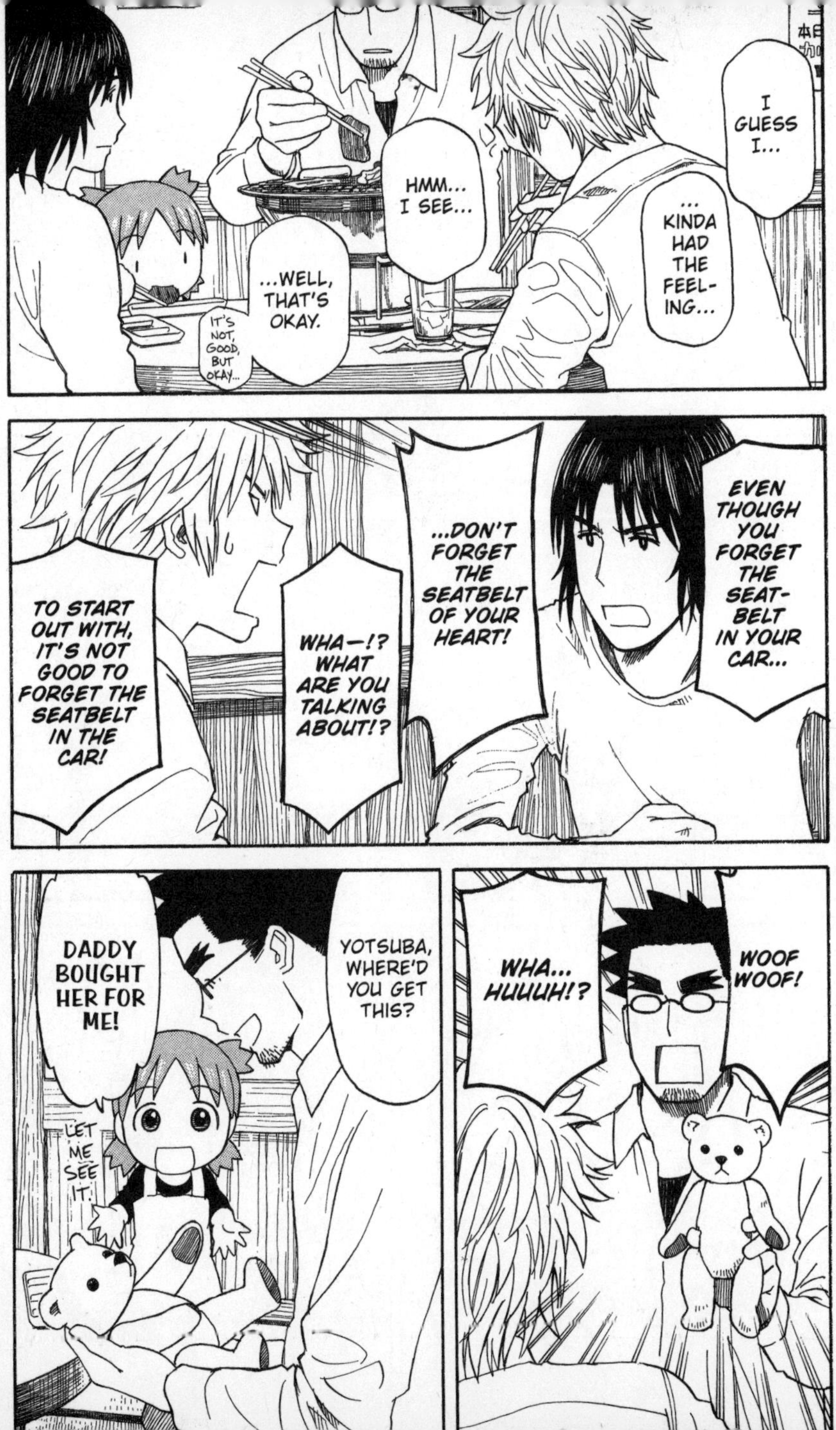
I GUESS I...
...KINDA HAD THE FEELING...
HMM... I SEE...
...WELL, THAT'S OKAY.
IT'S NOT GOOD, BUT OKAY...
EVEN THOUGH YOU FORGET THE SEATBELT IN YOUR CAR...
...DON'T FORGET THE SEATBELT OF YOUR HEART!
WHA—!? WHAT ARE YOU TALKING ABOUT!?
TO START OUT WITH, IT'S NOT GOOD TO FORGET THE SEATBELT IN THE CAR!
WOOF WOOF!
WHA... HUUUH!?
YOTSUBA, WHERE'D YOU GET THIS?
DADDY BOUGHT HER FOR ME!
LET ME SEE IT.

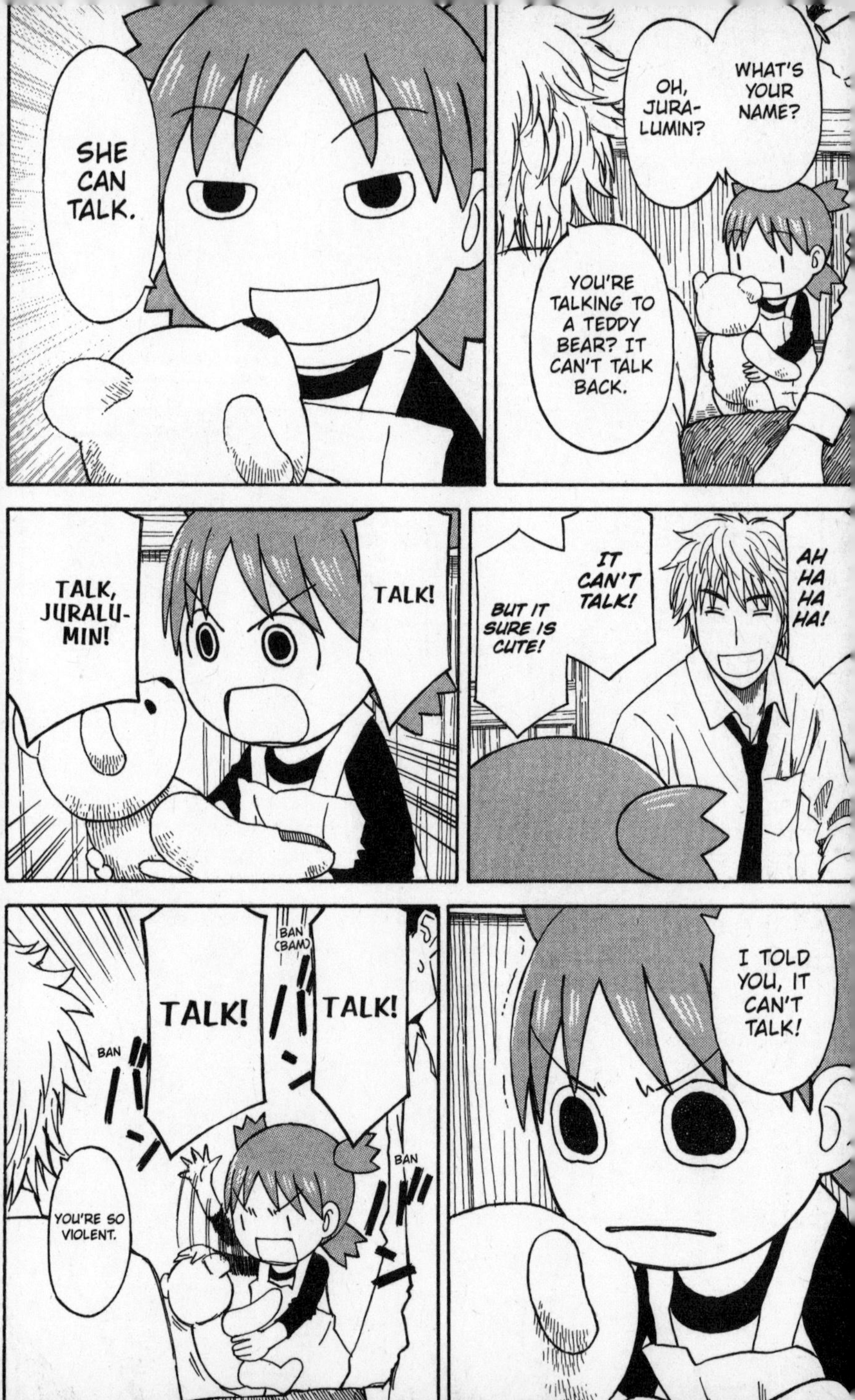
WHAT'S YOUR NAME?
OH, JURA-LUMIN?
YOU'RE TALKING TO A TEDDY BEAR? IT CAN'T TALK BACK.
SHE CAN TALK.
AH HA HA HA!
IT CAN'T TALK!
BUT IT SURE IS CUTE!
TALK!
TALK, JURALU-MIN!
I TOLD YOU, IT CAN'T TALK!
BAN (BAM)
TALK!
TALK!
BAN
BAN
YOU'RE SO VIOLENT.

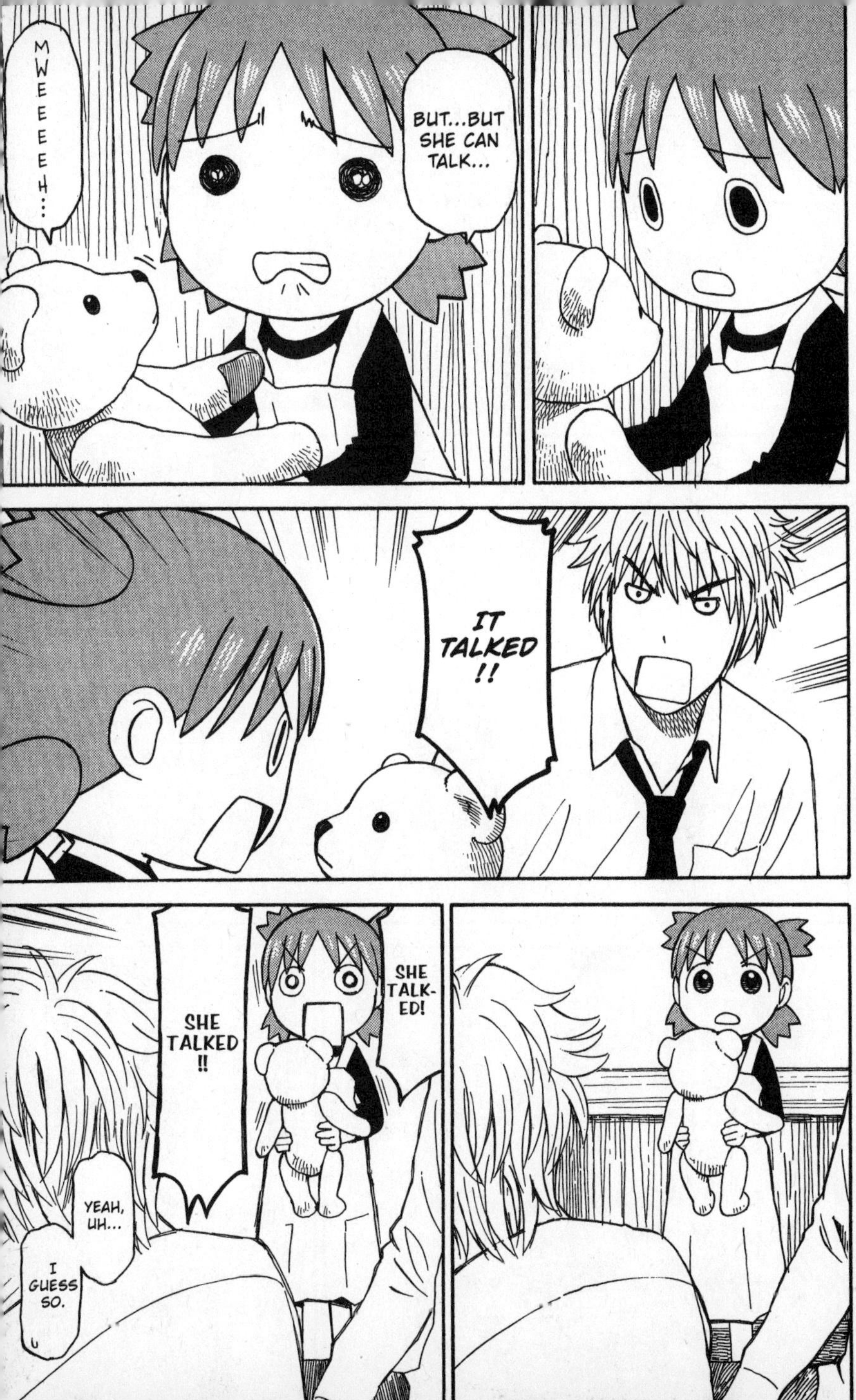
BUT...BUT SHE CAN TALK...
MWEEEEEH...
IT TALKED !!
SHE TALK-ED!
SHE TALKED !!
YEAH, UH...
I GUESS SO.

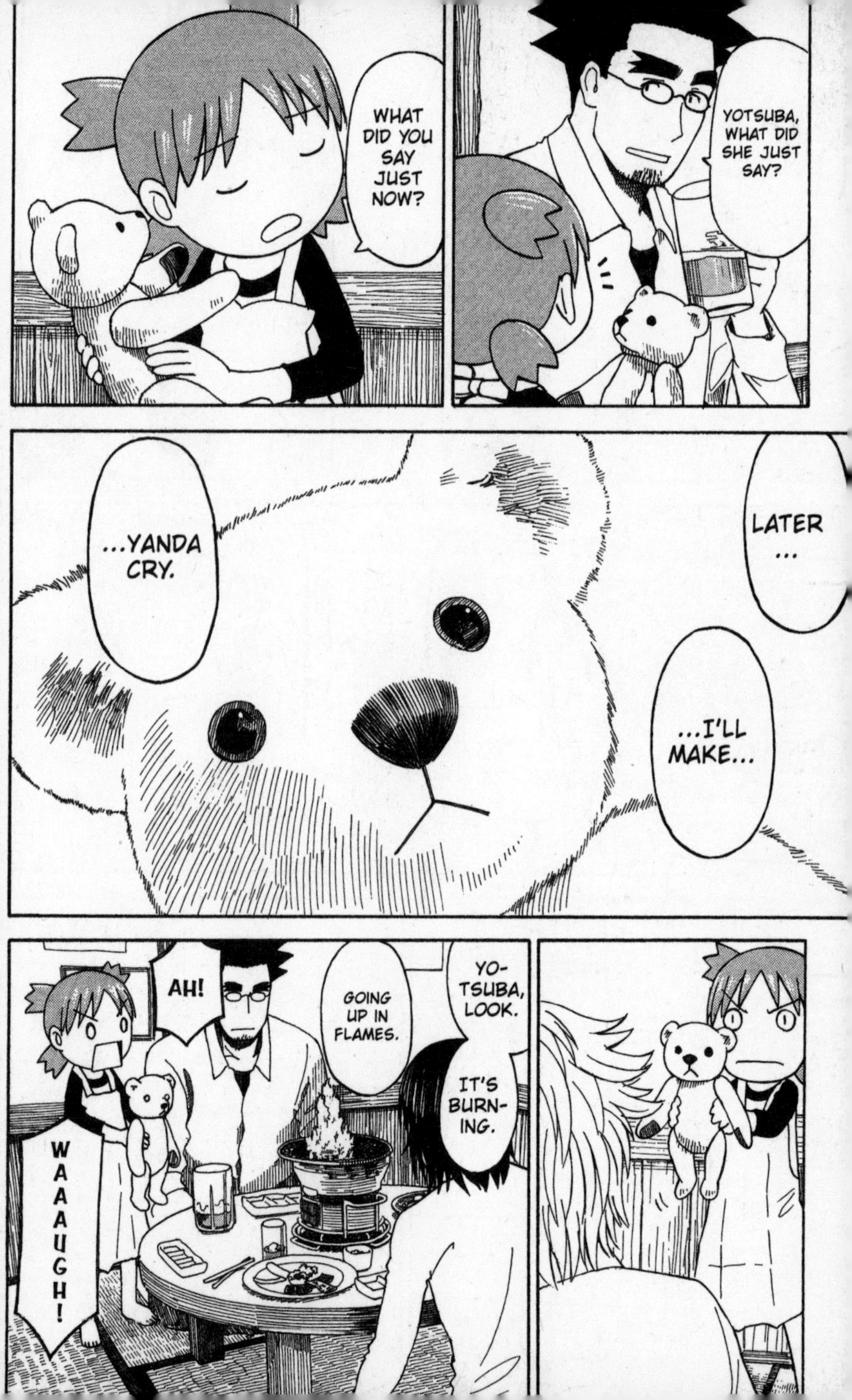
YOTSUBA, WHAT DID SHE JUST SAY?
WHAT DID YOU SAY JUST NOW?
LATER ...
...I'LL MAKE...
...YANDA CRY.
YO-TSUBA, LOOK.
IT'S BURN-ING.
GOING UP IN FLAMES.
AH!
WAAAAUGH!

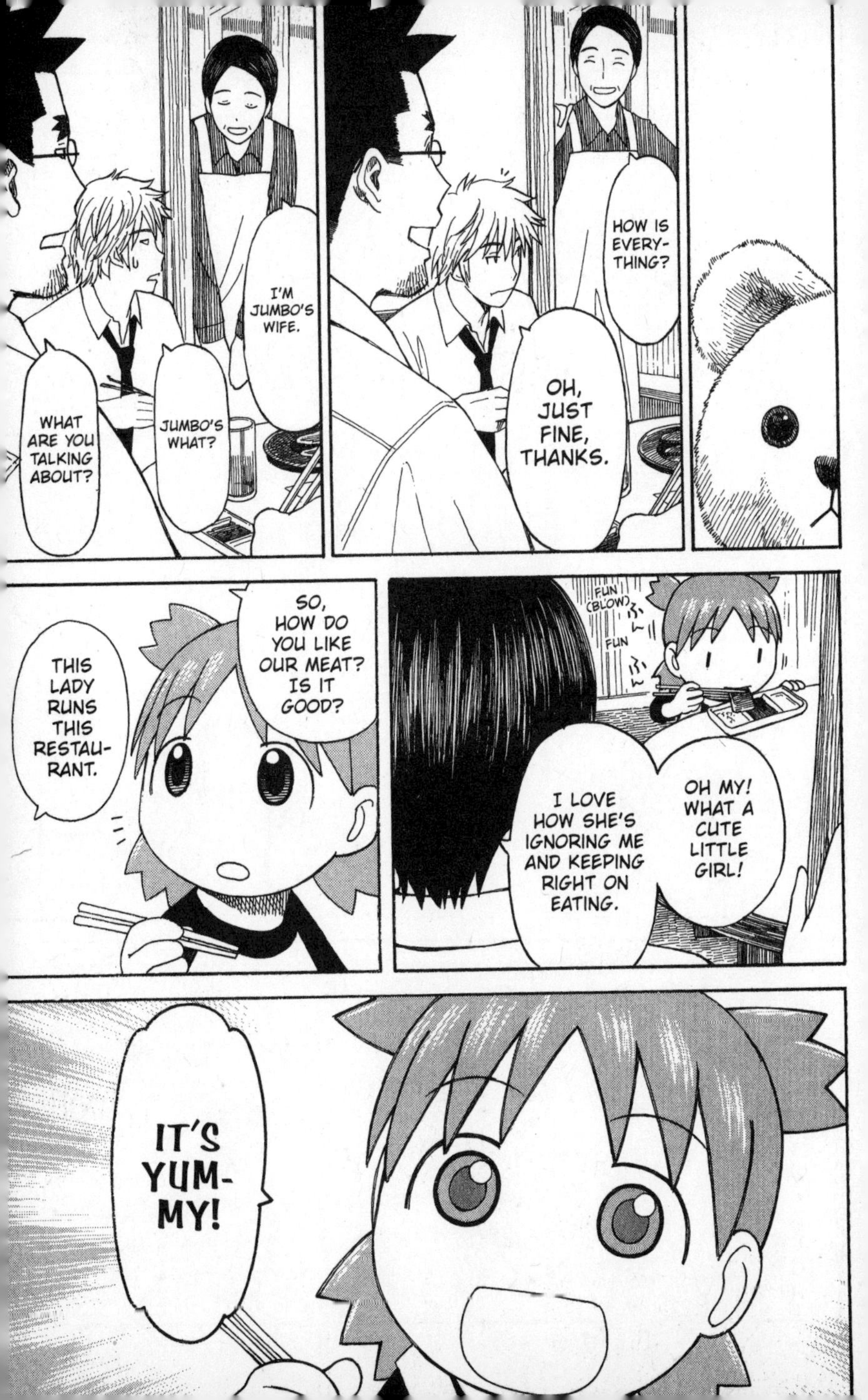
HOW IS EVERYTHING?
OH, JUST FINE, THANKS.
I'M JUMBO'S WIFE.
JUMBO'S WHAT?
WHAT ARE YOU TALKING ABOUT?
FUN (BLOW) FUN
OH MY! WHAT A CUTE LITTLE GIRL!
I LOVE HOW SHE'S IGNORING ME AND KEEPING RIGHT ON EATING.
SO, HOW DO YOU LIKE OUR MEAT? IS IT GOOD?
THIS LADY RUNS THIS RESTAURANT.
IT'S YUMMY!

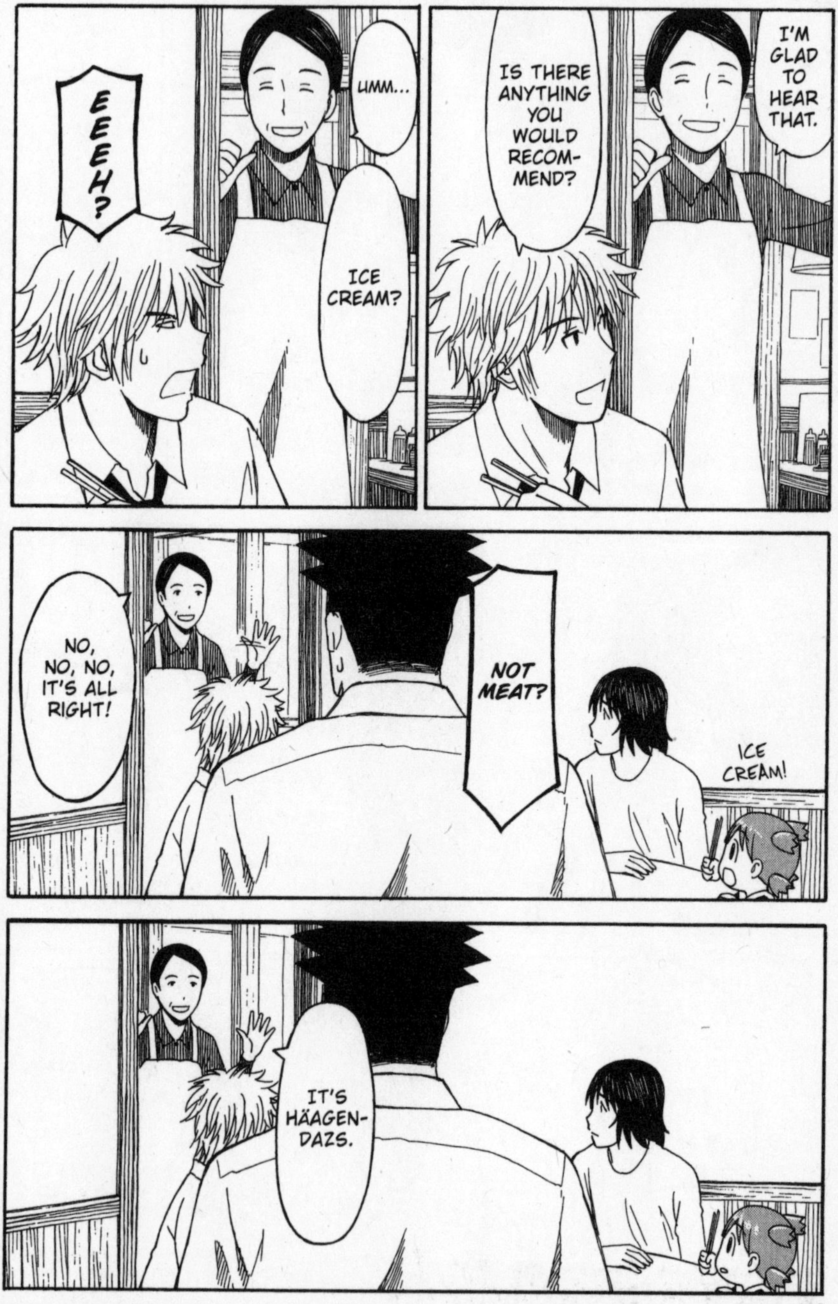
I'M GLAD TO HEAR THAT.
IS THERE ANYTHING YOU WOULD RECOMMEND?
UMM...
ICE CREAM?
EEEEH?
NOT MEAT?
ICE CREAM!
NO, NO, NO, IT'S ALL RIGHT!
IT'S HÄAGEN-DAZS.

YOTSUBA&!

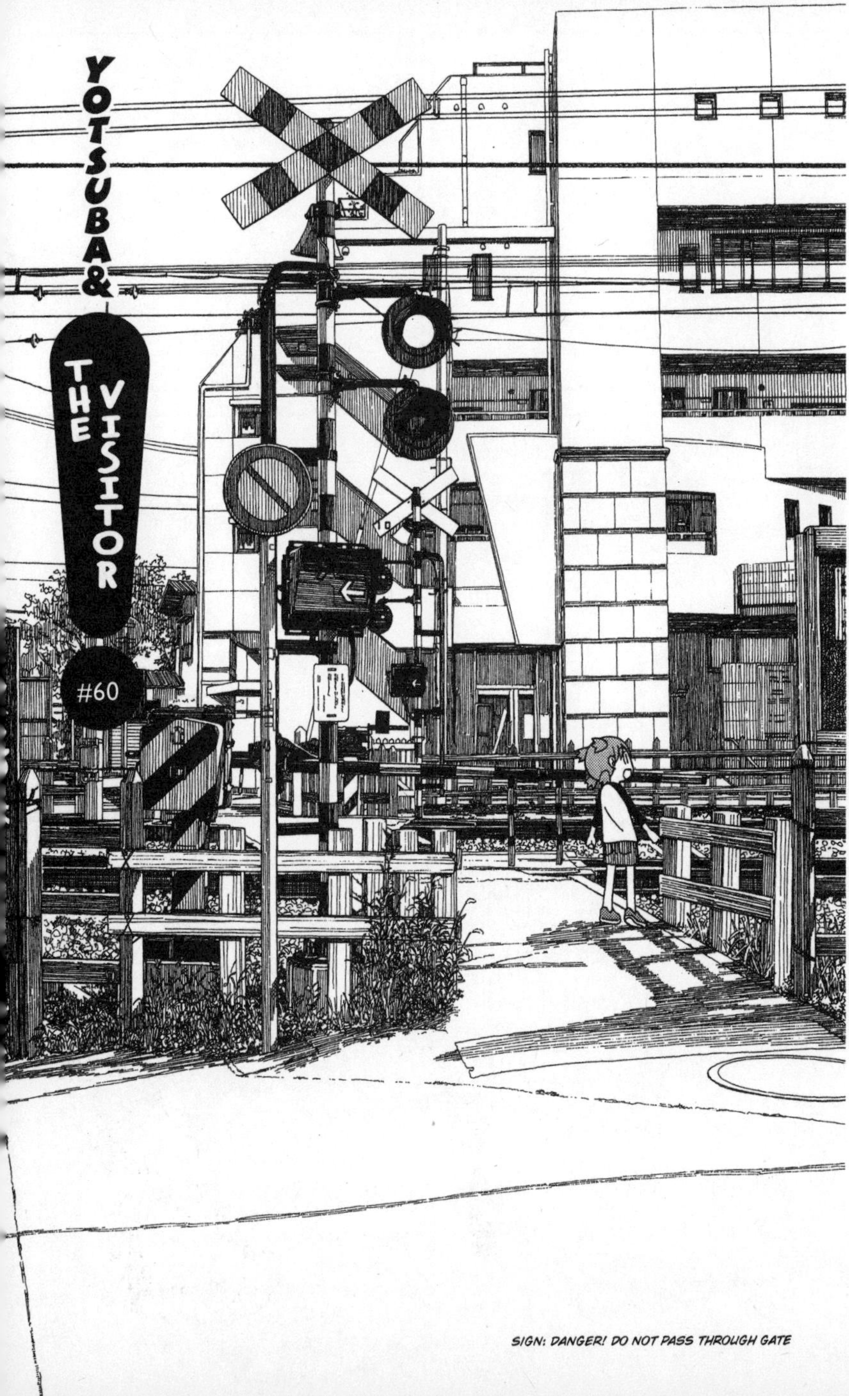
YOTSUBA&
THE VISITOR
#60

SIGN: DANGER! DO NOT PASS THROUGH GATE

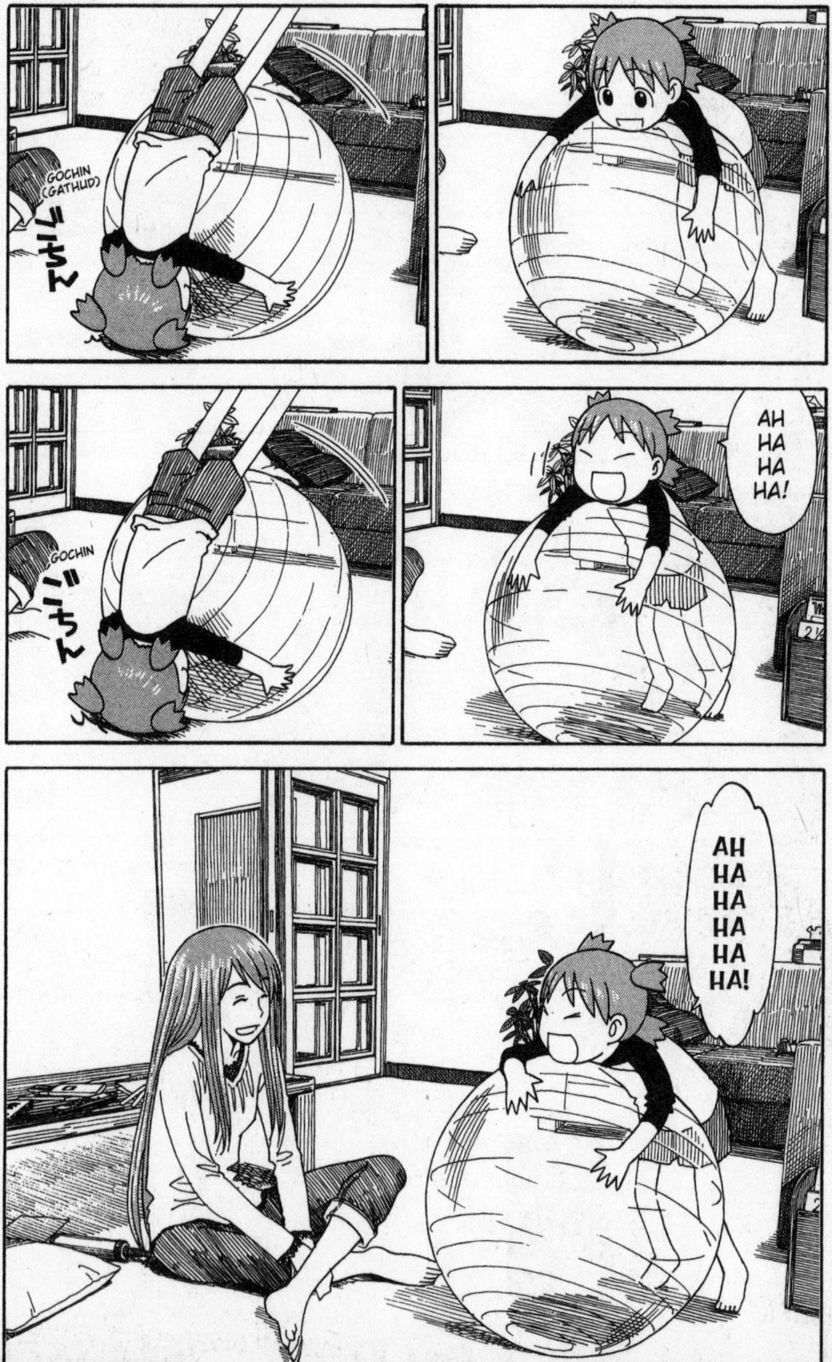
GOCHIN (GATHUD)
ごちん
AH HA HA HA!
GOCHIN
ごちん
AH HA HA HA HA HA!

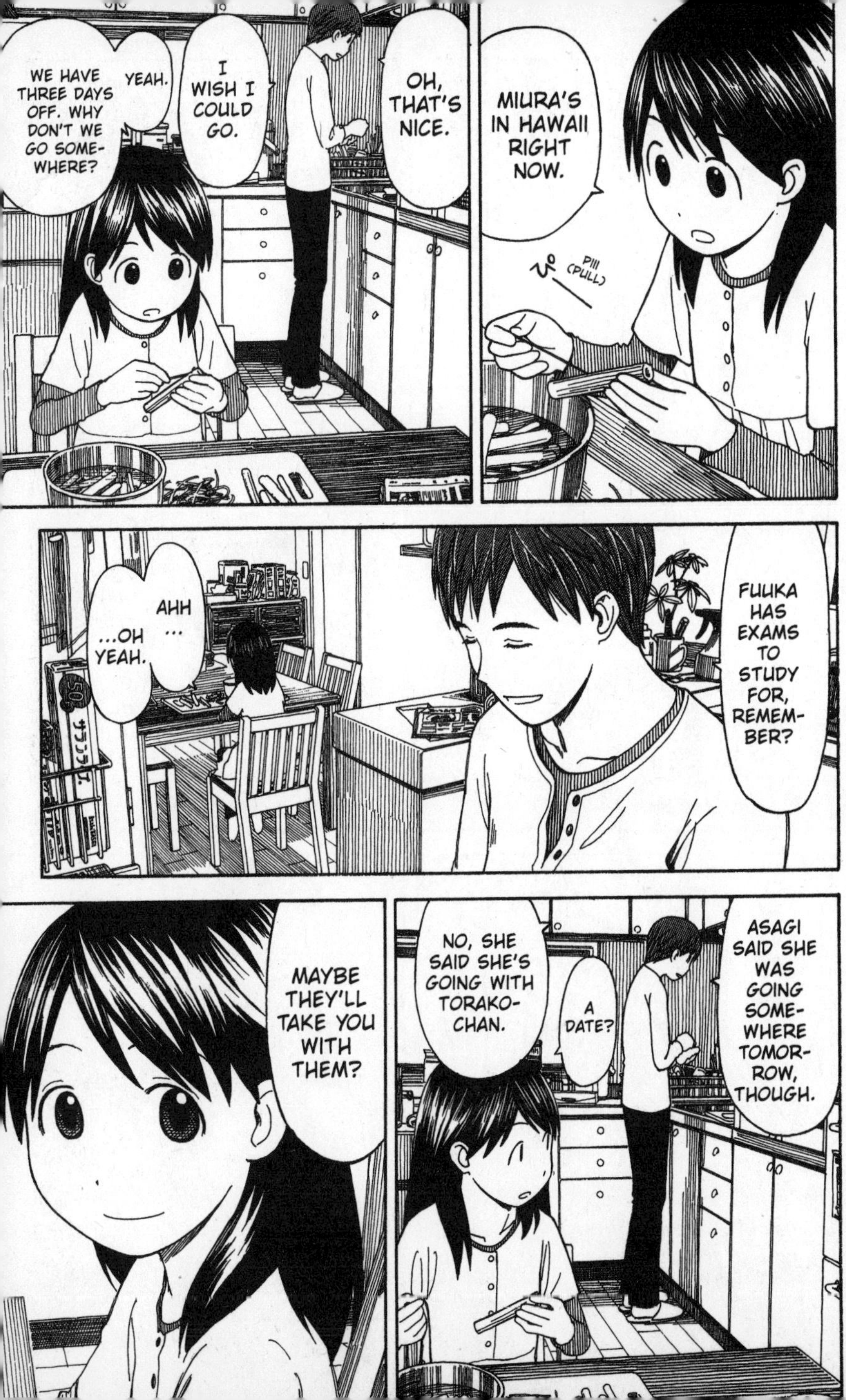
MIURA'S IN HAWAII RIGHT NOW.
PIII (PULL)
OH, THAT'S NICE.
I WISH I COULD GO.
YEAH.
WE HAVE THREE DAYS OFF. WHY DON'T WE GO SOME-WHERE?
FUUKA HAS EXAMS TO STUDY FOR, REMEM-BER?
AHH ...
...OH YEAH.
ASAGI SAID SHE WAS GOING SOME-WHERE TOMOR-ROW, THOUGH.
A DATE?
NO, SHE SAID SHE'S GOING WITH TORAKO-CHAN.
MAYBE THEY'LL TAKE YOU WITH THEM?

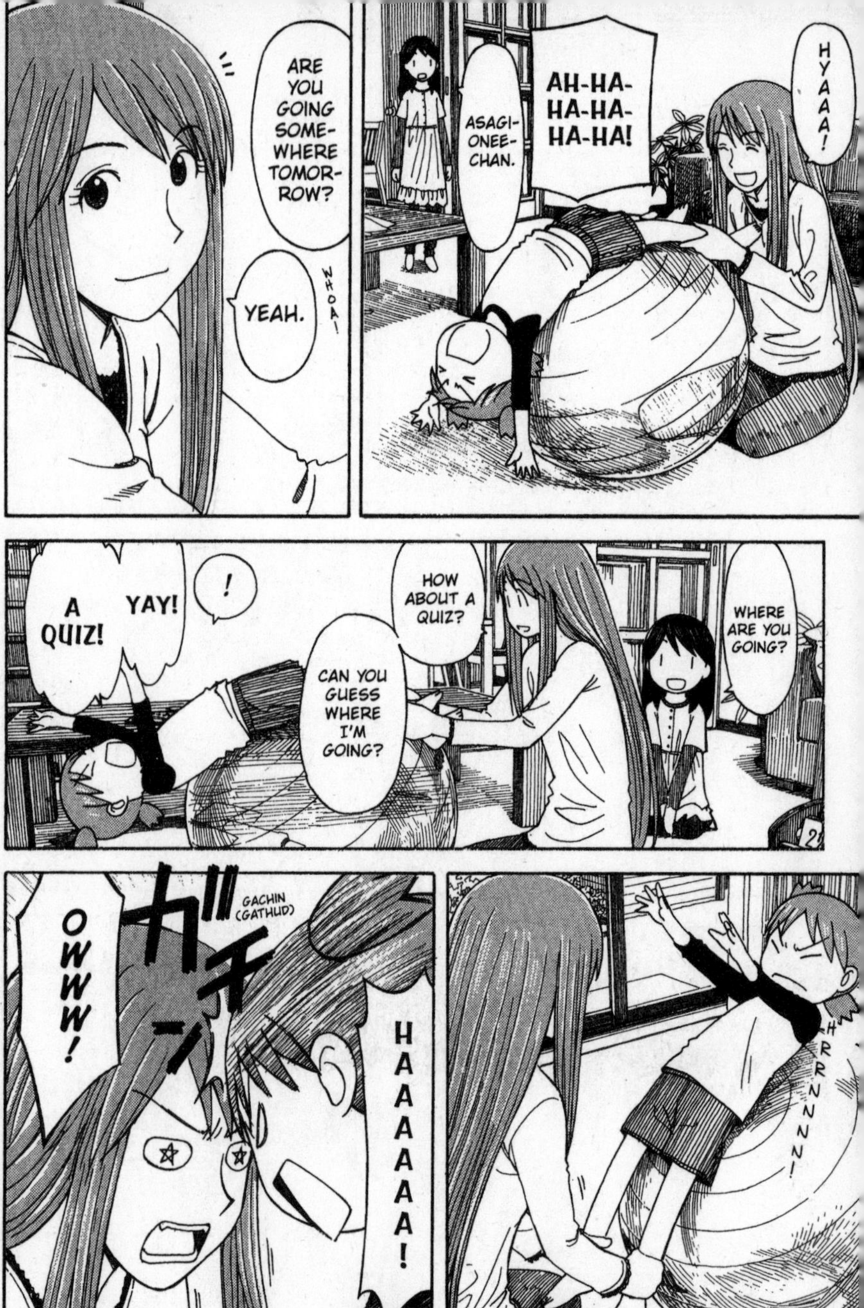
HYAAAA!
AH-HA-HA-HA-HA-HA!
ASAGI-ONEE-CHAN.
ARE YOU GOING SOMEWHERE TOMORROW?
WHOA!
YEAH.
WHERE ARE YOU GOING?
HOW ABOUT A QUIZ?
CAN YOU GUESS WHERE I'M GOING?
!
YAY! A QUIZ!
HRRNNNN!
GACHIN (GATHUD)
HAAAAAAAA!
OWWW!

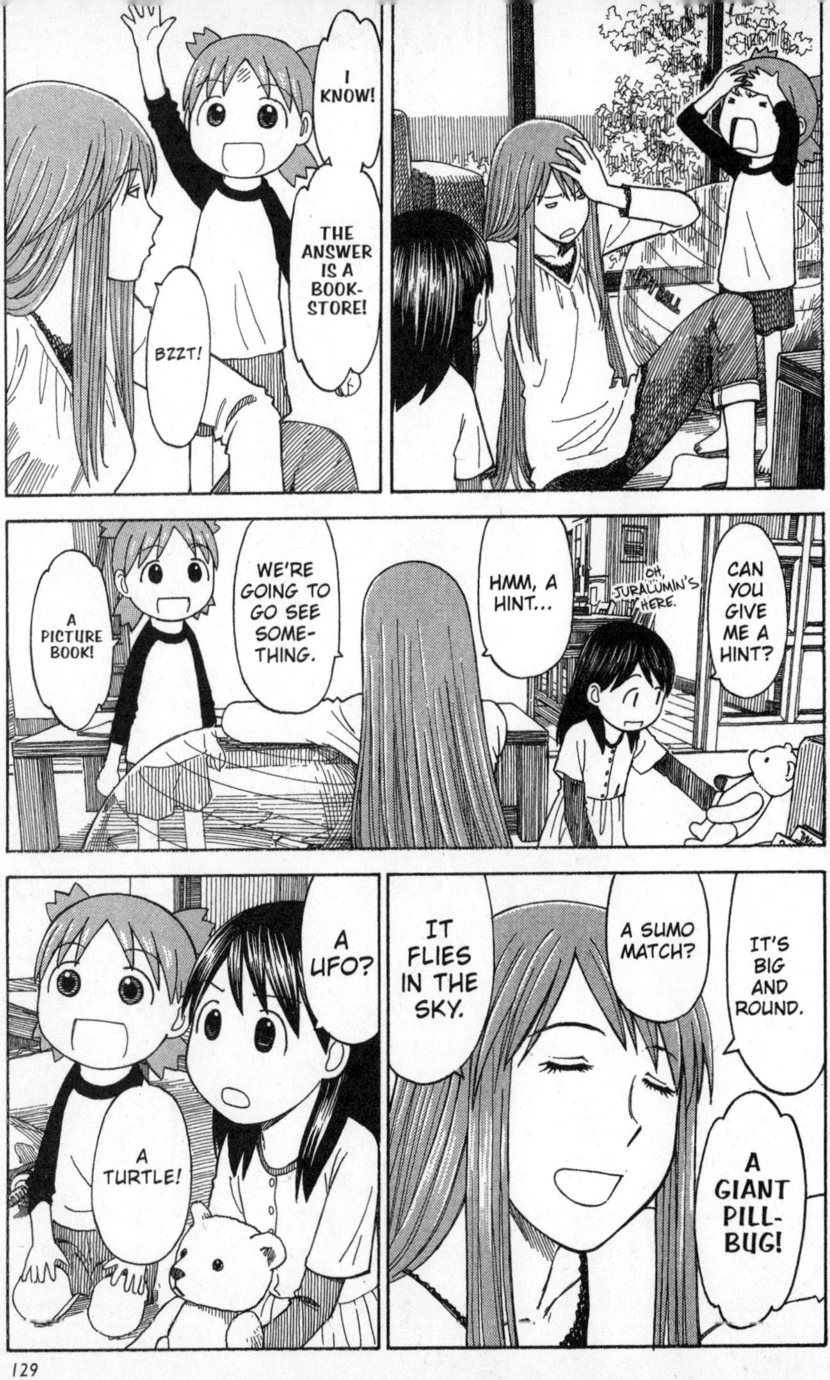
I KNOW!
THE ANSWER IS A BOOK-STORE!
BZZT!
CAN YOU GIVE ME A HINT?
OH, JURALUMIN'S HERE.
HMM, A HINT...
WE'RE GOING TO GO SEE SOME-THING.
A PICTURE BOOK!
IT'S BIG AND ROUND.
A SUMO MATCH?
IT FLIES IN THE SKY.
A GIANT PILL-BUG!
A UFO?
A TURTLE!

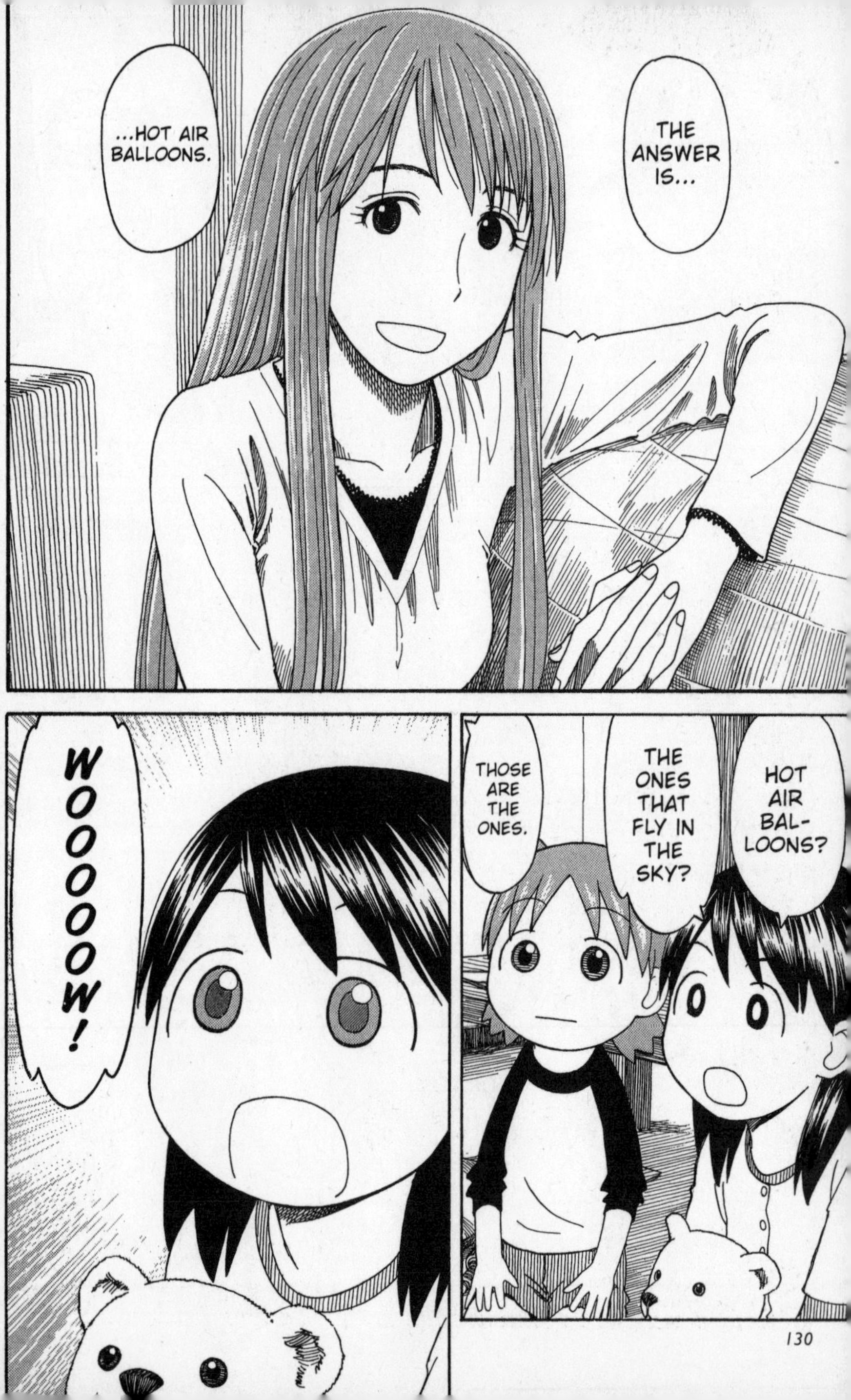
THE ANSWER IS...
...HOT AIR BALLOONS.
HOT AIR BAL-LOONS?
THE ONES THAT FLY IN THE SKY?
THOSE ARE THE ONES.
WOOOOOOOW!

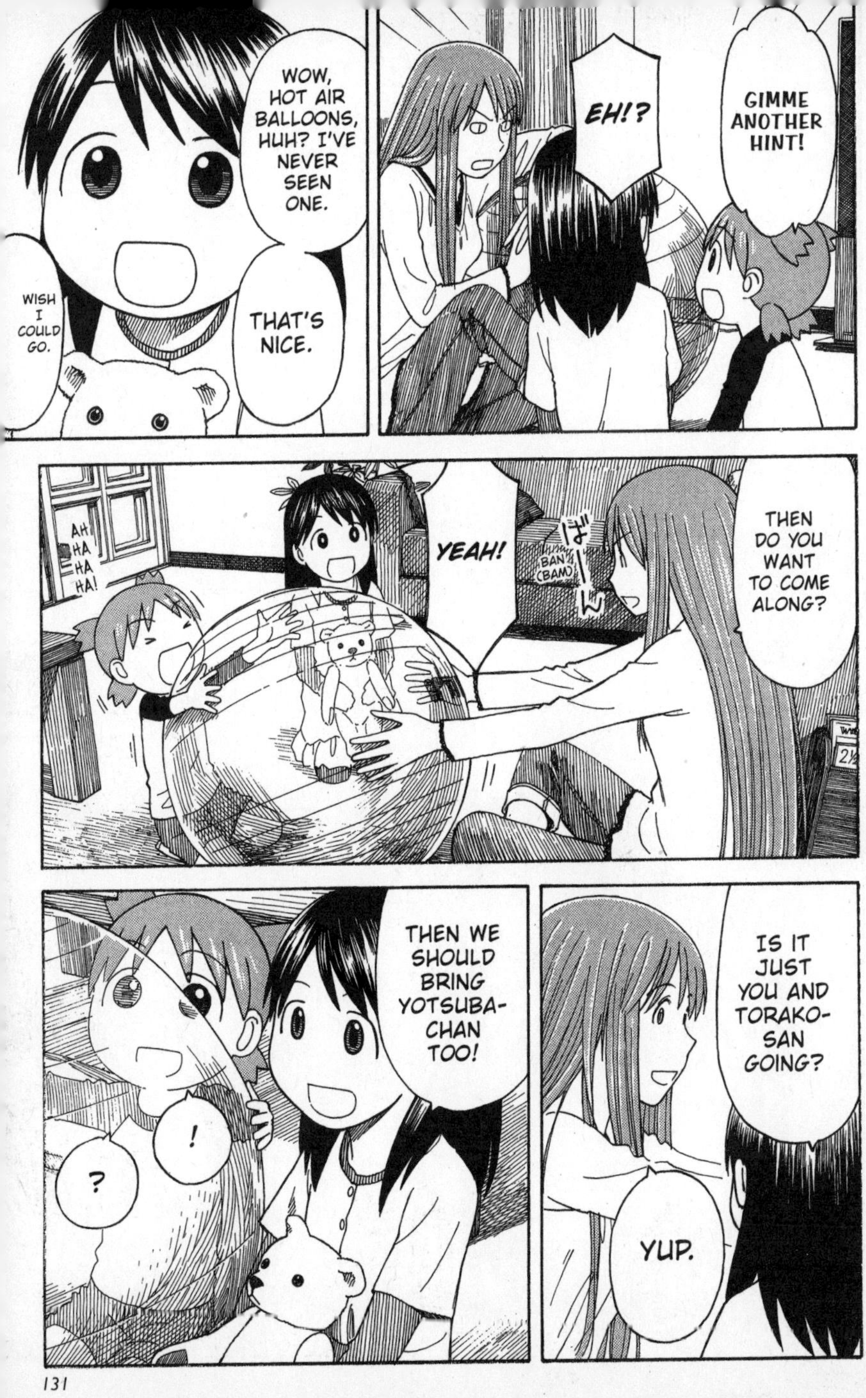
GIMME ANOTHER HINT!
EH!?
WOW, HOT AIR BALLOONS, HUH? I'VE NEVER SEEN ONE.
THAT'S NICE.
WISH I COULD GO.
THEN DO YOU WANT TO COME ALONG?
ばーん
BAN (BAM)
YEAH!
AH HA HA HA!
IS IT JUST YOU AND TORAKO-SAN GOING?
YUP.
THEN WE SHOULD BRING YOTSUBA-CHAN TOO!
!
?

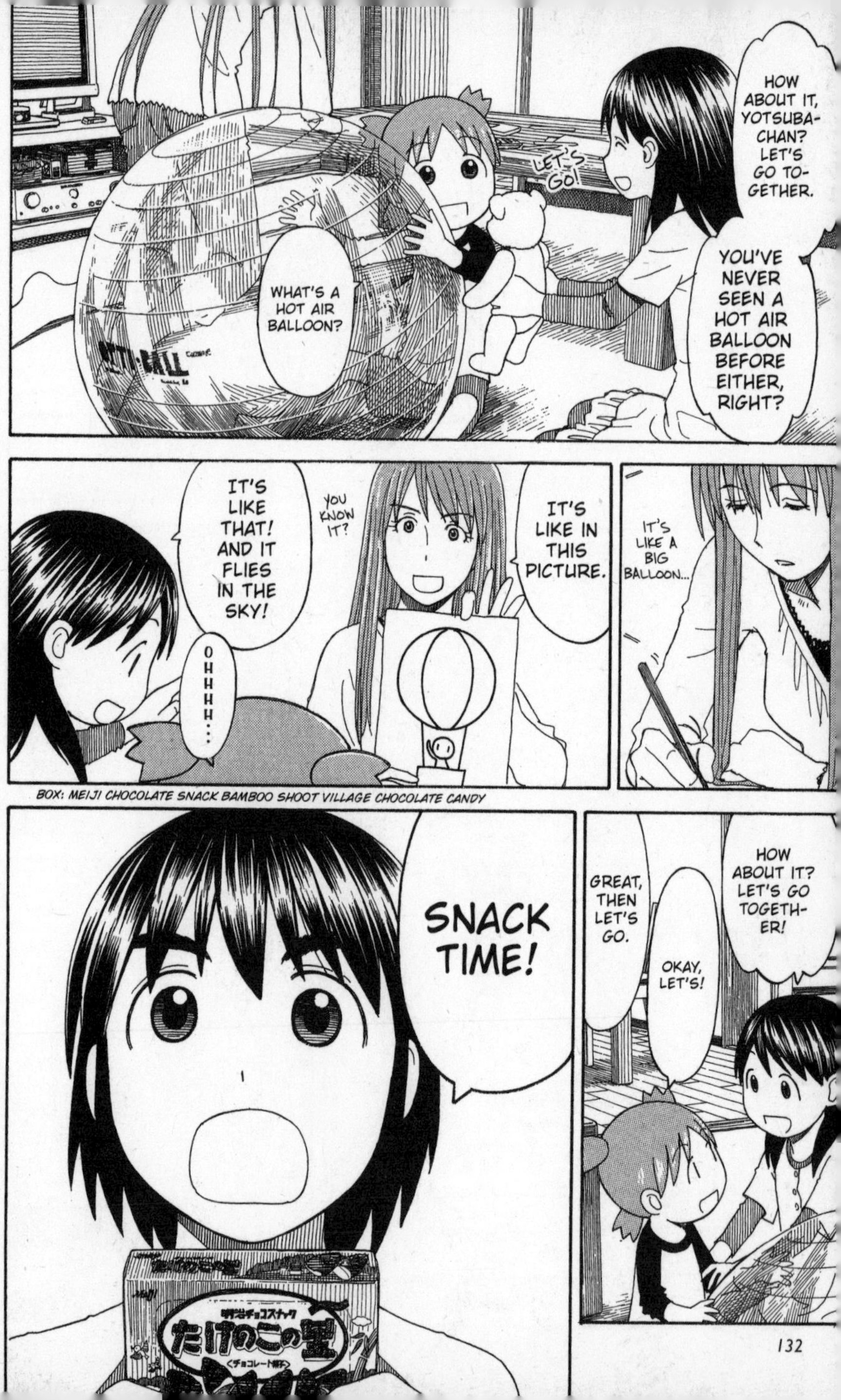
HOW ABOUT IT, YOTSUBA-CHAN? LET'S GO TOGETHER.
YOU'VE NEVER SEEN A HOT AIR BALLOON BEFORE EITHER, RIGHT?
LET'S GO!
WHAT'S A HOT AIR BALLOON?
IT'S LIKE A BIG BALLOON...
IT'S LIKE IN THIS PICTURE.
YOU KNOW IT?
IT'S LIKE THAT! AND IT FLIES IN THE SKY!
OHHHH...
BOX: MEIJI CHOCOLATE SNACK BAMBOO SHOOT VILLAGE CHOCOLATE CANDY
HOW ABOUT IT? LET'S GO TOGETHER!
GREAT, THEN LET'S GO.
OKAY, LET'S!
SNACK TIME!
明治チョコスナック
たけのこの里
<チョコレート菓子>

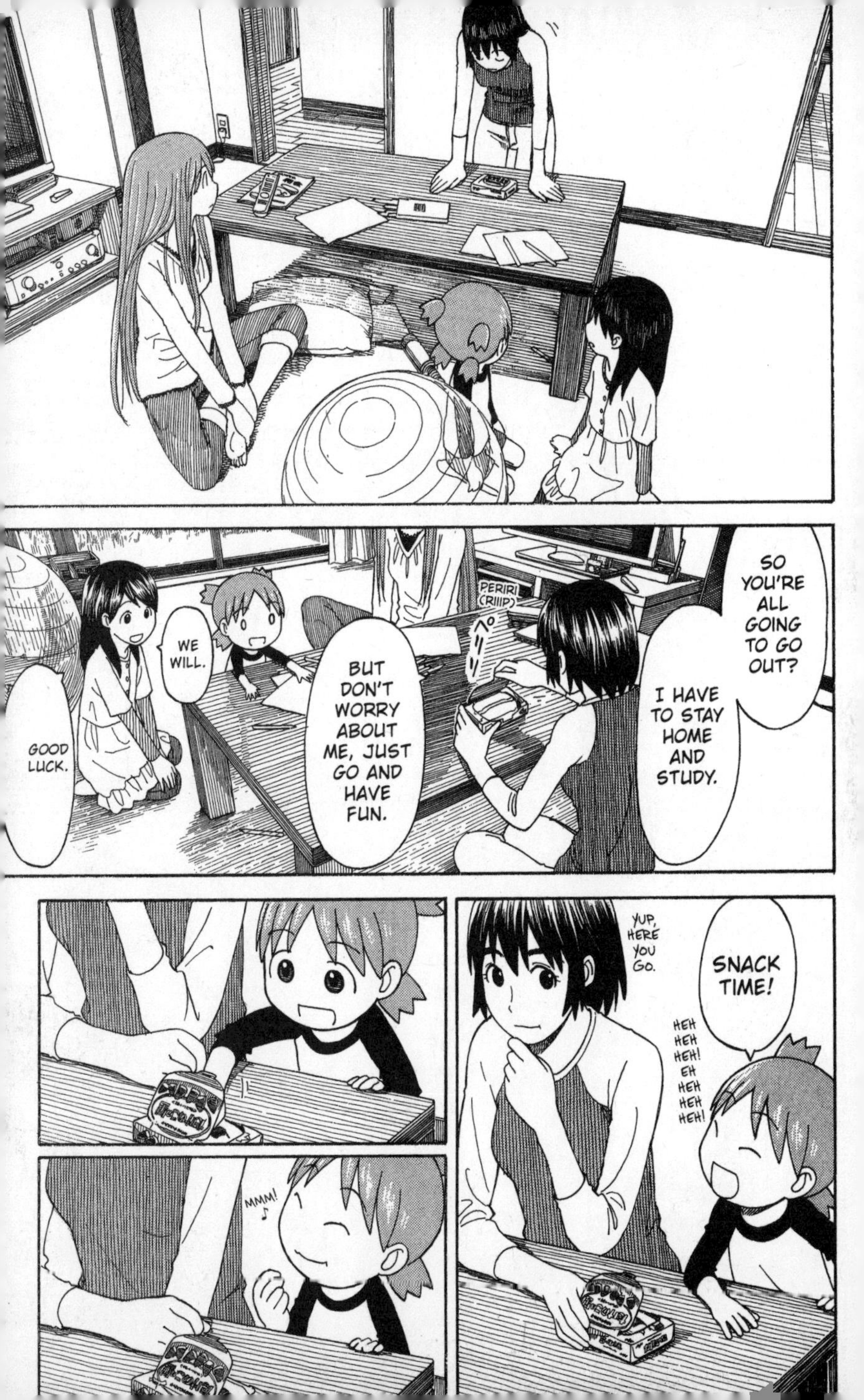
SO YOU'RE ALL GOING TO GO OUT?
I HAVE TO STAY HOME AND STUDY.
PERIRI (RIIIP)
BUT DON'T WORRY ABOUT ME, JUST GO AND HAVE FUN.
WE WILL.
GOOD LUCK.
SNACK TIME!
YUP, HERE YOU GO.
HEH HEH HEH! EH HEH HEH HEH!
MMM! ♪

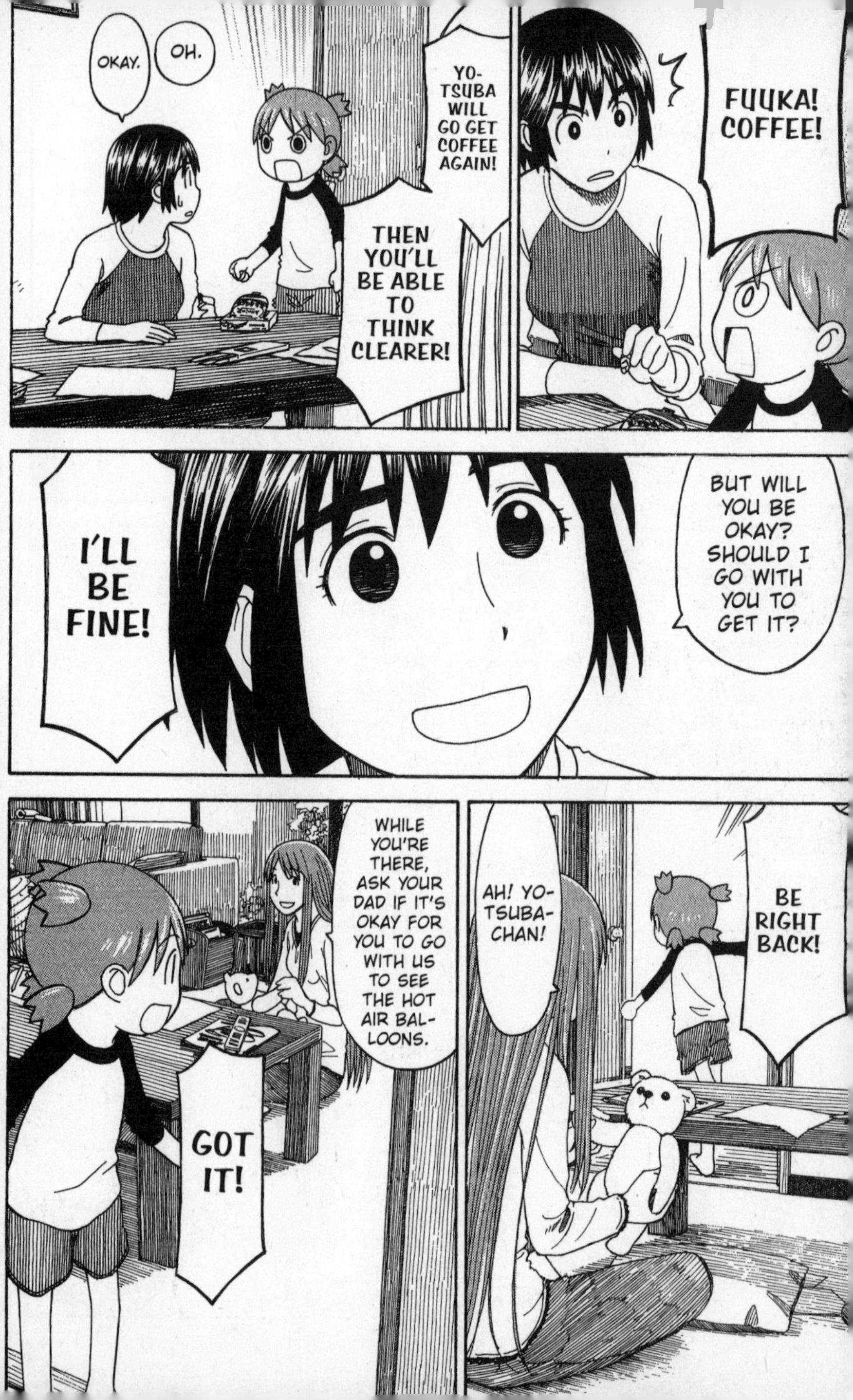
FUUKA! COFFEE!
YO-TSUBA WILL GO GET COFFEE AGAIN!
THEN YOU'LL BE ABLE TO THINK CLEARER!
OH.
OKAY.
BUT WILL YOU BE OKAY? SHOULD I GO WITH YOU TO GET IT?
I'LL BE FINE!
BE RIGHT BACK!
AH! YO-TSUBA-CHAN!
WHILE YOU'RE THERE, ASK YOUR DAD IF IT'S OKAY FOR YOU TO GO WITH US TO SEE THE HOT AIR BAL-LOONS.
GOT IT!

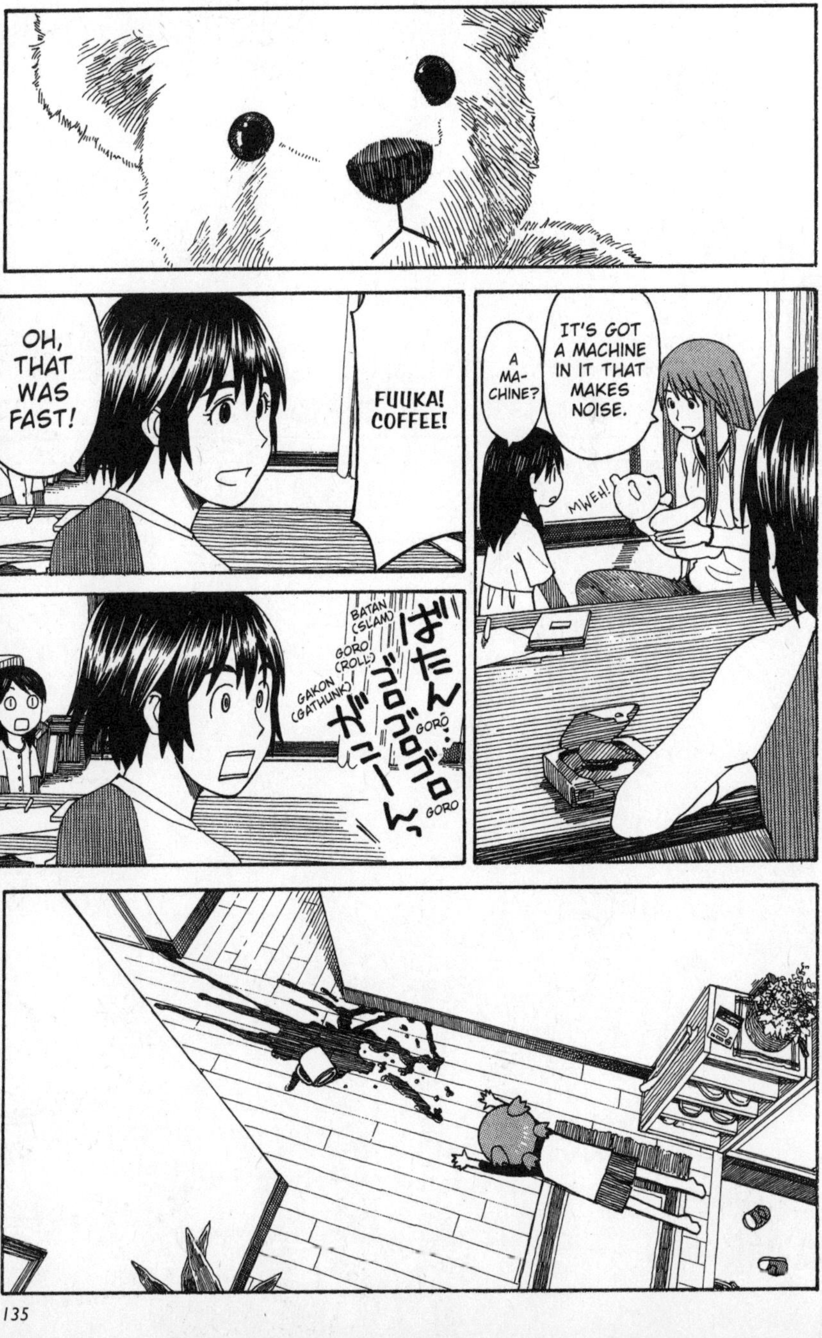
IT'S GOT A MACHINE IN IT THAT MAKES NOISE.
A MA-CHINE?
MWEH!
FUUKA! COFFEE!
OH, THAT WAS FAST!
ばたん BATAN (SLAM)
ゴロゴロゴロ GORO (ROLL) GORO GORO
がこーん GAKON (GATHUNK)

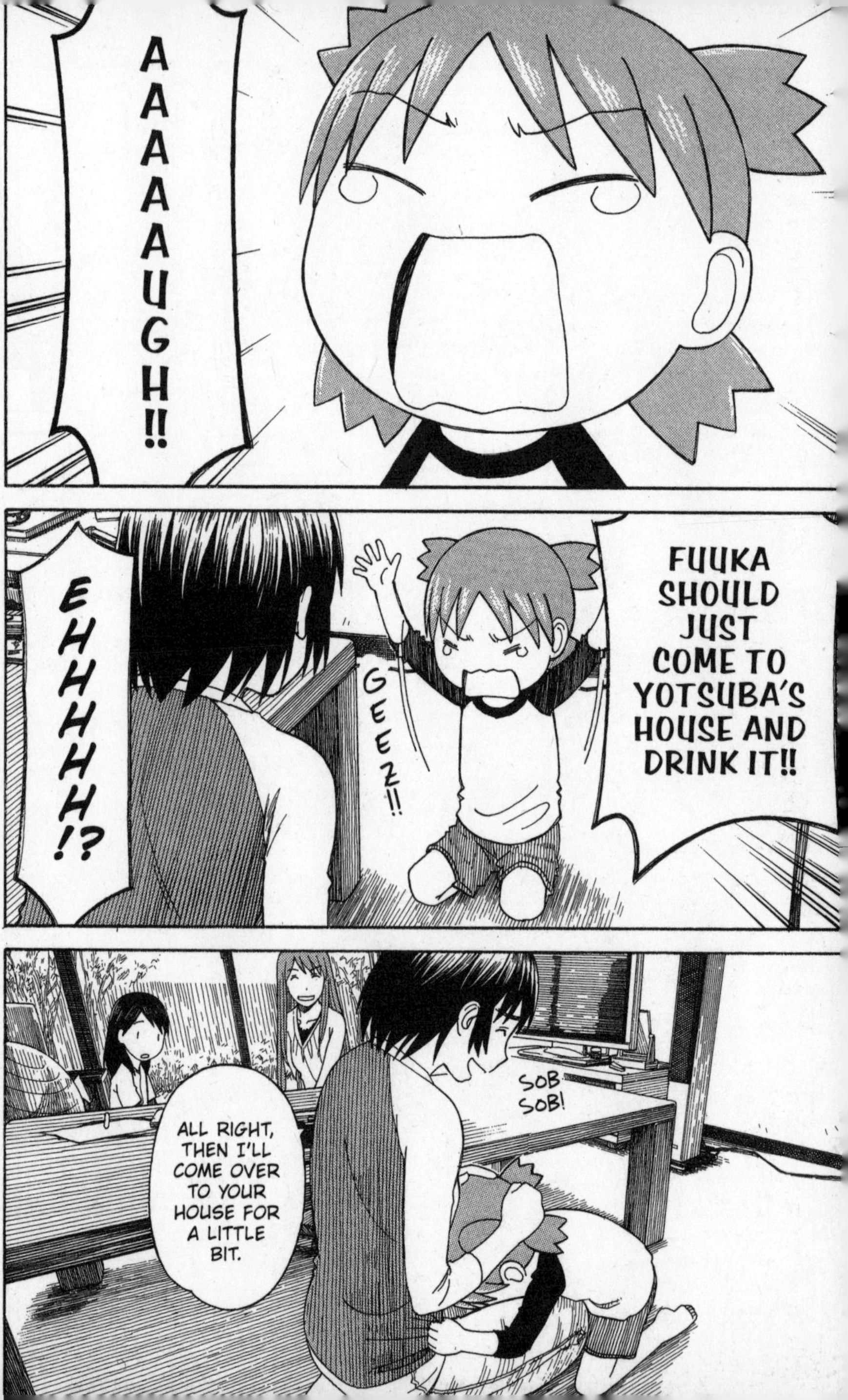
AAAAAAUGH!!
FUUKA SHOULD JUST COME TO YOTSUBA'S HOUSE AND DRINK IT!!
GEEZ!!
EHHHHHH!?
SOB SOB!
ALL RIGHT, THEN I'LL COME OVER TO YOUR HOUSE FOR A LITTLE BIT.

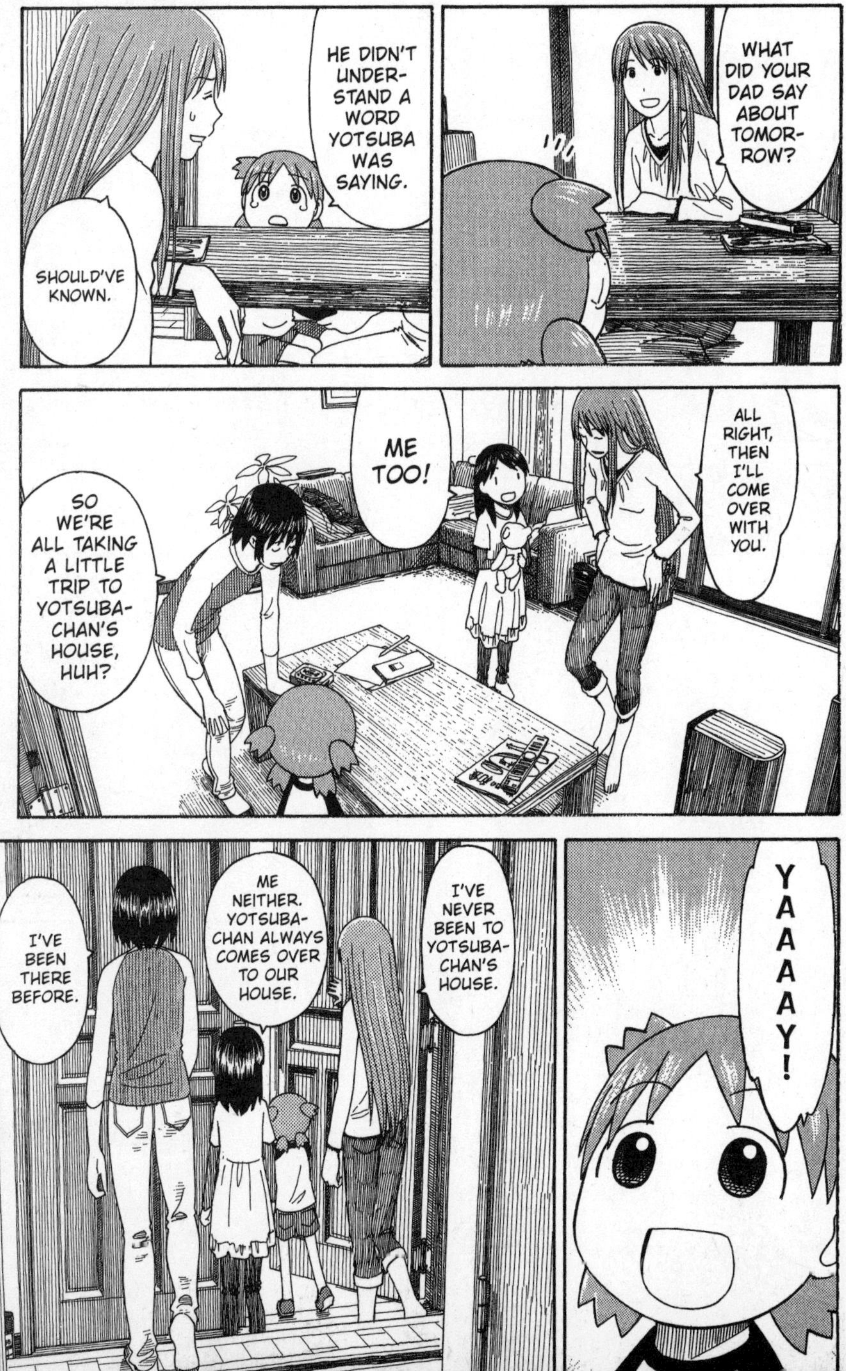
WHAT DID YOUR DAD SAY ABOUT TOMORROW?
HE DIDN'T UNDER-STAND A WORD YOTSUBA WAS SAYING.
SHOULD'VE KNOWN.
ALL RIGHT, THEN I'LL COME OVER WITH YOU.
ME TOO!
SO WE'RE ALL TAKING A LITTLE TRIP TO YOTSUBA-CHAN'S HOUSE, HUH?
YAAAAY!
I'VE NEVER BEEN TO YOTSUBA-CHAN'S HOUSE.
ME NEITHER. YOTSUBA-CHAN ALWAYS COMES OVER TO OUR HOUSE.
I'VE BEEN THERE BEFORE.

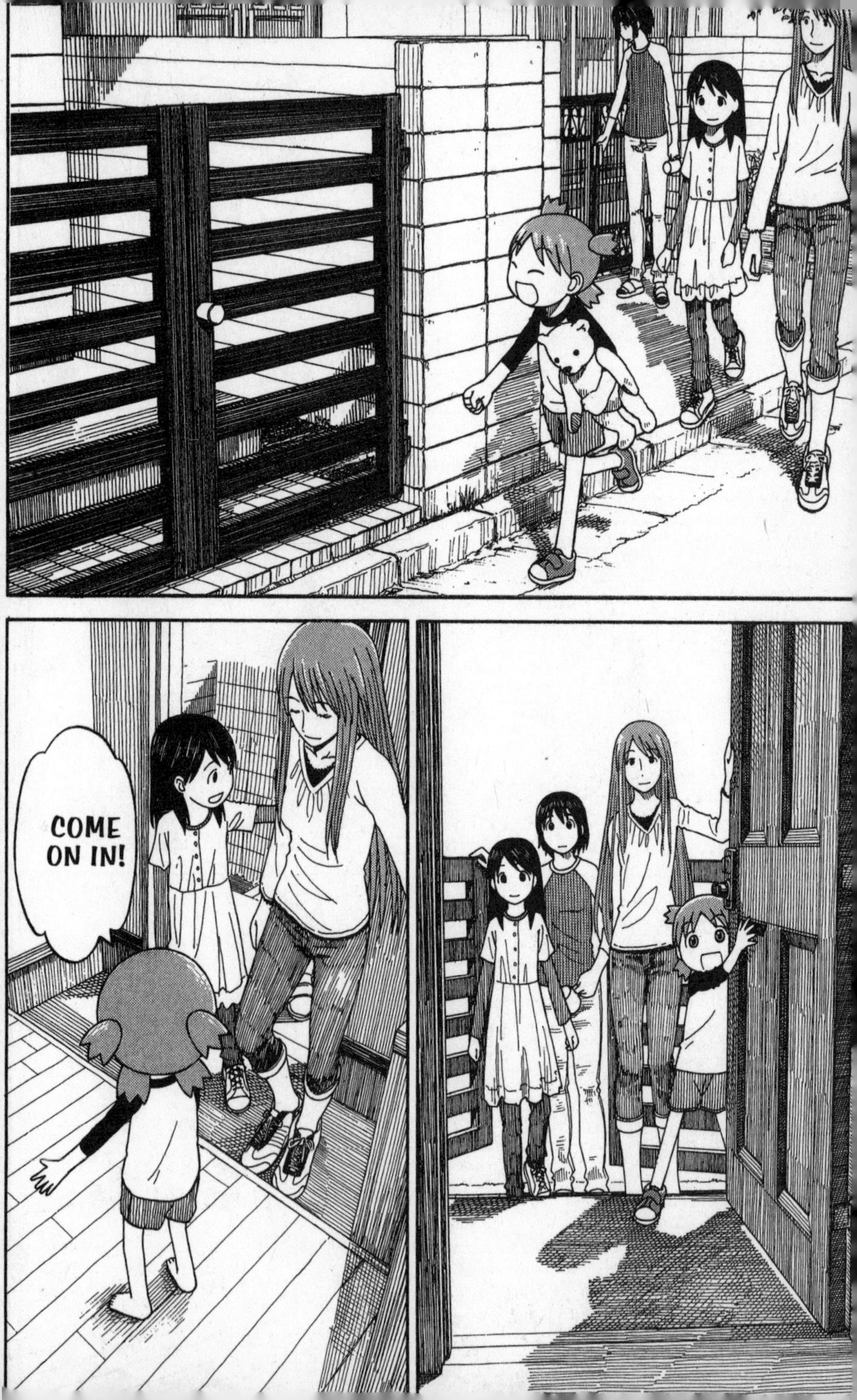
COME ON IN!

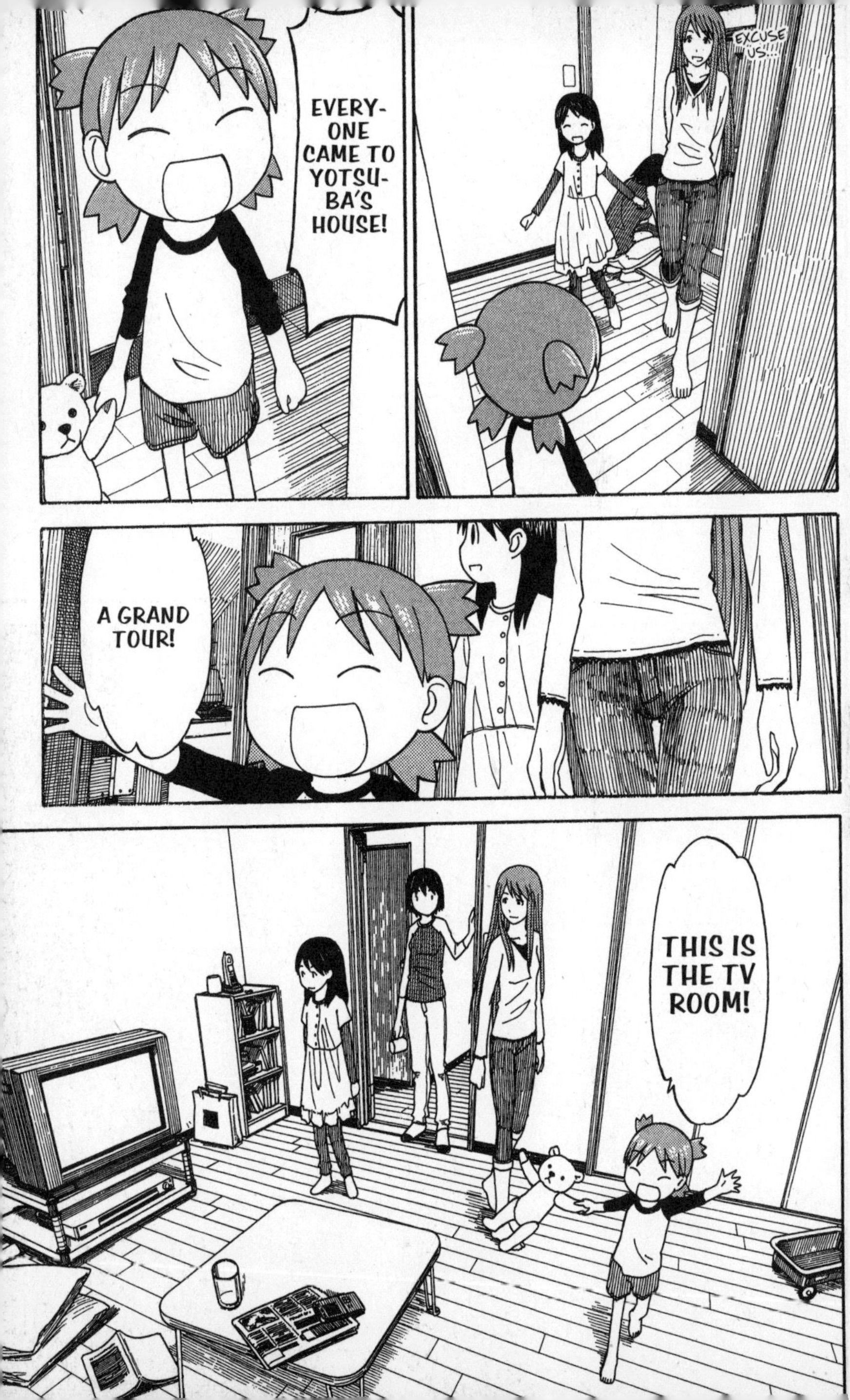
EXCUSE US...
EVERY-ONE CAME TO YOTSU-BA'S HOUSE!
A GRAND TOUR!
THIS IS THE TV ROOM!

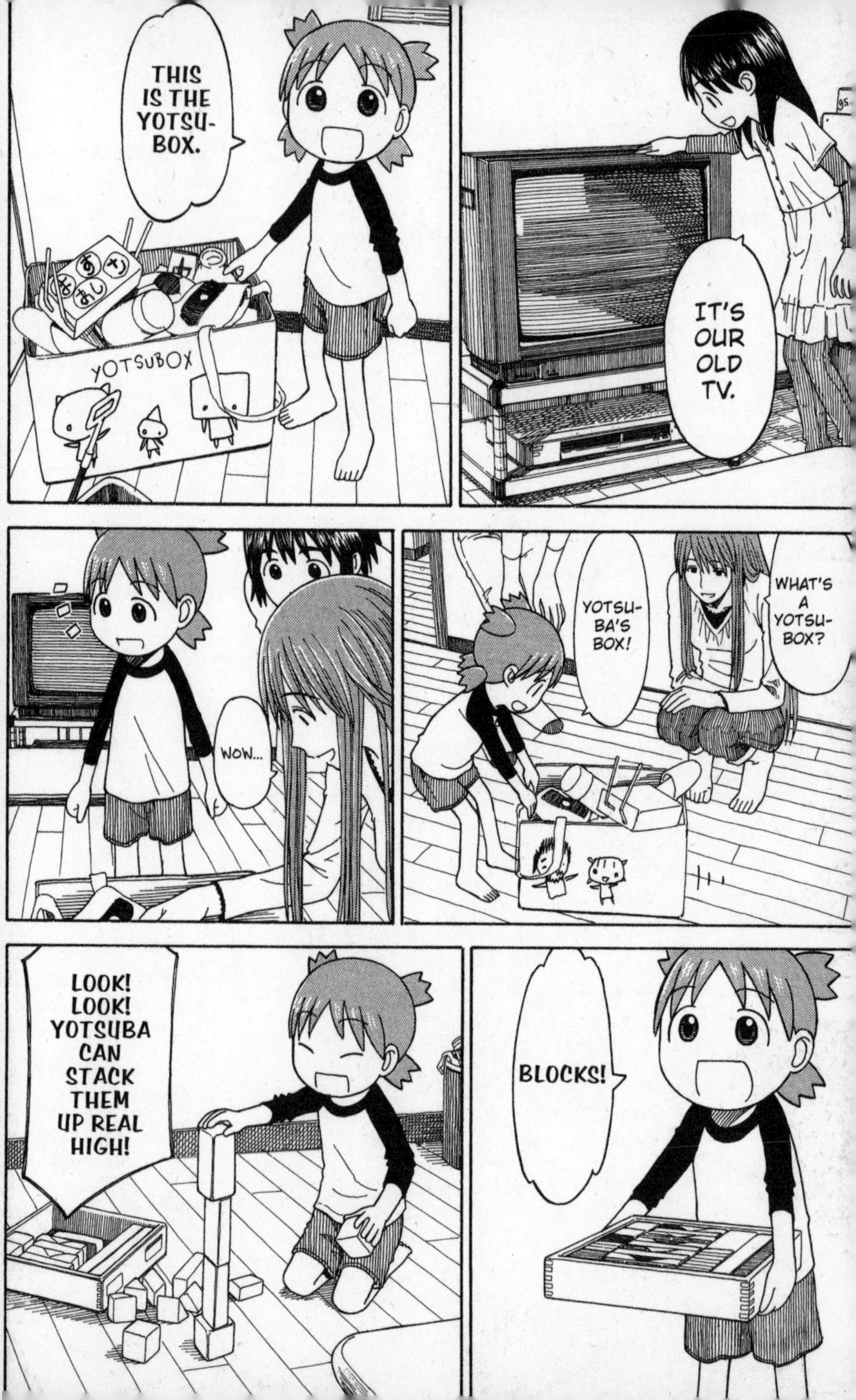
IT'S OUR OLD TV.
THIS IS THE YOTSU-BOX.
YOTSUBOX
WHAT'S A YOTSU-BOX?
YOTSU-BA'S BOX!
WOW...
BLOCKS!
LOOK! LOOK! YOTSUBA CAN STACK THEM UP REAL HIGH!

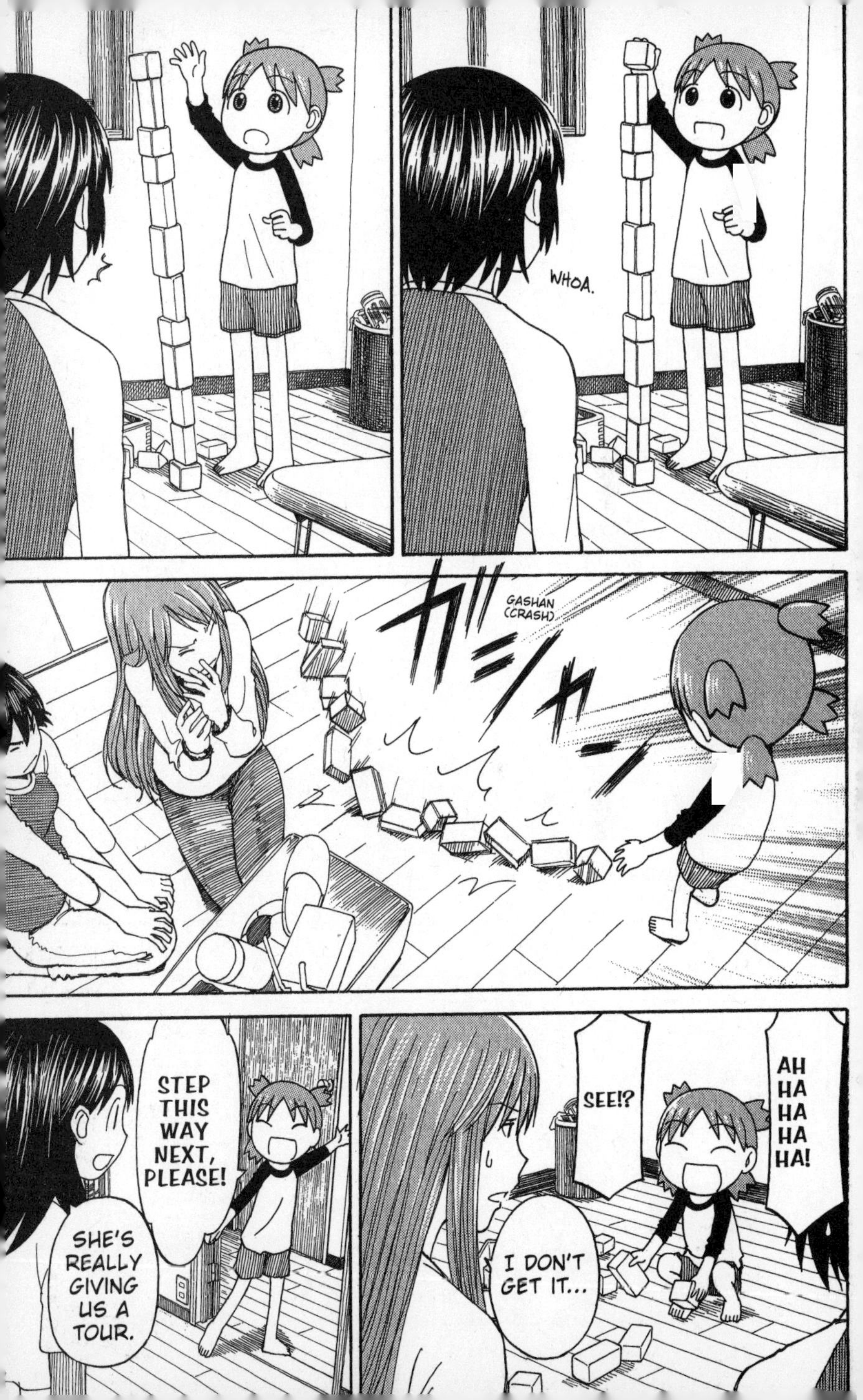
WHOA.
GASHAN
(CRASH)
AH HA HA HA HA!
SEE!?
I DON'T GET IT...
STEP THIS WAY NEXT, PLEASE!
SHE'S REALLY GIVING US A TOUR.

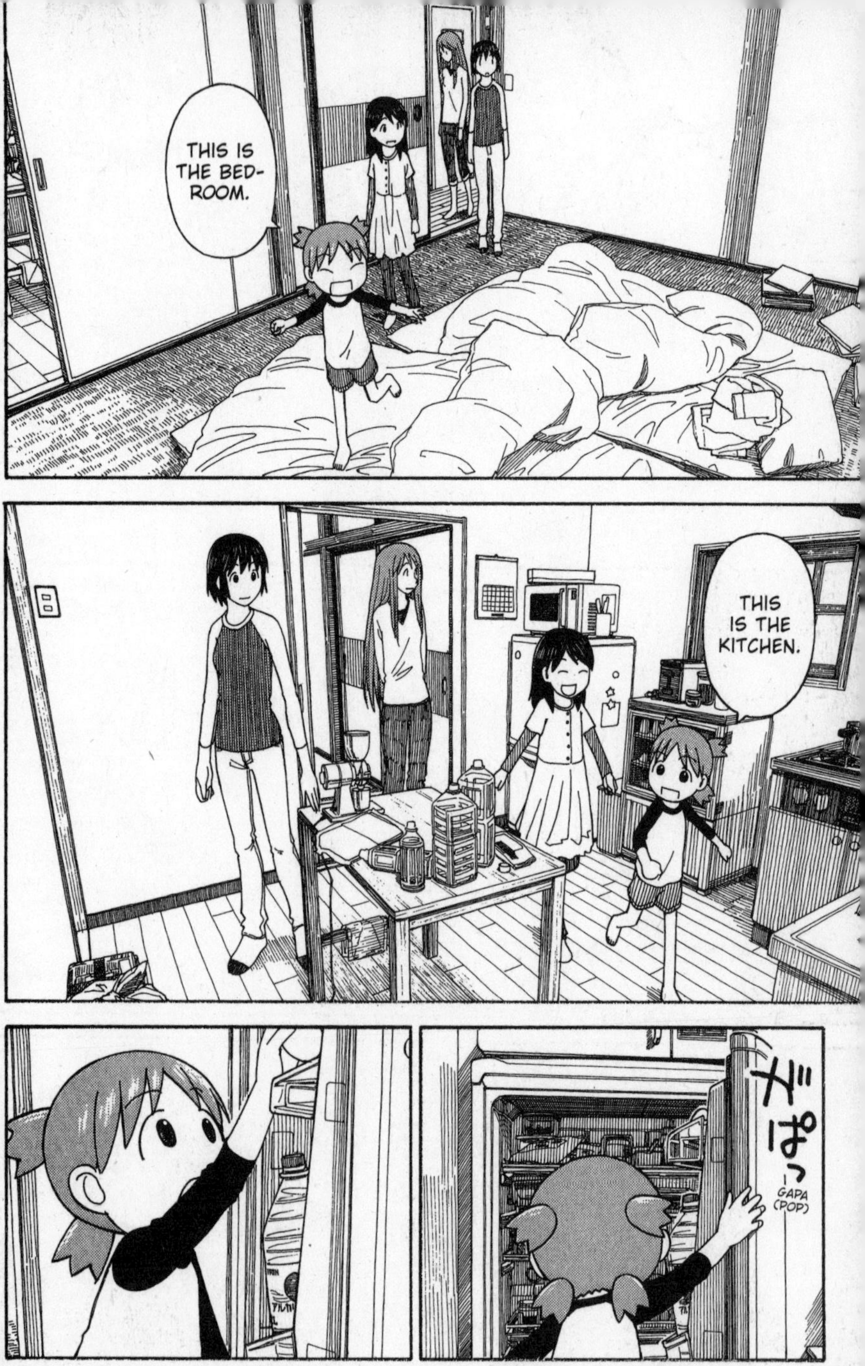
THIS IS THE BED-ROOM.
THIS IS THE KITCHEN.
ガぱっ
GAPA (POP)

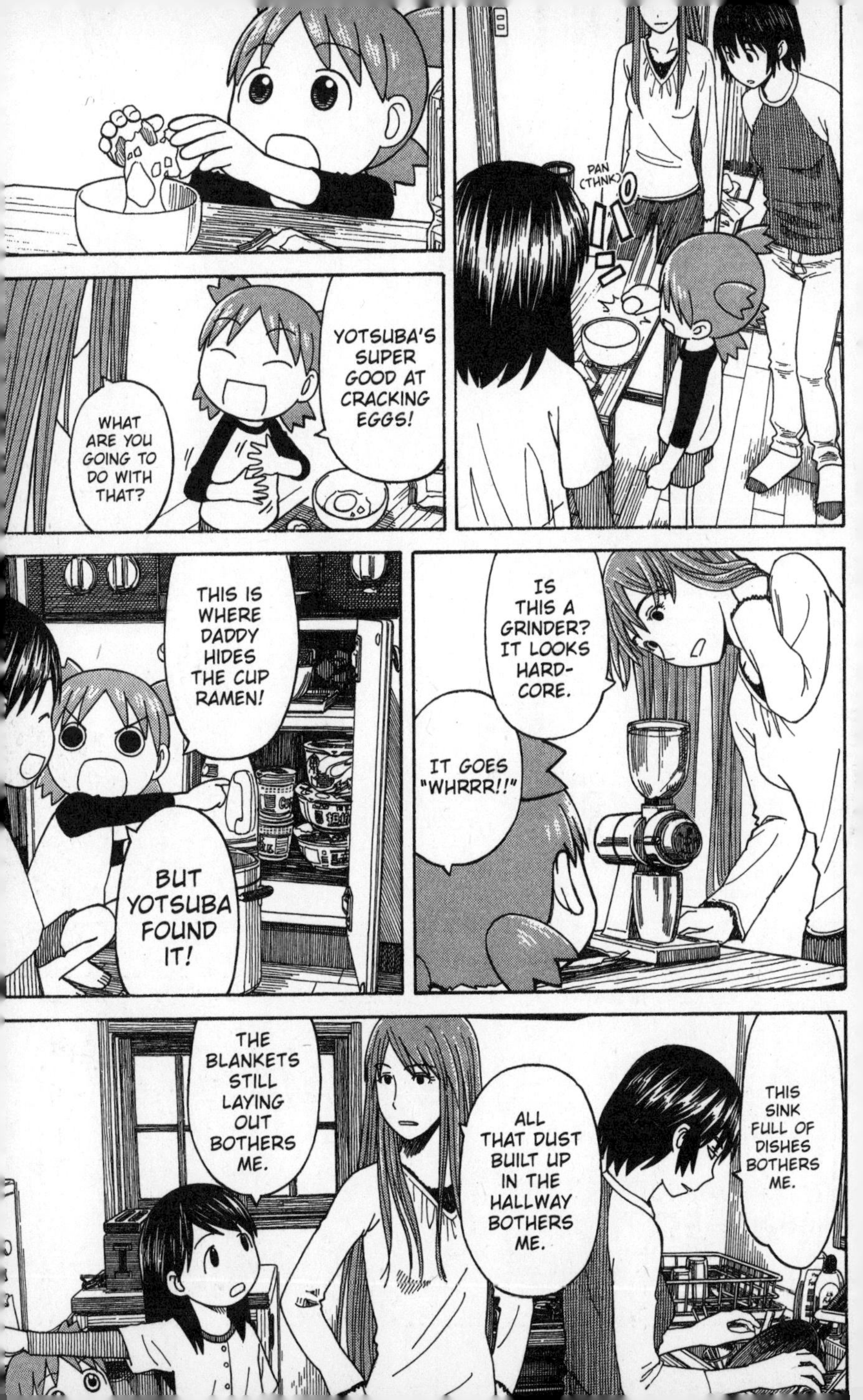
PAN (THNK)
YOTSUBA'S SUPER GOOD AT CRACKING EGGS!
WHAT ARE YOU GOING TO DO WITH THAT?
IS THIS A GRINDER? IT LOOKS HARD-CORE.
IT GOES "WHRRR!!"
THIS IS WHERE DADDY HIDES THE CUP RAMEN!
BUT YOTSUBA FOUND IT!
THIS SINK FULL OF DISHES BOTHERS ME.
ALL THAT DUST BUILT UP IN THE HALLWAY BOTHERS ME.
THE BLANKETS STILL LAYING OUT BOTHERS ME.

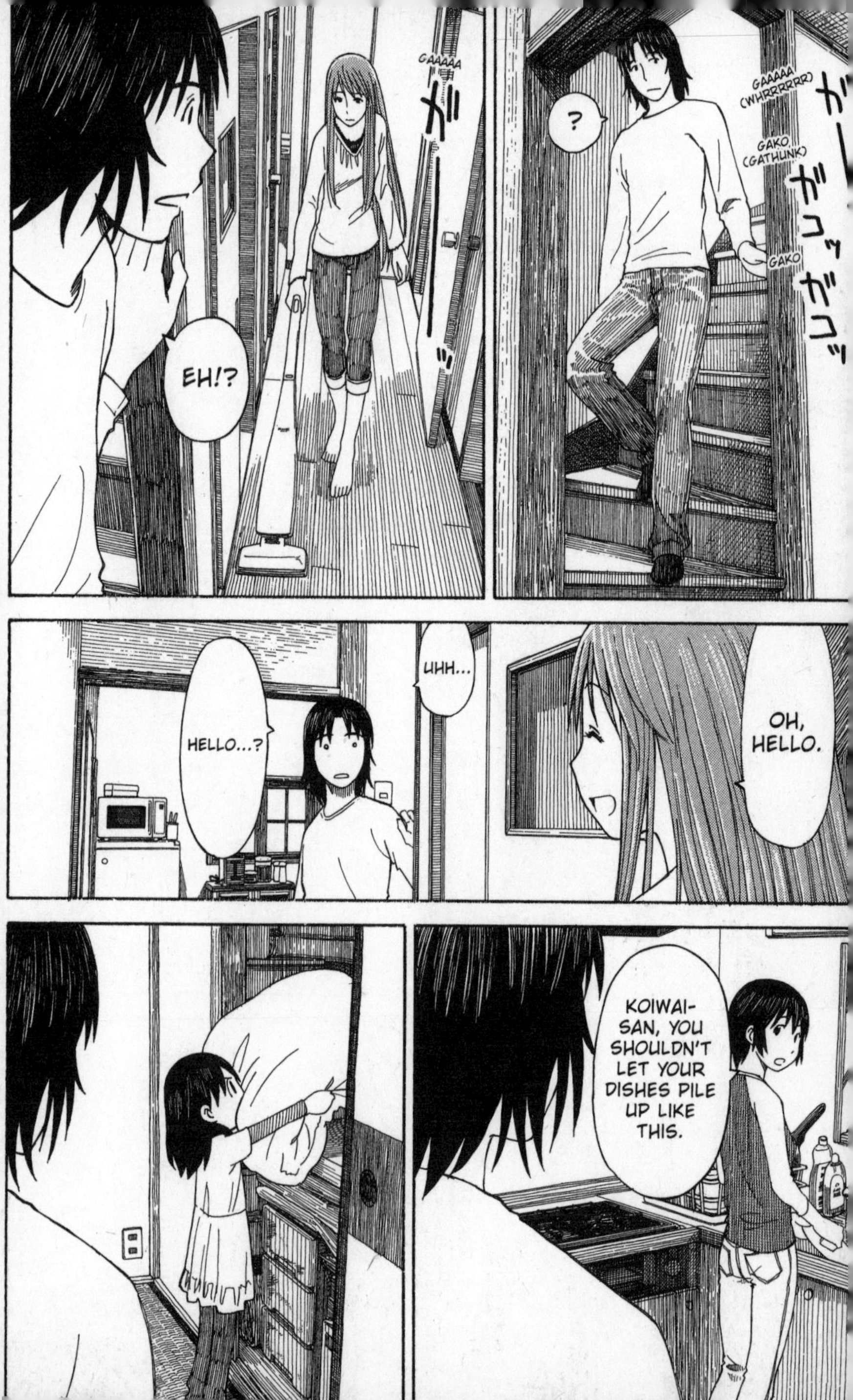
GAAAAA (WHRRRRRR)
GAKO (GATHUNK)
ガコッ
GAKO
ガコッ
?
GAAAAA
ガーー
EH!?
OH, HELLO.
UHH...
HELLO...?
KOIWAI-SAN, YOU SHOULDN'T LET YOUR DISHES PILE UP LIKE THIS.

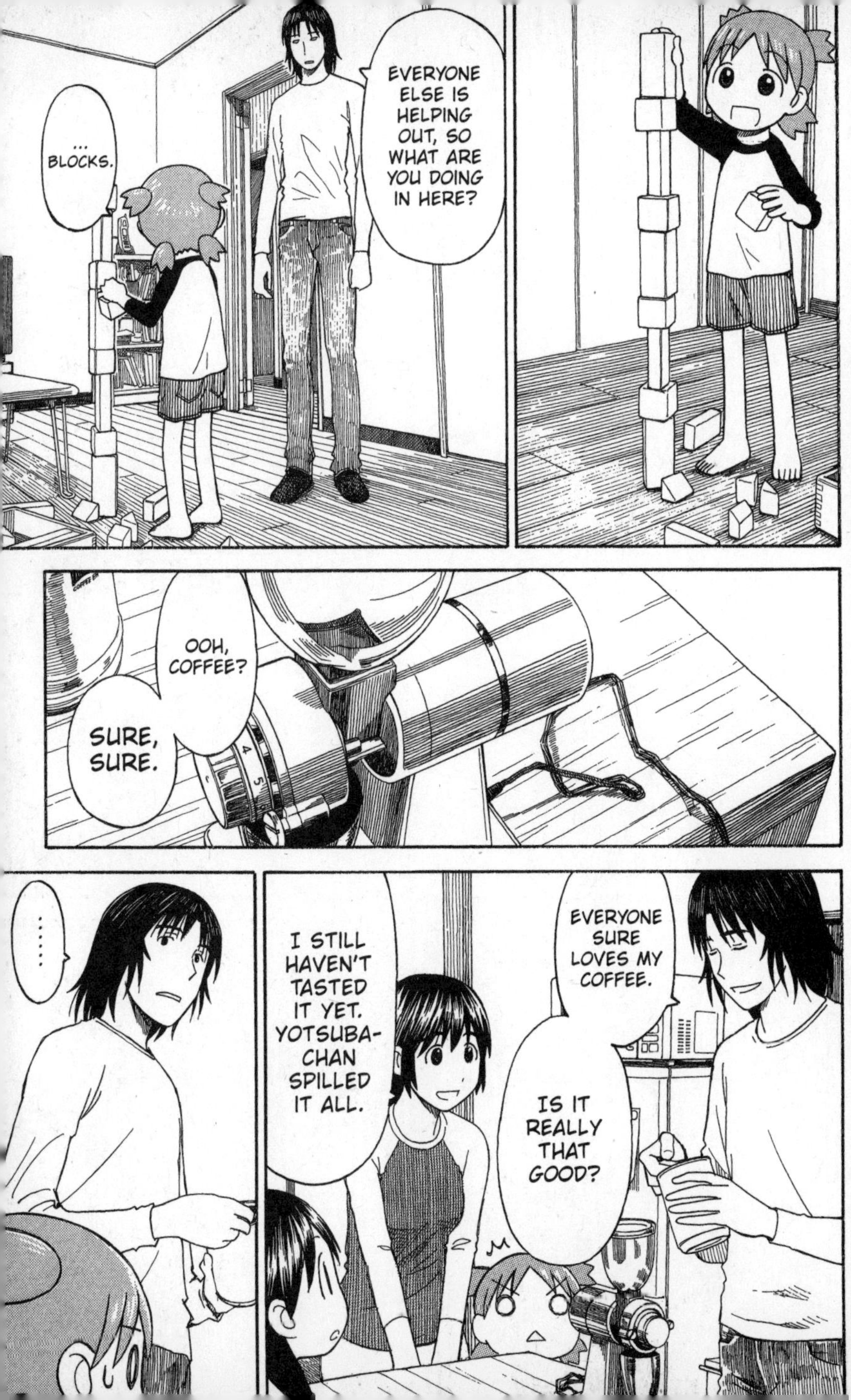
EVERYONE ELSE IS HELPING OUT, SO WHAT ARE YOU DOING IN HERE?
...BLOCKS.
OOH, COFFEE?
SURE, SURE.
EVERYONE SURE LOVES MY COFFEE.
IS IT REALLY THAT GOOD?
I STILL HAVEN'T TASTED IT YET. YOTSUBA-CHAN SPILLED IT ALL.
......

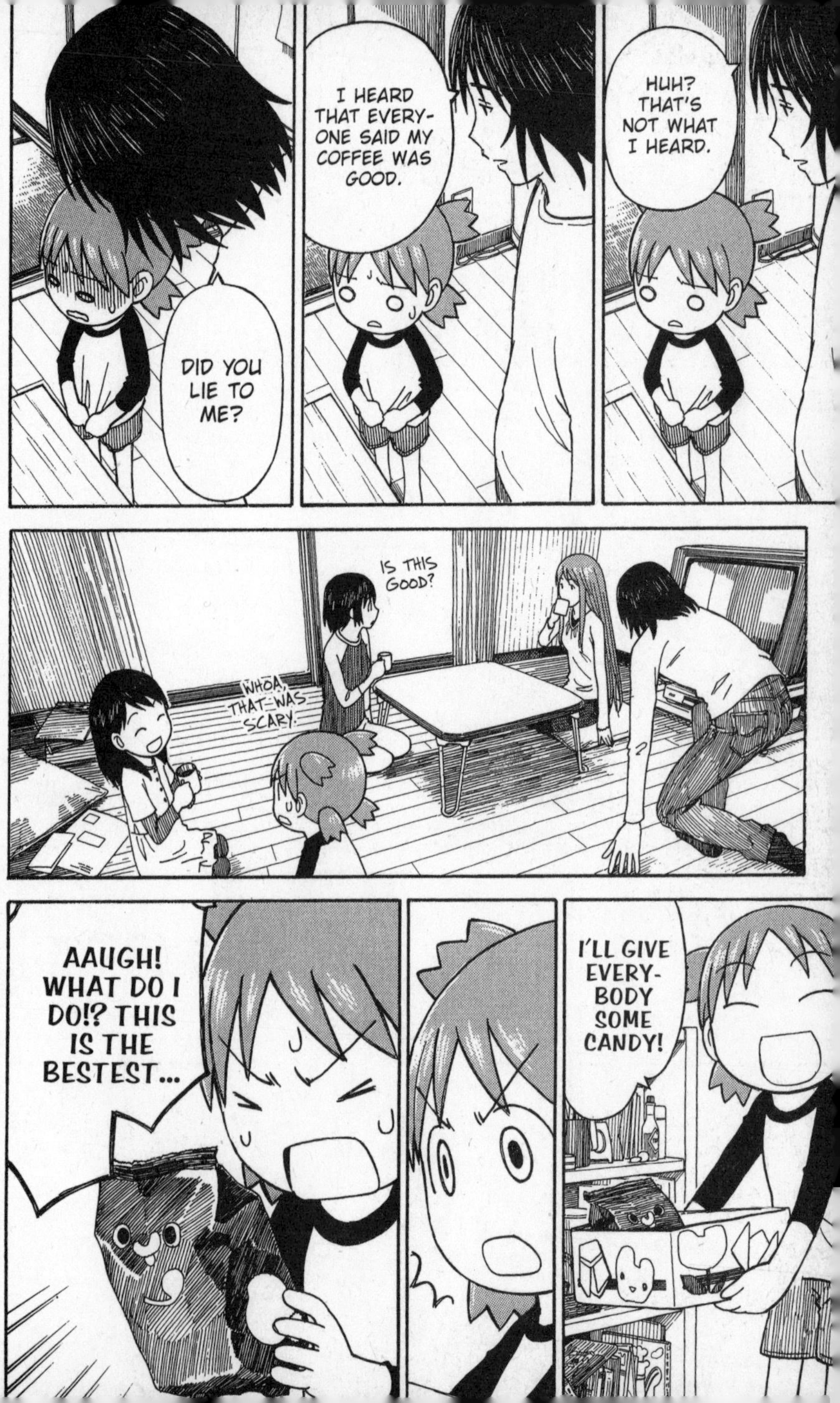
HUH? THAT'S NOT WHAT I HEARD.
I HEARD THAT EVERY-ONE SAID MY COFFEE WAS GOOD.
DID YOU LIE TO ME?
IS THIS GOOD?
WHOA, THAT WAS SCARY.
I'LL GIVE EVERY-BODY SOME CANDY!
AAUGH! WHAT DO I DO!? THIS IS THE BESTEST...

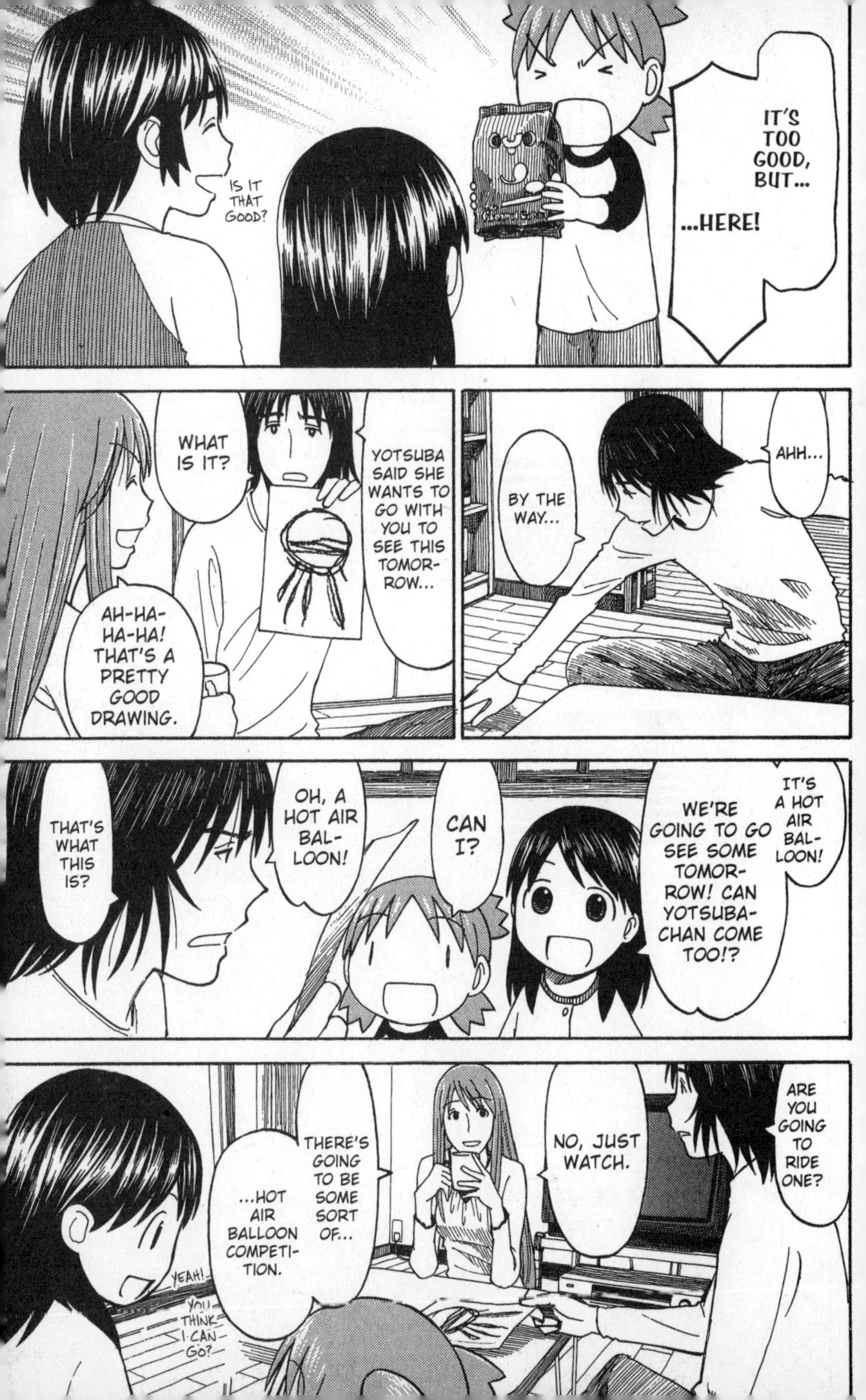
IT'S TOO GOOD, BUT...
...HERE!
IS IT THAT GOOD?
AHH...
BY THE WAY...
YOTSUBA SAID SHE WANTS TO GO WITH YOU TO SEE THIS TOMORROW...
WHAT IS IT?
AH-HA-HA-HA! THAT'S A PRETTY GOOD DRAWING.
IT'S A HOT AIR BALLOON!
WE'RE GOING TO GO SEE SOME TOMORROW! CAN YOTSUBA-CHAN COME TOO!?
CAN I?
OH, A HOT AIR BALLOON!
THAT'S WHAT THIS IS?
ARE YOU GOING TO RIDE ONE?
NO, JUST WATCH.
THERE'S GOING TO BE SOME SORT OF...
...HOT AIR BALLOON COMPETITION.
YEAH!
YOU THINK I CAN GO?

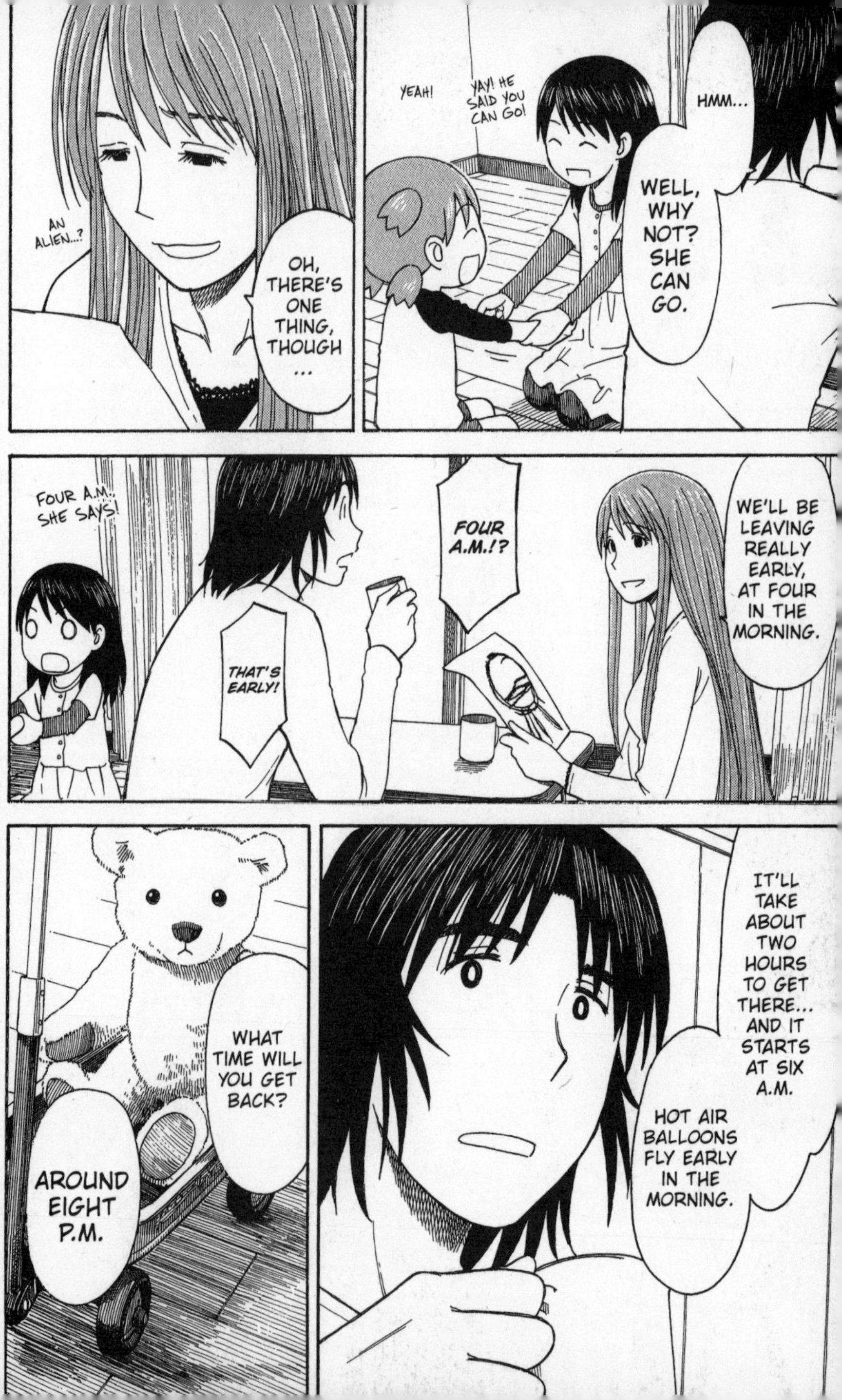
HMM...
WELL, WHY NOT? SHE CAN GO.
YAY! HE SAID YOU CAN GO!
YEAH!
OH, THERE'S ONE THING, THOUGH...
AN ALIEN...?
WE'LL BE LEAVING REALLY EARLY, AT FOUR IN THE MORNING.
FOUR A.M.!?
THAT'S EARLY!
FOUR A.M., SHE SAYS!
IT'LL TAKE ABOUT TWO HOURS TO GET THERE... AND IT STARTS AT SIX A.M.
HOT AIR BALLOONS FLY EARLY IN THE MORNING.
WHAT TIME WILL YOU GET BACK?
AROUND EIGHT P.M.

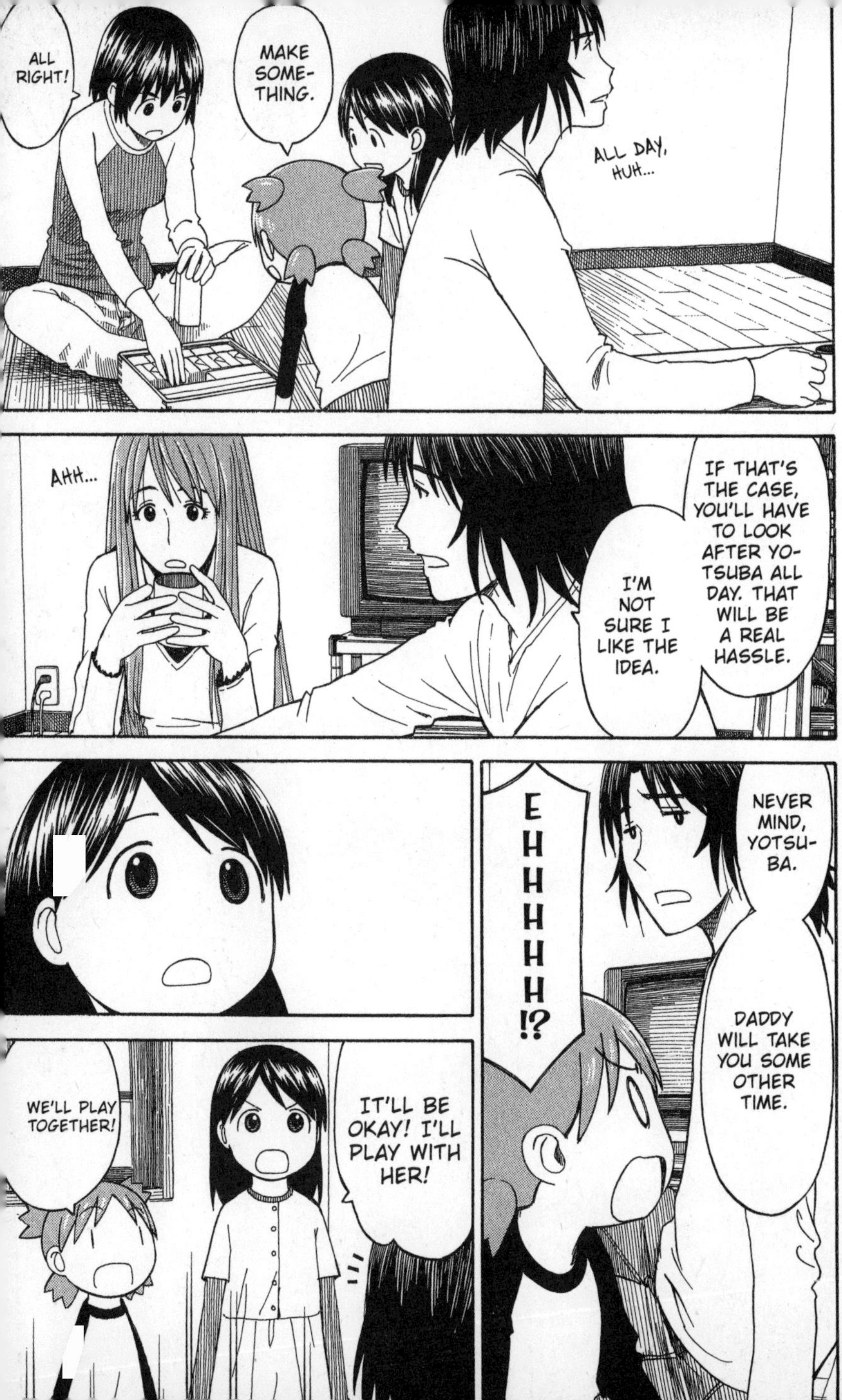
ALL DAY, HUH...
MAKE SOME-THING.
ALL RIGHT!
IF THAT'S THE CASE, YOU'LL HAVE TO LOOK AFTER YO-TSUBA ALL DAY. THAT WILL BE A REAL HASSLE.
I'M NOT SURE I LIKE THE IDEA.
AHH...
NEVER MIND, YOTSU-BA.
DADDY WILL TAKE YOU SOME OTHER TIME.
EHHHHHH!?
IT'LL BE OKAY! I'LL PLAY WITH HER!
WE'LL PLAY TOGETHER!

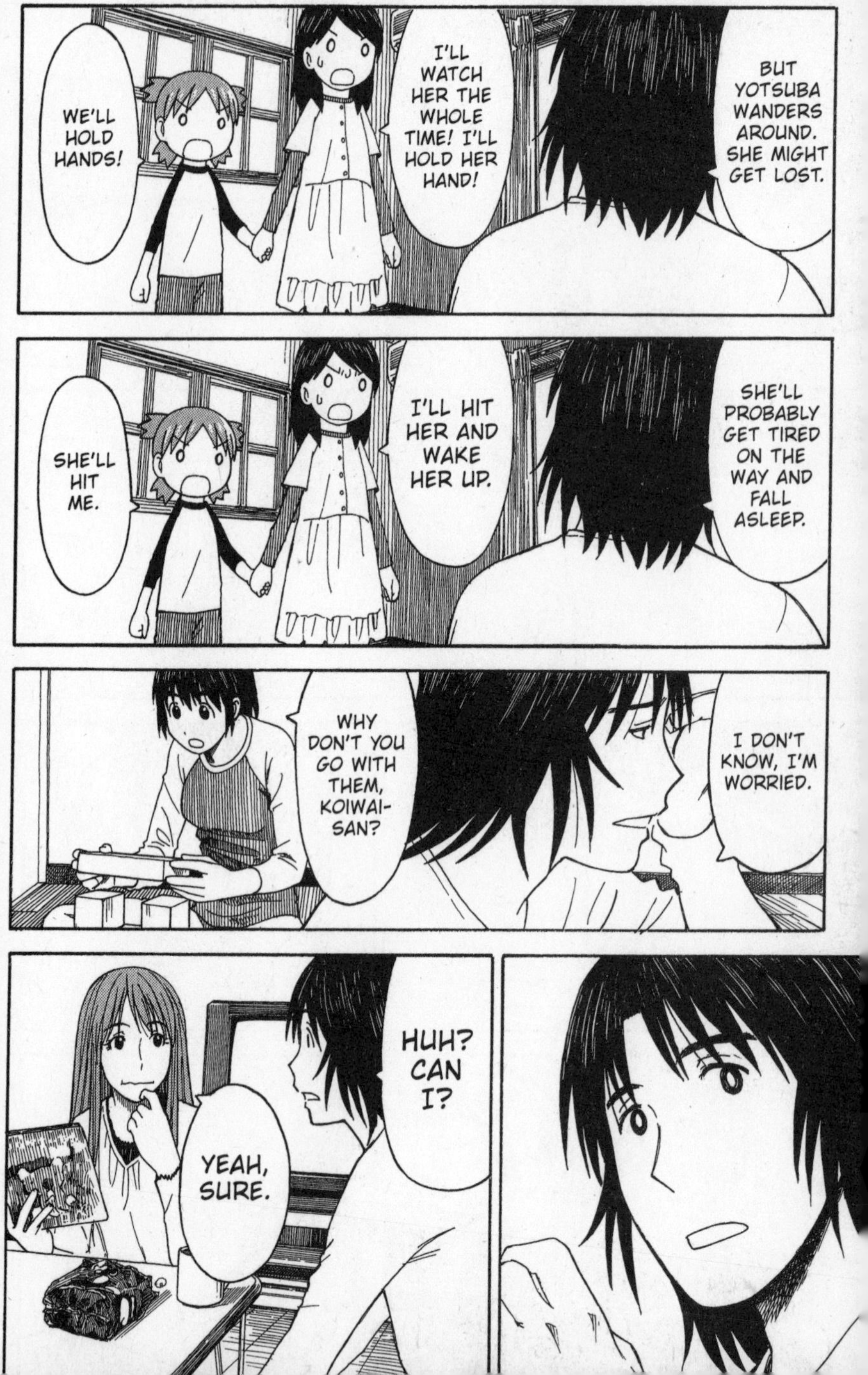
BUT YOTSUBA WANDERS AROUND. SHE MIGHT GET LOST.
I'LL WATCH HER THE WHOLE TIME! I'LL HOLD HER HAND!
WE'LL HOLD HANDS!
SHE'LL PROBABLY GET TIRED ON THE WAY AND FALL ASLEEP.
I'LL HIT HER AND WAKE HER UP.
SHE'LL HIT ME.
I DON'T KNOW, I'M WORRIED.
WHY DON'T YOU GO WITH THEM, KOIWAI-SAN?
HUH? CAN I?
YEAH, SURE.

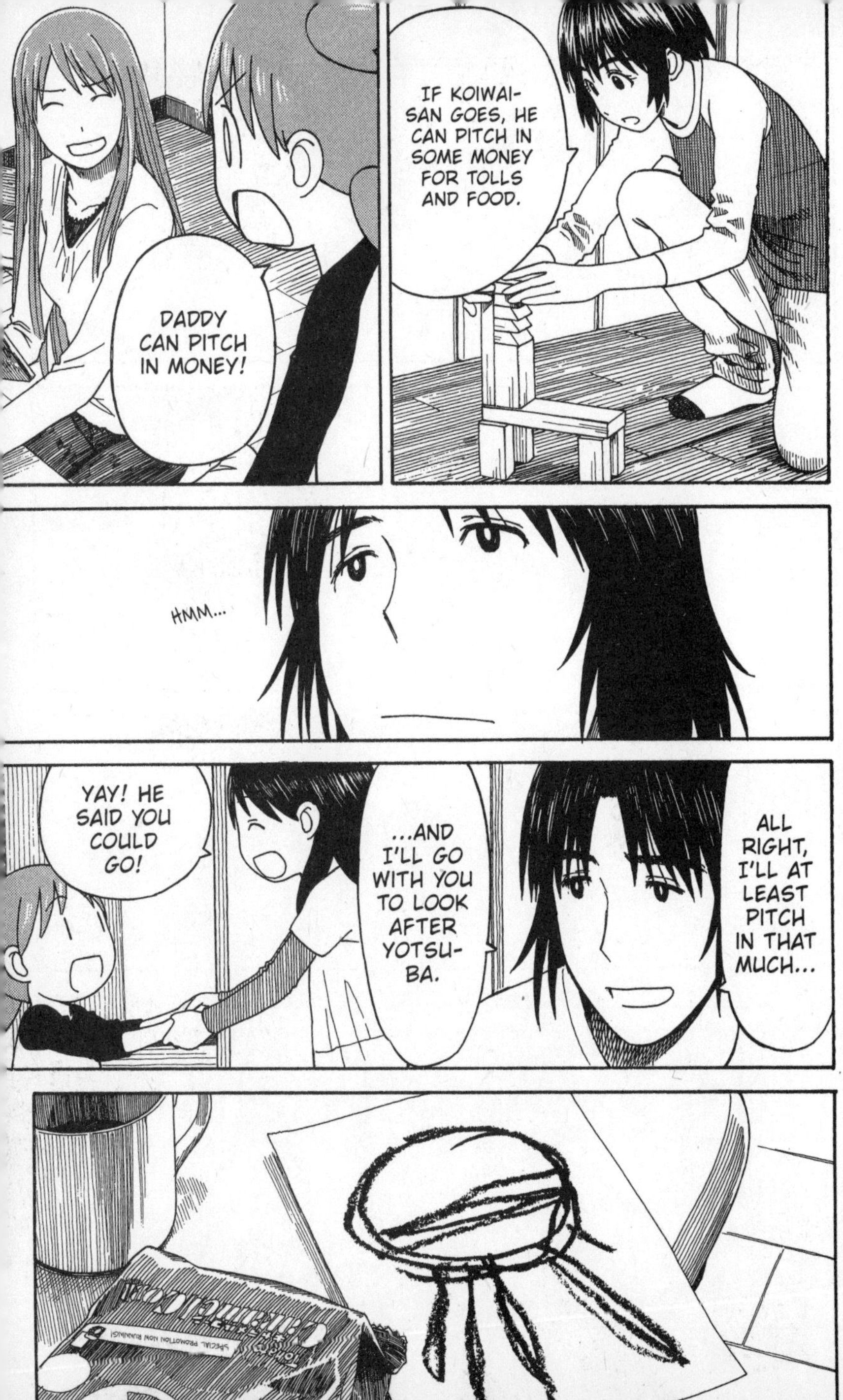
IF KOIWAI-SAN GOES, HE CAN PITCH IN SOME MONEY FOR TOLLS AND FOOD.
DADDY CAN PITCH IN MONEY!
HMM...
ALL RIGHT, I'LL AT LEAST PITCH IN THAT MUCH...
...AND I'LL GO WITH YOU TO LOOK AFTER YOTSUBA.
YAY! HE SAID YOU COULD GO!
SPECIAL PROMOTION NOW RUNNING!

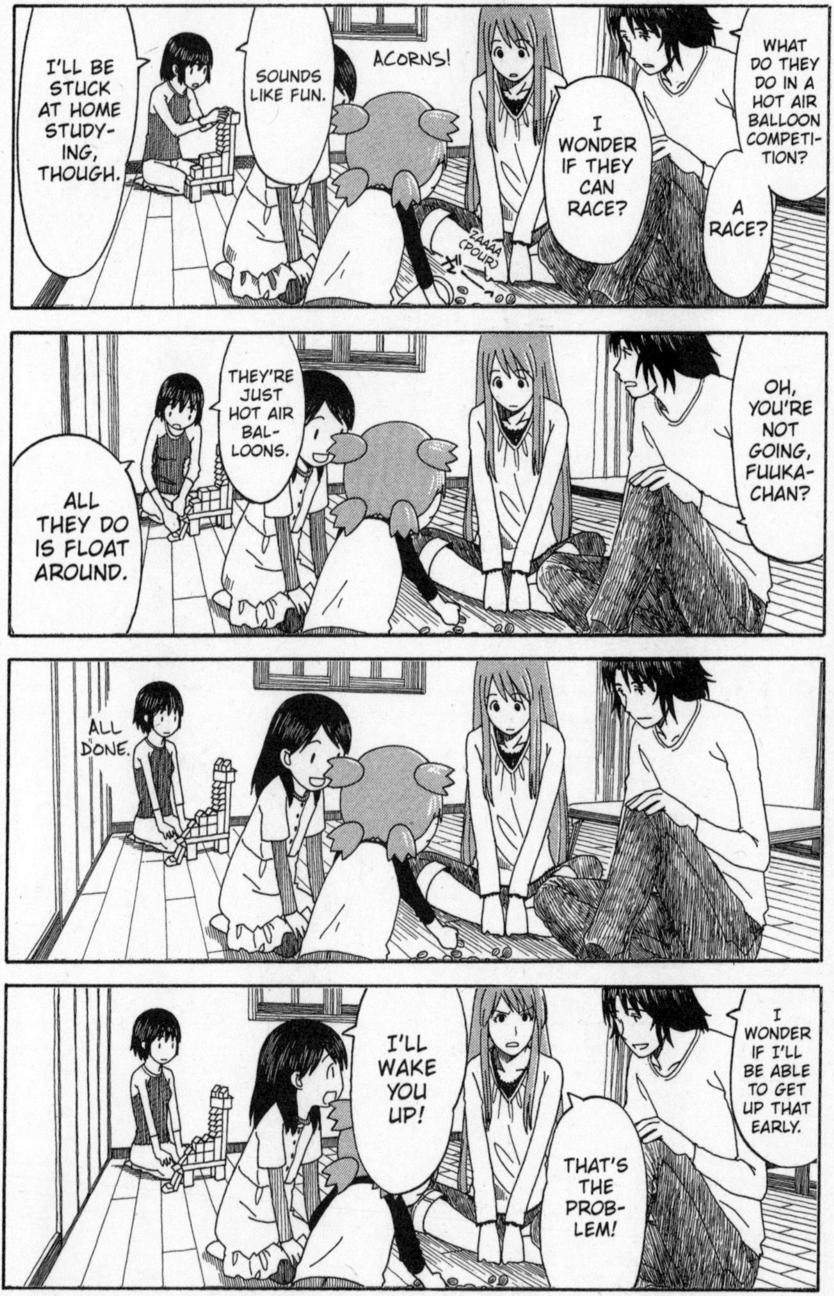

WHAT DO THEY DO IN A HOT AIR BALLOON COMPETITION?
A RACE?
I WONDER IF THEY CAN RACE?
ACORNS!
ZAAAA (POUR)
SOUNDS LIKE FUN.
I'LL BE STUCK AT HOME STUDYING, THOUGH.
OH, YOU'RE NOT GOING, FUUKA-CHAN?
THEY'RE JUST HOT AIR BALLOONS.
ALL THEY DO IS FLOAT AROUND.
ALL DONE.
I WONDER IF I'LL BE ABLE TO GET UP THAT EARLY.
THAT'S THE PROBLEM!
I'LL WAKE YOU UP!

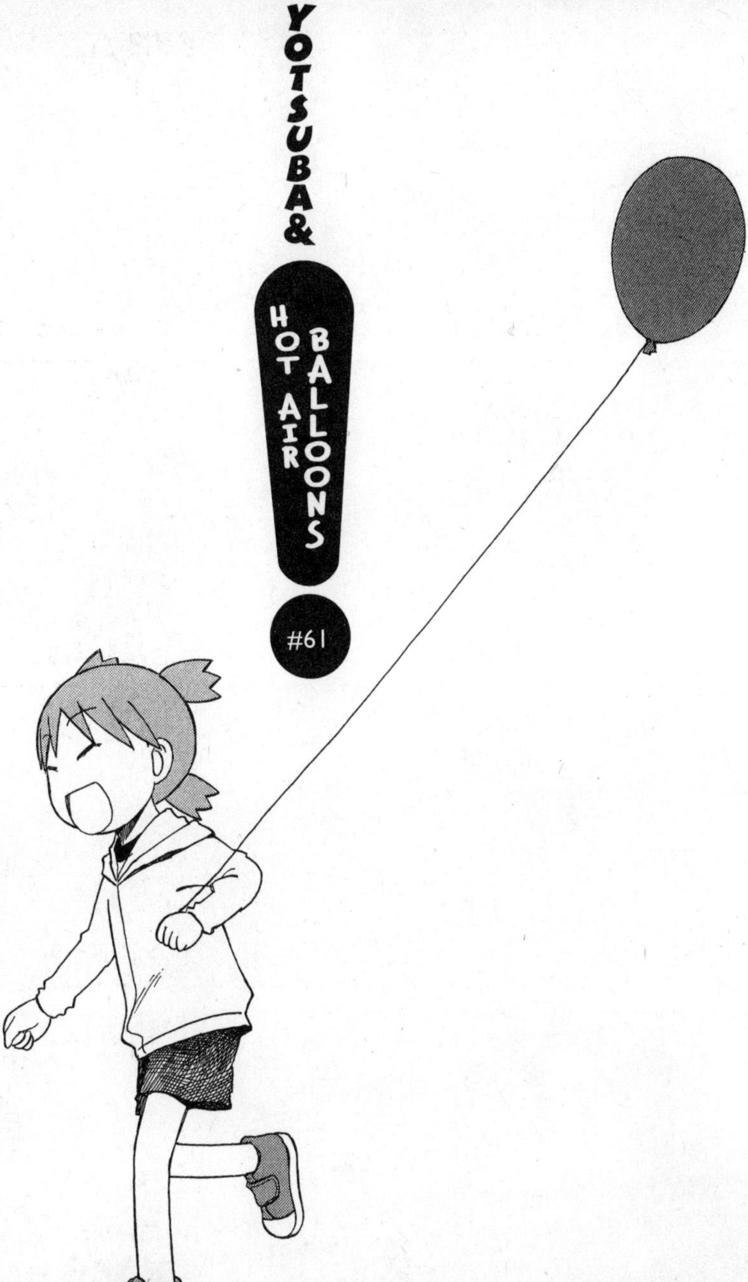
YOTSUBA&
HOT AIR BALLOONS!
#61

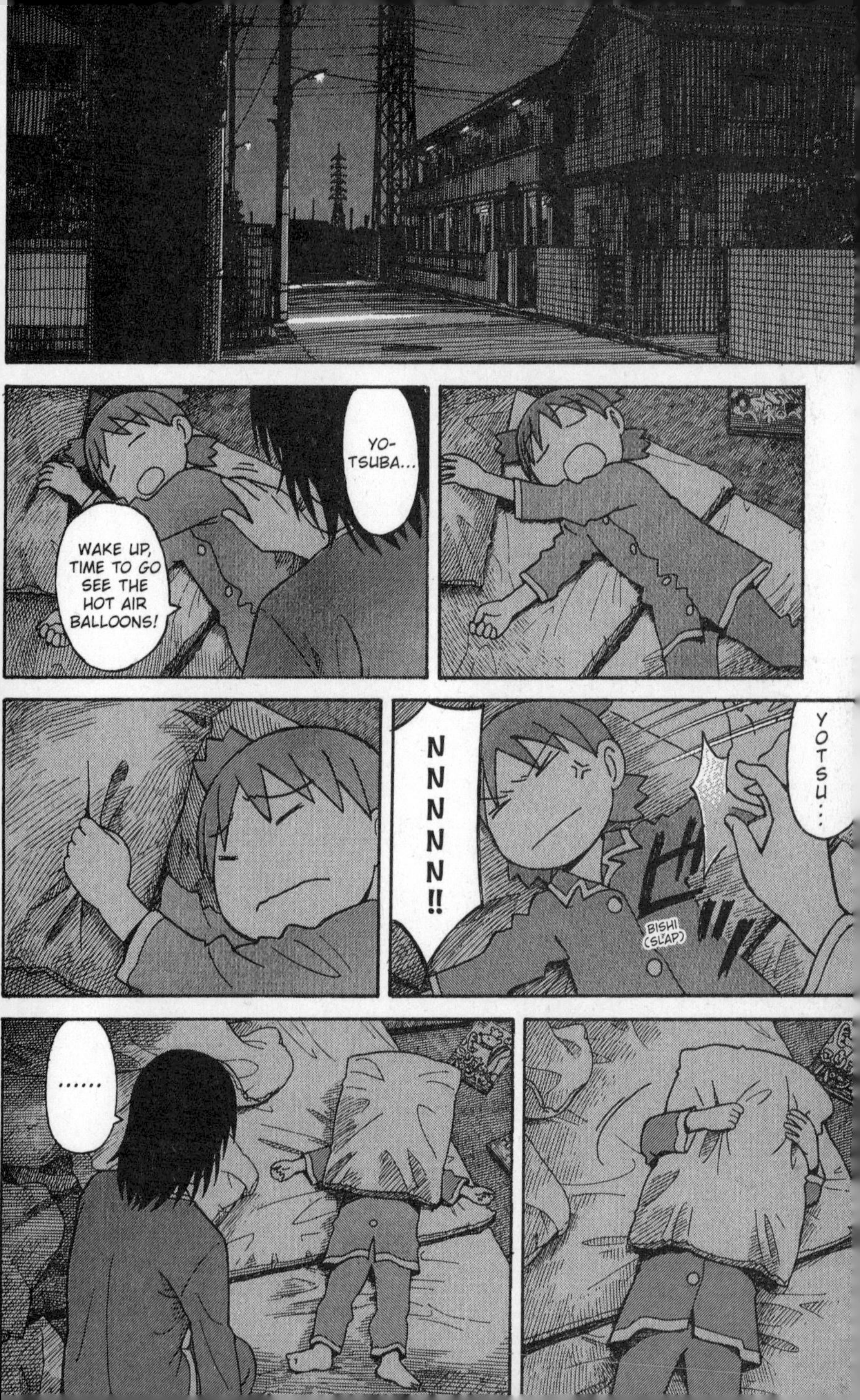
YO-TSUBA...
WAKE UP, TIME TO GO SEE THE HOT AIR BALLOONS!
YOTSU...
NNNNNN!!
BISHI (SLAP)
....

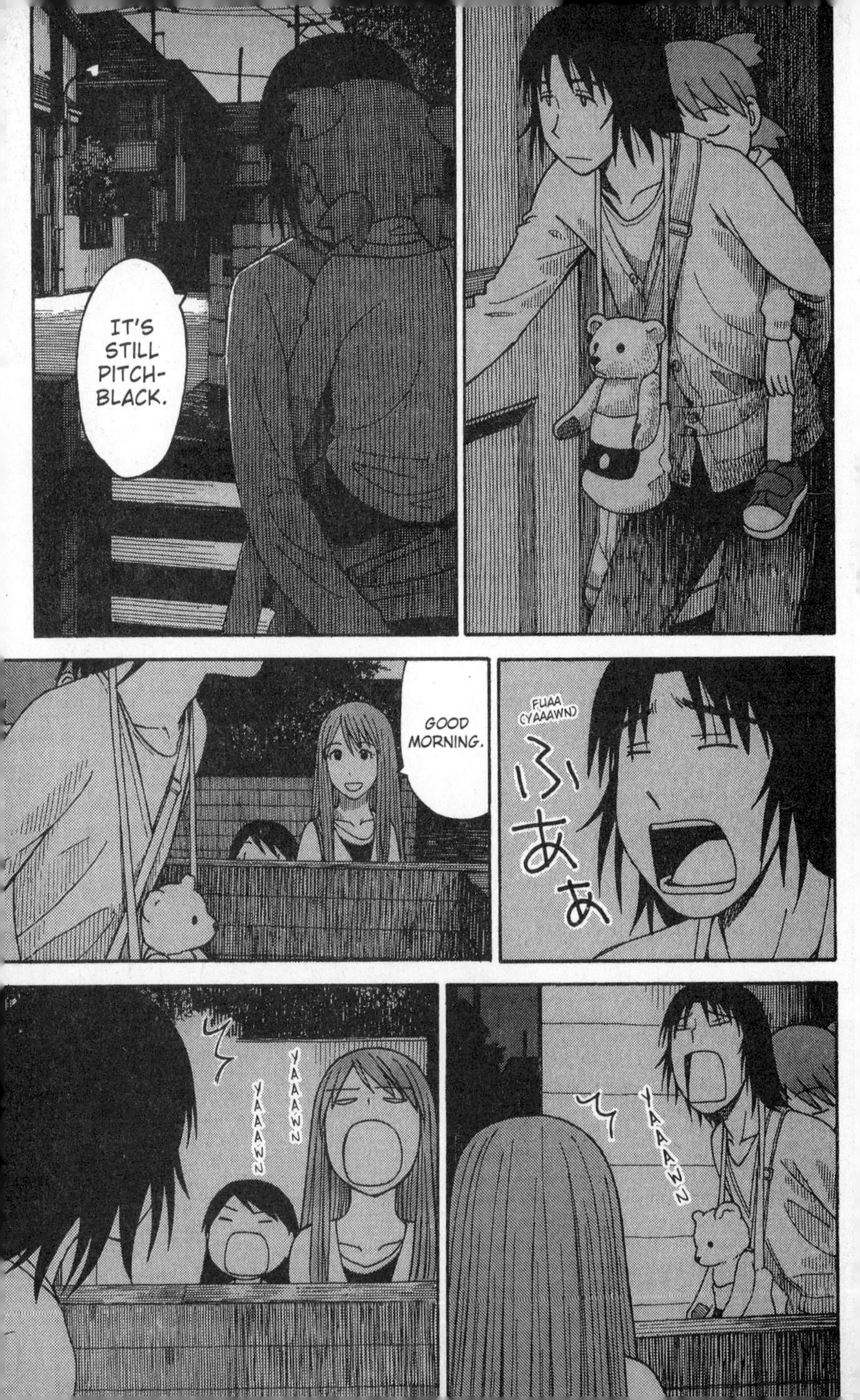
IT'S STILL PITCH-BLACK.
FUAA (YAAAWN)
ふあぁ
GOOD MORNING.
YAAAWN
YAAAWN
YAAAWN

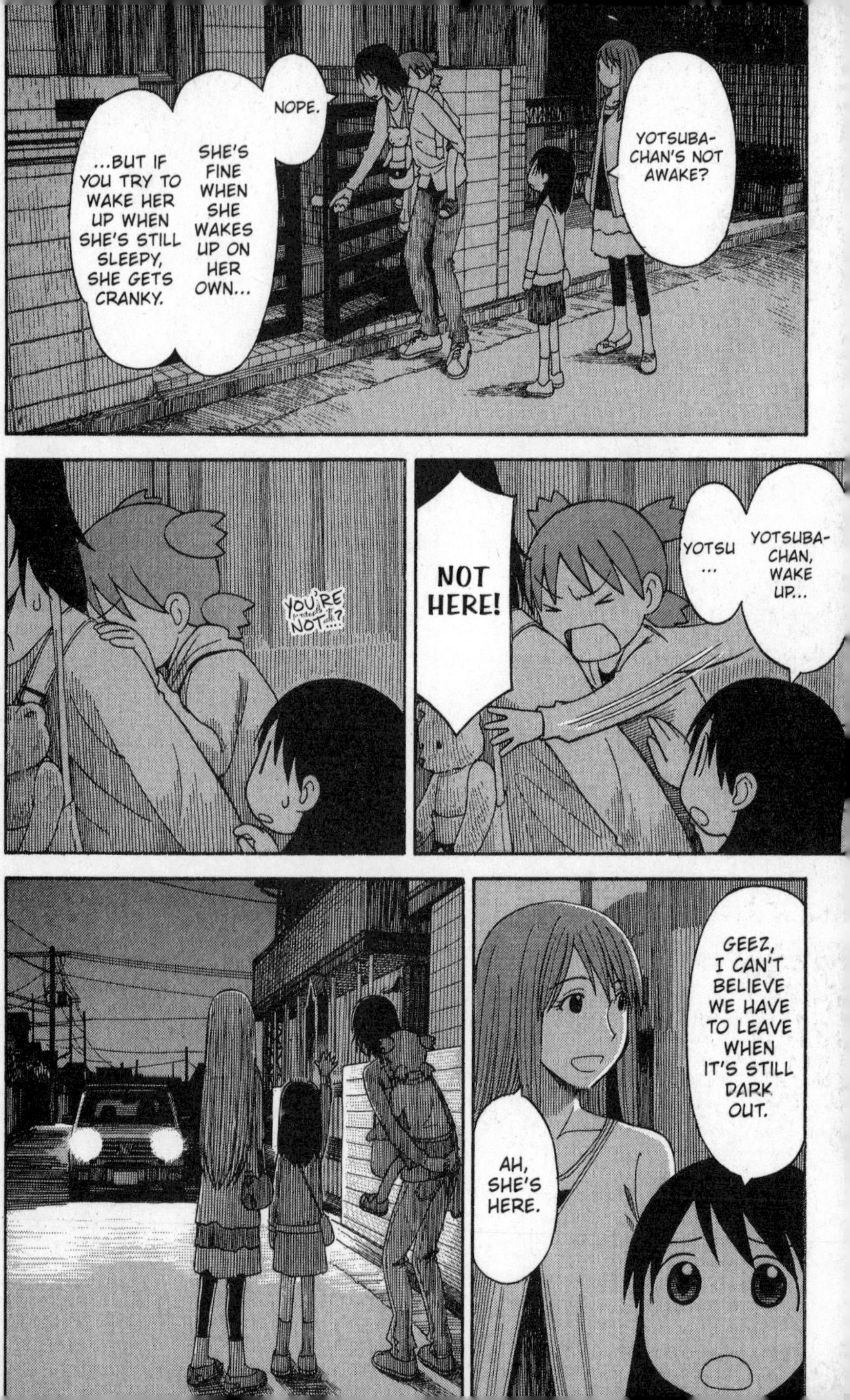
YOTSUBA-CHAN'S NOT AWAKE?
NOPE.
SHE'S FINE WHEN SHE WAKES UP ON HER OWN...
...BUT IF YOU TRY TO WAKE HER UP WHEN SHE'S STILL SLEEPY, SHE GETS CRANKY.
YOTSUBA-CHAN, WAKE UP...
YOTSU...
NOT HERE!
YOU'RE NOT...?
GEEZ, I CAN'T BELIEVE WE HAVE TO LEAVE WHEN IT'S STILL DARK OUT.
AH, SHE'S HERE.

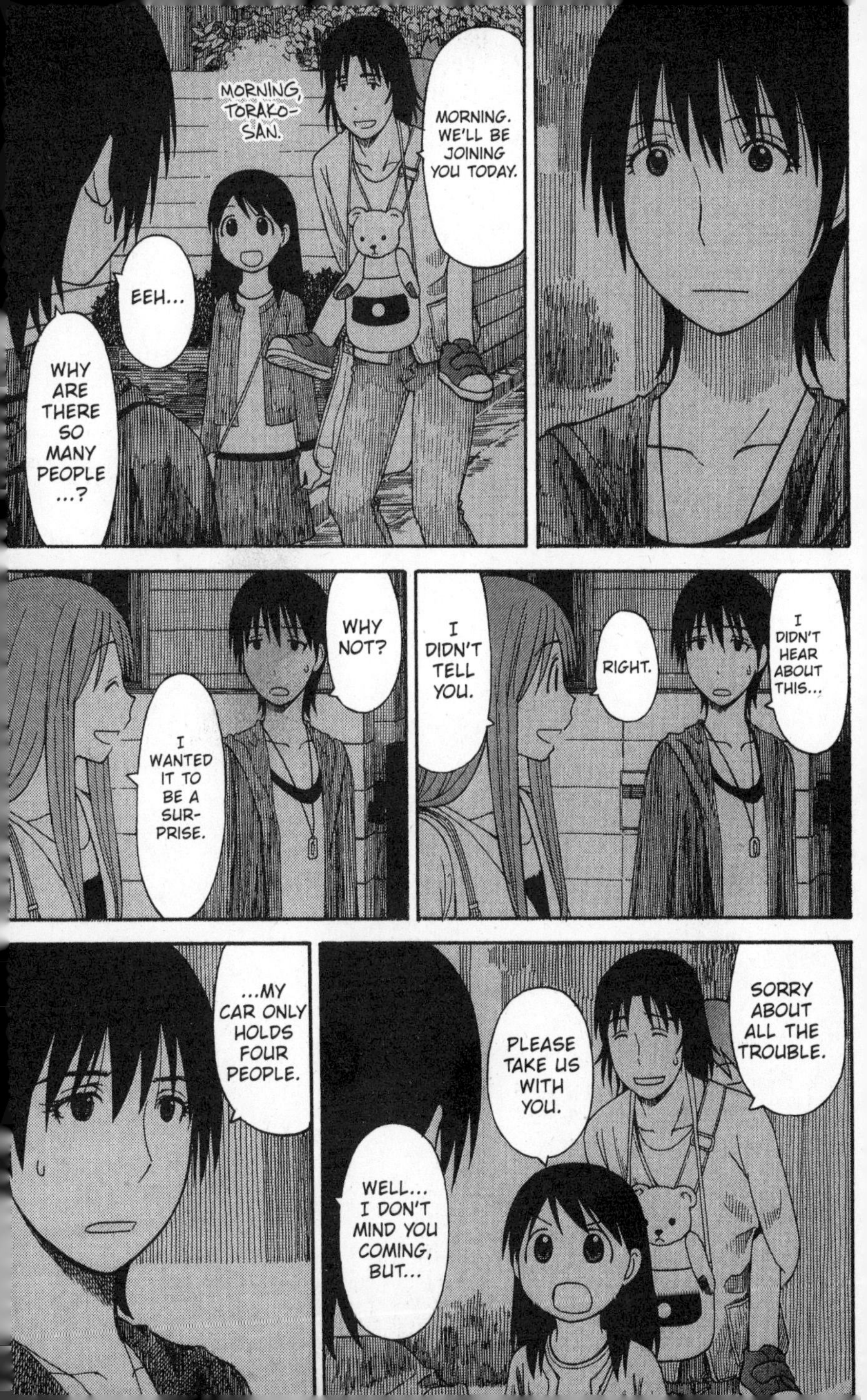
MORNING. WE'LL BE JOINING YOU TODAY.
MORNING, TORAKO-SAN.
EEH...
WHY ARE THERE SO MANY PEOPLE ...?
I DIDN'T HEAR ABOUT THIS...
RIGHT.
I DIDN'T TELL YOU.
WHY NOT?
I WANTED IT TO BE A SUR-PRISE.
SORRY ABOUT ALL THE TROUBLE.
PLEASE TAKE US WITH YOU.
WELL... I DON'T MIND YOU COMING, BUT...
...MY CAR ONLY HOLDS FOUR PEOPLE.

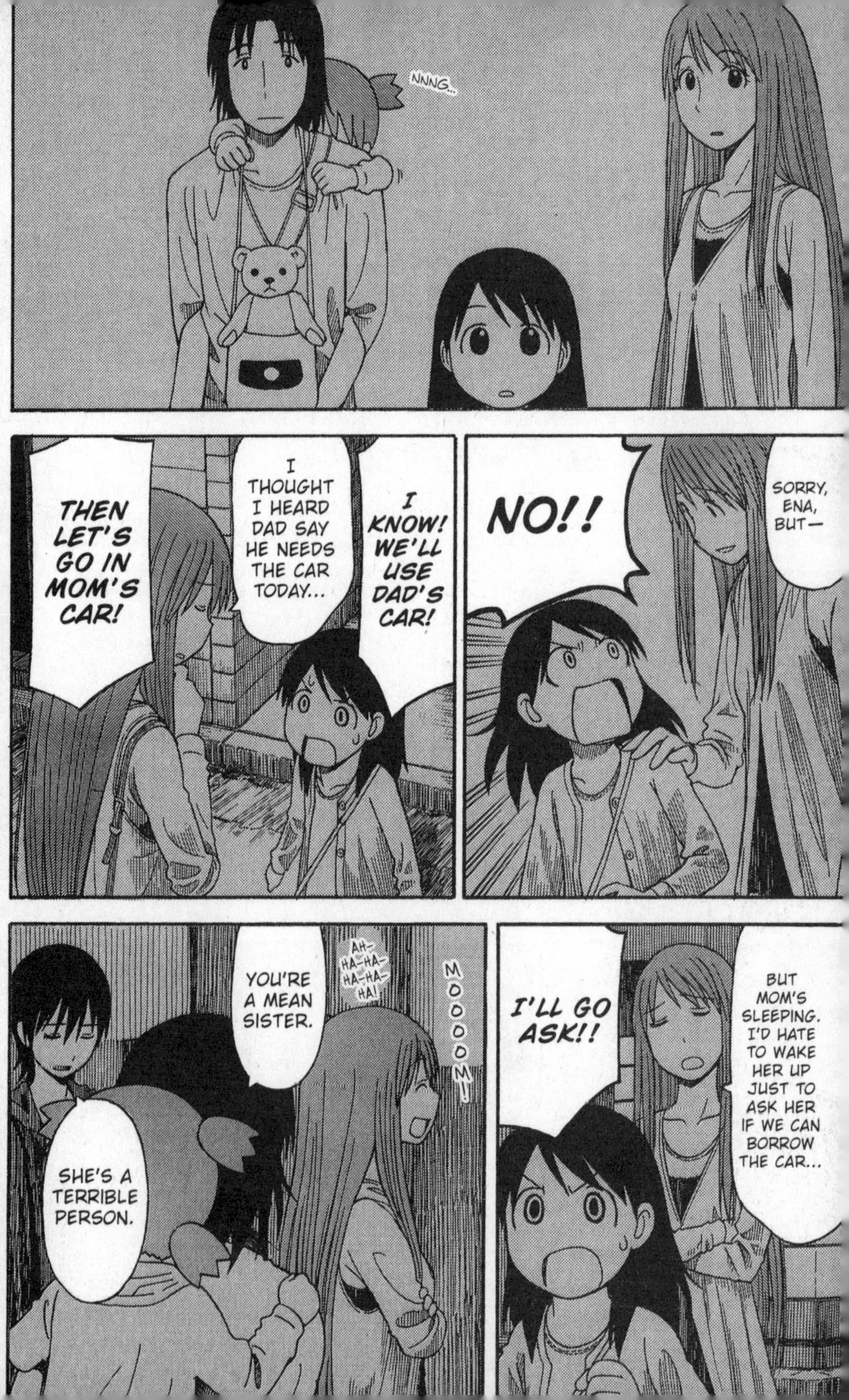
NNNG...
SORRY, ENA, BUT—
NO!!
I KNOW! WE'LL USE DAD'S CAR!
I THOUGHT I HEARD DAD SAY HE NEEDS THE CAR TODAY...
THEN LET'S GO IN MOM'S CAR!
BUT MOM'S SLEEPING. I'D HATE TO WAKE HER UP JUST TO ASK HER IF WE CAN BORROW THE CAR...
I'LL GO ASK!!
MOOOOOM!
AH-HA-HA-HA-HA-HA!
YOU'RE A MEAN SISTER.
SHE'S A TERRIBLE PERSON.

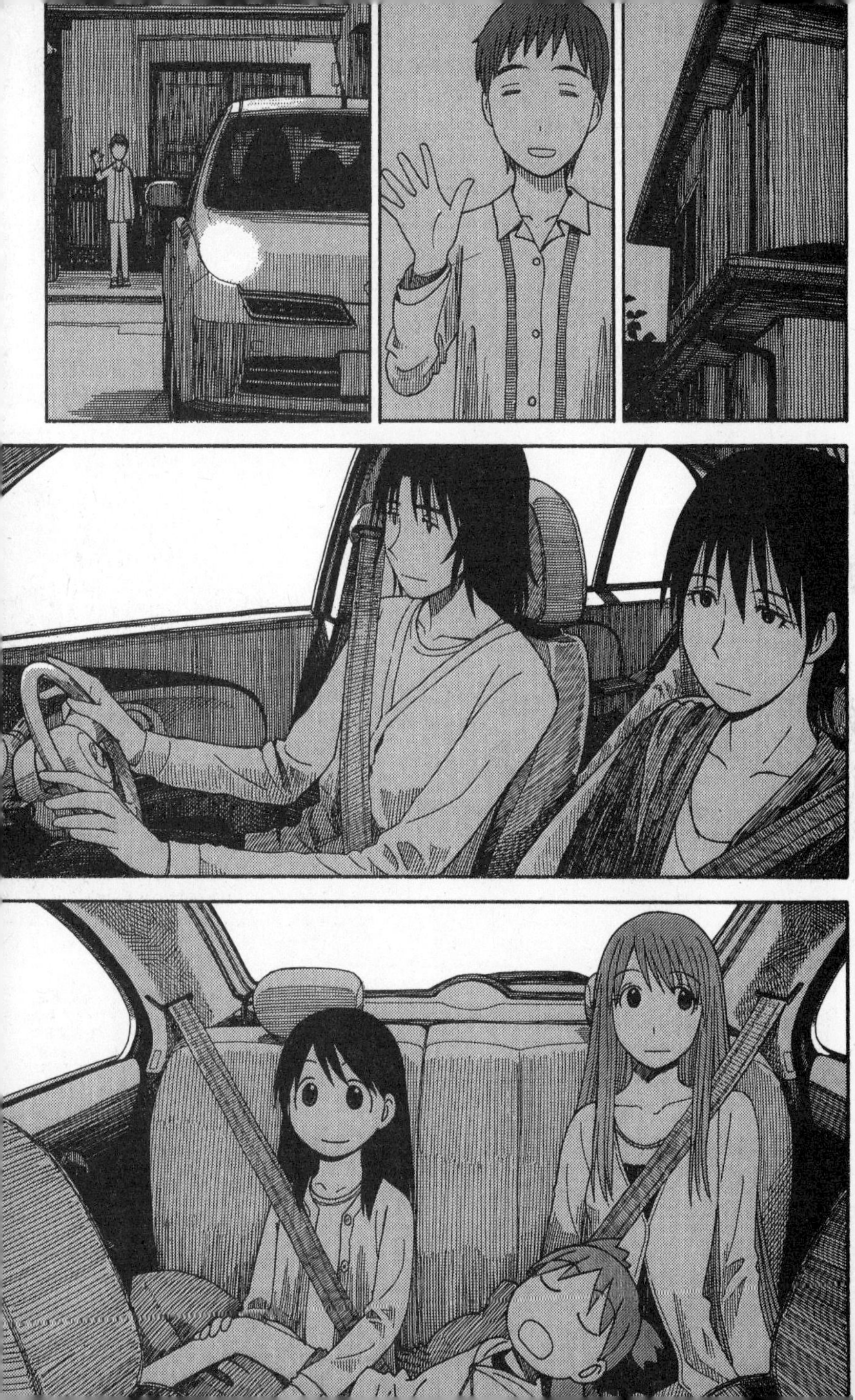

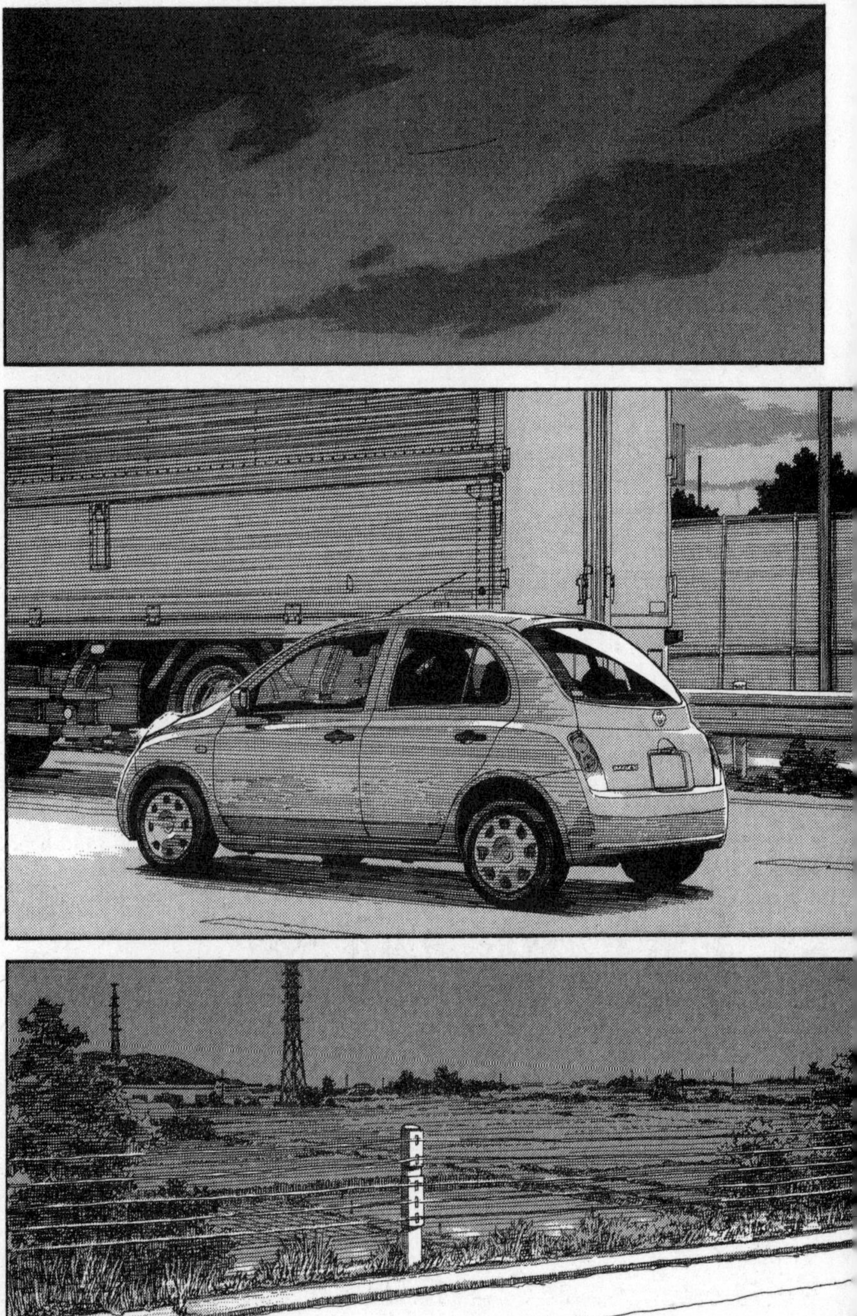

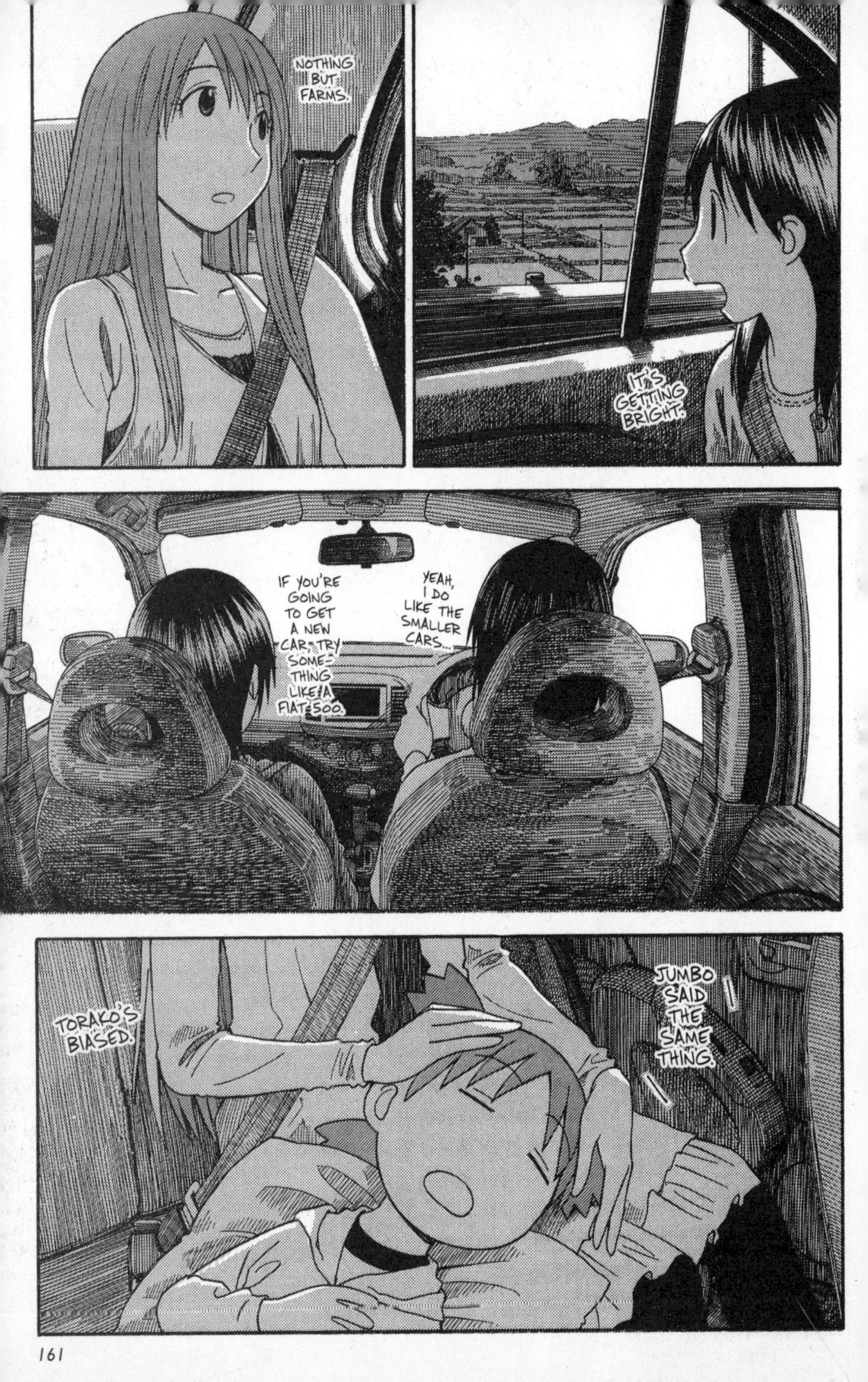
IT'S GETTING BRIGHT.
NOTHING BUT FARMS.
YEAH, I DO LIKE THE SMALLER CARS...
IF YOU'RE GOING TO GET A NEW CAR, TRY SOME-THING LIKE A FIAT 500.
JUMBO SAID THE SAME THING.
TORAKO'S BIASED.

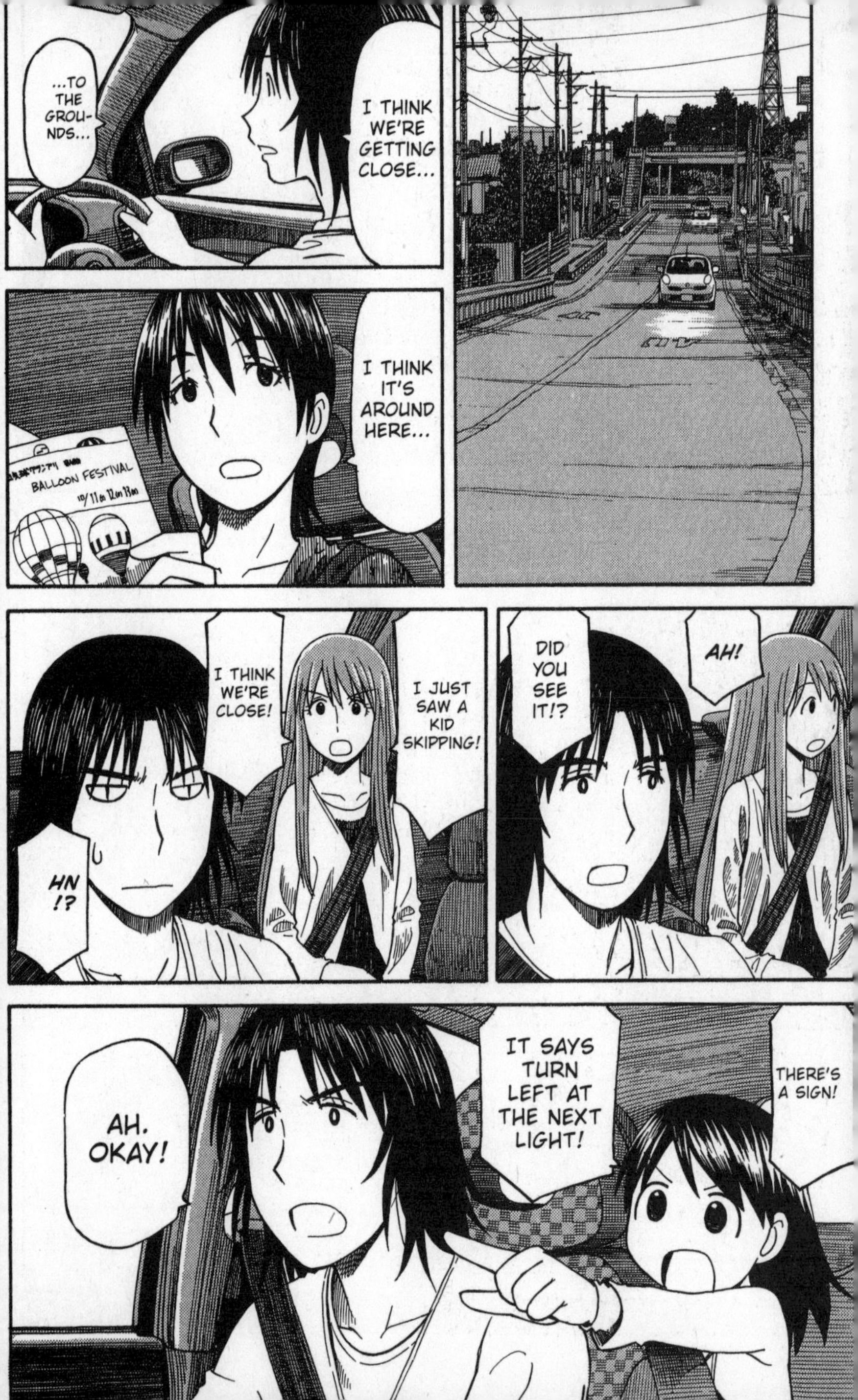
I THINK WE'RE GETTING CLOSE...
...TO THE GROUNDS...
I THINK IT'S AROUND HERE...
BALLOON FESTIVAL
AH!
DID YOU SEE IT!?
I JUST SAW A KID SKIPPING!
I THINK WE'RE CLOSE!
HN!?
THERE'S A SIGN!
IT SAYS TURN LEFT AT THE NEXT LIGHT!
AH. OKAY!

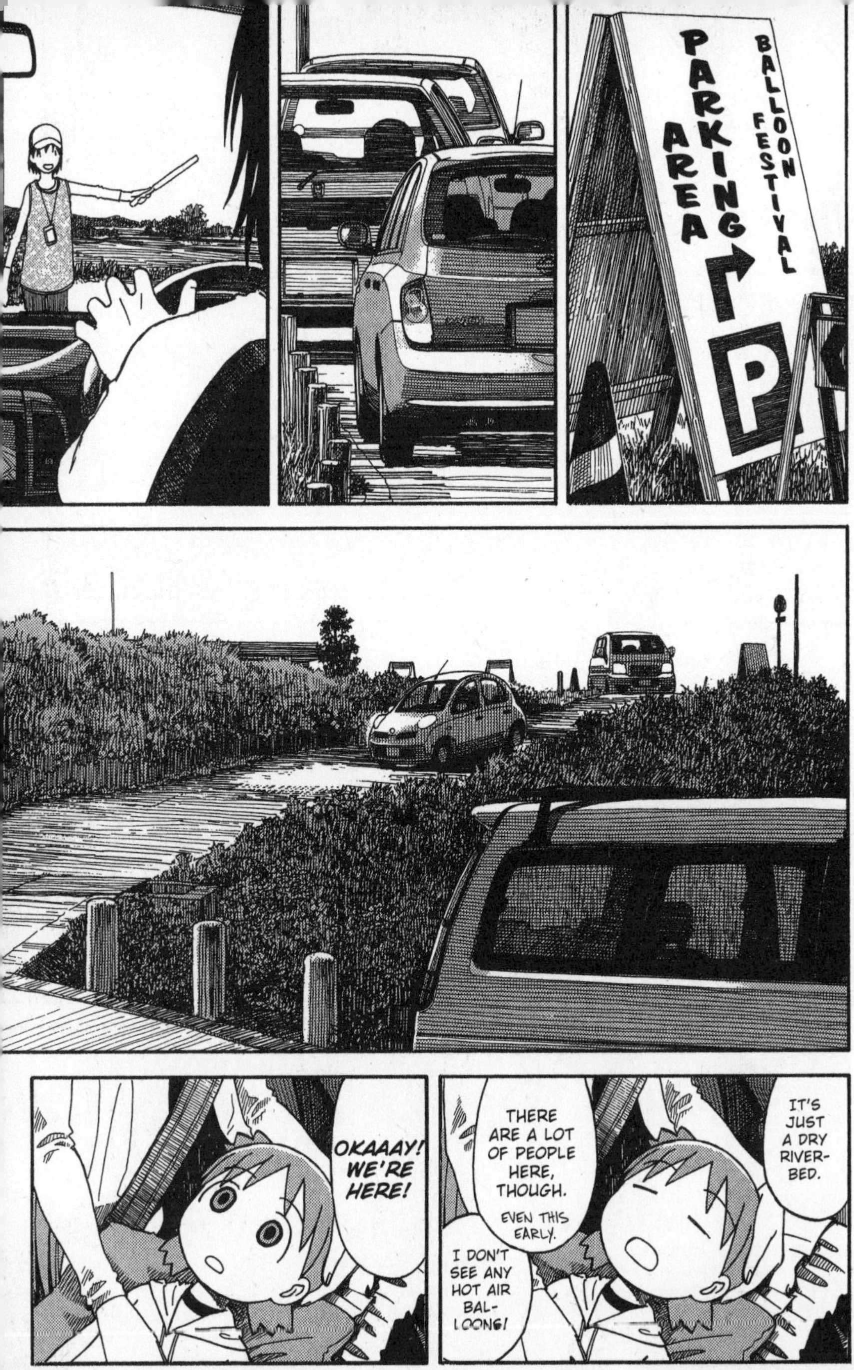
BALLOON FESTIVAL
PARKING AREA
IT'S JUST A DRY RIVERBED.
THERE ARE A LOT OF PEOPLE HERE, THOUGH.
EVEN THIS EARLY.
I DON'T SEE ANY HOT AIR BAL-LOONS!
OKAAAY! WE'RE HERE!

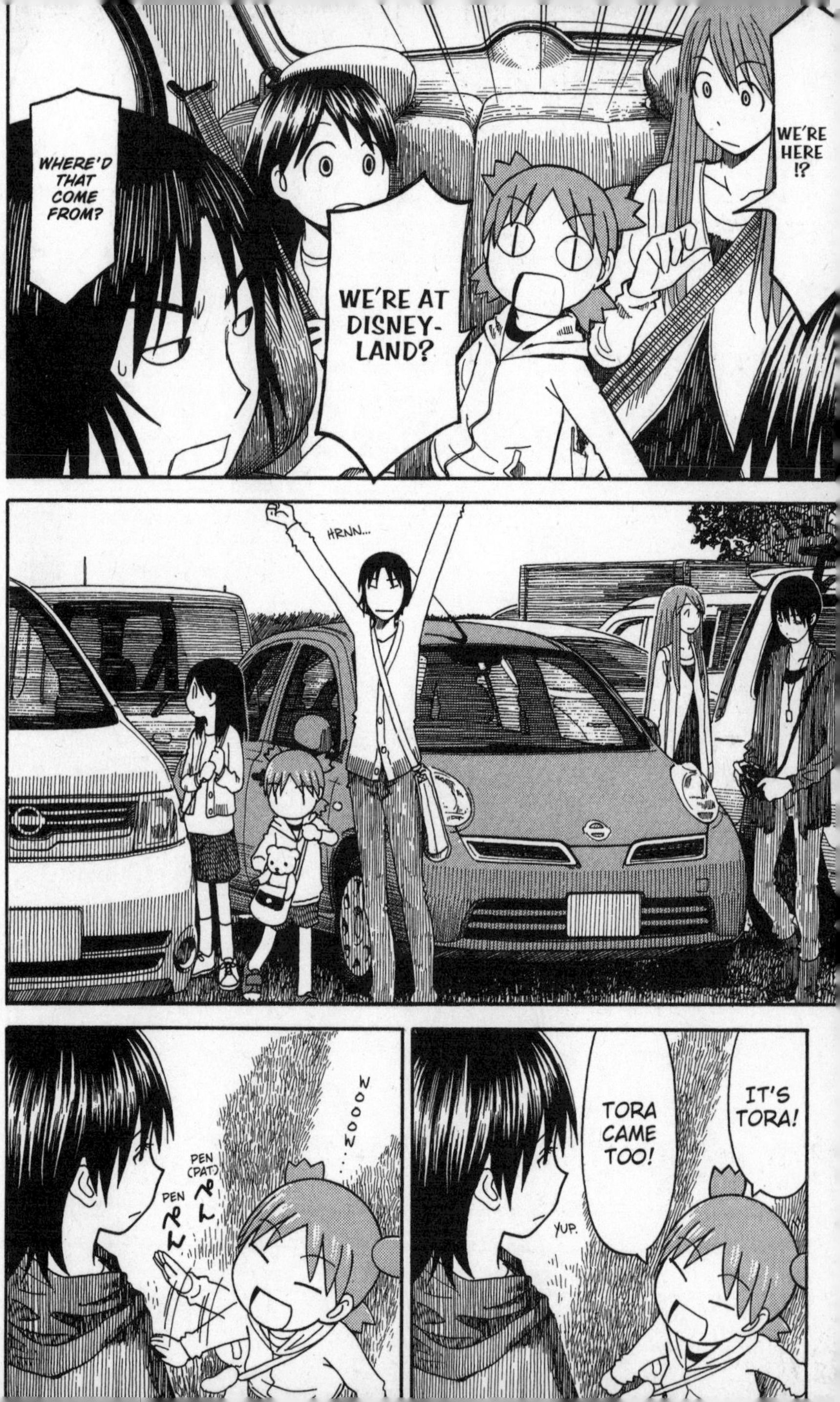
WE'RE HERE !?
WE'RE AT DISNEY-LAND?
WHERE'D THAT COME FROM?
HRNN...
IT'S TORA!
TORA CAME TOO!
YUP.
WOOOW...
PEN (PAT) ぺん
PEN ぺん

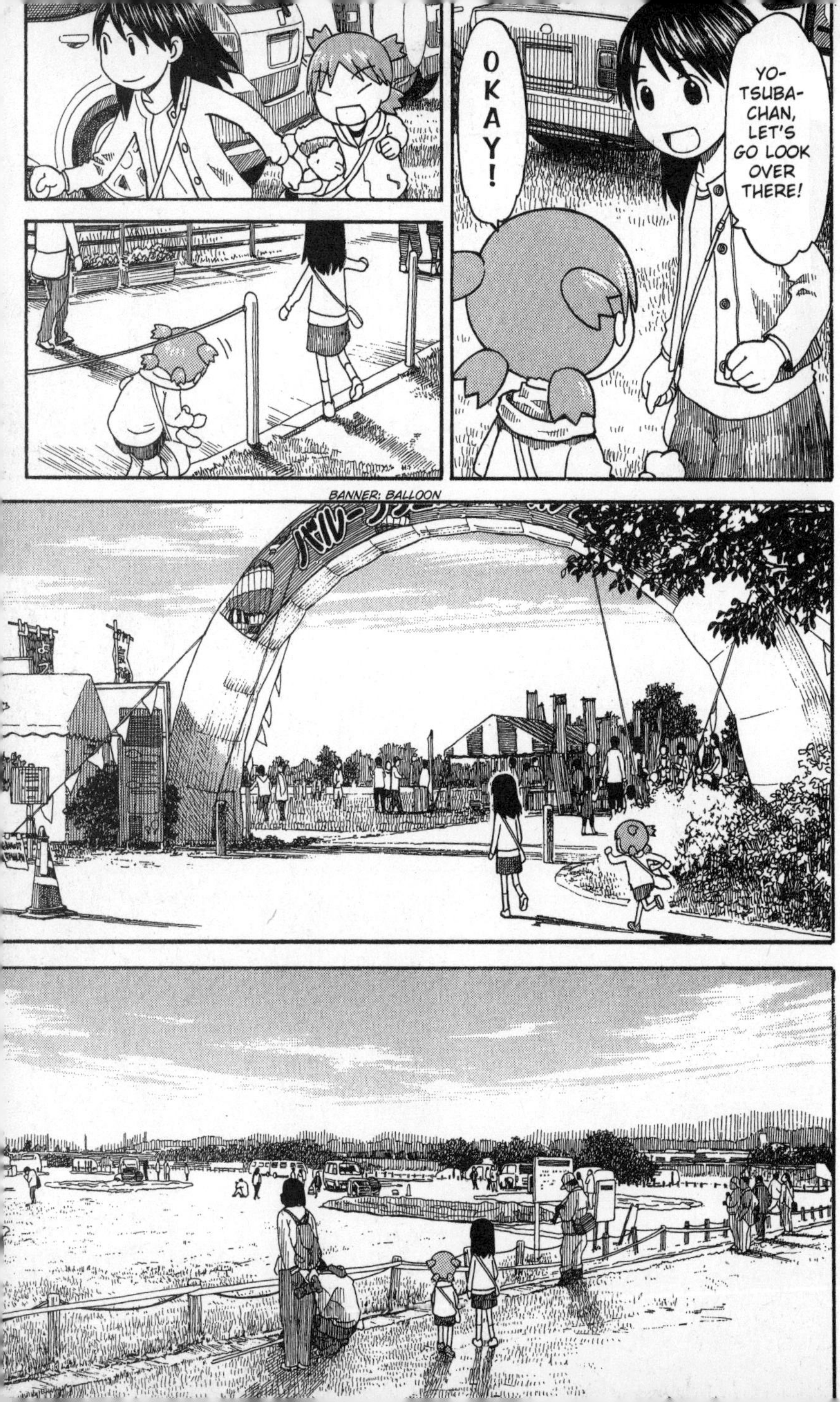
YO-TSUBA-CHAN, LET'S GO LOOK OVER THERE!
OKAY!
BANNER: BALLOON

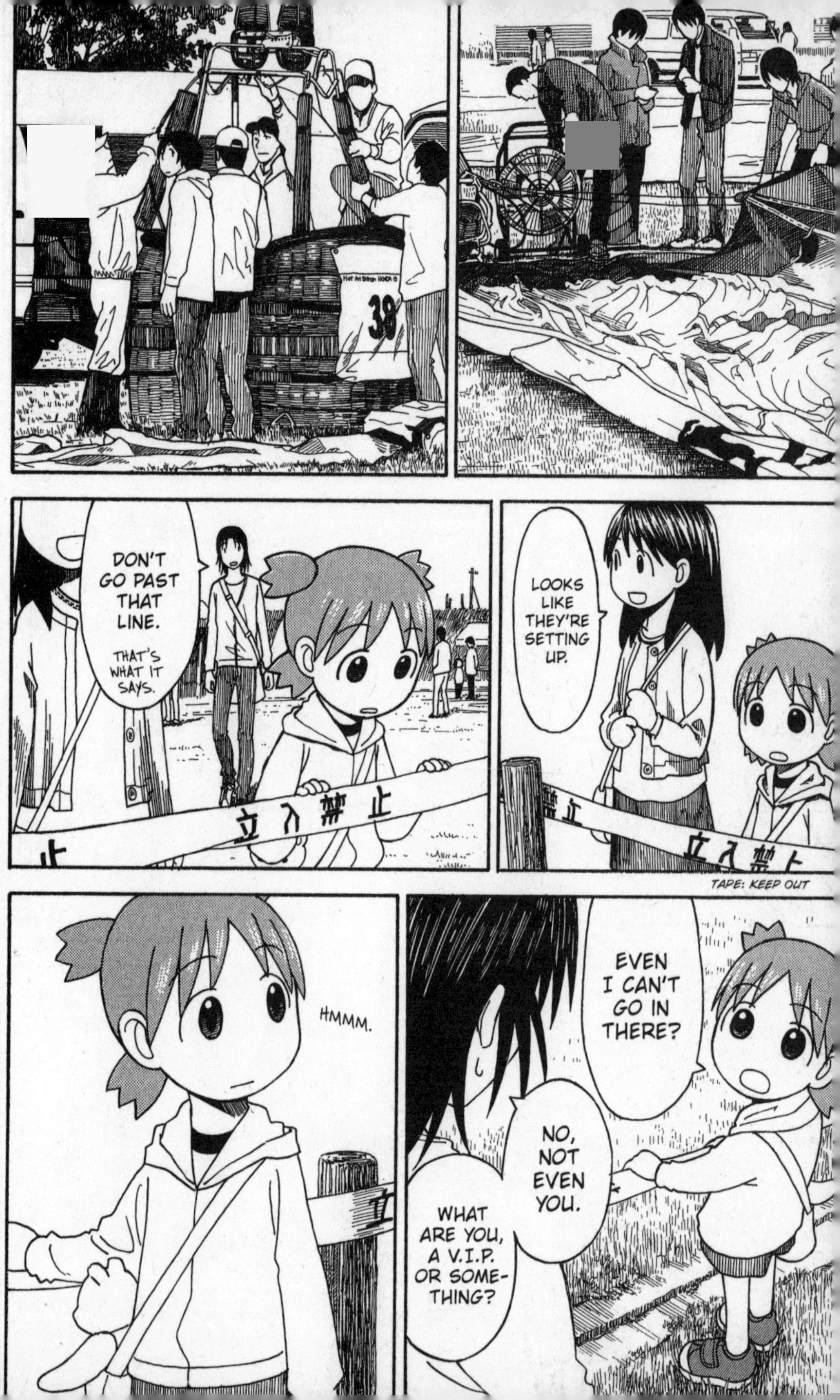
Hot Air Balloon
38
LOOKS LIKE THEY'RE SETTING UP.
立入禁止
DON'T GO PAST THAT LINE.
THAT'S WHAT IT SAYS.
立入禁止
TAPE: KEEP OUT
EVEN I CAN'T GO IN THERE?
NO, NOT EVEN YOU.
WHAT ARE YOU, A V.I.P. OR SOME-THING?
HMMM.

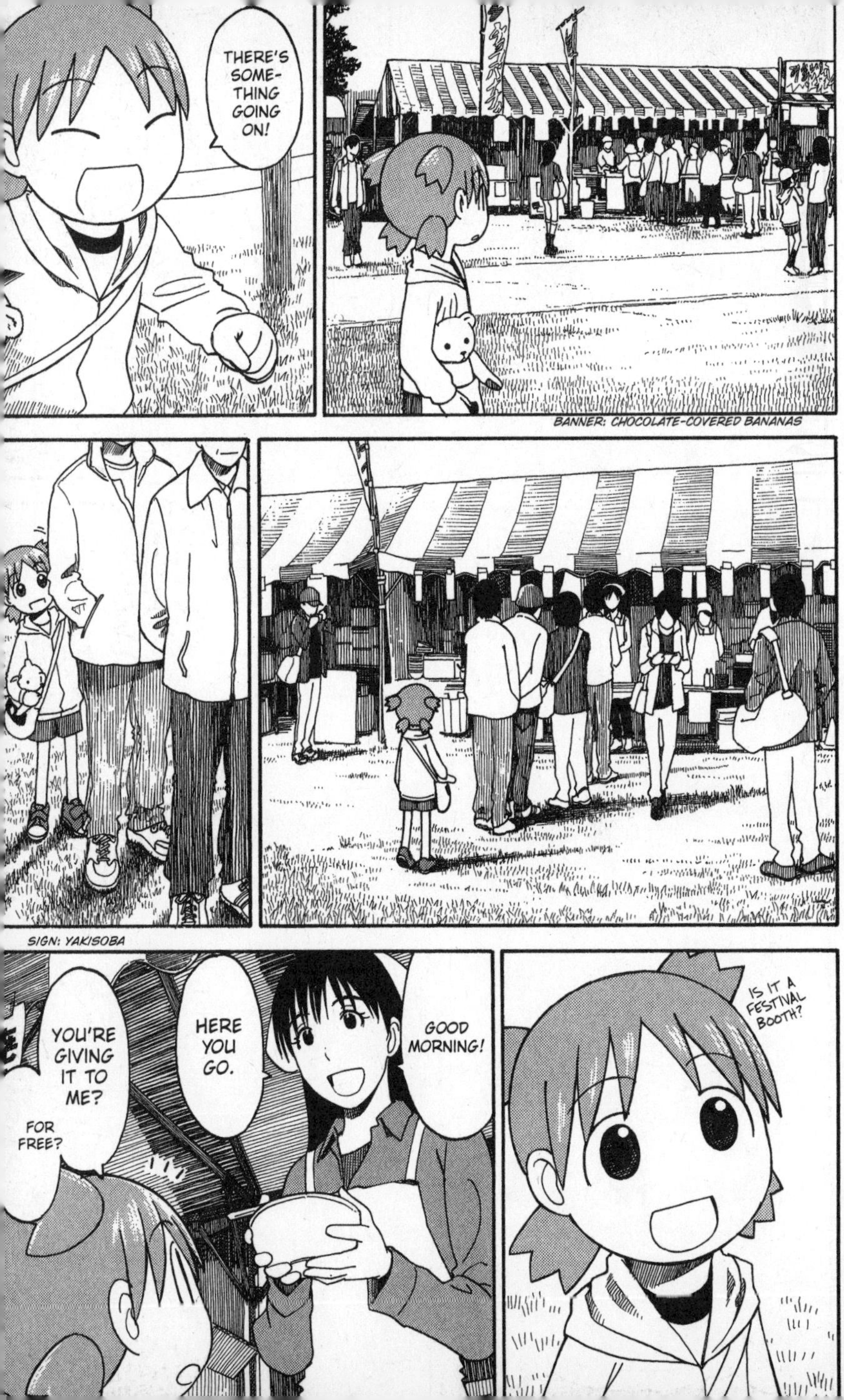
BANNER: CHOCOLATE-COVERED BANANAS
THERE'S SOME-THING GOING ON!
SIGN: YAKISOBA
IS IT A FESTIVAL BOOTH?
GOOD MORNING!
HERE YOU GO.
YOU'RE GIVING IT TO ME?
FOR FREE?

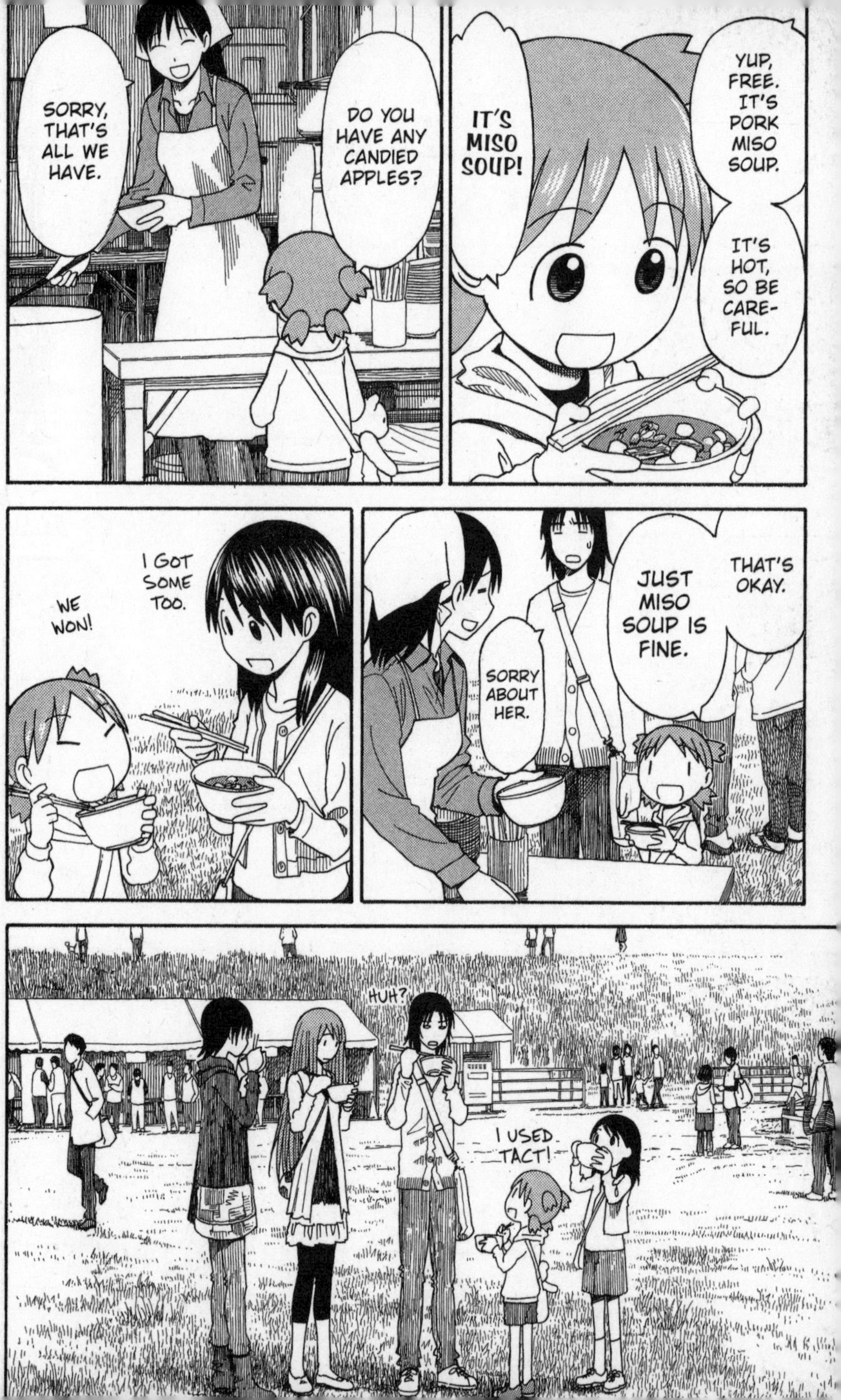
YUP, FREE. IT'S PORK MISO SOUP.
IT'S HOT, SO BE CAREFUL.
IT'S MISO SOUP!
DO YOU HAVE ANY CANDIED APPLES?
SORRY, THAT'S ALL WE HAVE.
THAT'S OKAY.
JUST MISO SOUP IS FINE.
SORRY ABOUT HER.
I GOT SOME TOO.
WE WON!
I USED TACT!
HUH?

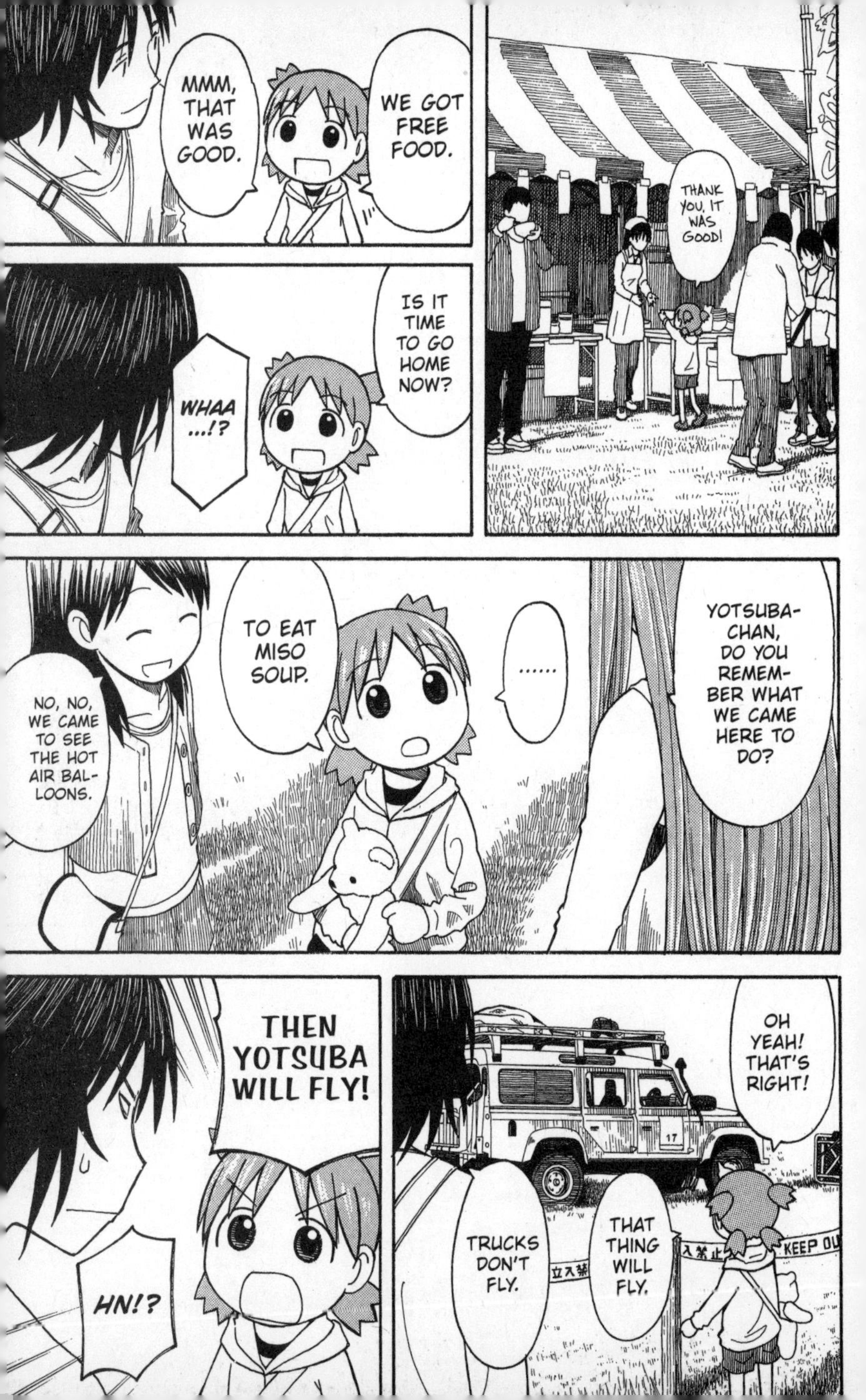
THANK YOU, IT WAS GOOD!
WE GOT FREE FOOD.
MMM, THAT WAS GOOD.
IS IT TIME TO GO HOME NOW?
WHAA ...!?
YOTSUBA-CHAN, DO YOU REMEMBER WHAT WE CAME HERE TO DO?
......
TO EAT MISO SOUP.
NO, NO, WE CAME TO SEE THE HOT AIR BALLOONS.
OH YEAH! THAT'S RIGHT!
THAT THING WILL FLY.
TRUCKS DON'T FLY.
THEN YOTSUBA WILL FLY!
HN!?

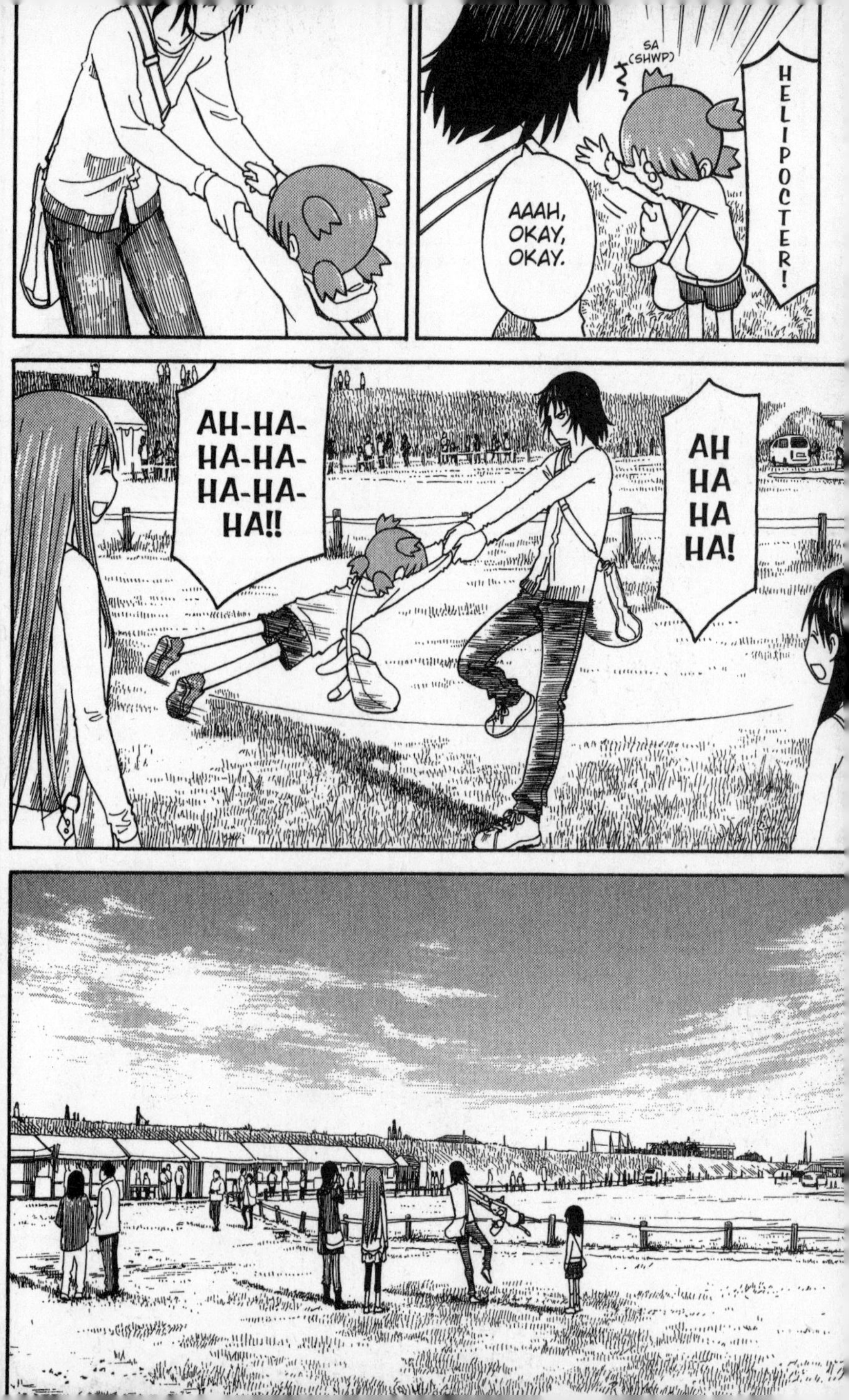
HELIPOCTER!
SA (SHWP)
AAAH, OKAY, OKAY.
AH HA HA HA!
AH-HA-HA-HA-HA-HA-HA!!

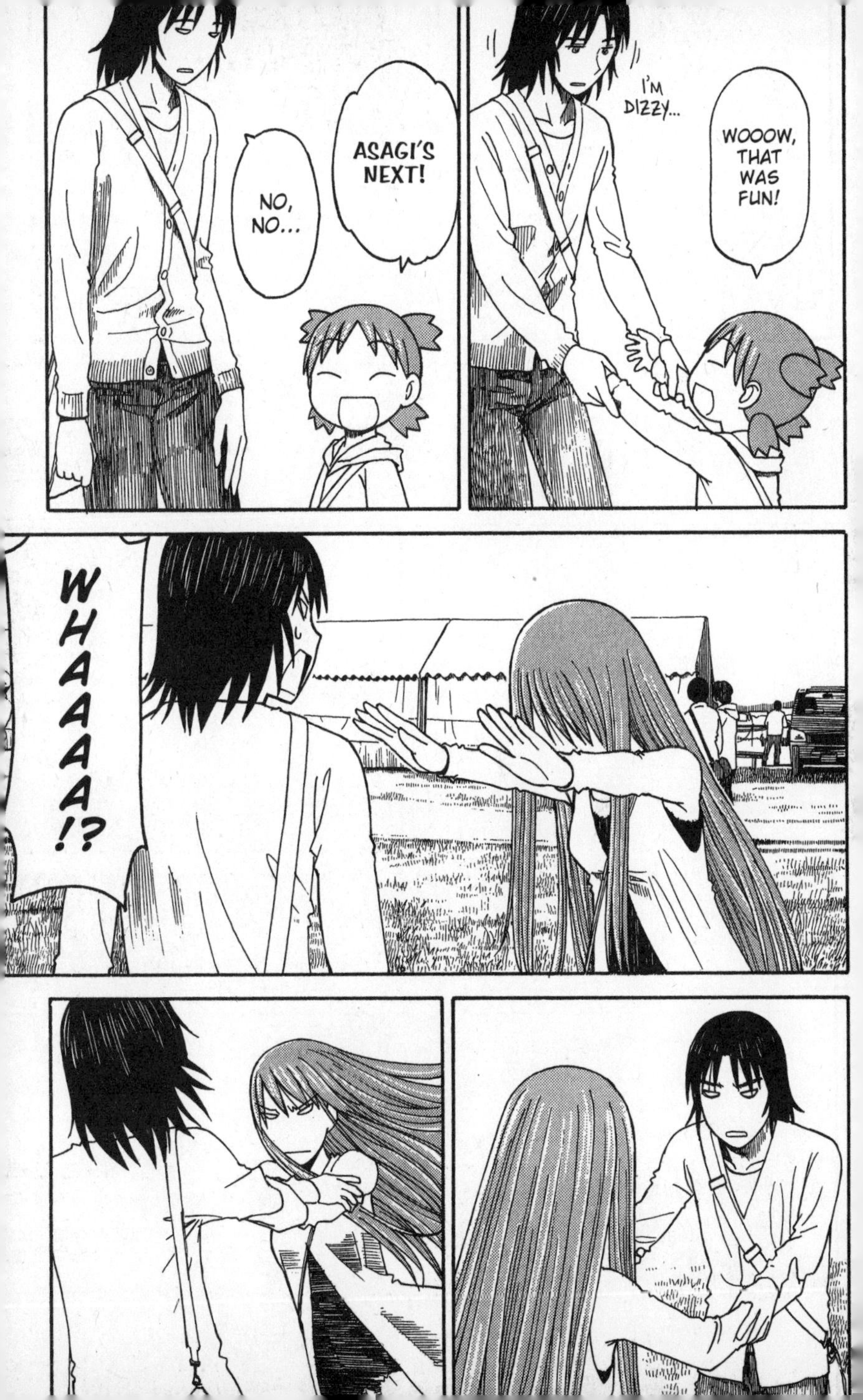
WOOOW, THAT WAS FUN!
I'M DIZZY...
ASAGI'S NEXT!
NO, NO...
WHAAAAA!?

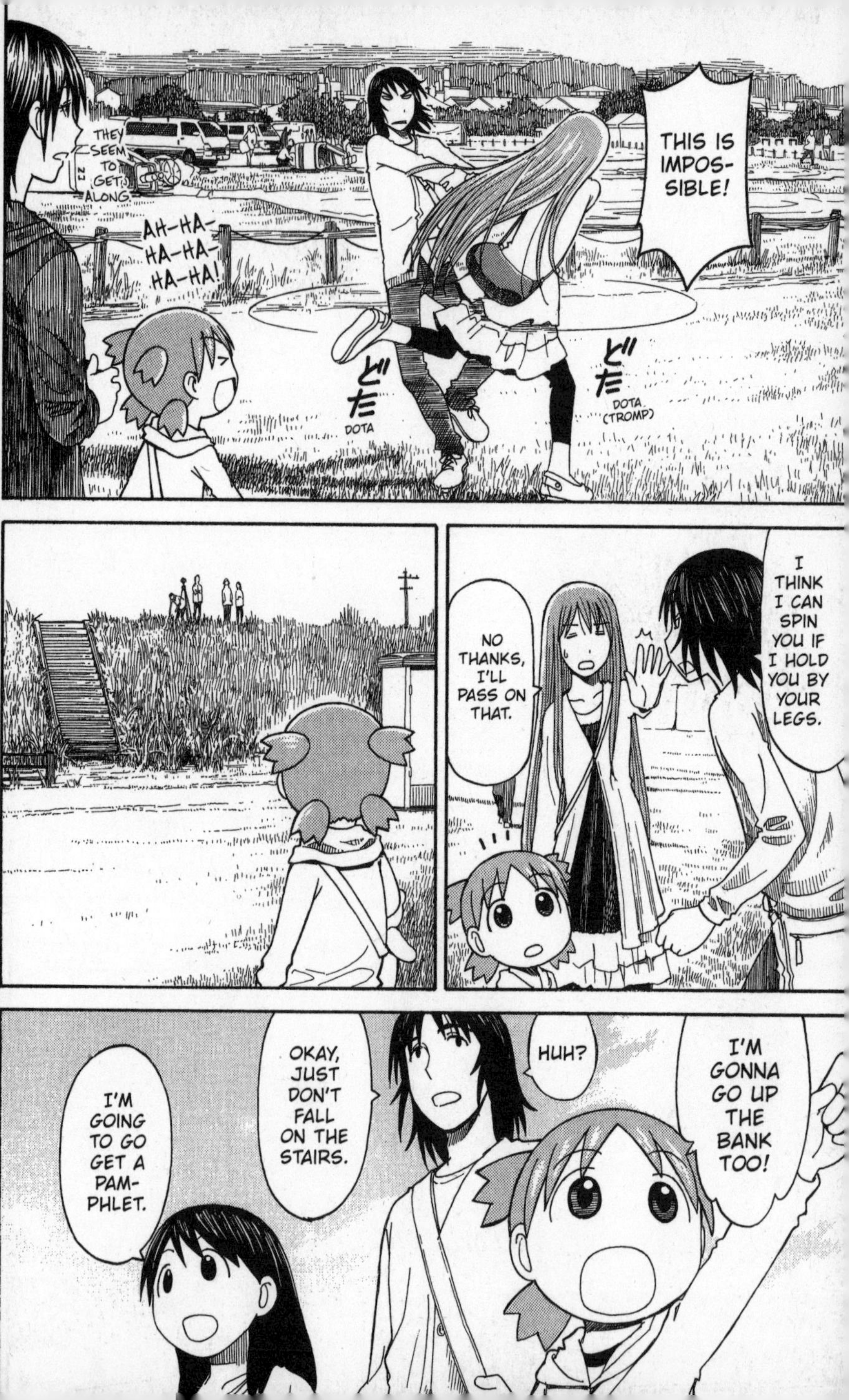
THIS IS IMPOSSIBLE!
どた
DOTA (TROMP)
どた
DOTA
AH-HA-HA-HA-HA-HA!
THEY SEEM TO GET ALONG.
I THINK I CAN SPIN YOU IF I HOLD YOU BY YOUR LEGS.
NO THANKS, I'LL PASS ON THAT.
I'M GONNA GO UP THE BANK TOO!
HUH?
OKAY, JUST DON'T FALL ON THE STAIRS.
I'M GOING TO GO GET A PAMPHLET.

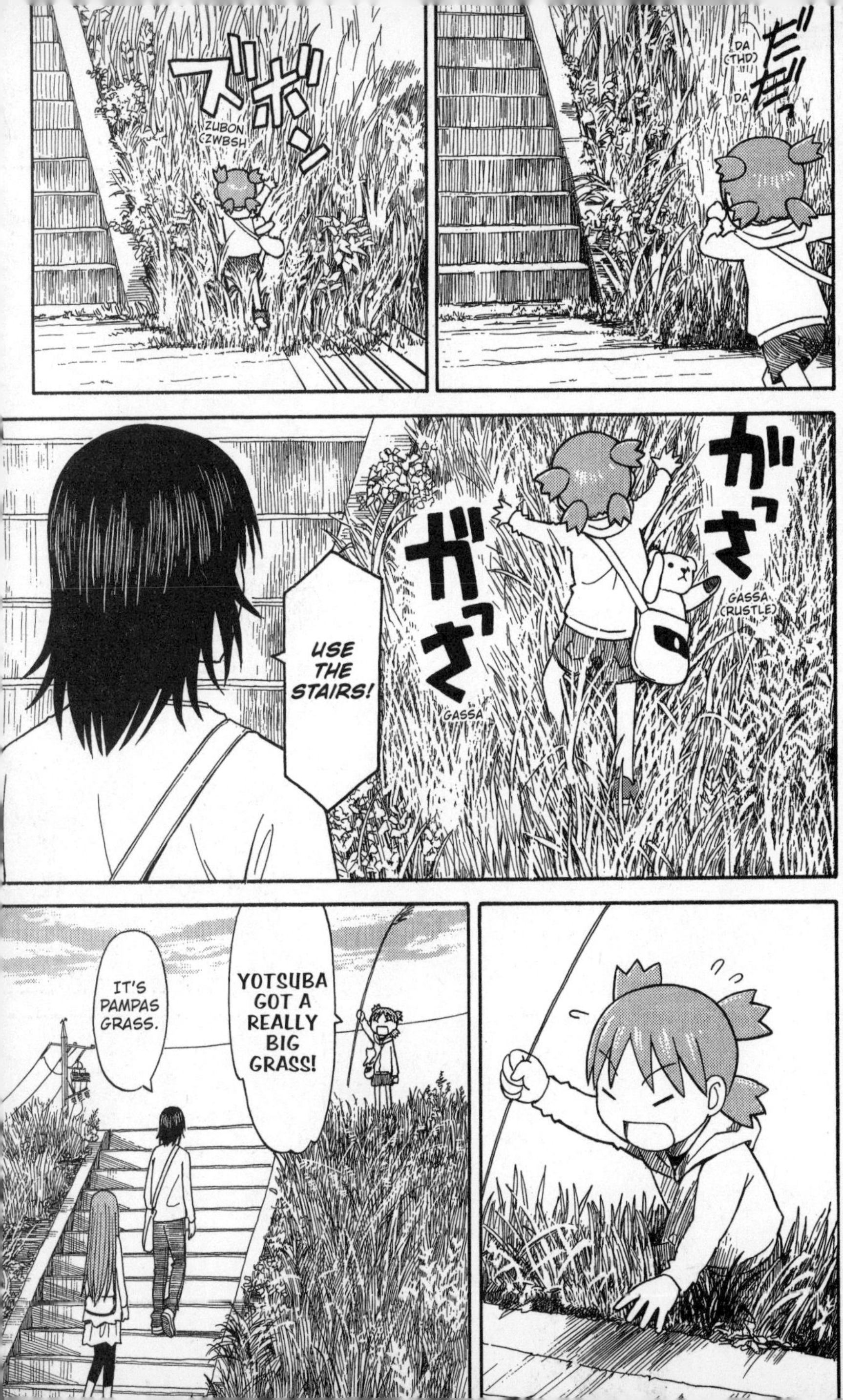
ダッ ダッ
DA (THD) DA
ズボン
ZUBON (ZWBSH)
がっさ
GASSA (RUSTLE)
がっさ
GASSA
USE THE STAIRS!
YOTSUBA GOT A REALLY BIG GRASS!
IT'S PAMPAS GRASS.

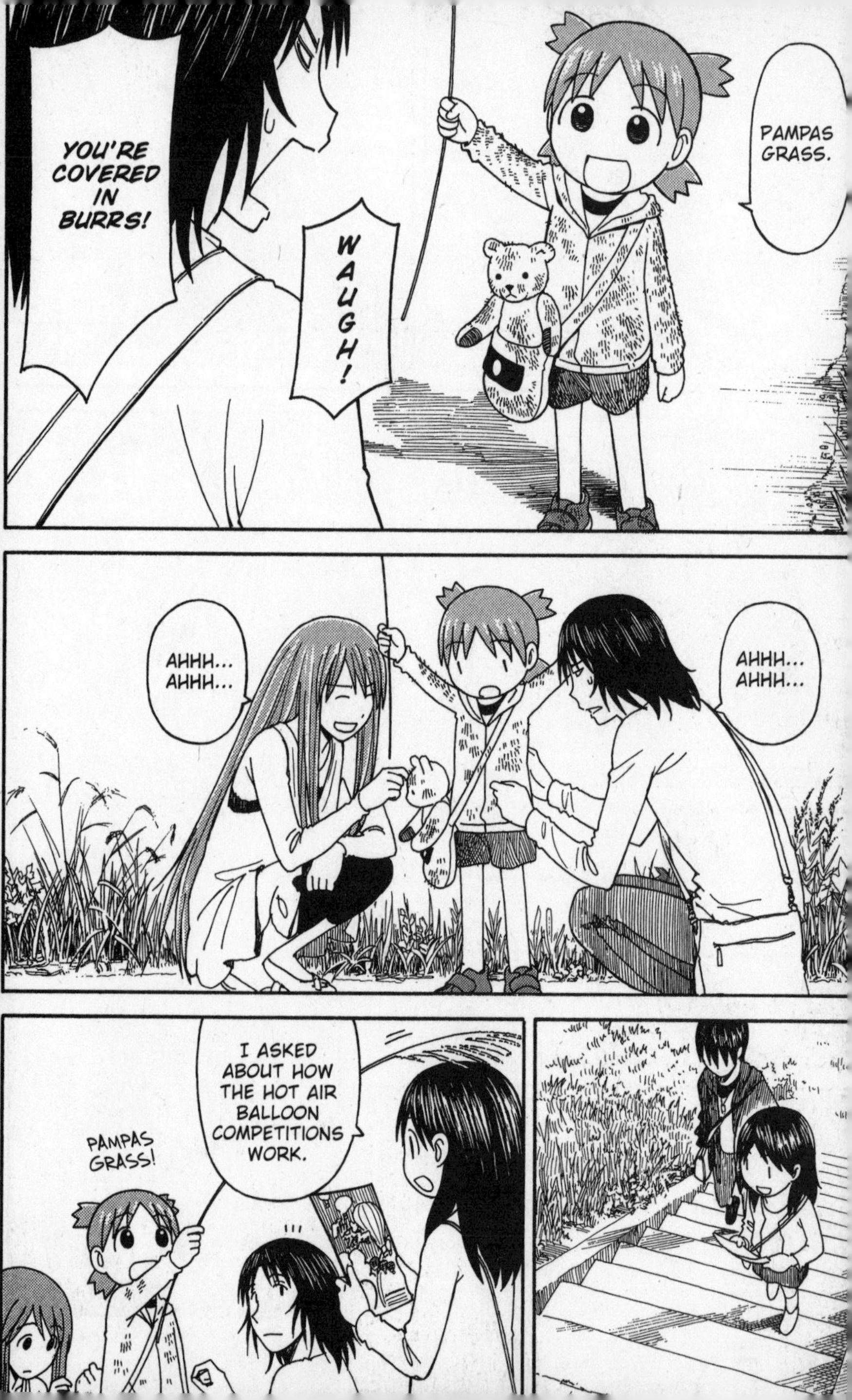
PAMPAS GRASS.
WAUGH!
YOU'RE COVERED IN BURRS!
AHHH... AHHH...
AHHH... AHHH...
I ASKED ABOUT HOW THE HOT AIR BALLOON COMPETITIONS WORK.
PAMPAS GRASS!

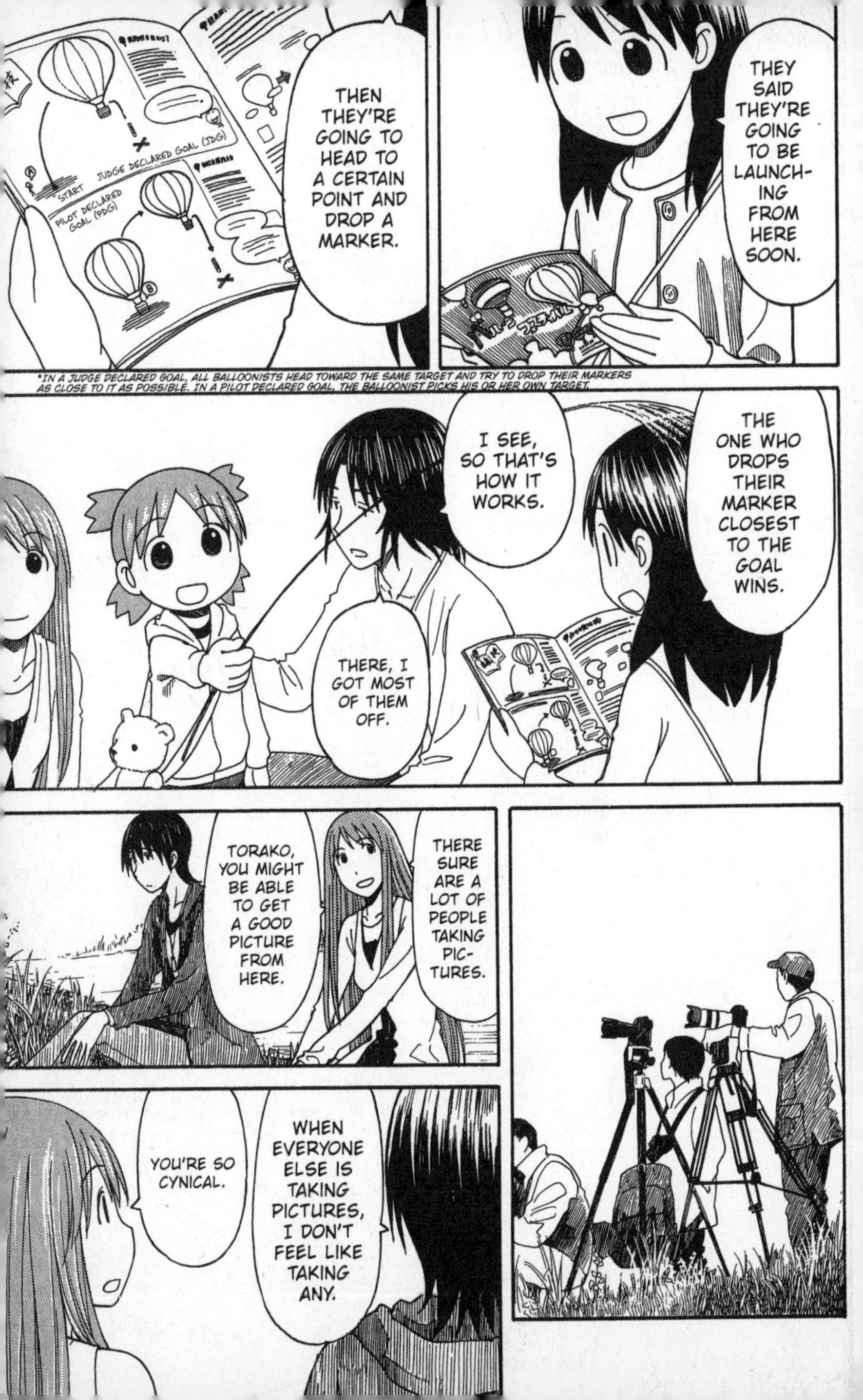
THEY SAID THEY'RE GOING TO BE LAUNCH-ING FROM HERE SOON.
JUDGE DECLARED GOAL (JDG)
START
PILOT DECLARED GOAL (PDG)
THEN THEY'RE GOING TO HEAD TO A CERTAIN POINT AND DROP A MARKER.
THE ONE WHO DROPS THEIR MARKER CLOSEST TO THE GOAL WINS.
I SEE, SO THAT'S HOW IT WORKS.
THERE, I GOT MOST OF THEM OFF.
THERE SURE ARE A LOT OF PEOPLE TAKING PIC-TURES.
TORAKO, YOU MIGHT BE ABLE TO GET A GOOD PICTURE FROM HERE.
WHEN EVERYONE ELSE IS TAKING PICTURES, I DON'T FEEL LIKE TAKING ANY.
YOU'RE SO CYNICAL.

*IN A JUDGE DECLARED GOAL, ALL BALLOONISTS HEAD TOWARD THE SAME TARGET AND TRY TO DROP THEIR MARKERS AS CLOSE TO IT AS POSSIBLE. IN A PILOT DECLARED GOAL, THE BALLOONIST PICKS HIS OR HER OWN TARGET.

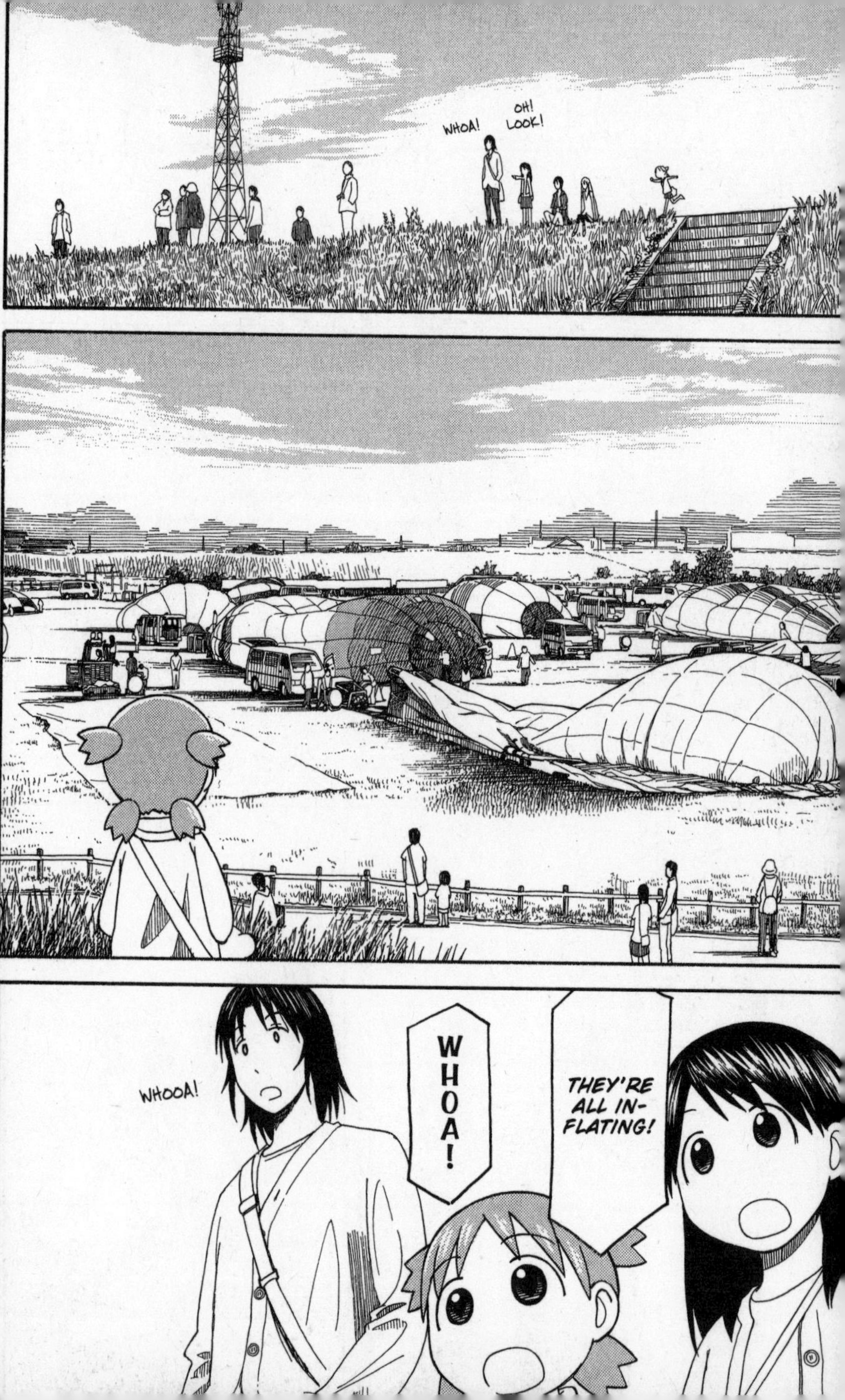
OH! LOOK!
WHOA!
THEY'RE ALL IN-FLATING!
WHOA!
WHOOA!

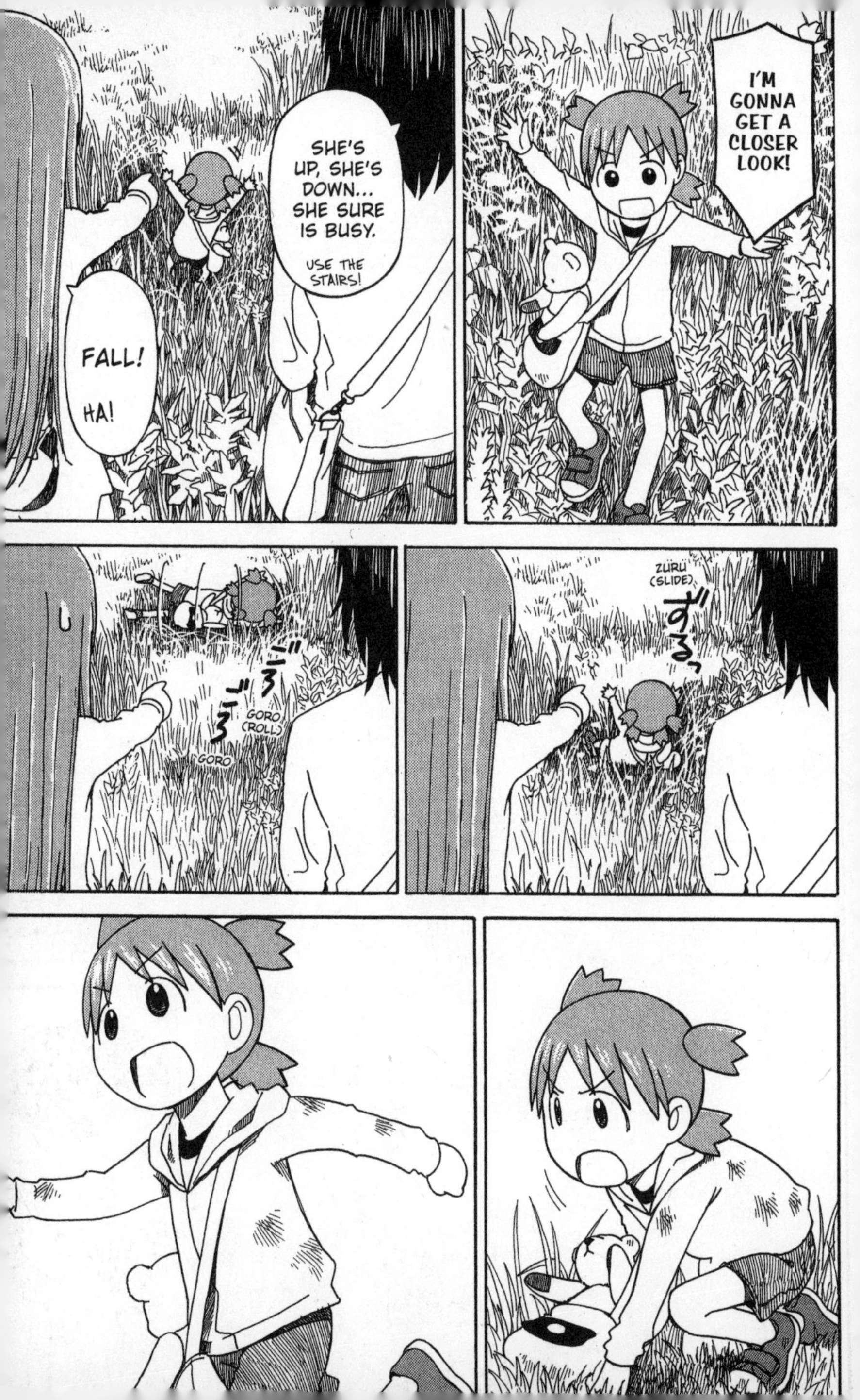
I'M GONNA GET A CLOSER LOOK!
SHE'S UP, SHE'S DOWN... SHE SURE IS BUSY.
USE THE STAIRS!
FALL!
HA!
ZURU (SLIDE)
ずるっ
ごろ
GORO (ROLL)
ごろ
GORO

ゴッオォォ
GOOOO
(ROOOOAR)

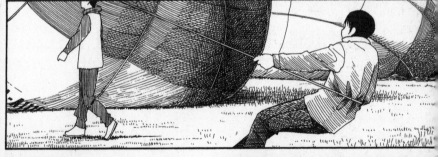

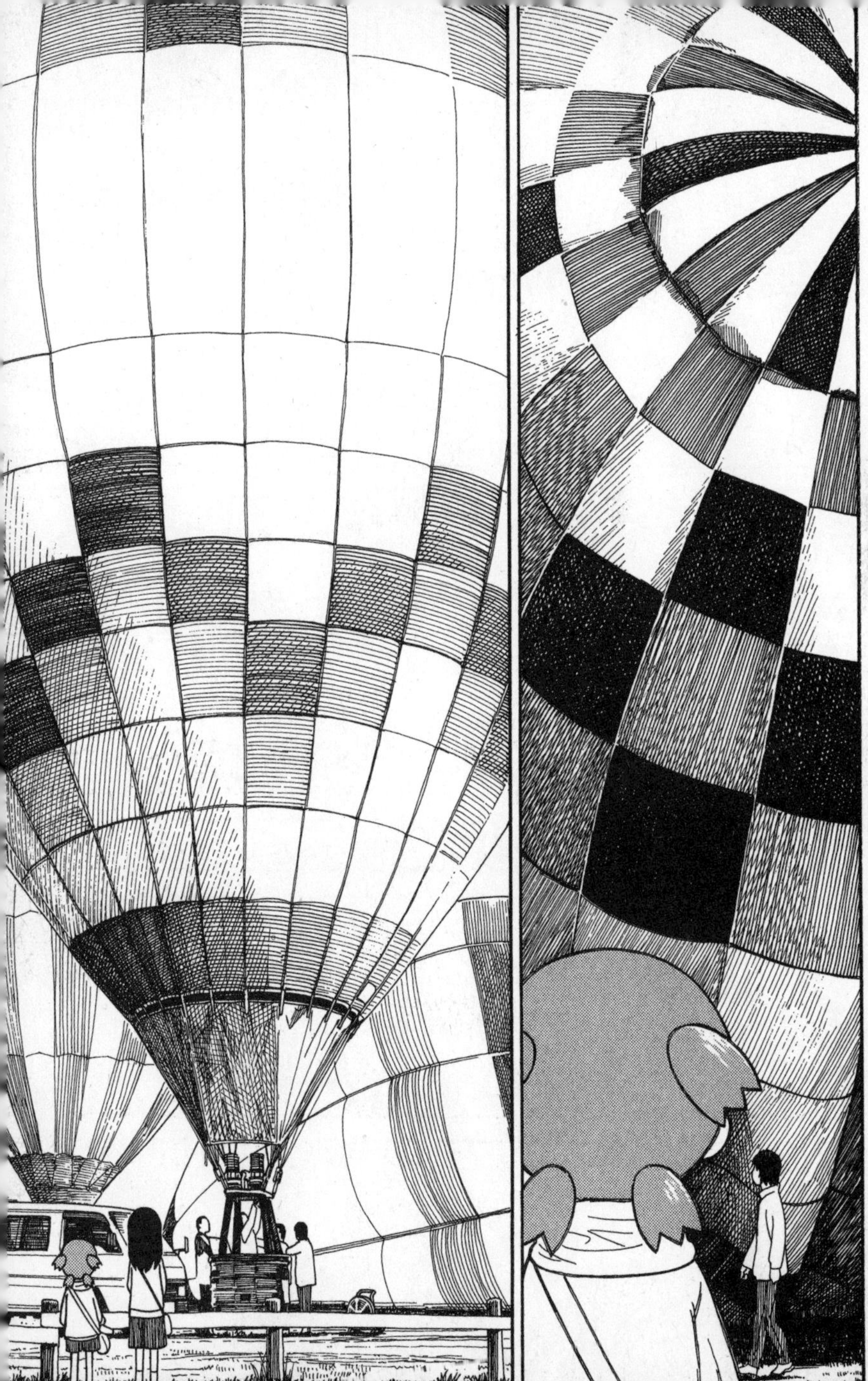

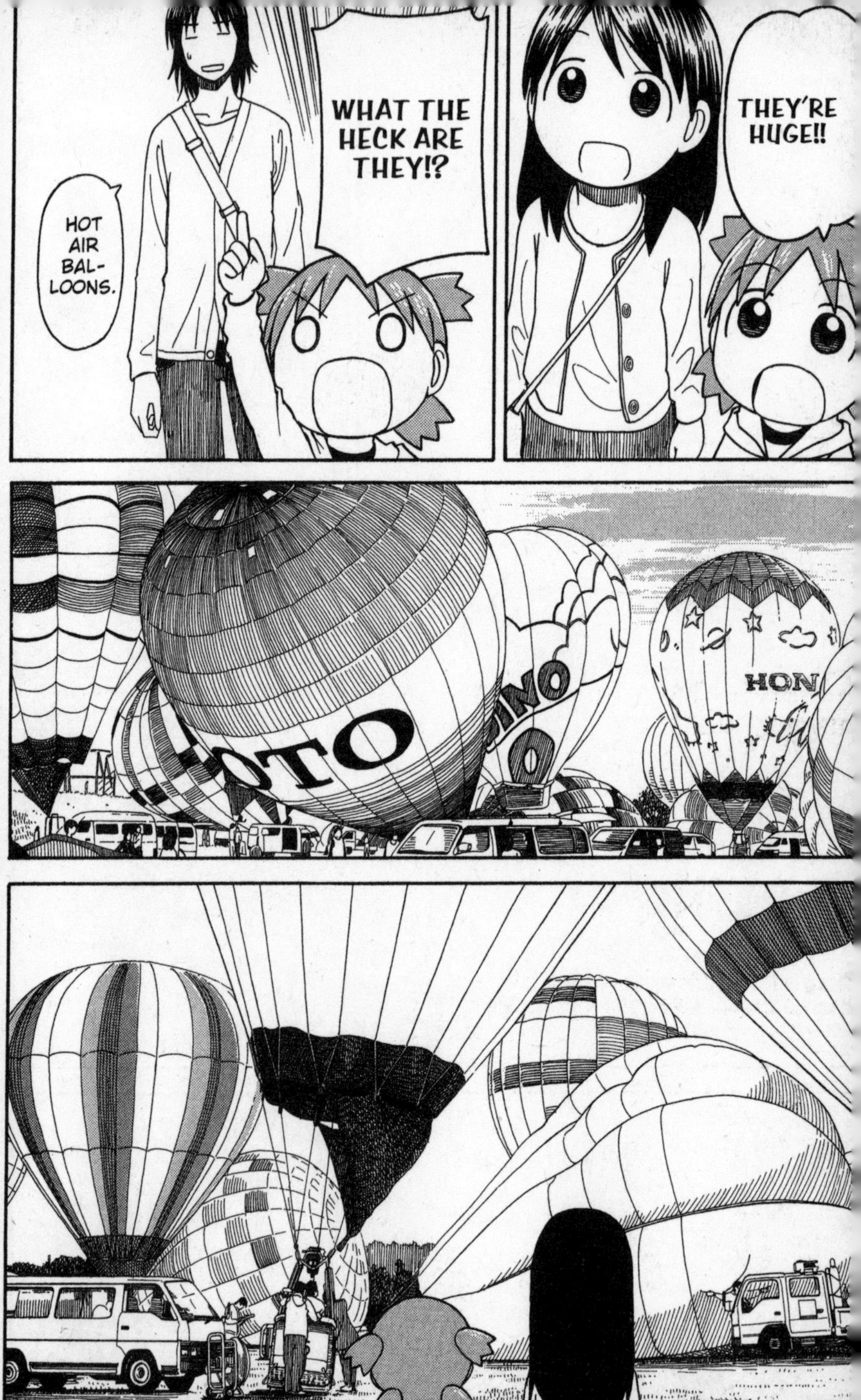
THEY'RE HUGE!!
WHAT THE HECK ARE THEY!?
HOT AIR BAL-LOONS.

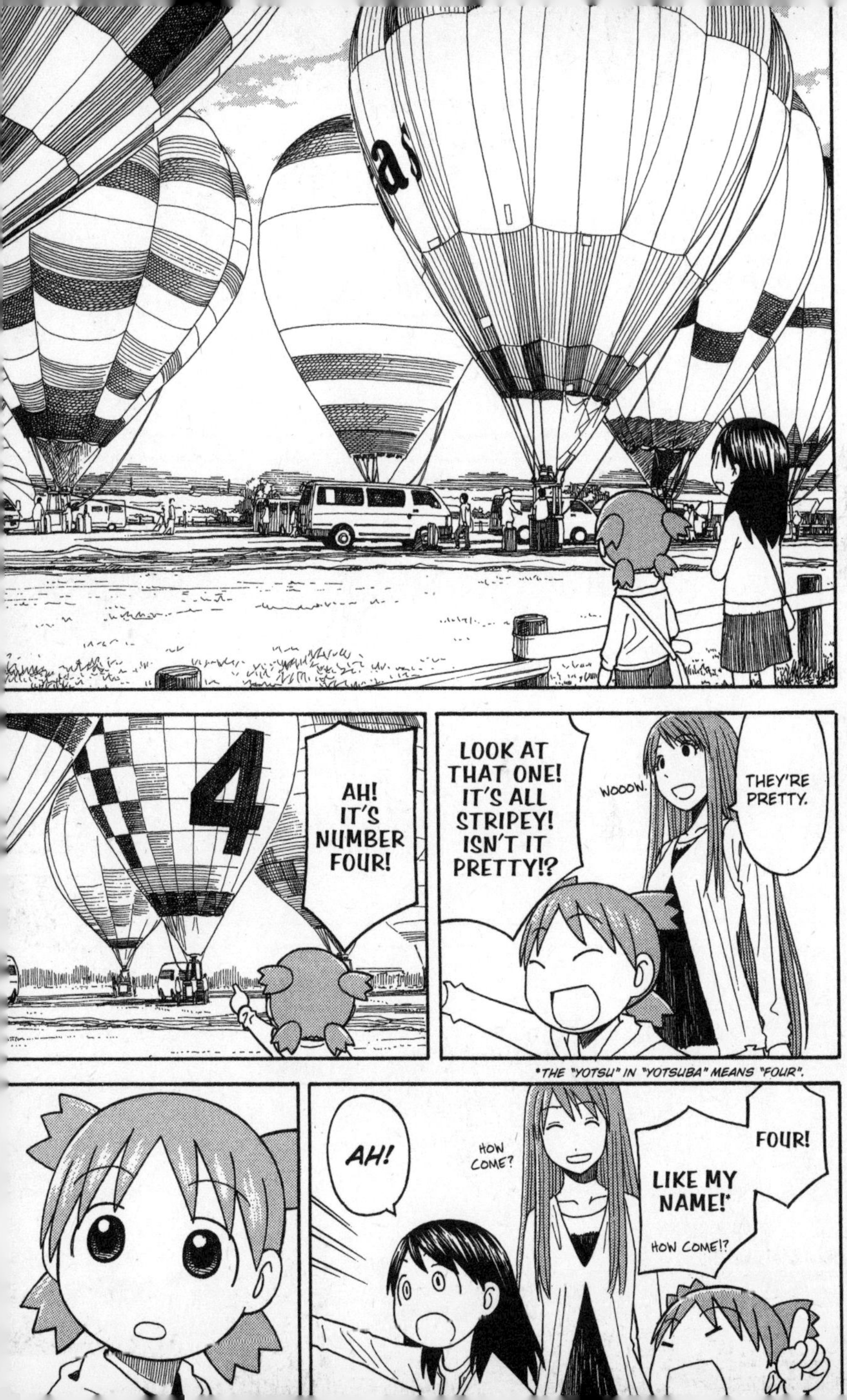
THEY'RE PRETTY.
WOOOW.
LOOK AT THAT ONE! IT'S ALL STRIPEY! ISN'T IT PRETTY!?
AH! IT'S NUMBER FOUR!
*THE "YOTSU" IN "YOTSUBA" MEANS "FOUR".
FOUR!
LIKE MY NAME!*
HOW COME?
AH!
HOW COME!?

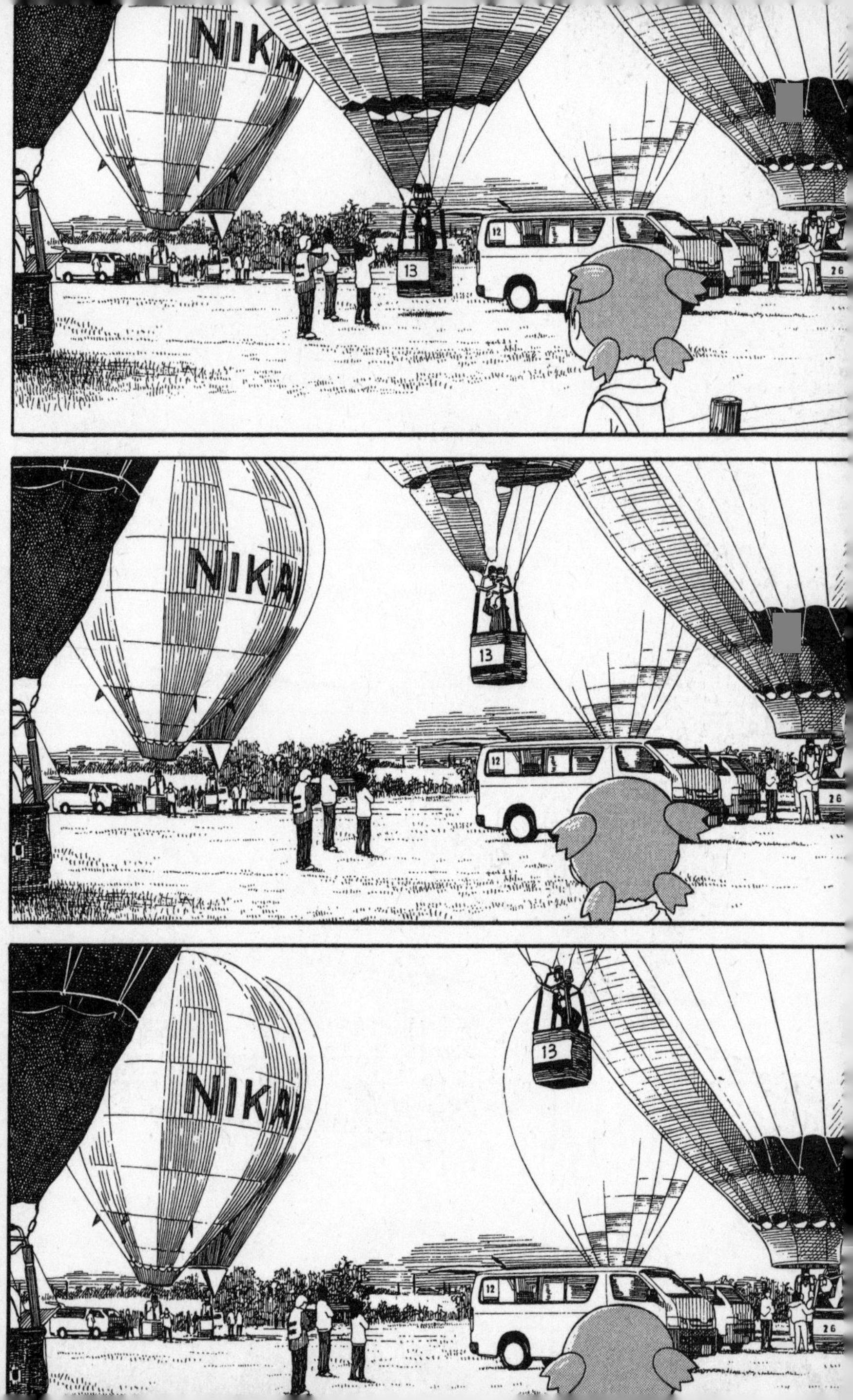
26
12
13
NIKA
26
12
13
NIKA
26
12
13
NIKA

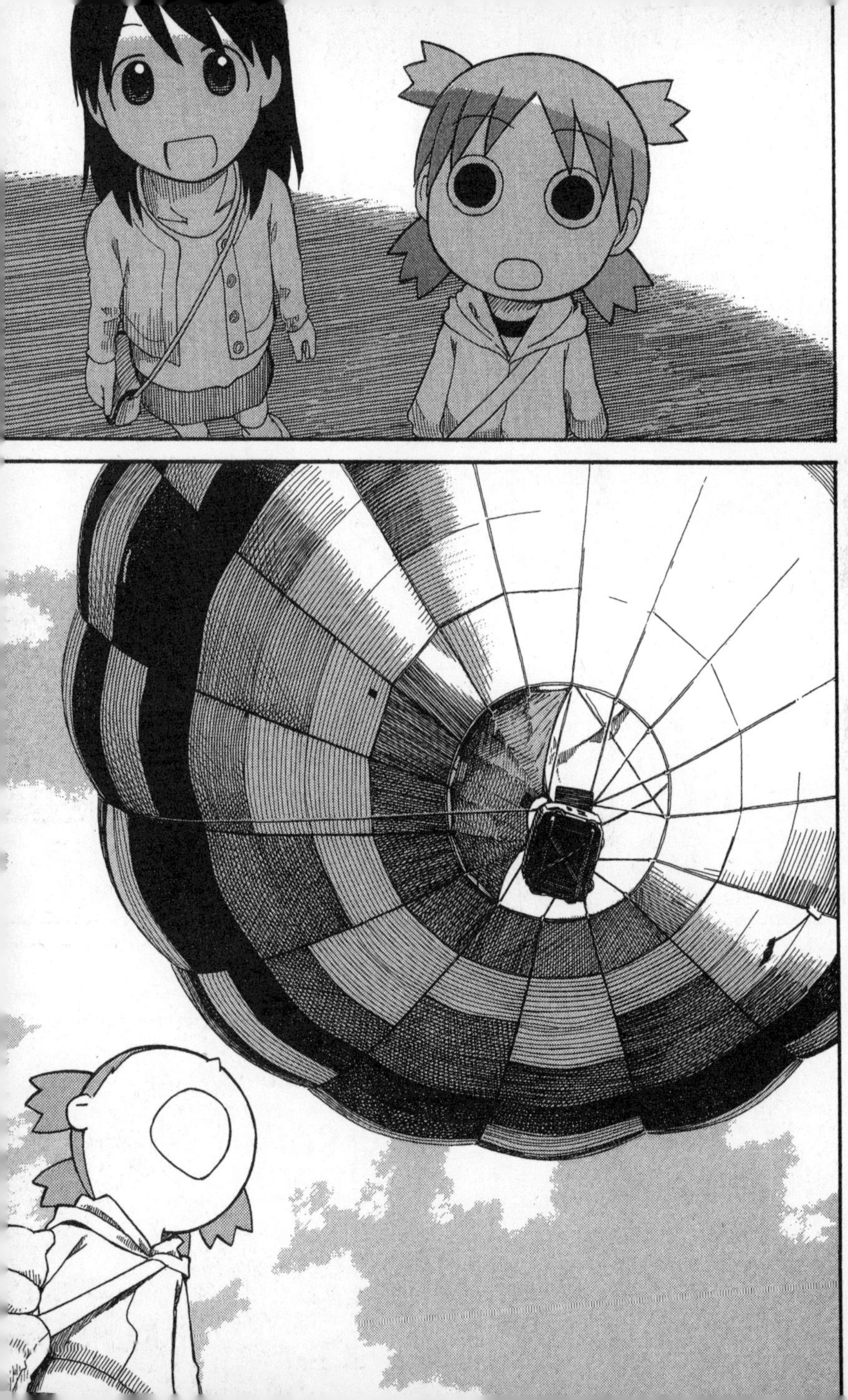

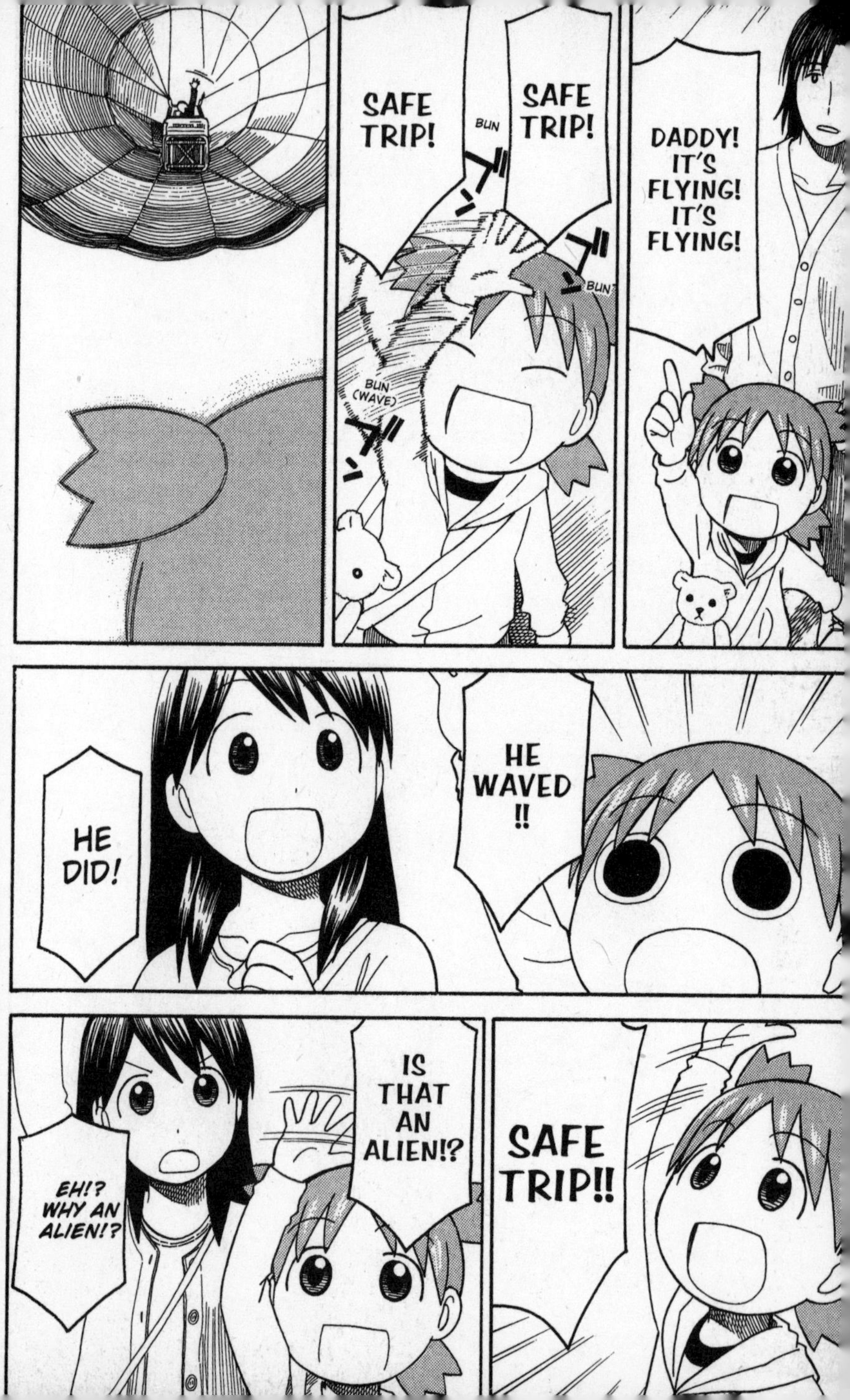
DADDY! IT'S FLYING! IT'S FLYING!
SAFE TRIP!
BUN
SAFE TRIP!
BUN
BUN (WAVE)
HE WAVED !!
HE DID!
SAFE TRIP!!
IS THAT AN ALIEN!?
EH!? WHY AN ALIEN!?

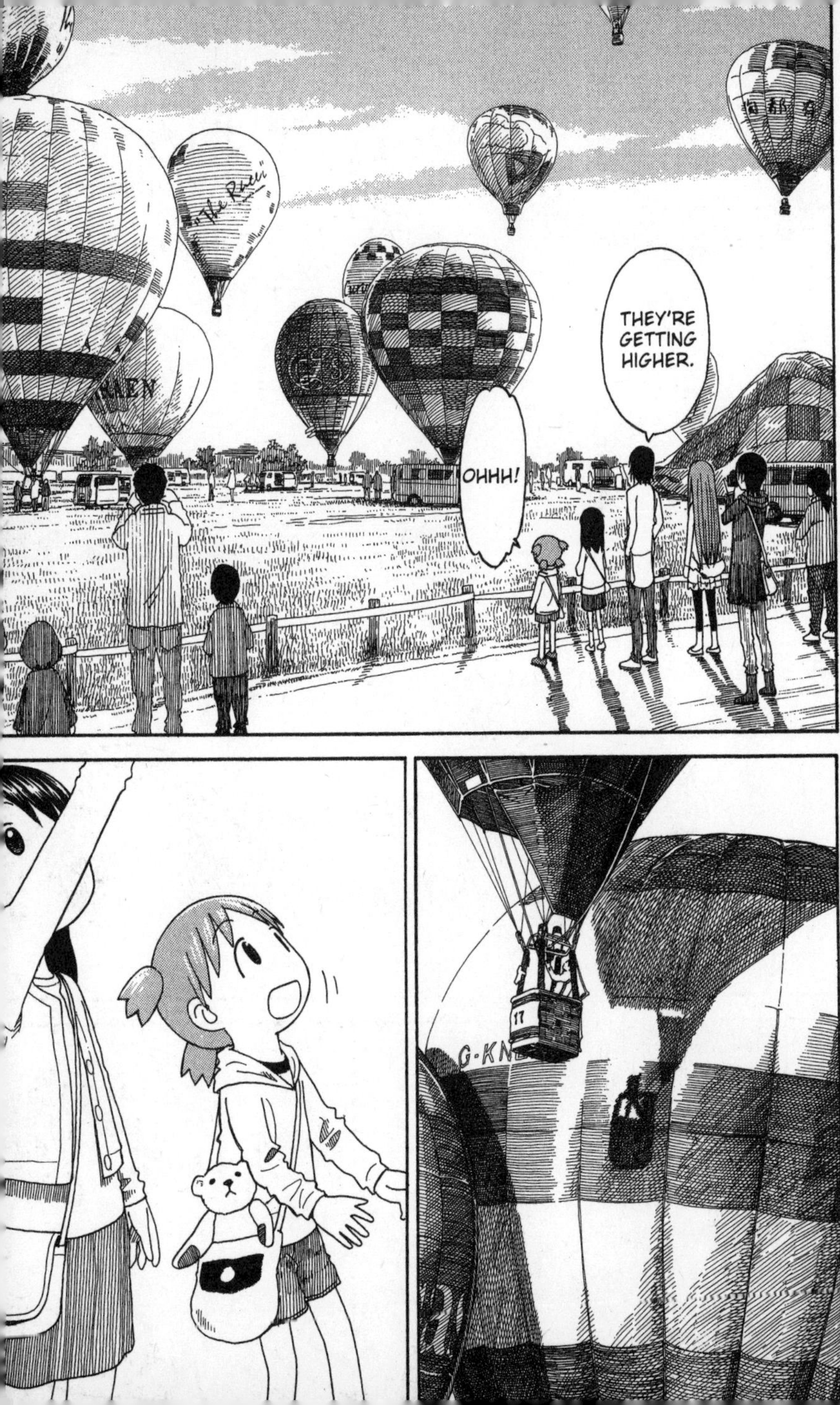
THEY'RE GETTING HIGHER.
OHHH!

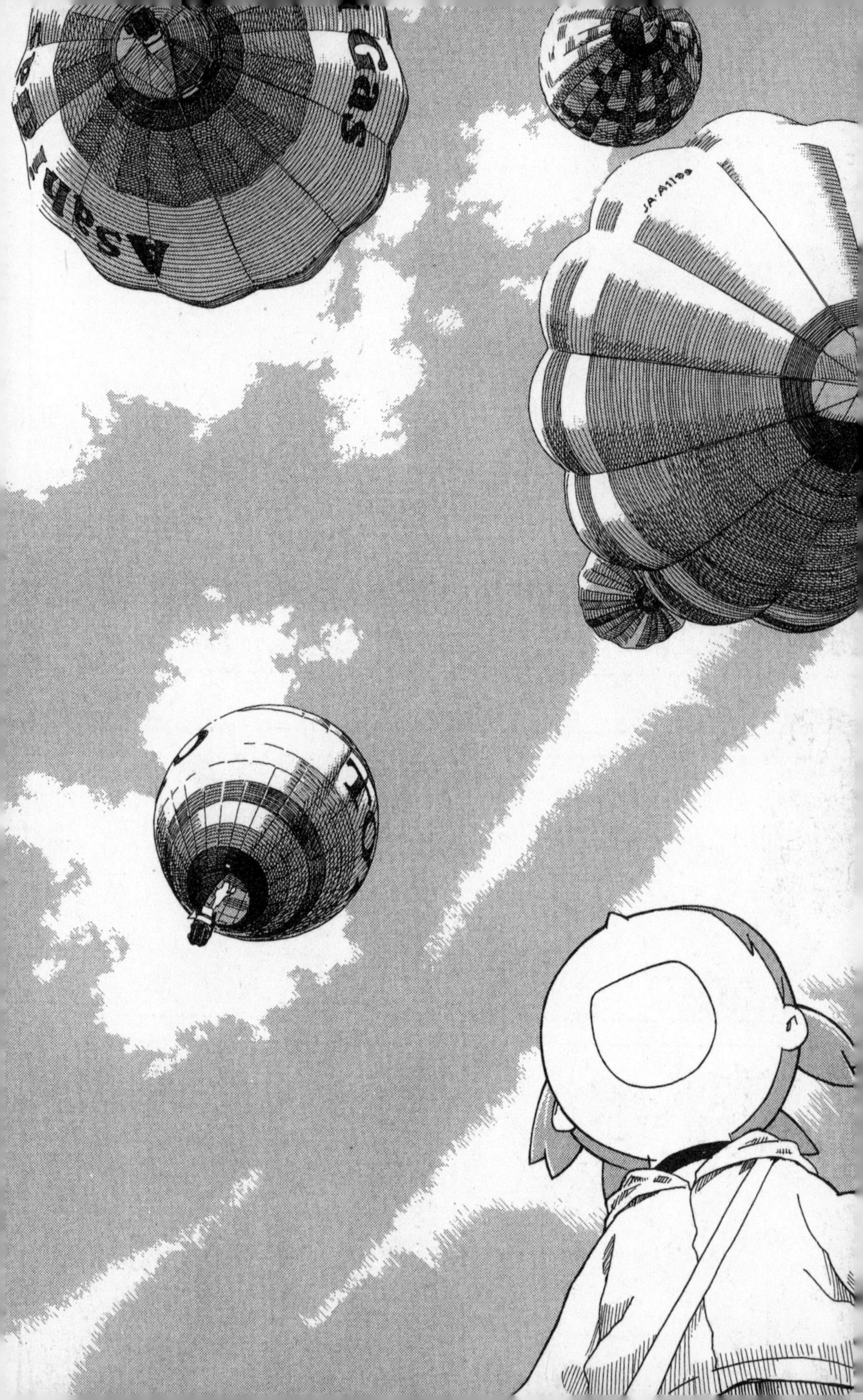

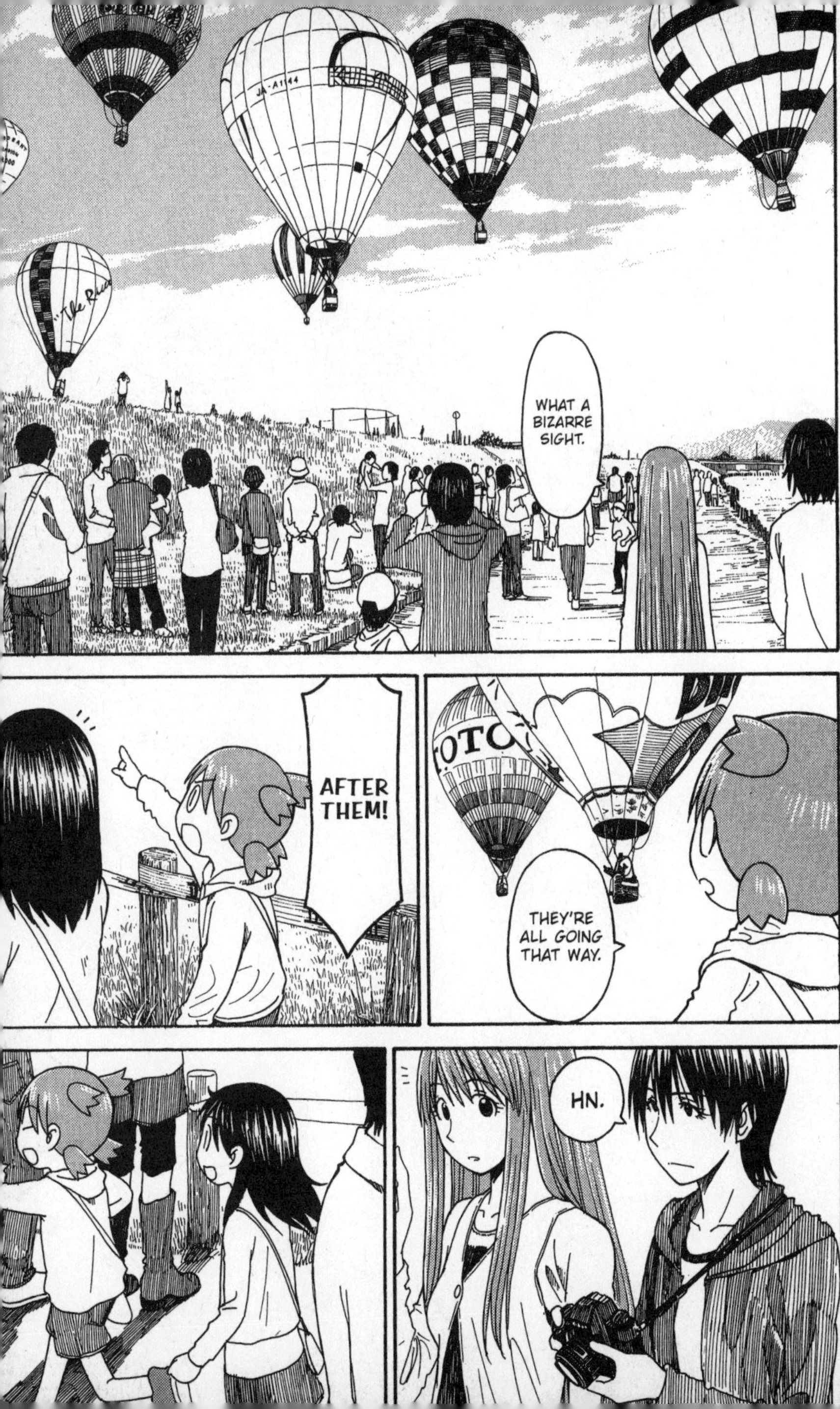
WHAT A BIZARRE SIGHT.
THEY'RE ALL GOING THAT WAY.
AFTER THEM!
HN.

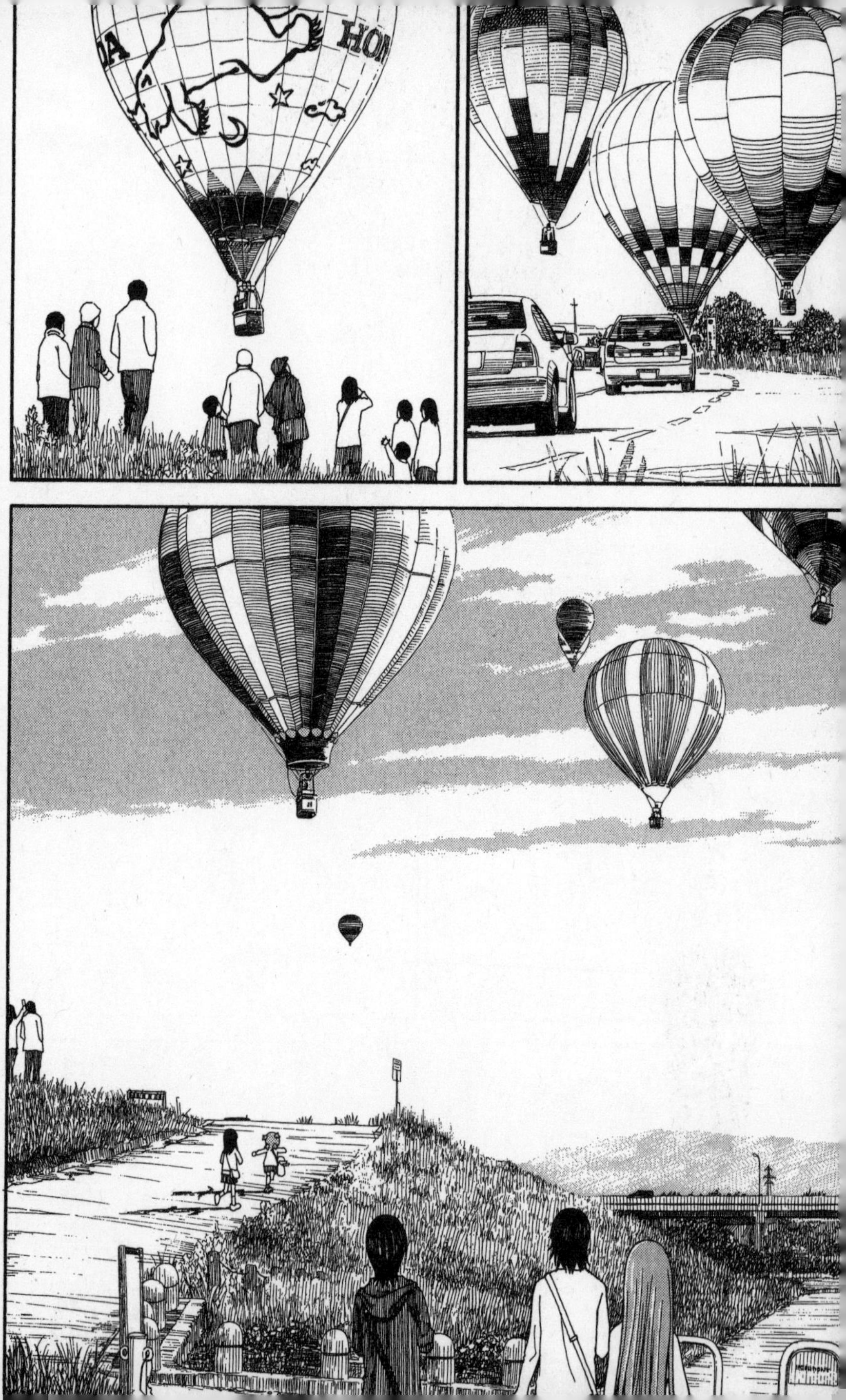

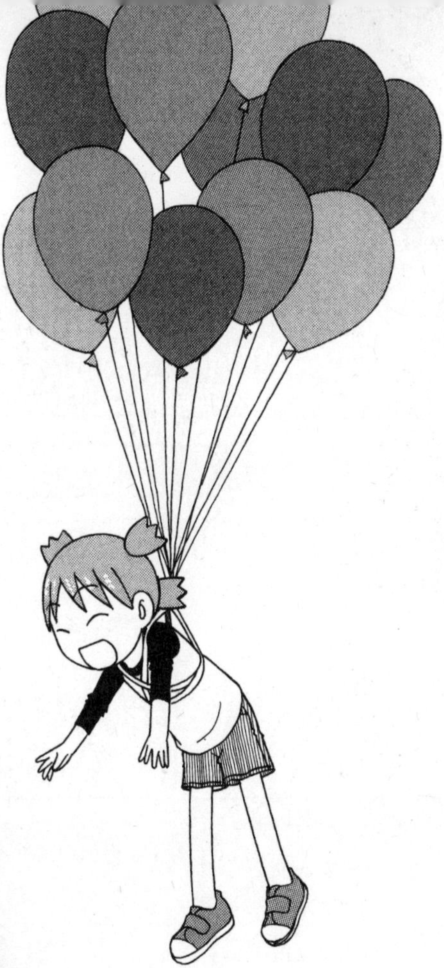

YOTSUBA& THE SKY!

#62

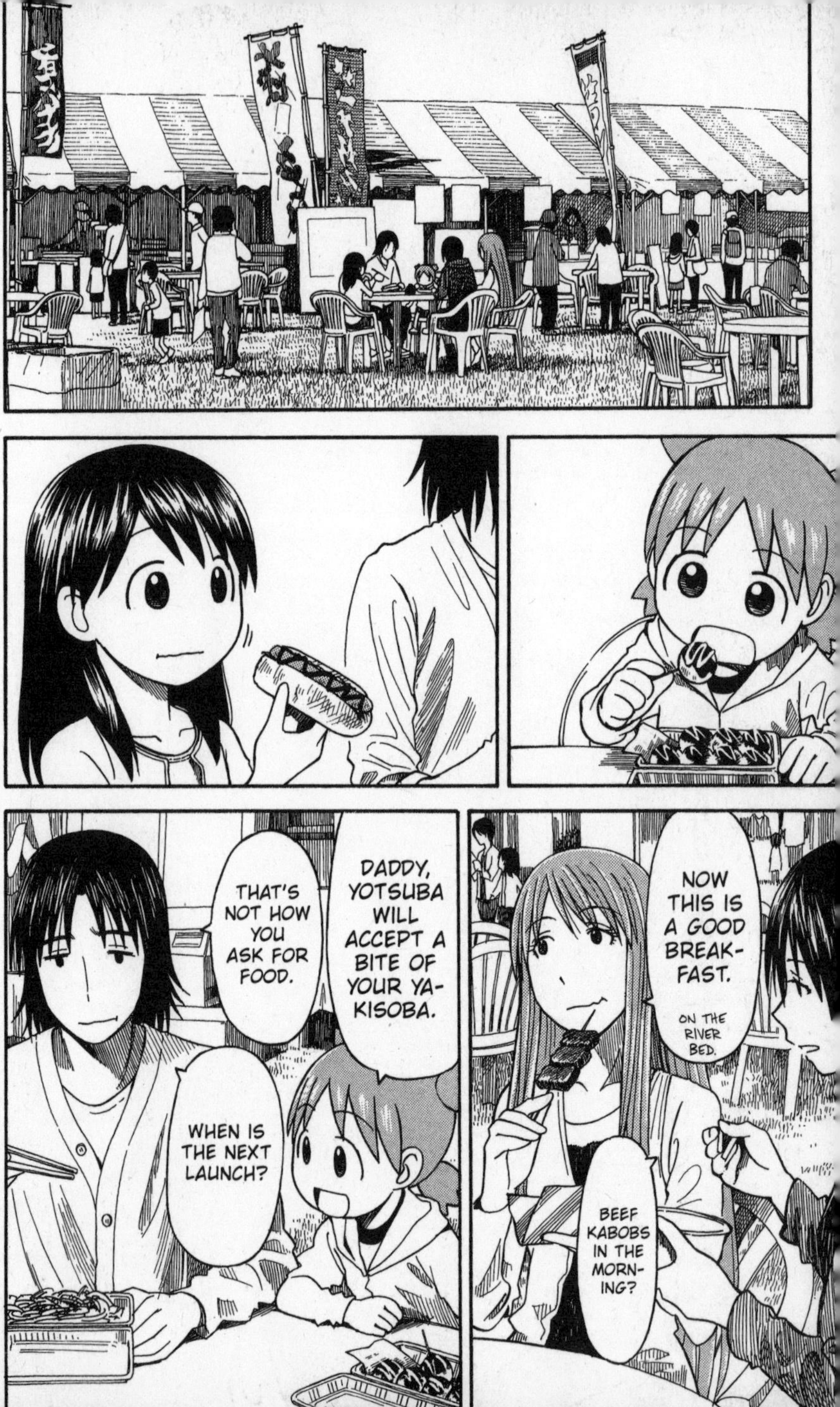
NOW THIS IS A GOOD BREAK-FAST.
ON THE RIVER BED.
BEEF KABOBS IN THE MORN-ING?
DADDY, YOTSUBA WILL ACCEPT A BITE OF YOUR YA-KISOBA.
THAT'S NOT HOW YOU ASK FOR FOOD.
WHEN IS THE NEXT LAUNCH?

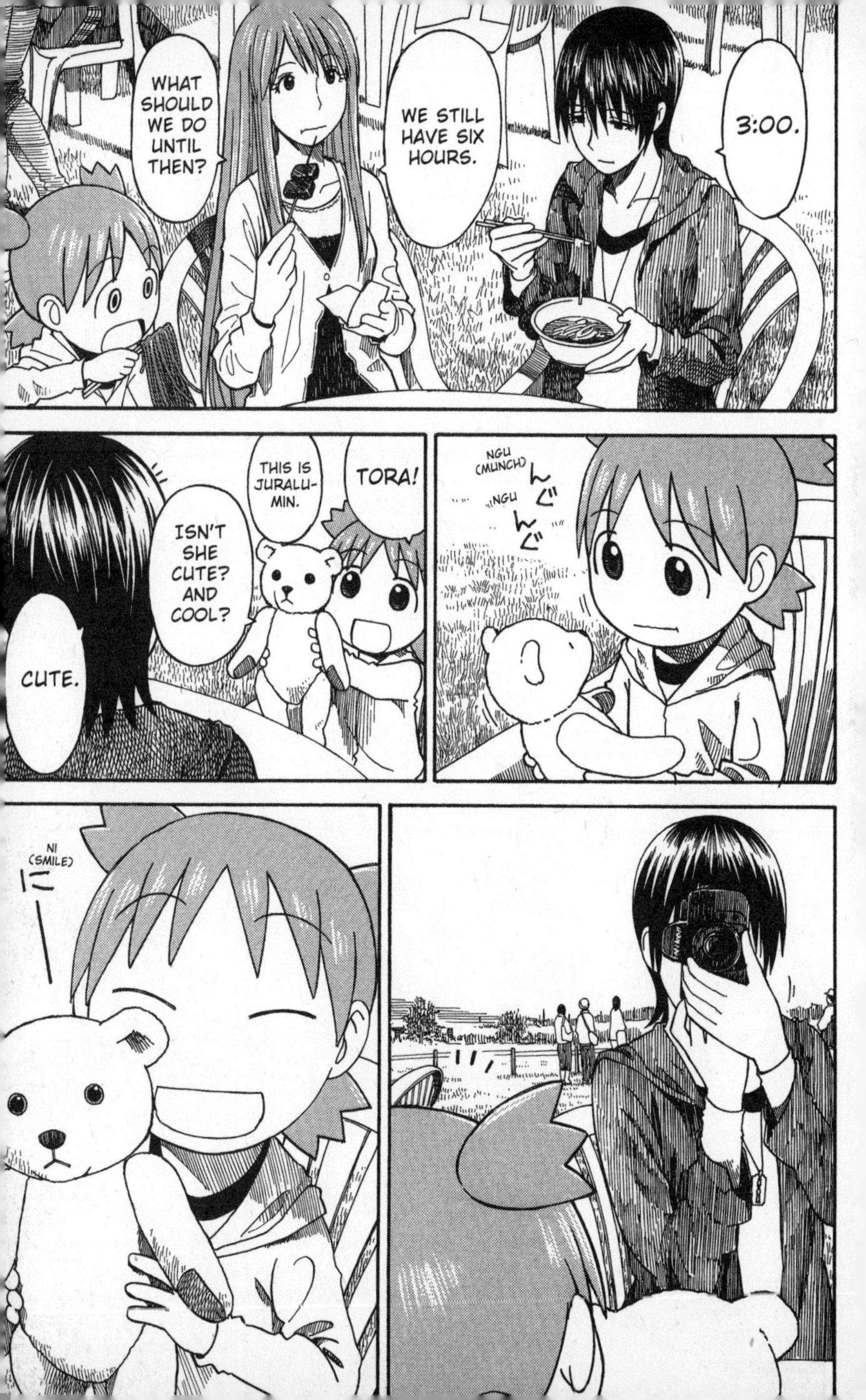
3:00.
WE STILL HAVE SIX HOURS.
WHAT SHOULD WE DO UNTIL THEN?
NGU (MUNCH)
んぐ
NGU
んぐ
TORA!
THIS IS JURALU-MIN.
ISN'T SHE CUTE? AND COOL?
CUTE.
NI (SMILE)
に

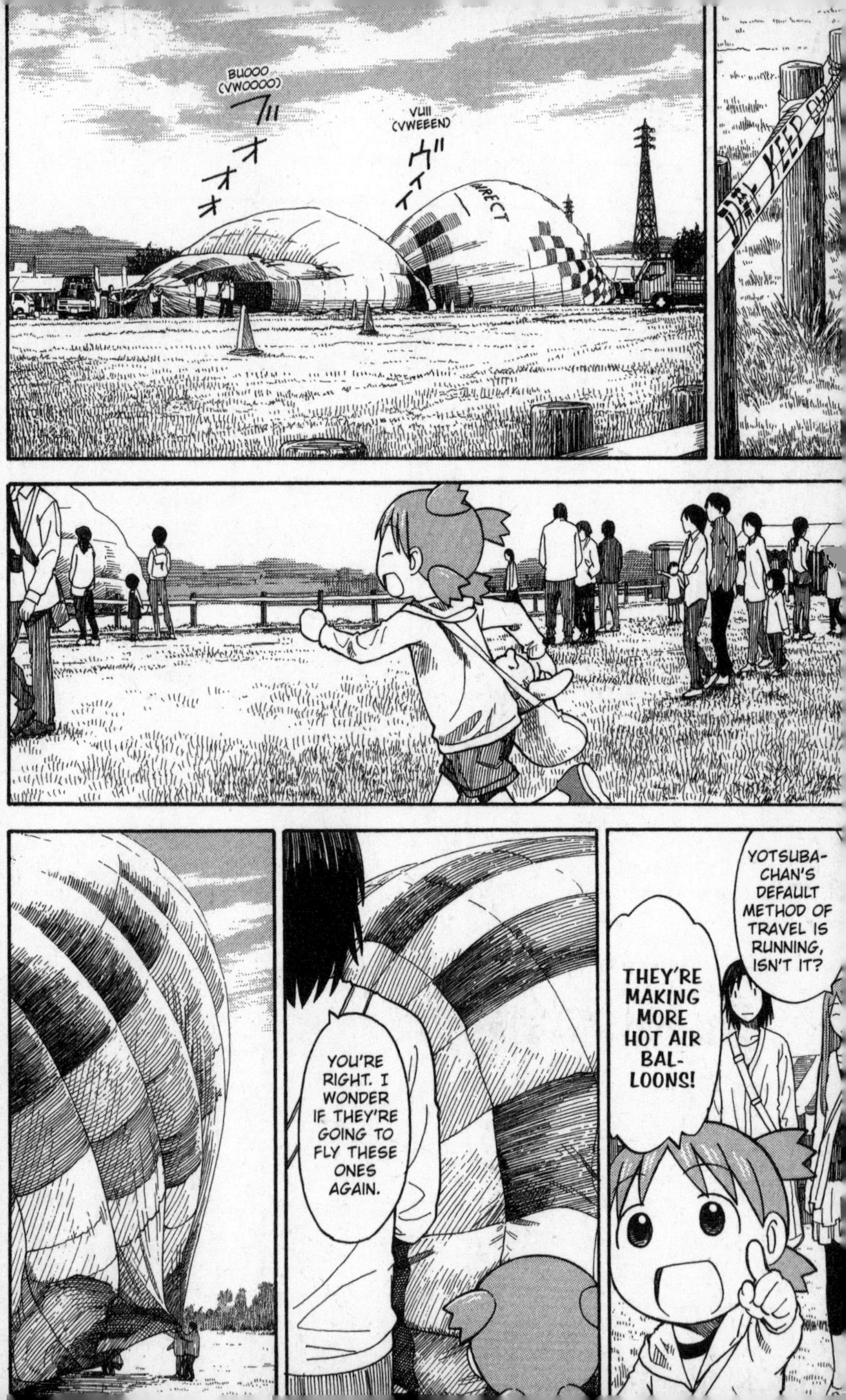
KEEP
VUII (VWEEEN)
ヴィイ
BUOOO (VWOOOO)
ブォオオ
YOTSUBA-CHAN'S DEFAULT METHOD OF TRAVEL IS RUNNING, ISN'T IT?
THEY'RE MAKING MORE HOT AIR BAL-LOONS!
YOU'RE RIGHT. I WONDER IF THEY'RE GOING TO FLY THESE ONES AGAIN.

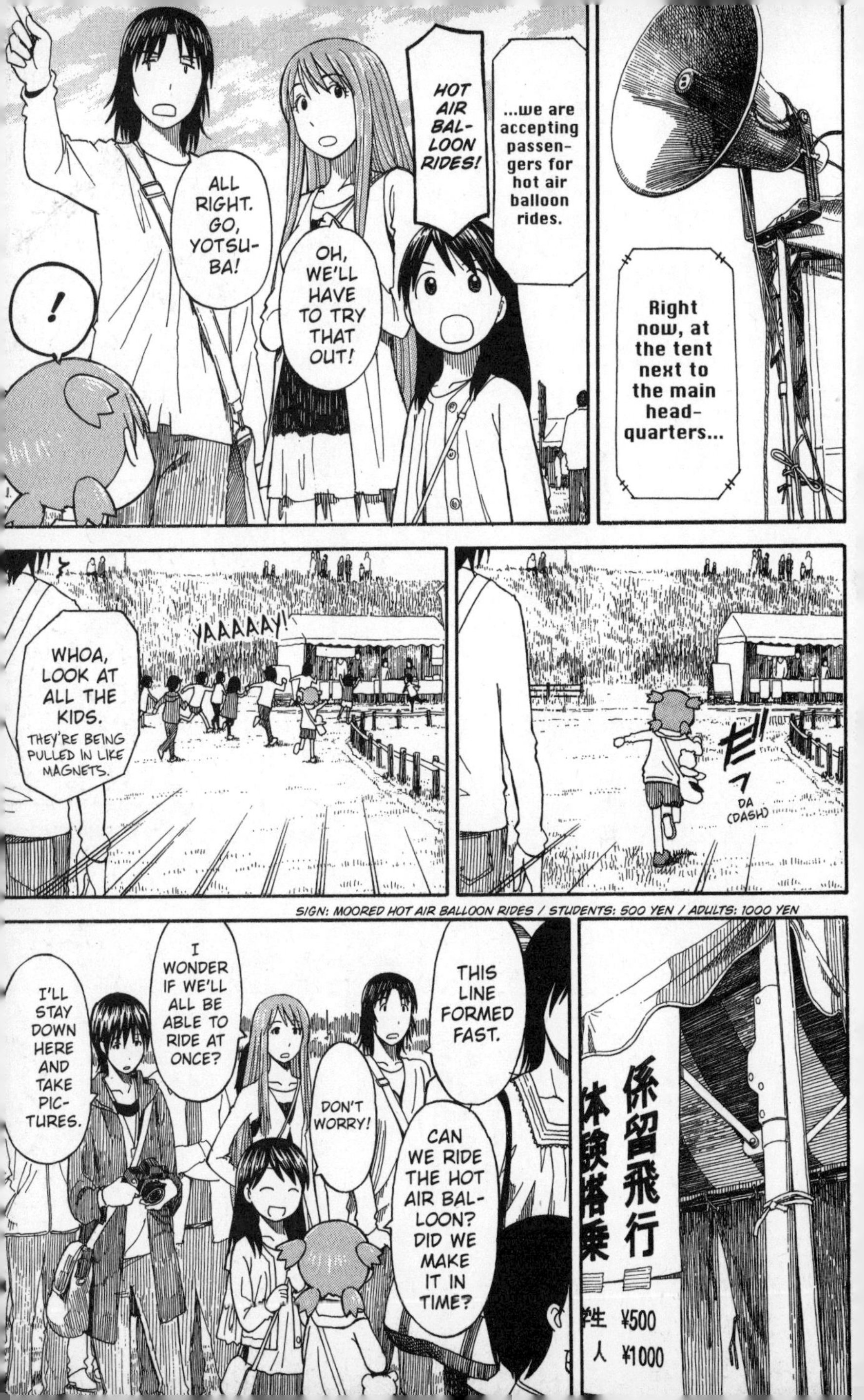
Right now, at the tent next to the main head-quarters...
...we are accepting passengers for hot air balloon rides.
HOT AIR BALLOON RIDES!
OH, WE'LL HAVE TO TRY THAT OUT!
ALL RIGHT. GO, YOTSUBA!
!
DA (DASH)
YAAAAAY!
WHOA, LOOK AT ALL THE KIDS. THEY'RE BEING PULLED IN LIKE MAGNETS.
SIGN: MOORED HOT AIR BALLOON RIDES / STUDENTS: 500 YEN / ADULTS: 1000 YEN
係留飛行
体験搭乗
生 ¥500
人 ¥1000
THIS LINE FORMED FAST.
CAN WE RIDE THE HOT AIR BALLOON? DID WE MAKE IT IN TIME?
DON'T WORRY!
I WONDER IF WE'LL ALL BE ABLE TO RIDE AT ONCE?
I'LL STAY DOWN HERE AND TAKE PICTURES.

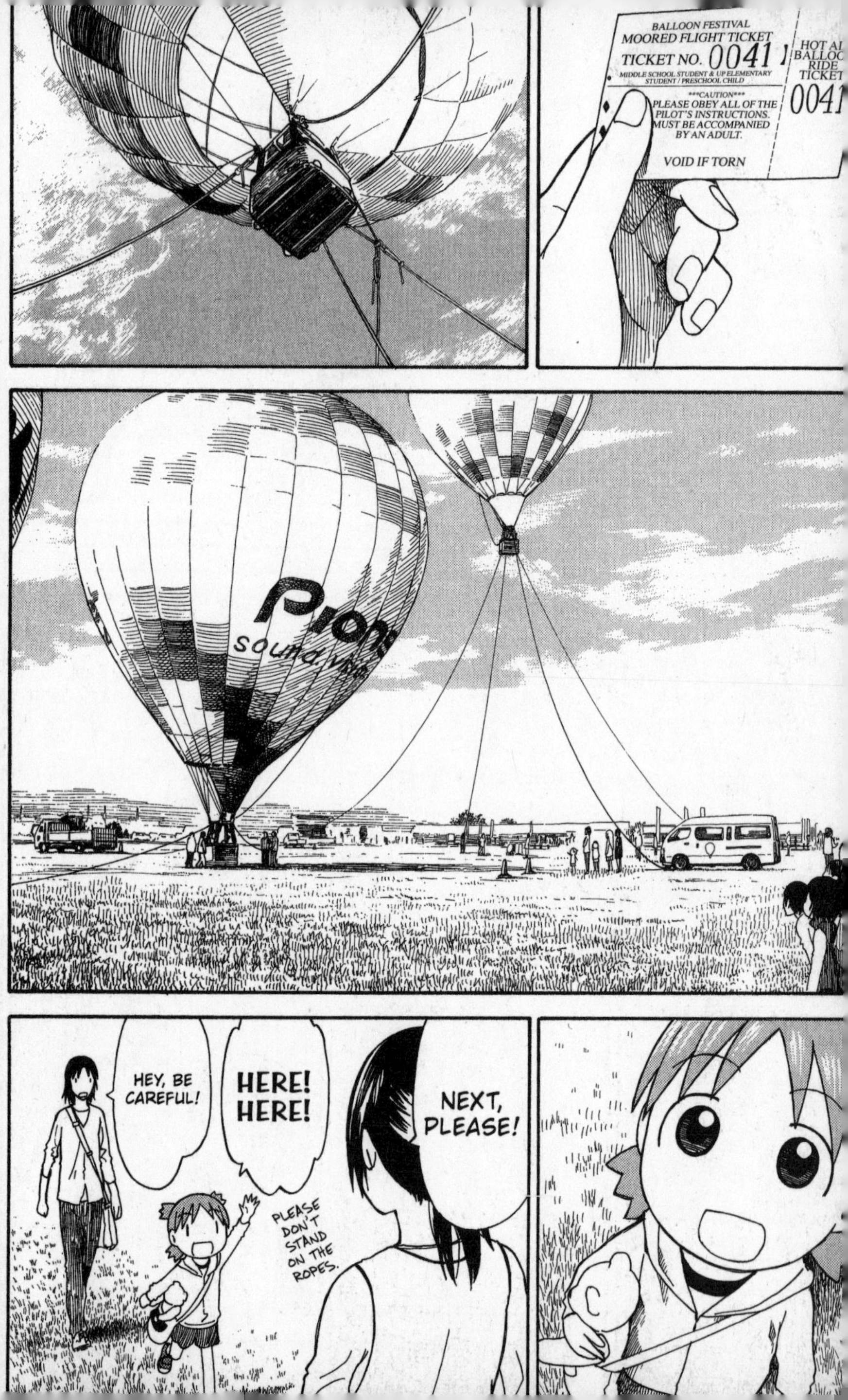
BALLOON FESTIVAL
MOORED FLIGHT TICKET
TICKET NO. 0041
MIDDLE SCHOOL STUDENT & UP ELEMENTARY STUDENT / PRESCHOOL CHILD
CAUTION
PLEASE OBEY ALL OF THE PILOT'S INSTRUCTIONS. MUST BE ACCOMPANIED BY AN ADULT.
VOID IF TORN
RIDE
TICKET
NEXT, PLEASE!
HERE! HERE!
HEY, BE CAREFUL!
PLEASE DON'T STAND ON THE ROPES.

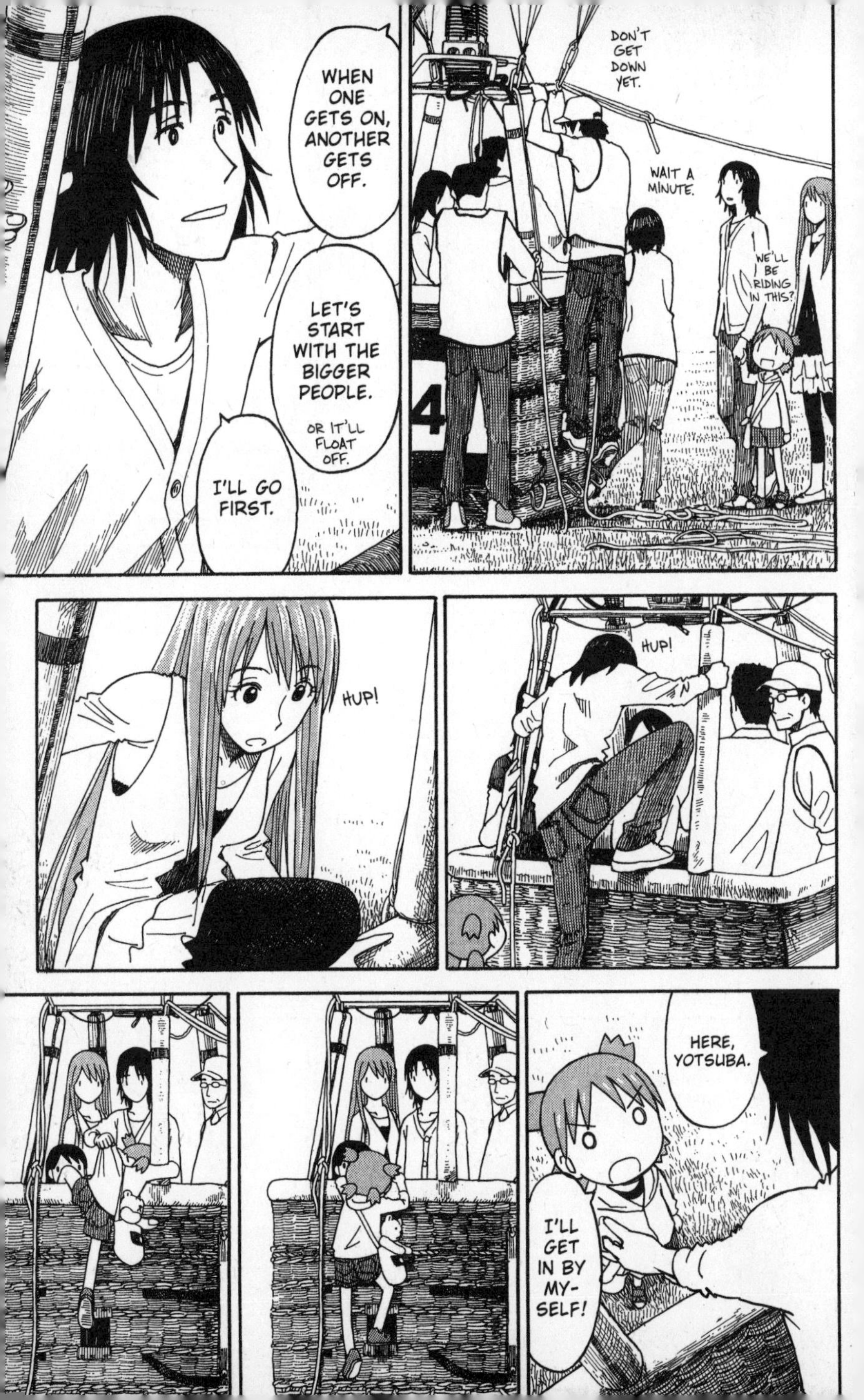
DON'T GET DOWN YET.
WAIT A MINUTE.
WE'LL BE RIDING IN THIS?
WHEN ONE GETS ON, ANOTHER GETS OFF.
LET'S START WITH THE BIGGER PEOPLE.
OR IT'LL FLOAT OFF.
I'LL GO FIRST.
HUP!
HUP!
HERE, YOTSUBA.
I'LL GET IN BY MY-SELF!

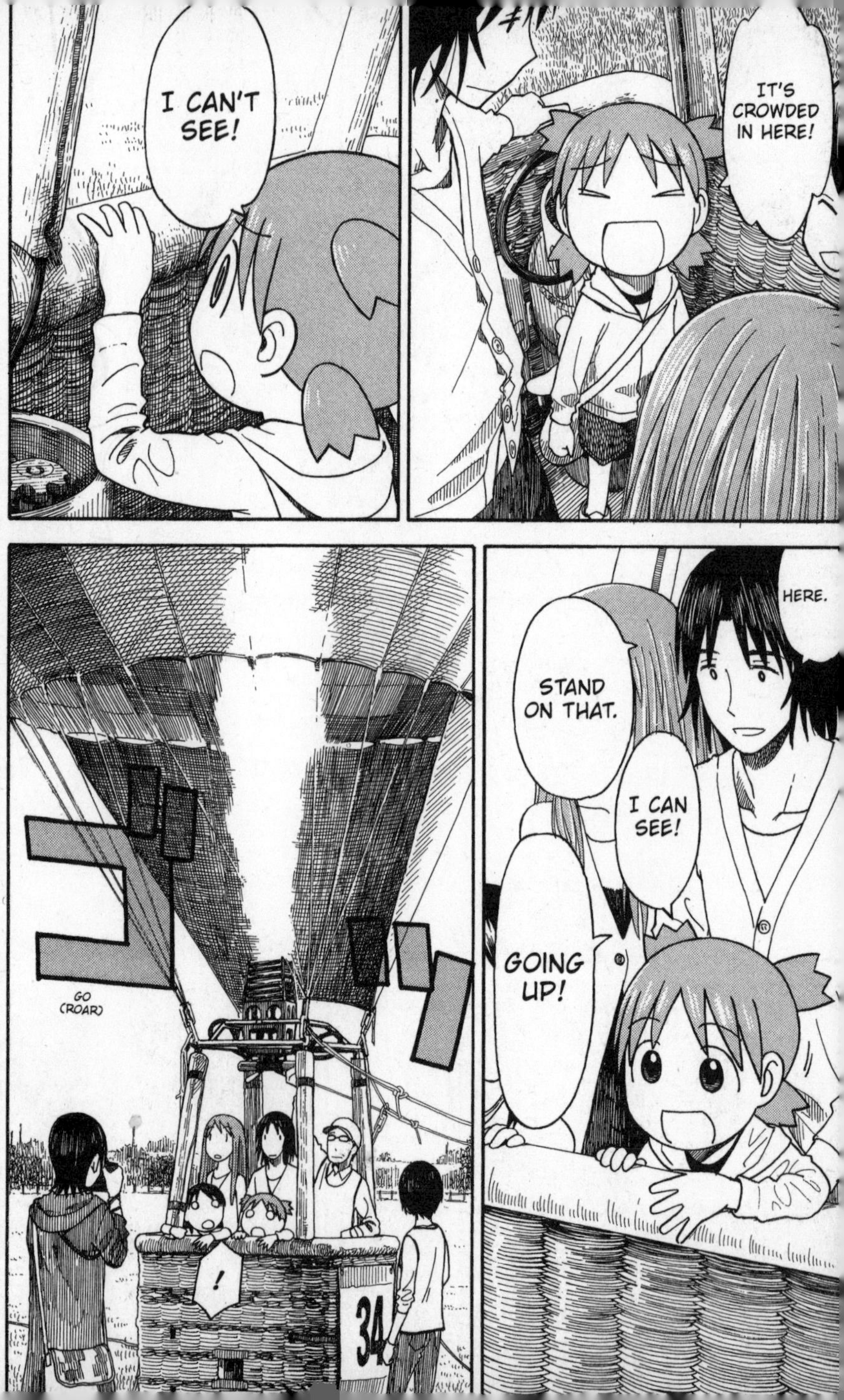
IT'S CROWDED IN HERE!
I CAN'T SEE!
HERE.
STAND ON THAT.
I CAN SEE!
GOING UP!
GO (ROAR)
!
34

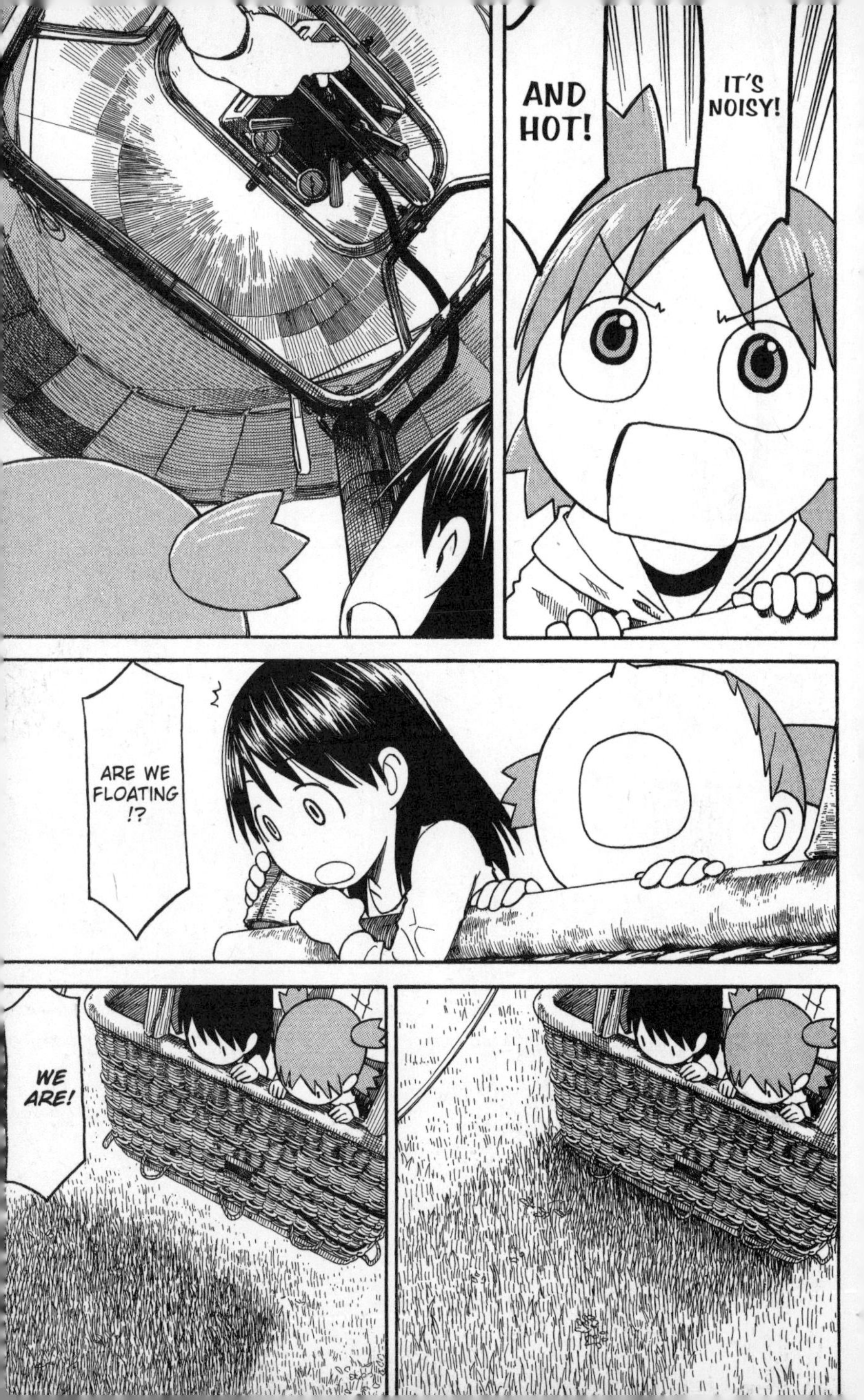
IT'S NOISY!
AND HOT!
ARE WE FLOATING !?
WE ARE!

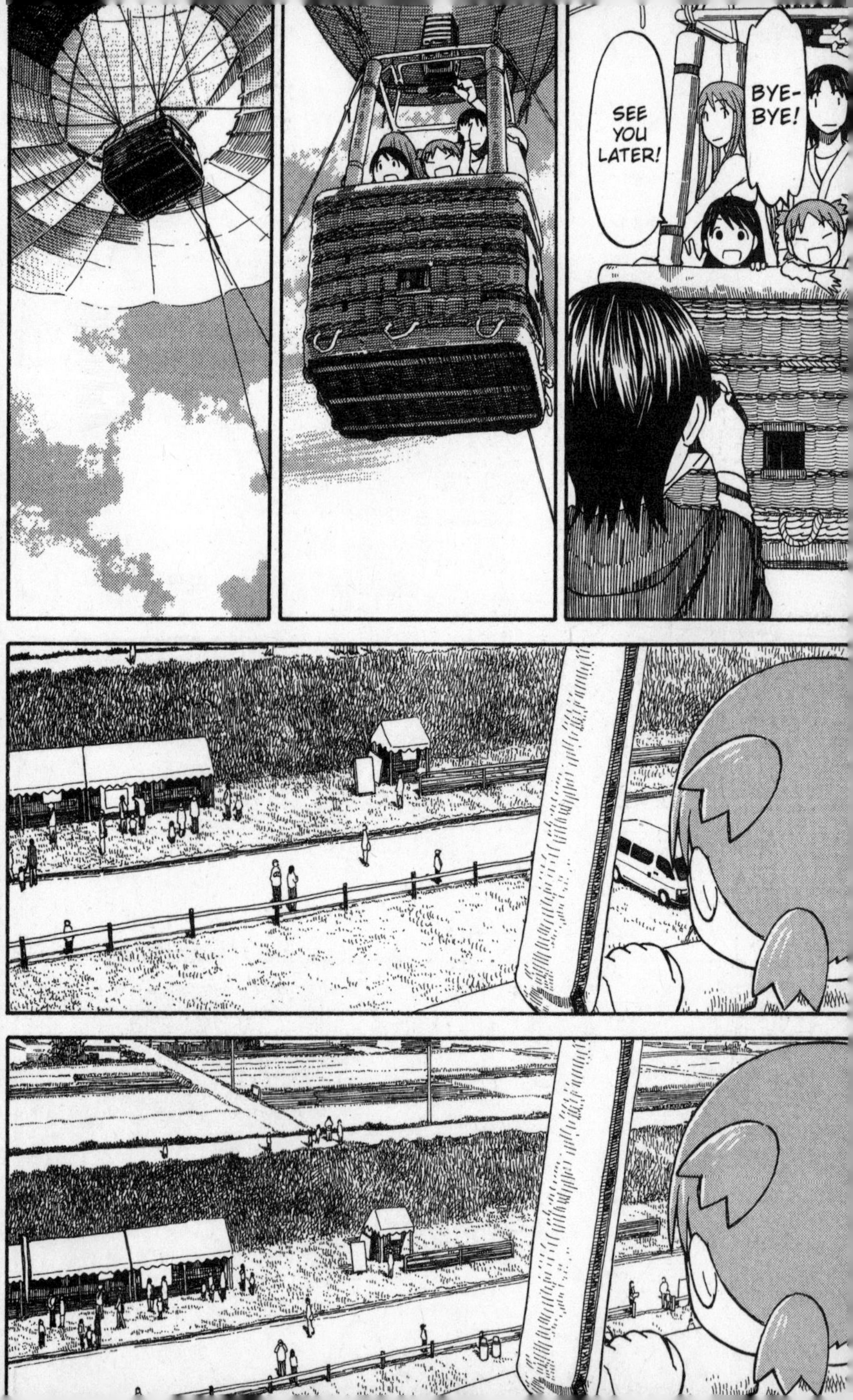
BYE-BYE!
SEE YOU LATER!

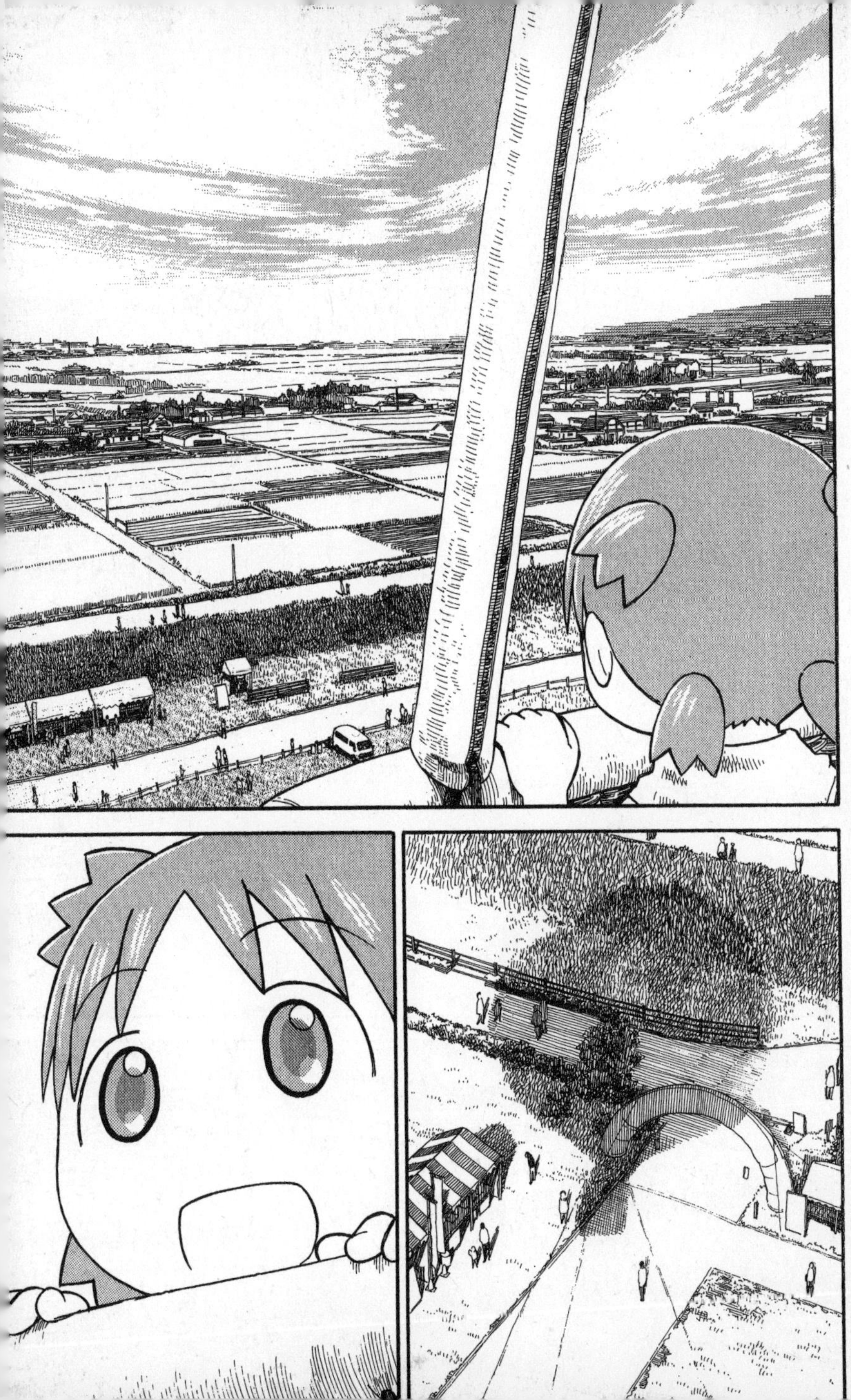

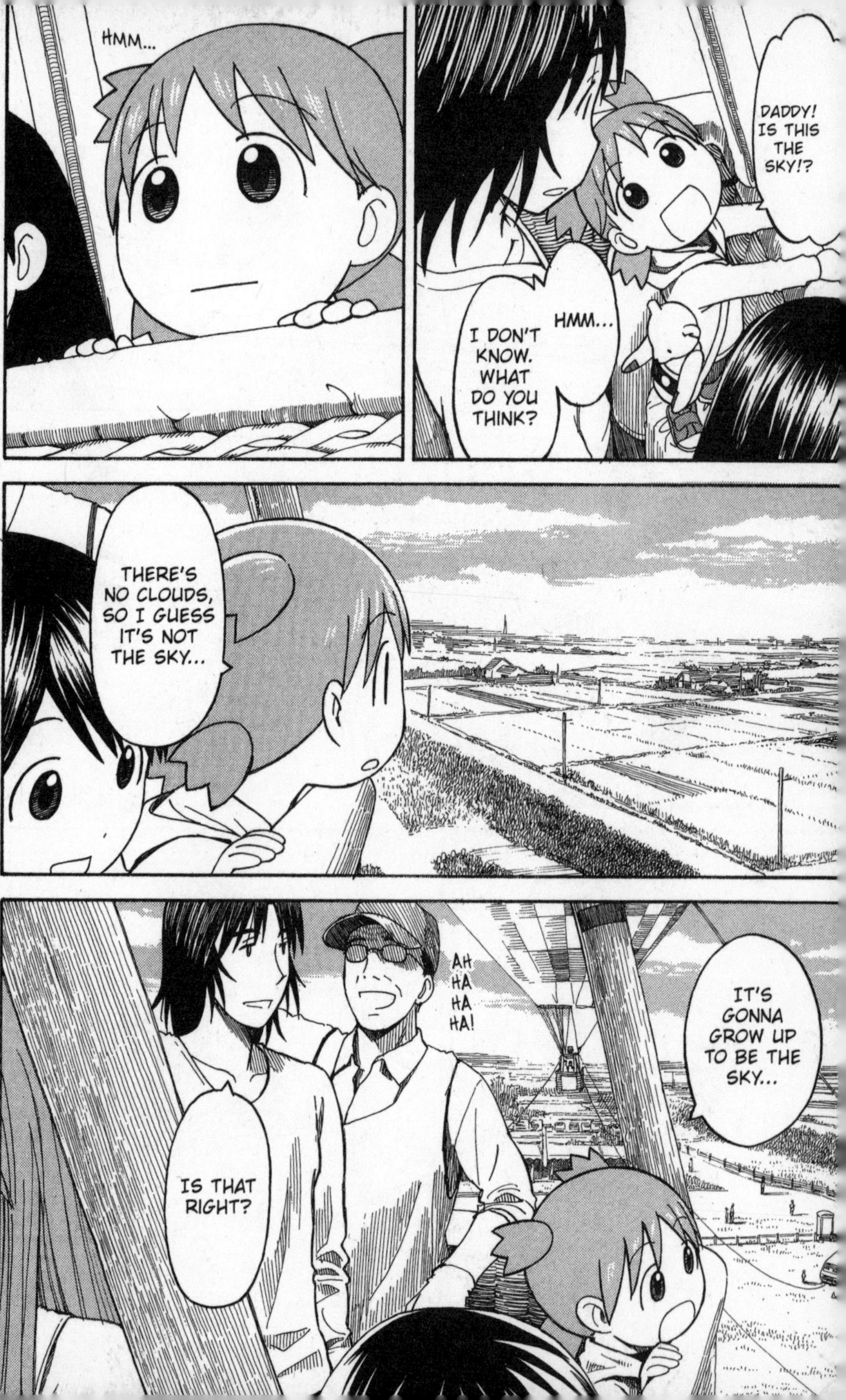
DADDY! IS THIS THE SKY!?
HMM... I DON'T KNOW. WHAT DO YOU THINK?
HMM...
THERE'S NO CLOUDS, SO I GUESS IT'S NOT THE SKY...
IT'S GONNA GROW UP TO BE THE SKY...
AH HA HA HA!
IS THAT RIGHT?

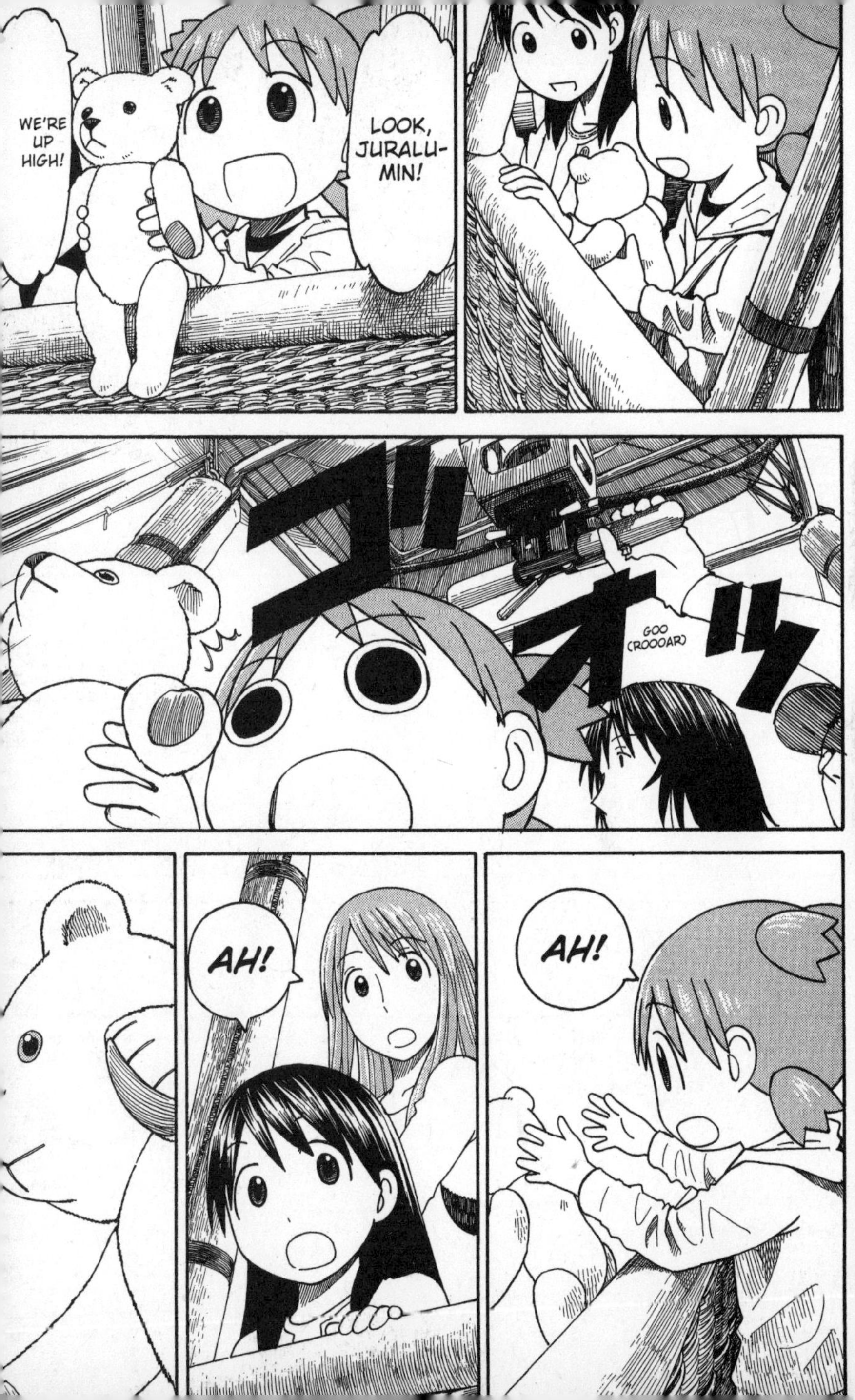
LOOK, JURALU-MIN!
WE'RE UP HIGH!
GOO (ROOOAR)
AH!
AH!

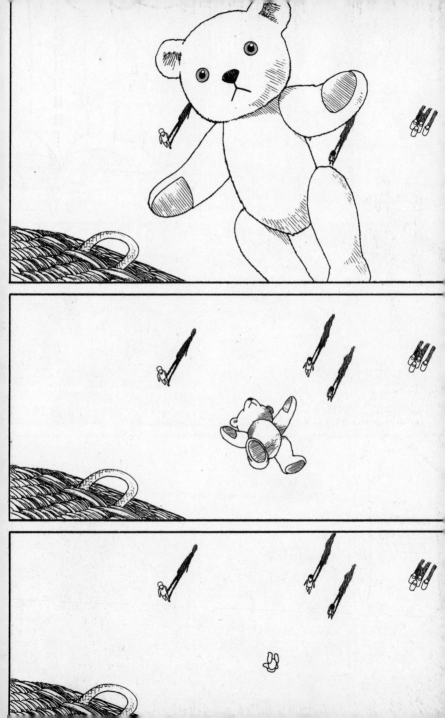

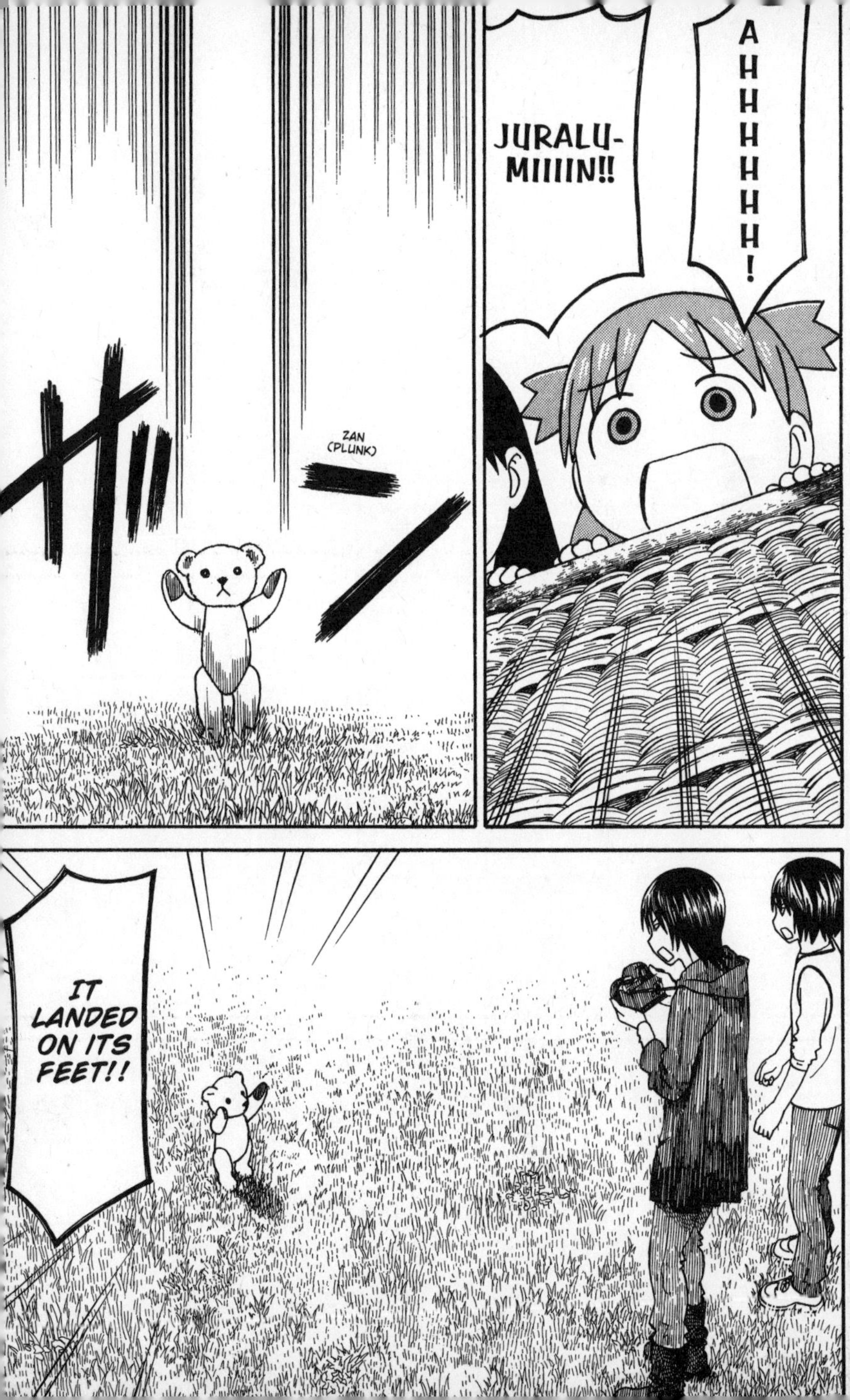
AHHHHHH!
JURALU-MIIIIN!!
ZAN (PLUNK)
IT LANDED ON ITS FEET!!

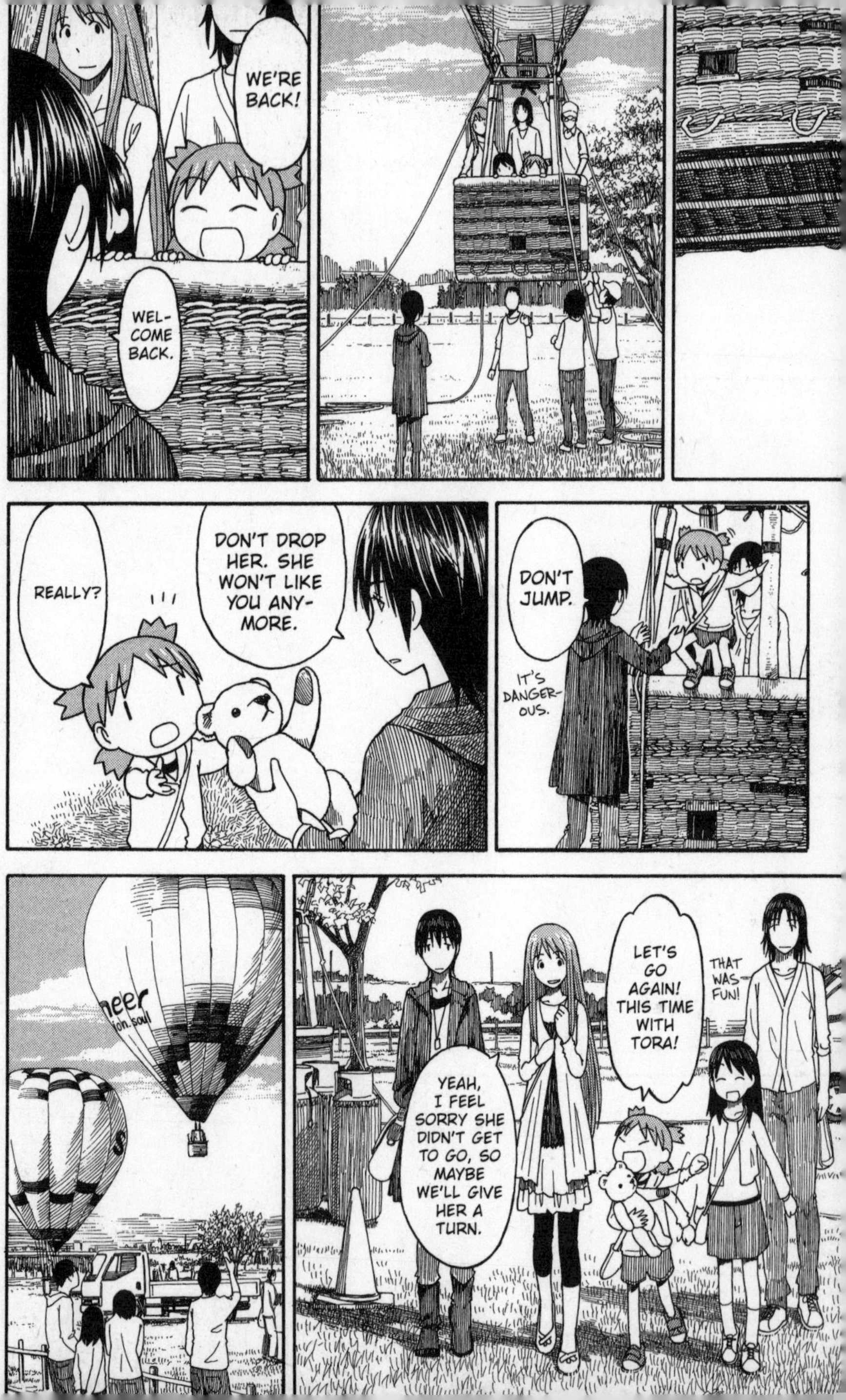
WE'RE BACK!
WEL-COME BACK.
DON'T JUMP.
IT'S DANGER-OUS.
DON'T DROP HER. SHE WON'T LIKE YOU ANY-MORE.
REALLY?
THAT WAS FUN!
LET'S GO AGAIN! THIS TIME WITH TORA!
YEAH, I FEEL SORRY SHE DIDN'T GET TO GO, SO MAYBE WE'LL GIVE HER A TURN.

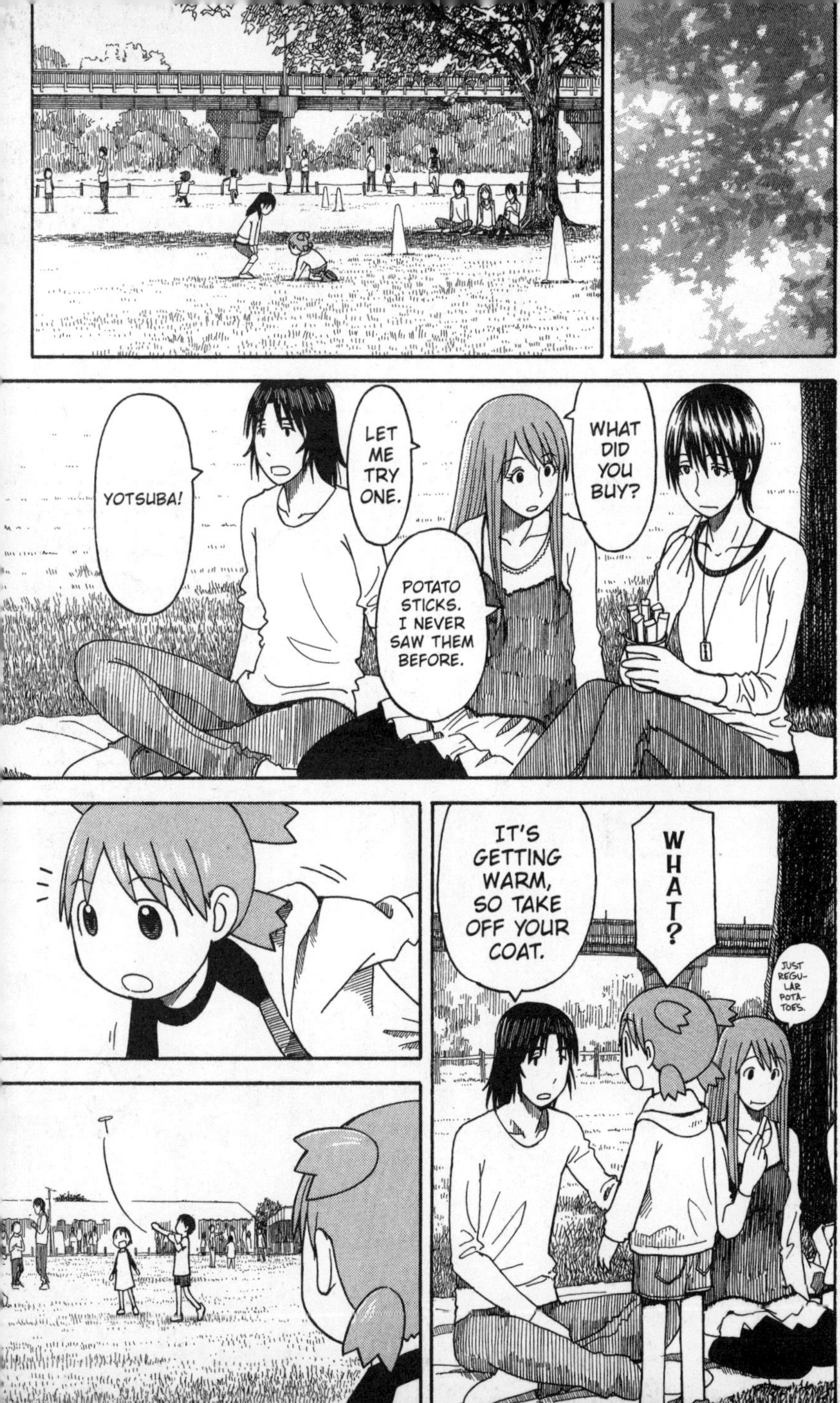
WHAT DID YOU BUY?
POTATO STICKS. I NEVER SAW THEM BEFORE.
LET ME TRY ONE.
YOTSUBA!
WHAT?
IT'S GETTING WARM, SO TAKE OFF YOUR COAT.
JUST REGULAR POTATOES.

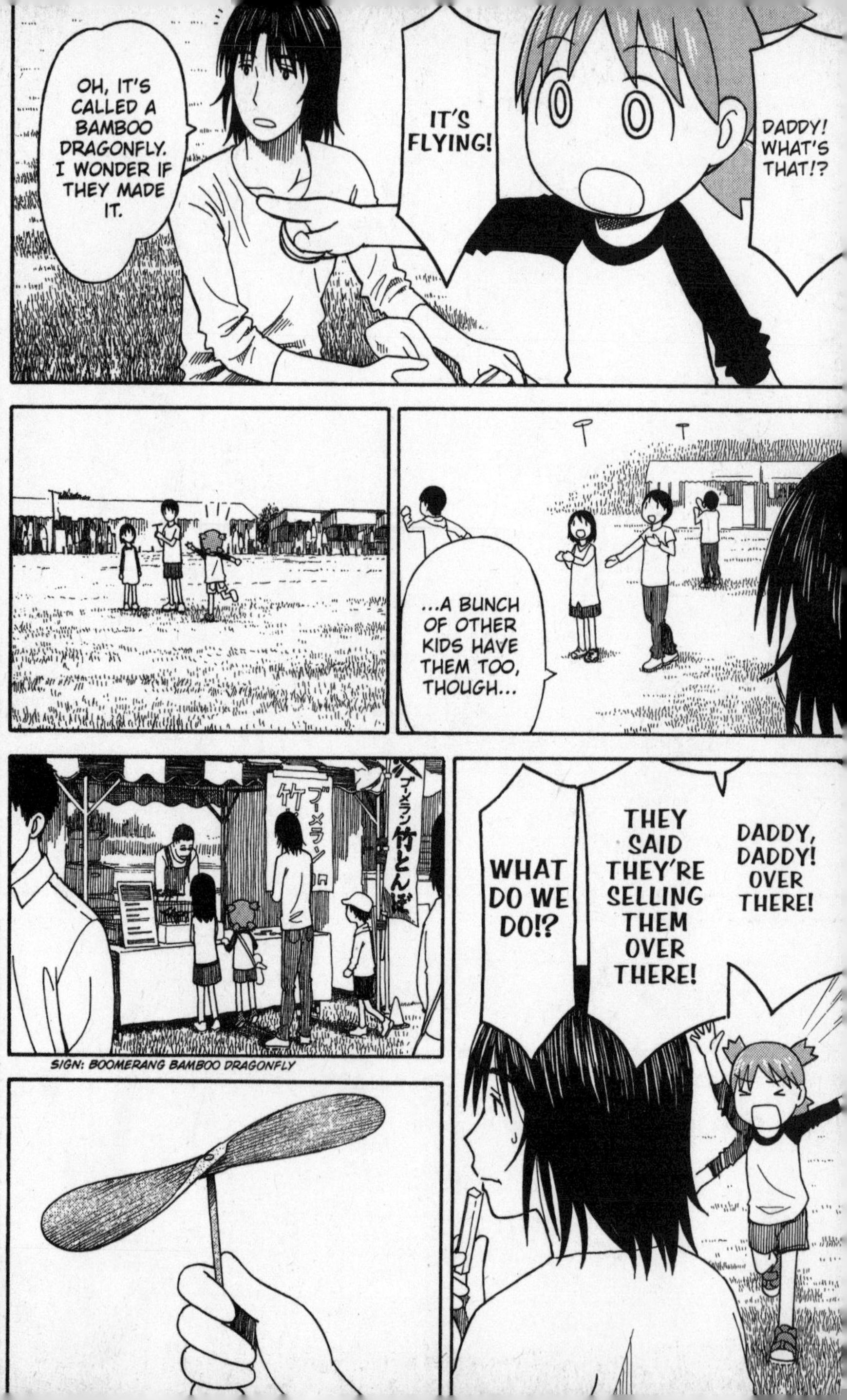
DADDY! WHAT'S THAT!?
IT'S FLYING!
OH, IT'S CALLED A BAMBOO DRAGONFLY. I WONDER IF THEY MADE IT.
...A BUNCH OF OTHER KIDS HAVE THEM TOO, THOUGH...
DADDY, DADDY! OVER THERE!
THEY SAID THEY'RE SELLING THEM OVER THERE!
WHAT DO WE DO!?
ブーメラン竹とんぼ
SIGN: BOOMERANG BAMBOO DRAGONFLY

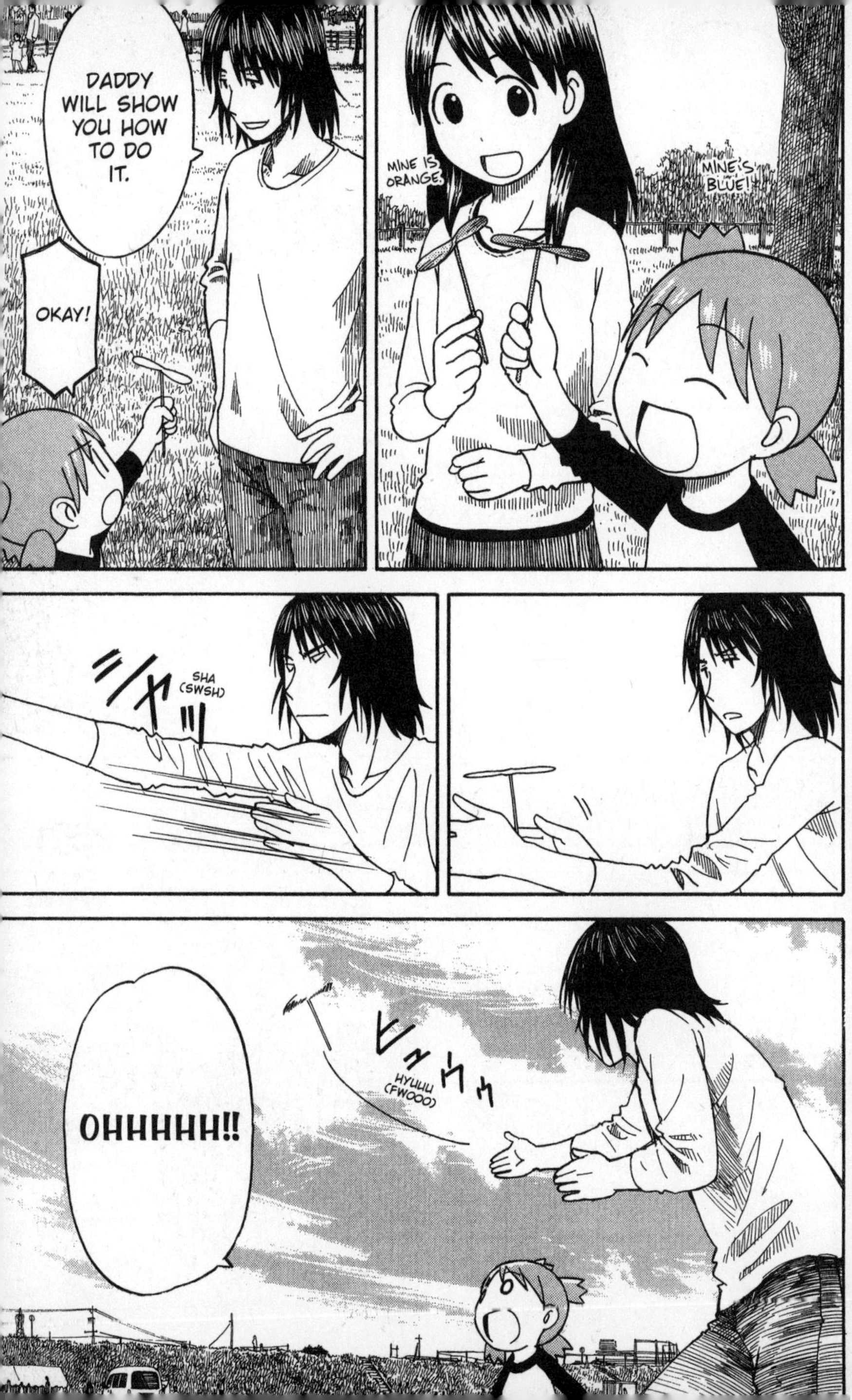
MINE'S BLUE!
MINE IS ORANGE.
DADDY WILL SHOW YOU HOW TO DO IT.
OKAY!
SHA (SWSH)
HYUUU (FWOOO)
OHHHHH!!

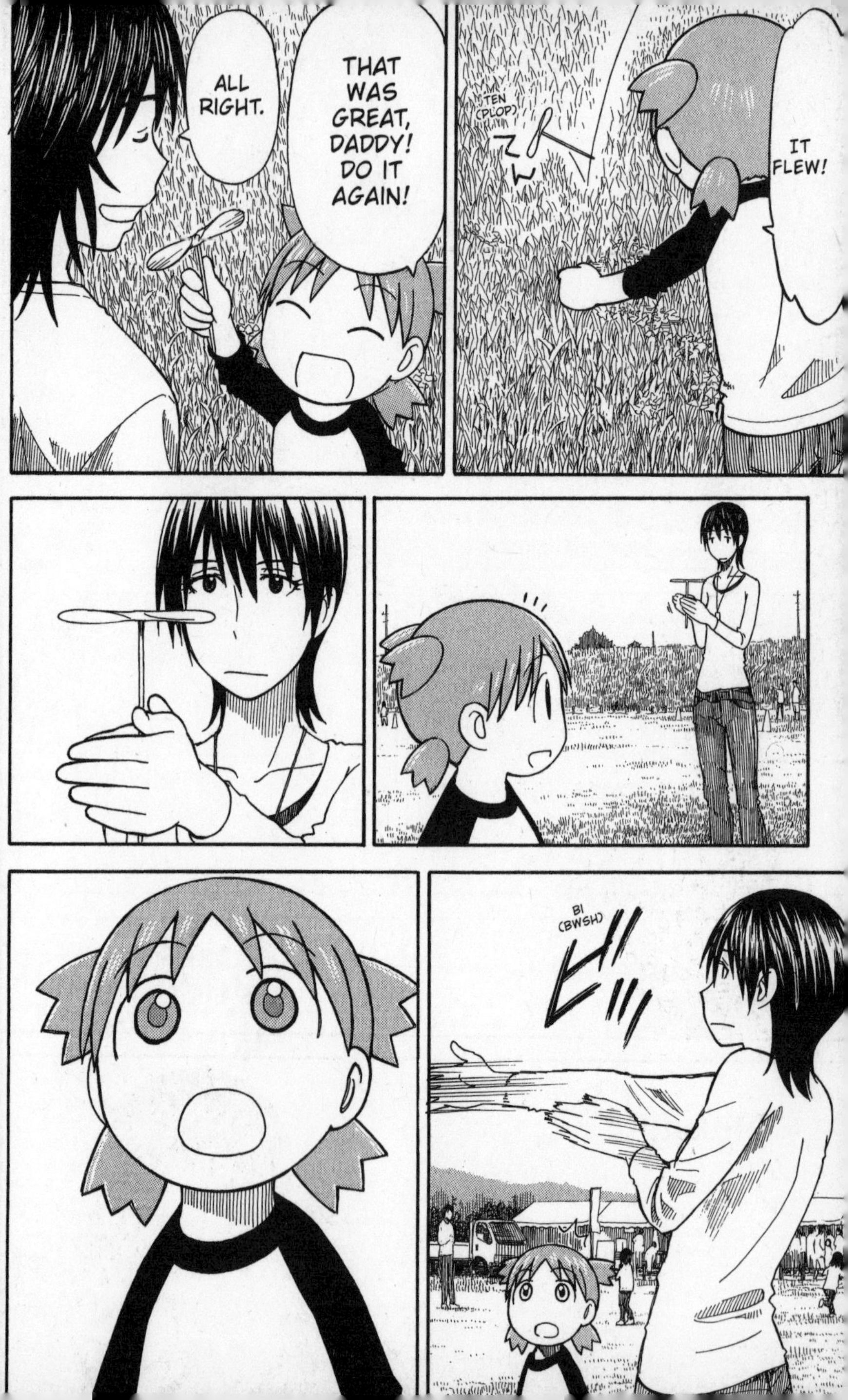
TEN (PLOP)
IT FLEW!
THAT WAS GREAT, DADDY! DO IT AGAIN!
ALL RIGHT.
BI (BWSH)

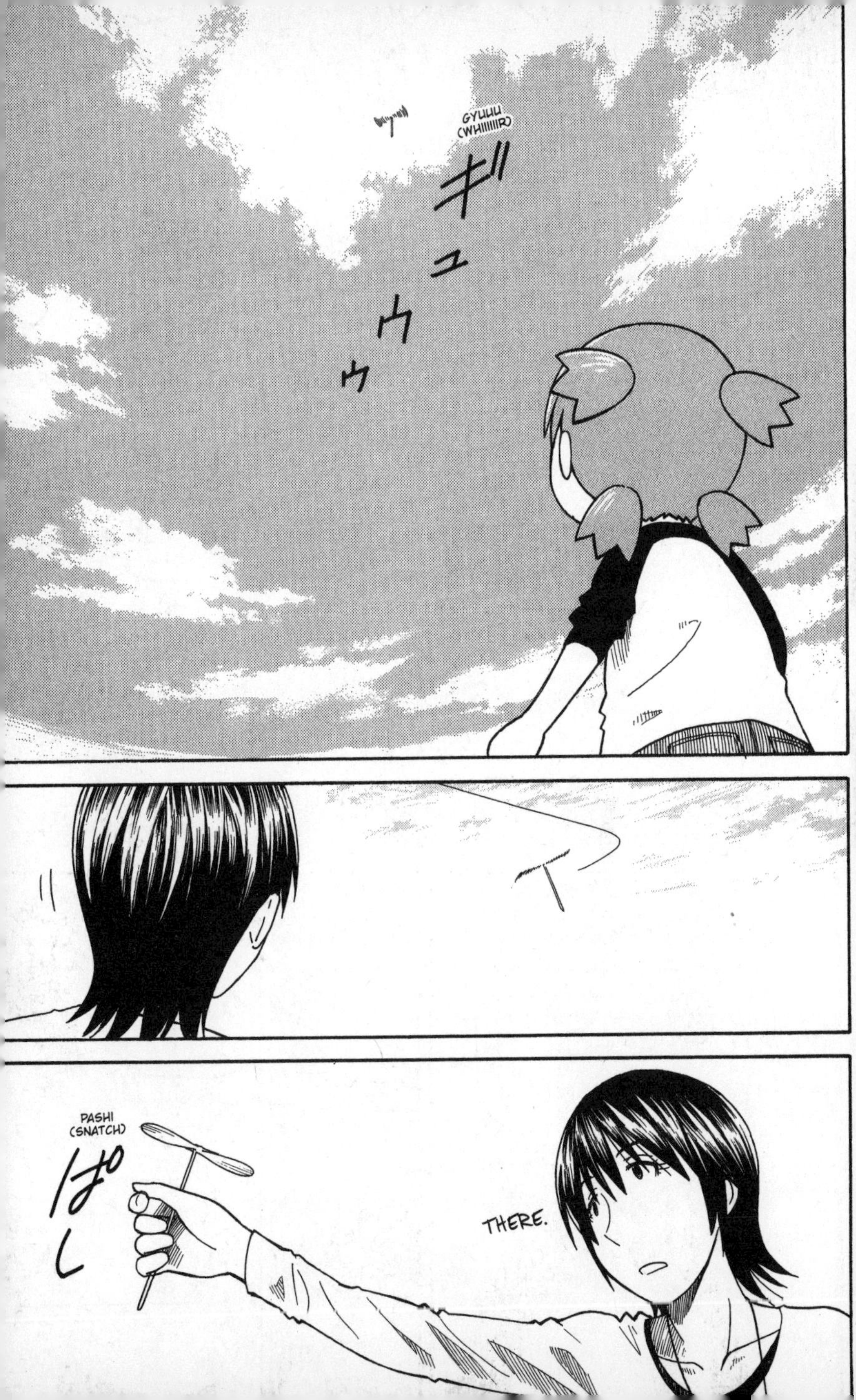
GYUUU (WHIIIIIR)
ギュウゥ
PASHI (SNATCH)
ぱし
THERE.

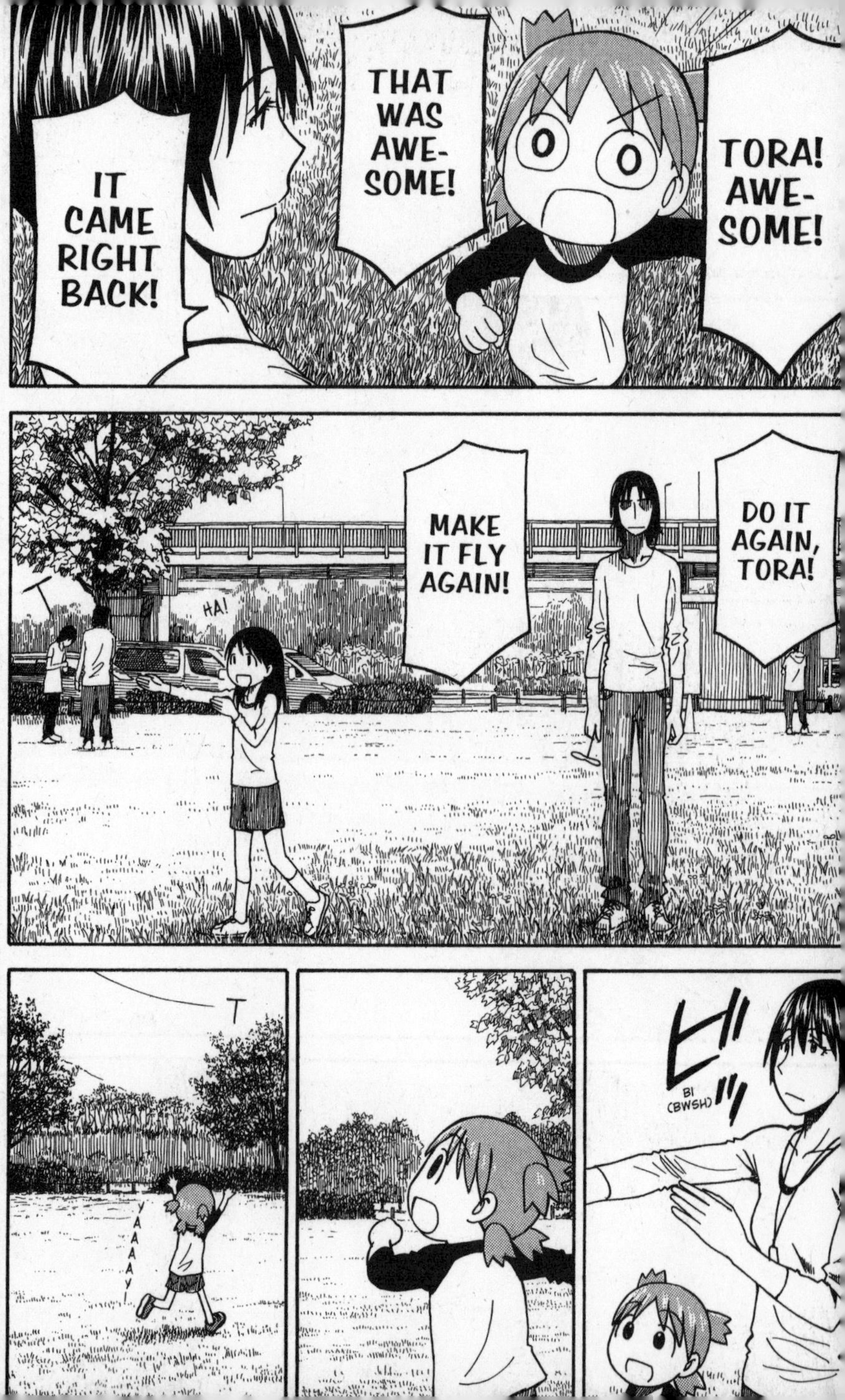
TORA! AWESOME!
THAT WAS AWESOME!
IT CAME RIGHT BACK!
DO IT AGAIN, TORA!
MAKE IT FLY AGAIN!
HA!
ビ
BI (BWSH)
YAAAAY!

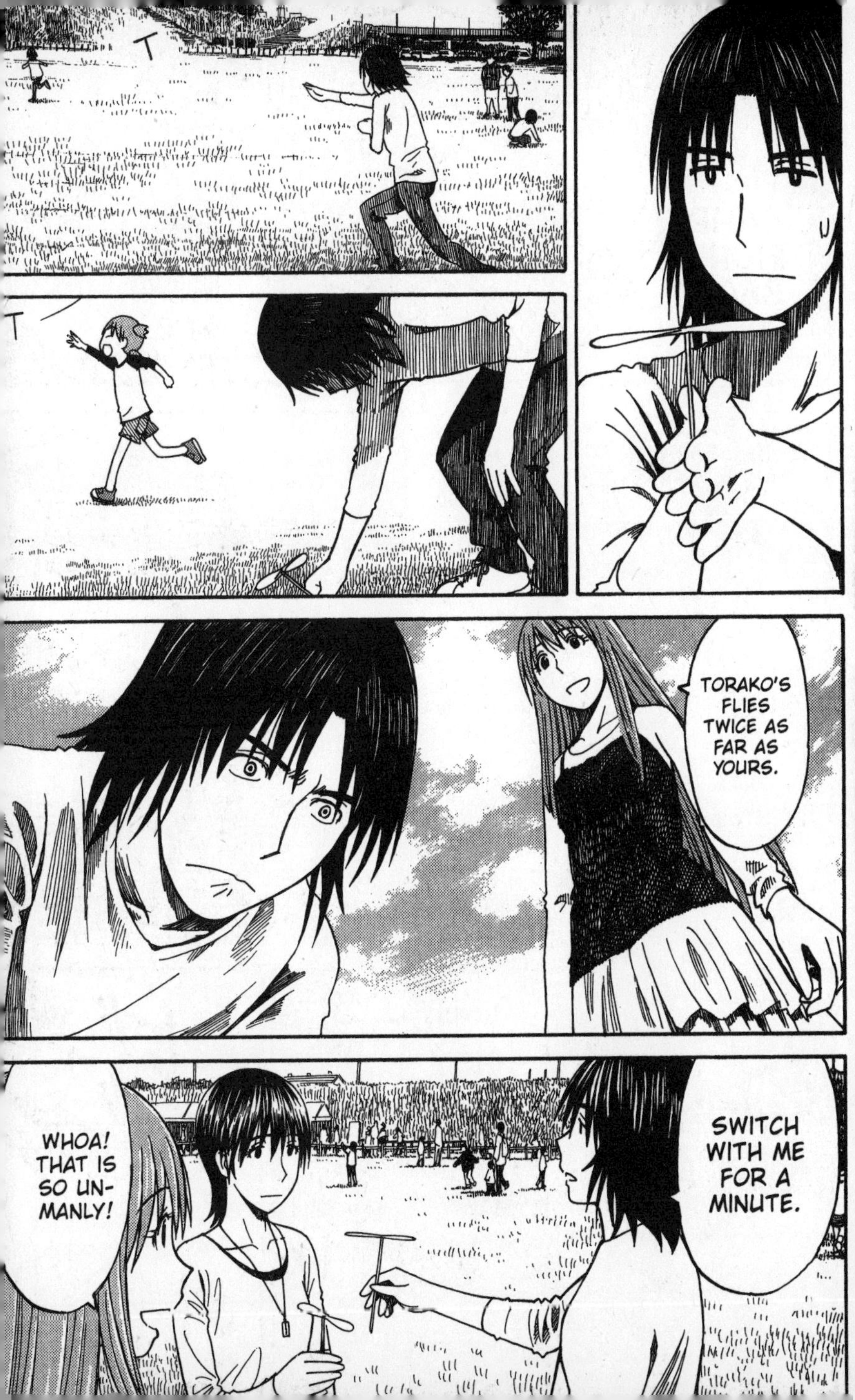
T
T
TORAKO'S FLIES TWICE AS FAR AS YOURS.
SWITCH WITH ME FOR A MINUTE.
WHOA! THAT IS SO UN-MANLY!

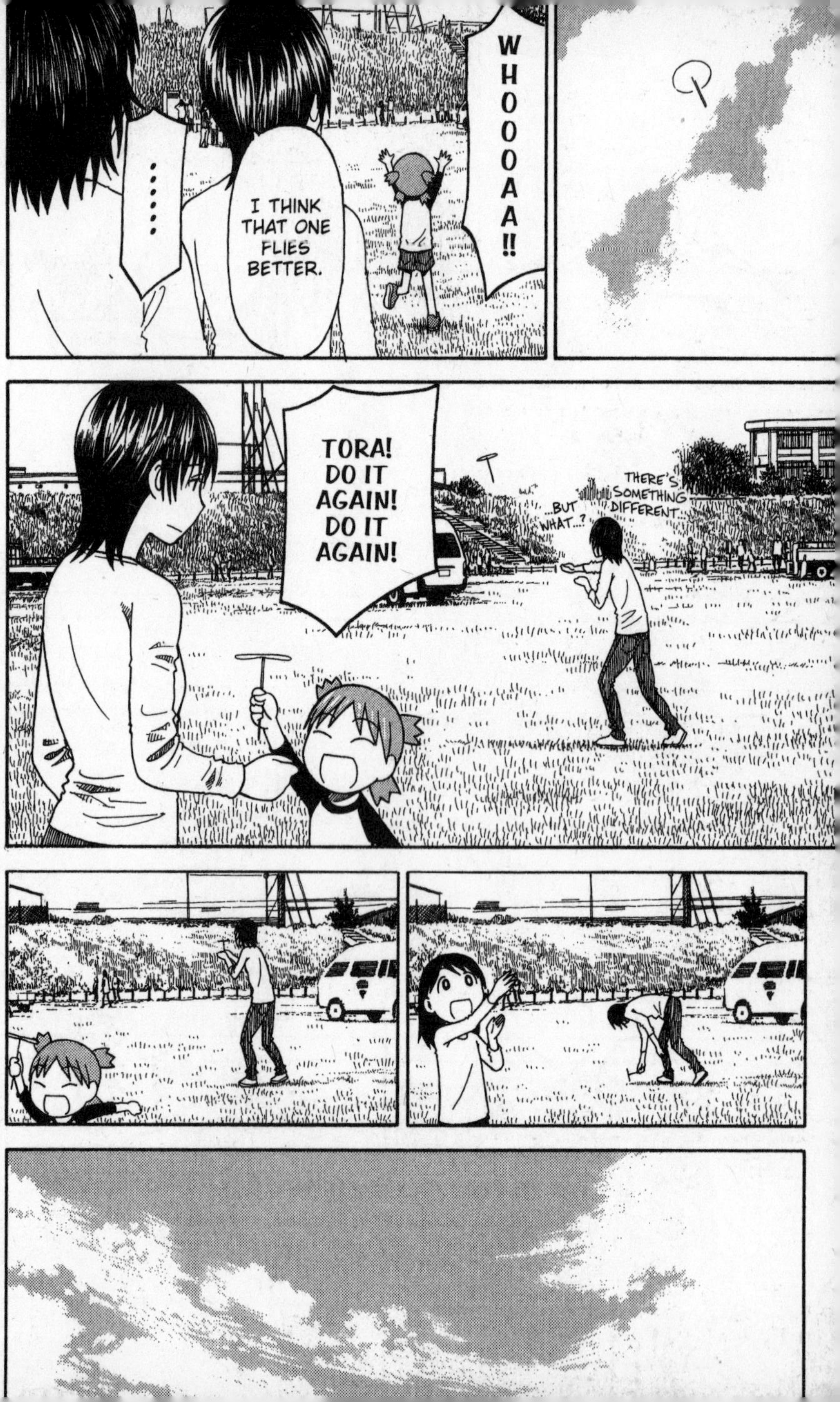
WHOOOOAA!!
I THINK THAT ONE FLIES BETTER.
......
THERE'S SOMETHING DIFFERENT
...BUT WHAT...?
TORA! DO IT AGAIN! DO IT AGAIN!

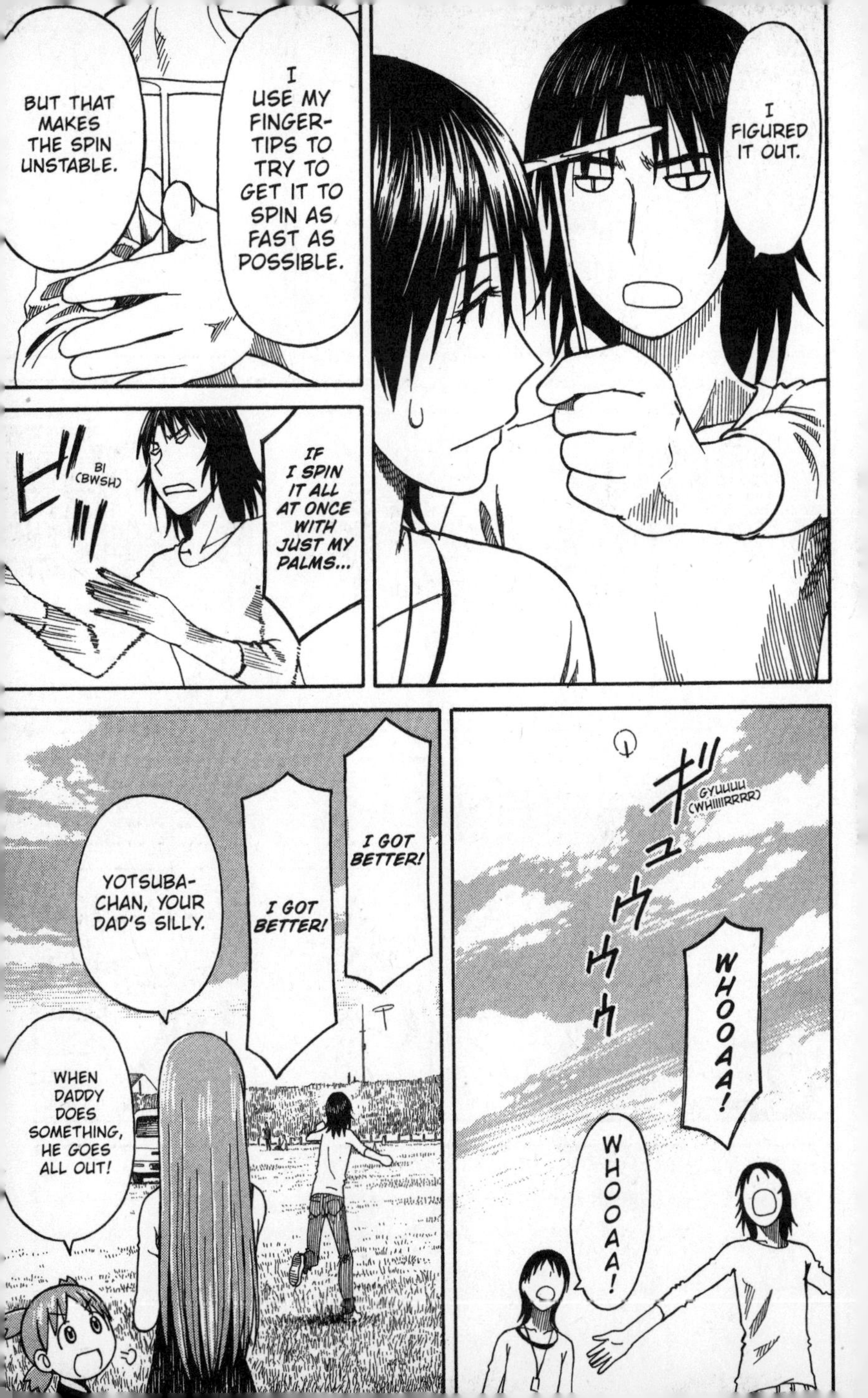
I FIGURED IT OUT.
I USE MY FINGER-TIPS TO TRY TO GET IT TO SPIN AS FAST AS POSSIBLE.
BUT THAT MAKES THE SPIN UNSTABLE.
IF I SPIN IT ALL AT ONCE WITH JUST MY PALMS...
BI (BWSH)
GYUUUU (WHIIIIRRRR)
WHOOOAA!
WHOOOAA!
I GOT BETTER!
I GOT BETTER!
YOTSUBA-CHAN, YOUR DAD'S SILLY.
WHEN DADDY DOES SOMETHING, HE GOES ALL OUT!

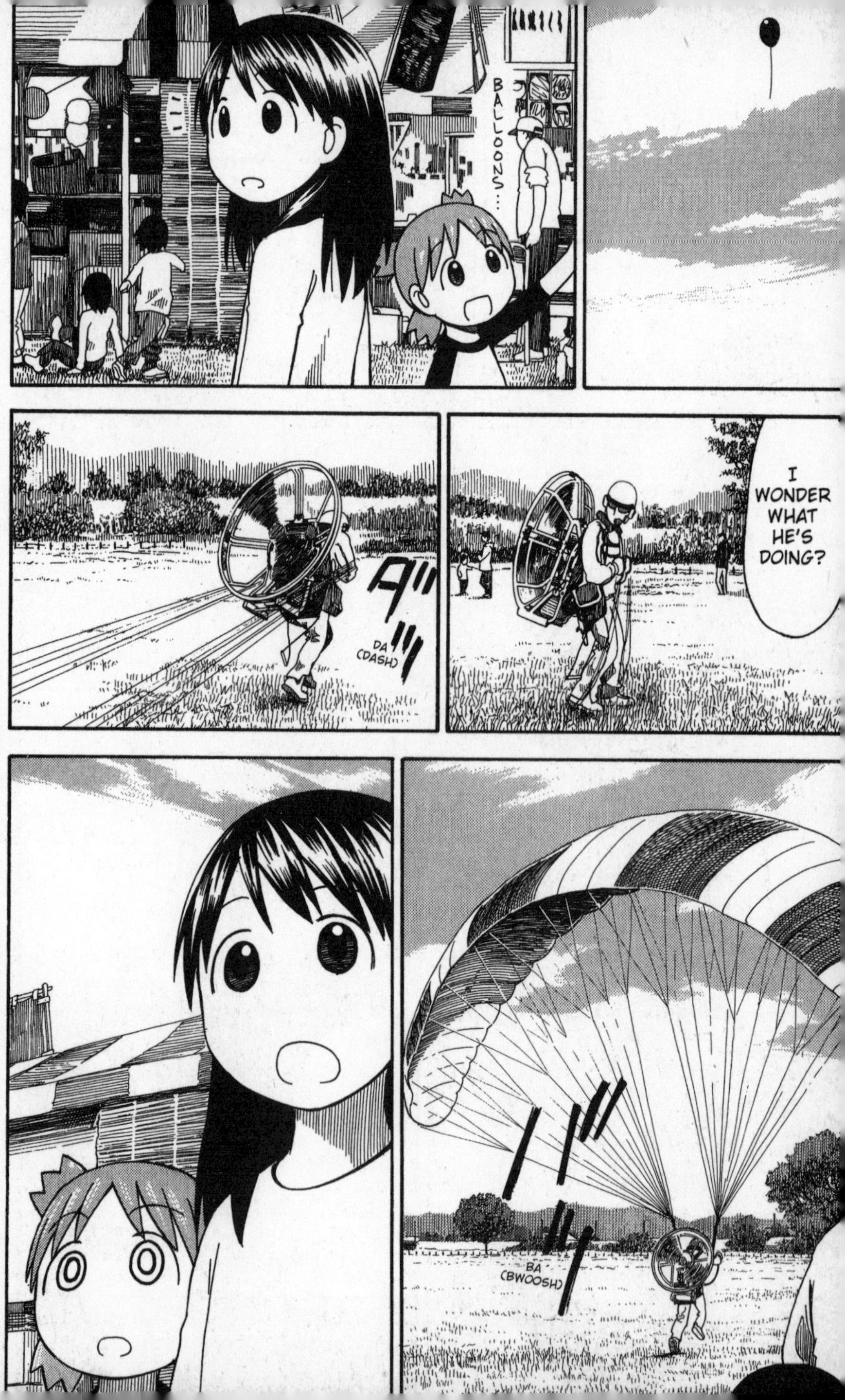
BALLOONS...
I WONDER WHAT HE'S DOING?
DA (DASH)
BA (BWOOSH)

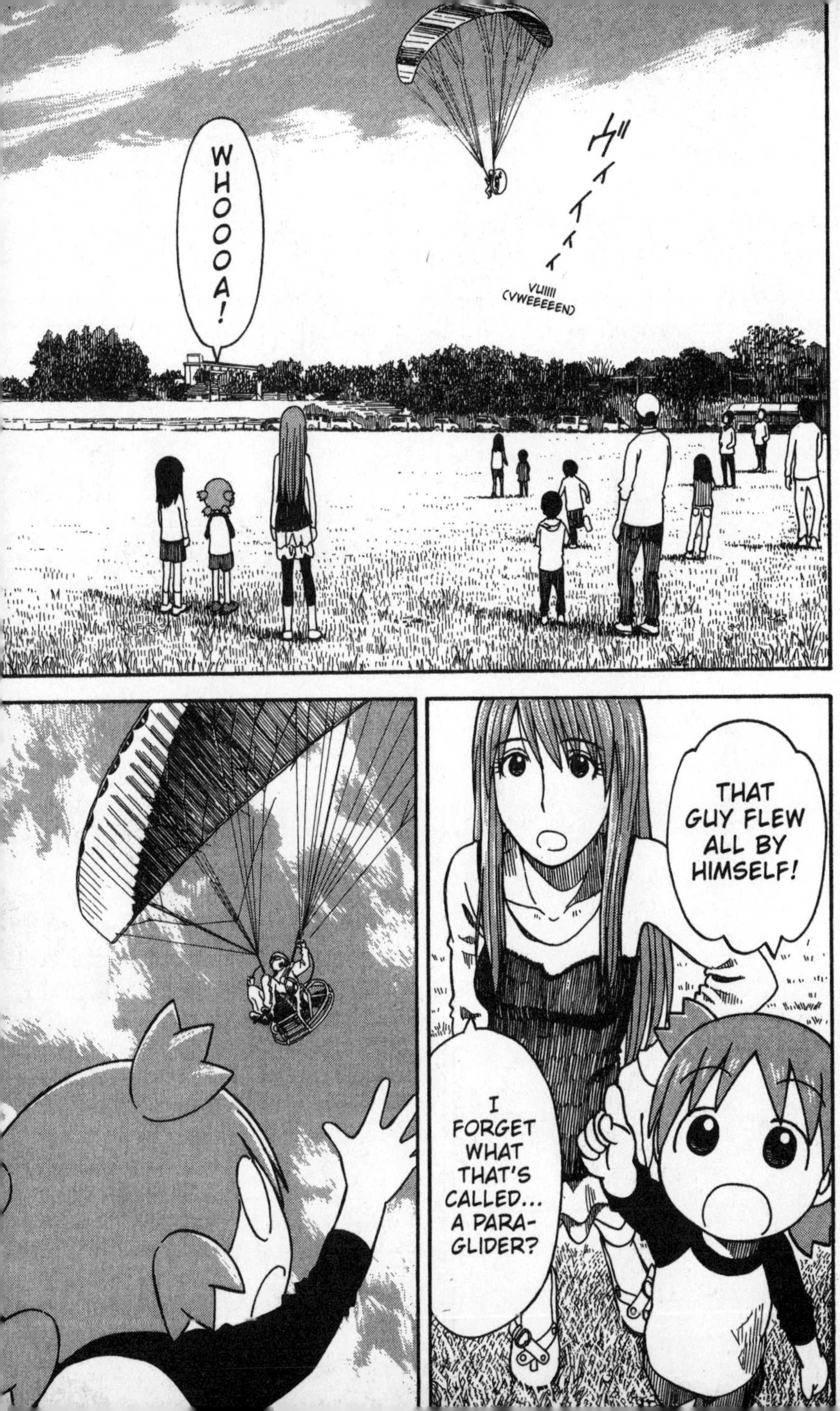
ヴィイイイイ
VUIIII (VWEEEEEN)
WHOOOOA!
THAT GUY FLEW ALL BY HIMSELF!
I FORGET WHAT THAT'S CALLED... A PARA-GLIDER?

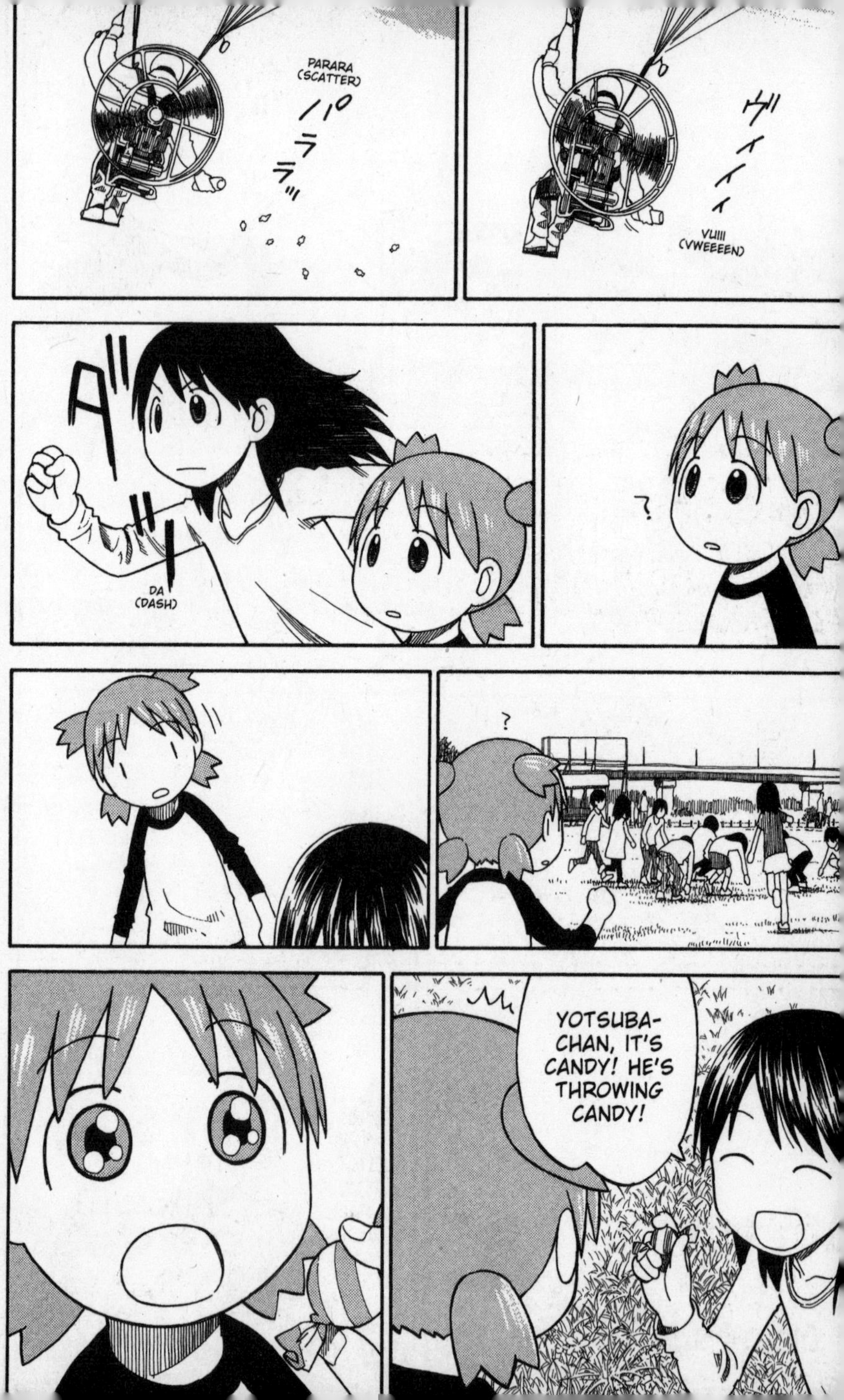
ヴィイイイ
VUIII
(VWEEEEN)
パラララッ
PARARA
(SCATTER)
?
ダッ
DA
(DASH)
?
YOTSUBA-CHAN, IT'S CANDY! HE'S THROWING CANDY!

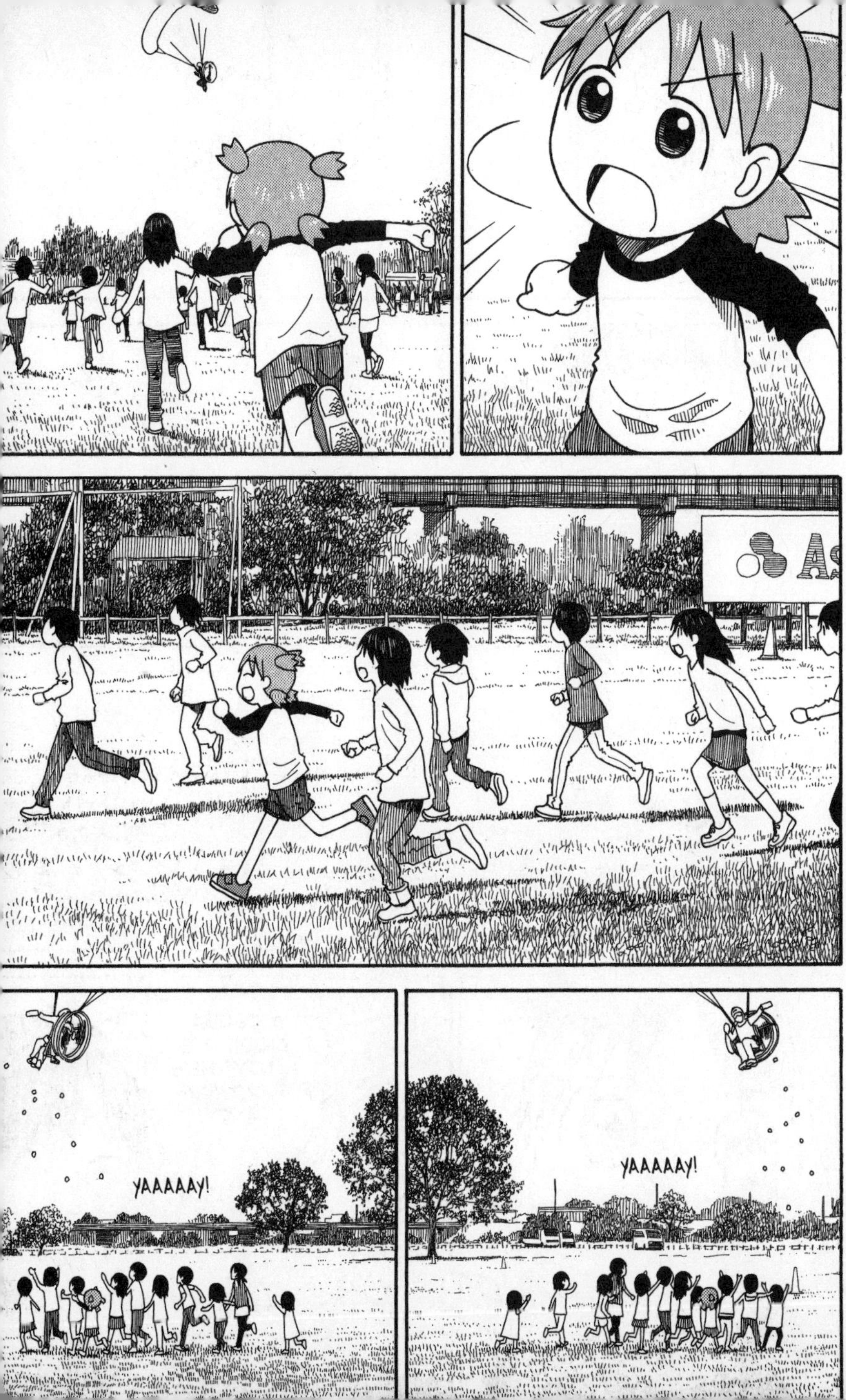
YAAAAY!
YAAAAY!

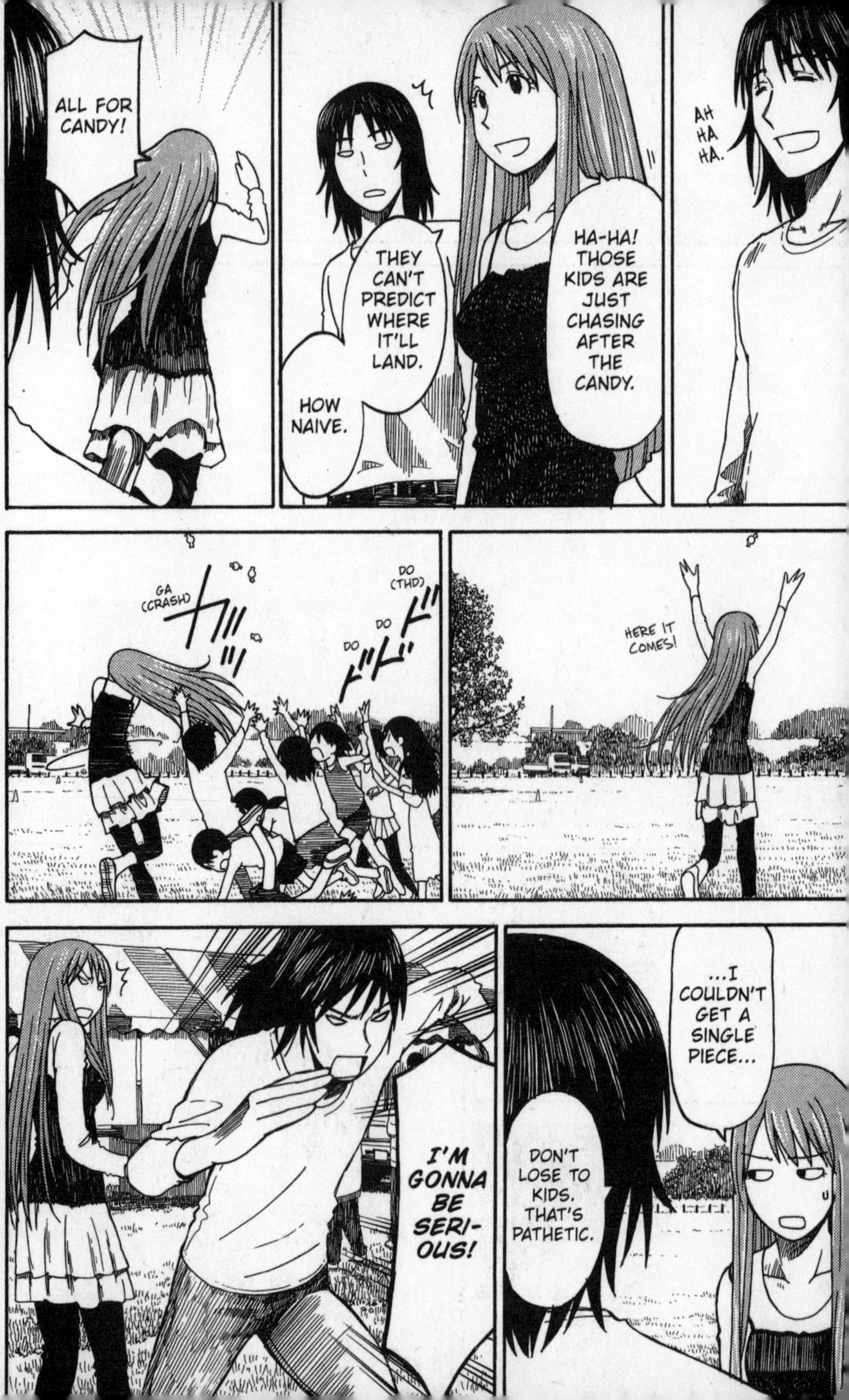
AH HA HA.
HA-HA! THOSE KIDS ARE JUST CHASING AFTER THE CANDY.
THEY CAN'T PREDICT WHERE IT'LL LAND.
HOW NAIVE.
ALL FOR CANDY!
HERE IT COMES!
DO (THD)
DO
DO
GA (CRASH)
...I COULDN'T GET A SINGLE PIECE...
DON'T LOSE TO KIDS. THAT'S PATHETIC.
I'M GONNA BE SERI-OUS!

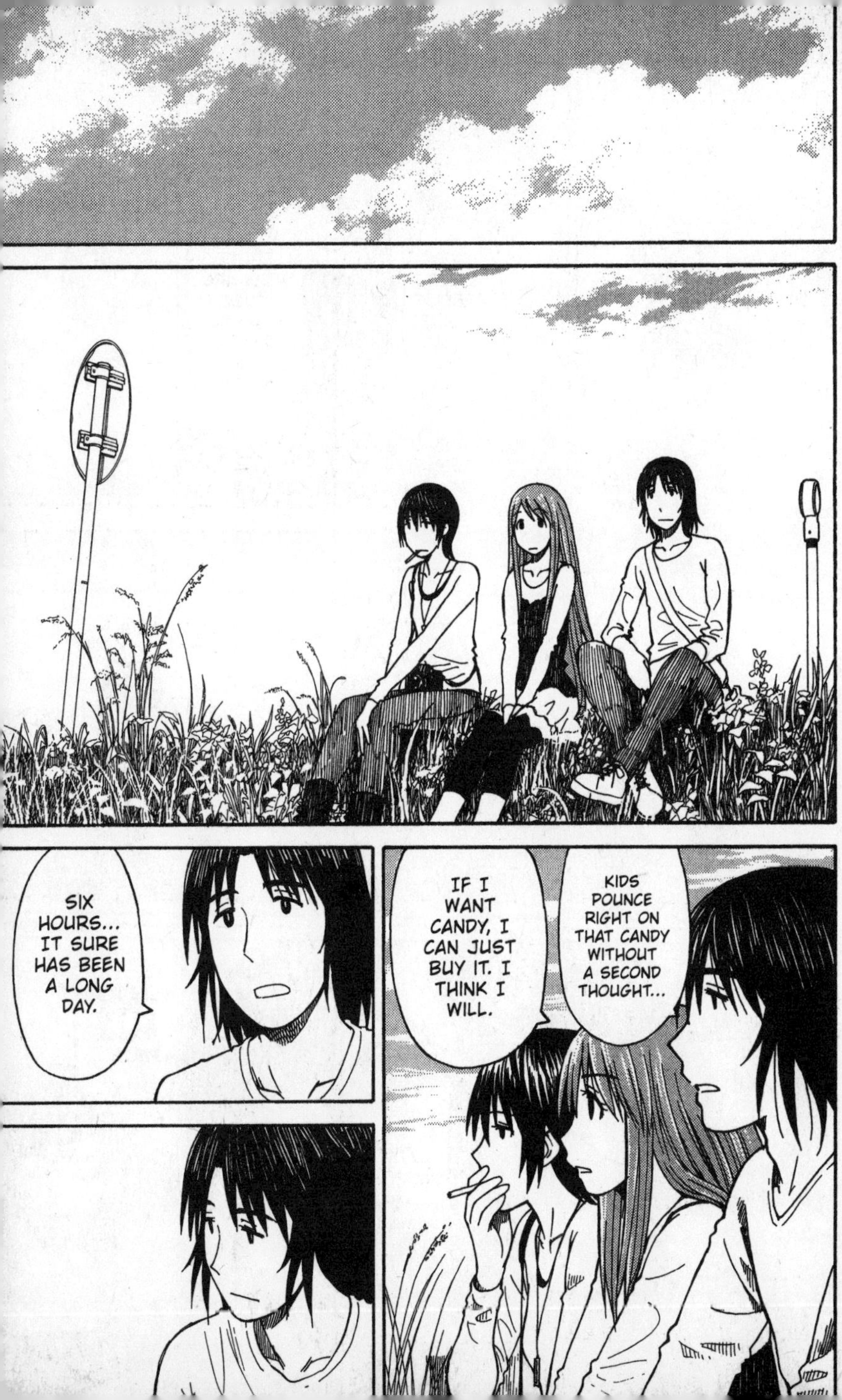
KIDS POUNCE RIGHT ON THAT CANDY WITHOUT A SECOND THOUGHT...
IF I WANT CANDY, I CAN JUST BUY IT. I THINK I WILL.
SIX HOURS... IT SURE HAS BEEN A LONG DAY.

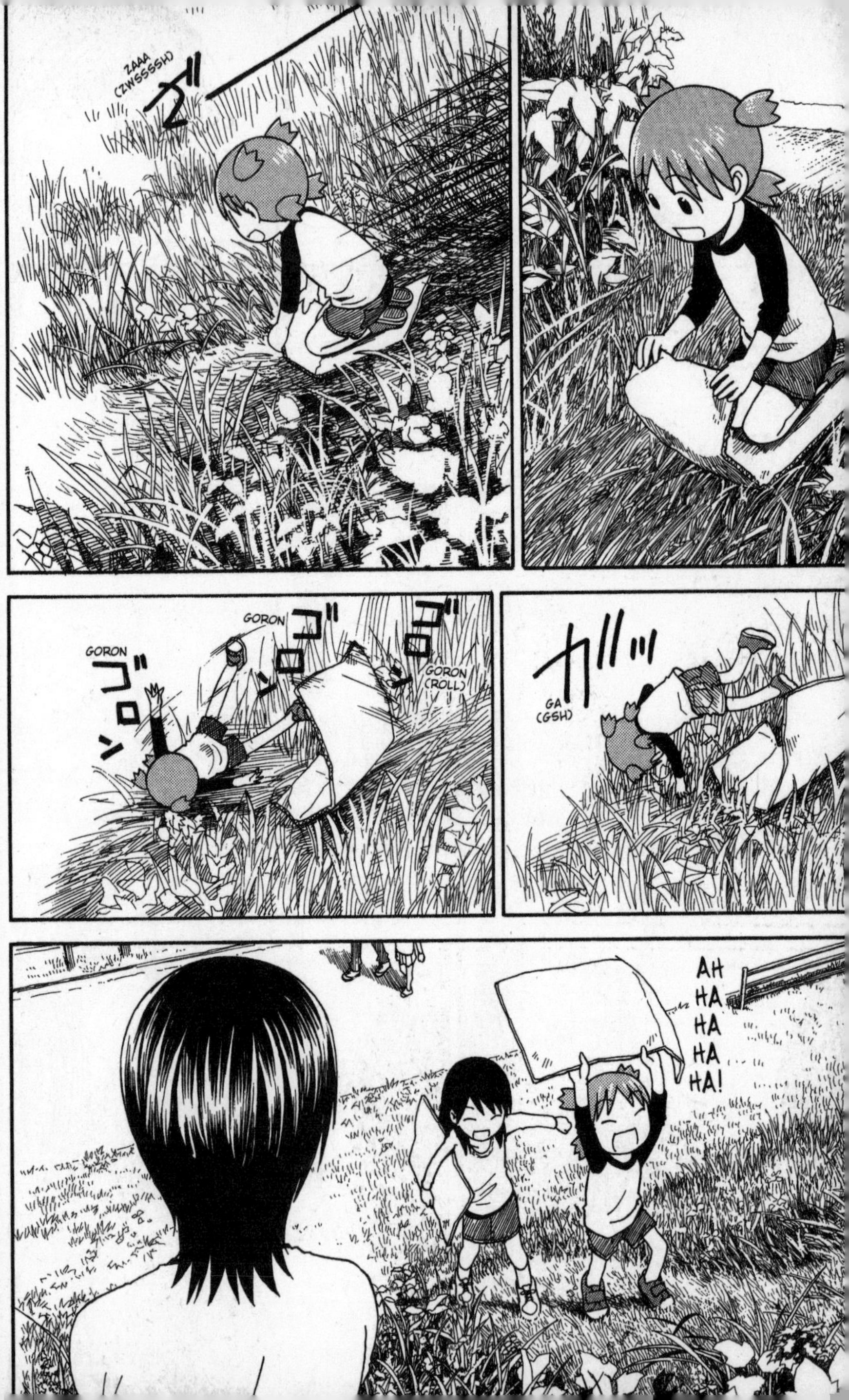
ZAAA
(ZWSSSSH)
ガッ
GA
(GSH)
ゴロン
GORON
(ROLL)
ゴロン
GORON
ゴロン
GORON
AH HA HA HA HA!

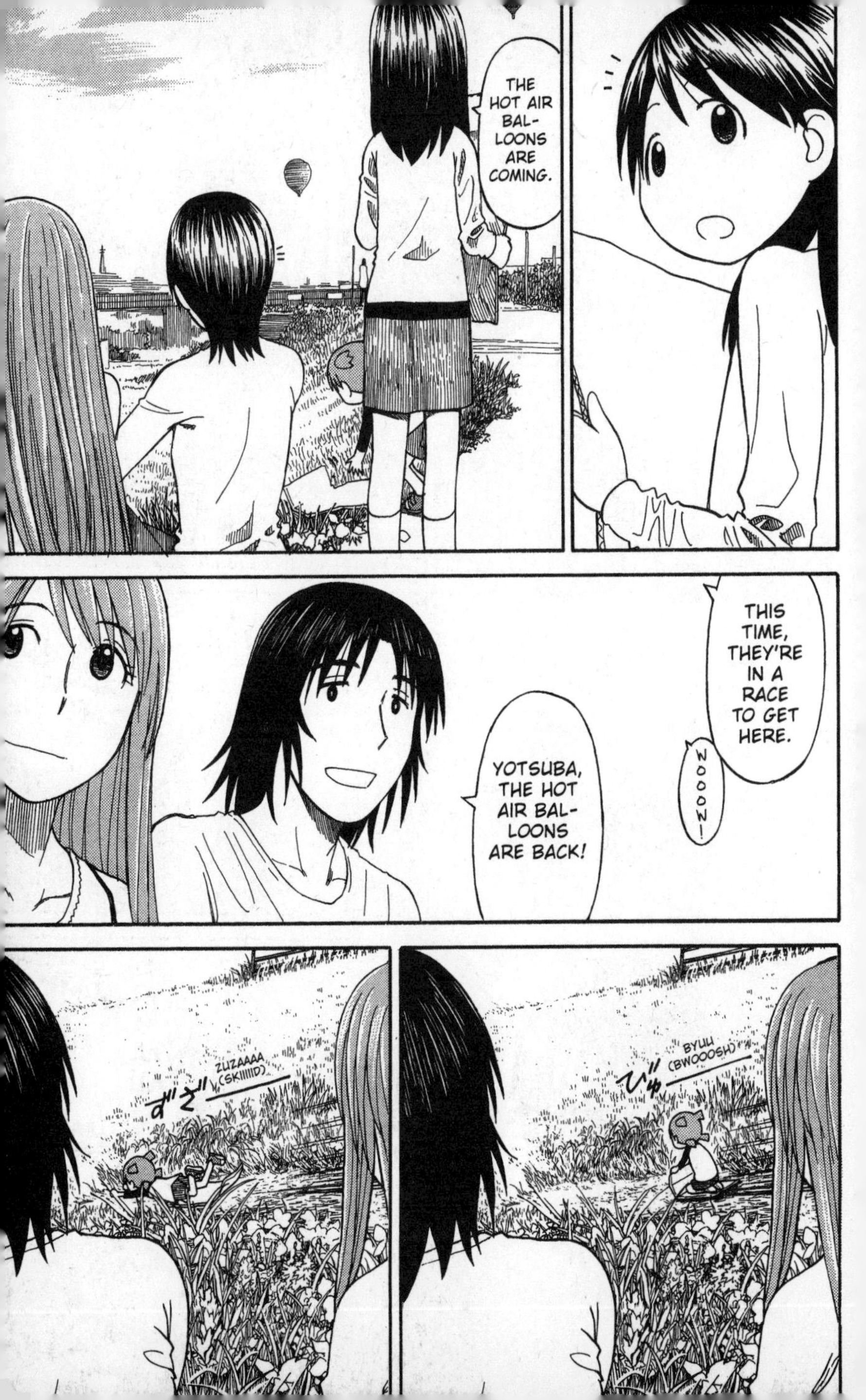
THE HOT AIR BAL-LOONS ARE COMING.
THIS TIME, THEY'RE IN A RACE TO GET HERE.
WOOOW!
YOTSUBA, THE HOT AIR BAL-LOONS ARE BACK!
びゅ
BYUU (BWOOOSH)
ずざ
ZUZAAAA (SKIIIIID)

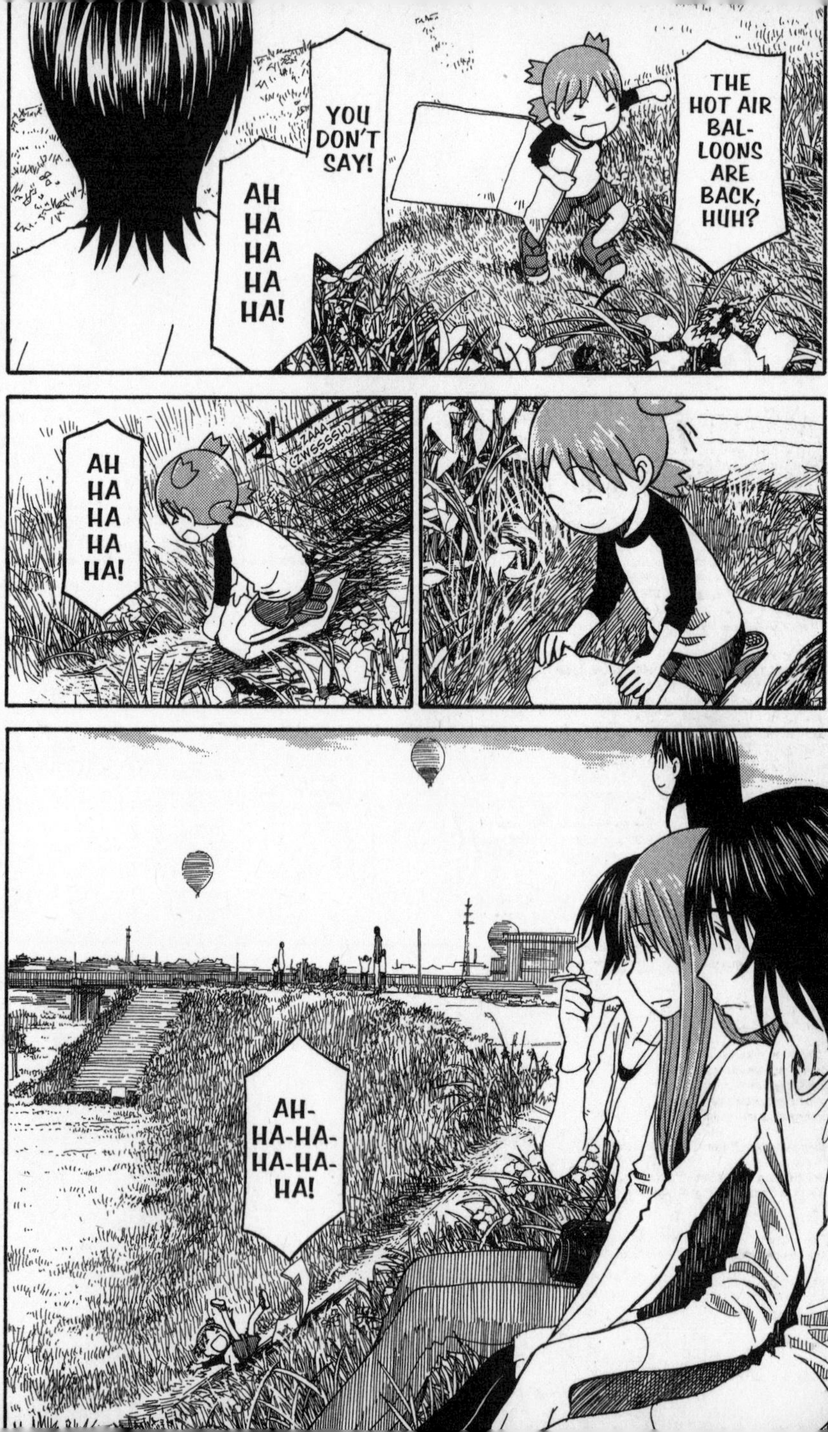
THE HOT AIR BALLOONS ARE BACK, HUH?
YOU DON'T SAY!
AH HA HA HA HA!
ZAAA (ZWSSSSH)
AH HA HA HA HA!
AH-HA-HA-HA-HA-HA!

YOTSUBA&! 9

KIYOHIKO AZUMA

Translation: Amy Forsyth
Lettering: Terri Delgado

YOTSUBA&! Vol. 9
© KIYOHIKO AZUMA / YOTUBA SUTAZIO 2009
Edited by ASCII MEDIA WORKS
First published in Japan in 2009 by
KADOKAWA CORPORATION, Tokyo.
English translation rights arranged with
KADOKAWA CORPORATION, Tokyo,
through Tuttle-Mori Agency, Inc., Tokyo.

English translation © 2010 by Yen Press, LLC

Yen Press
1290 Avenue of the Americas
New York, NY 10104

Visit us at yenpress.com
facebook.com/yenpress
twitter.com/yenpress
yenpress.tumblr.com
instagram.com/yenpress

First Yen Press Edition: December 2010

ISBN: 978-0-316-12679-3

10

WOR

Printed in the United States of America

YOTSUBA&!

ENJOY EVERYTHING.

TO BE CONTINUED!

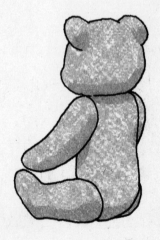